EMPIRE AND JIHAD

# EMPIRE AND JIHAD
## The Anglo-Arab Wars of 1870–1920

Neil Faulkner

YALE UNIVERSITY PRESS
NEW HAVEN AND LONDON

For information about this and other Yale University Press publications, please contact:
U.S. Office: sales.press@yale.edu yalebooks.com
Europe Office: sales@yaleup.co.uk yalebooks.co.uk

Set in Minion Pro by IDSUK (DataConnection) Ltd
Printed in Great Britain by TJ Books, Padstow, Cornwall

Library of Congress Control Number: 2021936885

ISBN 978-0-300-22749-9

A catalogue record for this book is available from the British Library.

10 9 8 7 6 5 4 3 2 1

# CONTENTS

# MAPS AND PLATES

## Maps

*Plates*

The plates in this book are taken from a range of contemporary published primary sources. They include the following:

Archer, T., 1886, *The War in Egypt and the Soudan: An Episode in the History of the British Empire; a Descriptive Account of the Scenes and Events of that Great Drama, and Sketches of the Principal Actors in it*, 4 volumes, London, Blackie & Son; Baker, S.B., 1879, *Ismailia: A Narrative of the Expedition to Central Africa for the Suppression of the Slave Trade Organised by Ismail, Khedive of Egypt*, London, Macmillan; Grant, J., 1886, *Cassell's History of the War in the Soudan*, 6 volumes, London, Cassell; *Illustrated London News*, various issues; Schweinfurth, G., 1874, *The Heart of Africa: Three Years' Travels and Adventures in the Unexplored Regions of Central Africa from 1868 to 1871*, 2 volumes, New York, Harper & Brothers; Slatin, R. and Wingate, F.R., 1895/1930, *Fire and Sword in the Sudan: A Personal Narrative of Fighting and Serving the Dervishes, 1879–1895*, London, Edward Arnold; Stanley, H.M., 1872, *How I Found Livingstone: Travels, Adventures, and Discoveries in Central Africa; Including Four Months' Residence with Dr Livingstone*, London, Sampson Low, Marston, Low, and Searle.

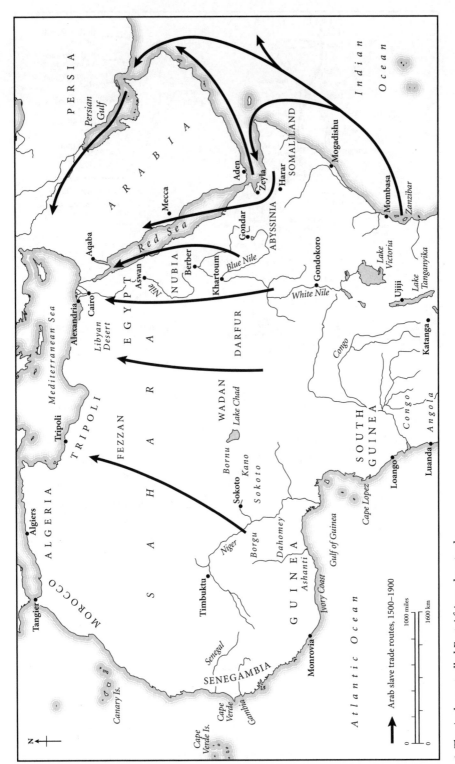

1. The Arab-controlled East African slave trade

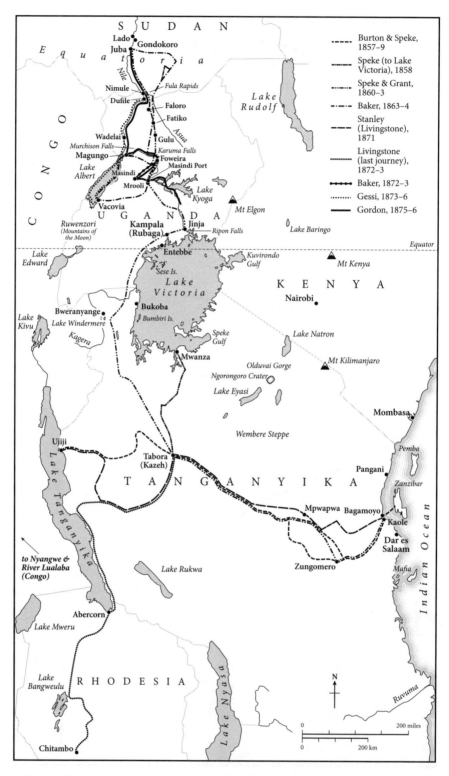

2. Central Africa, showing the main routes followed by the great explorers

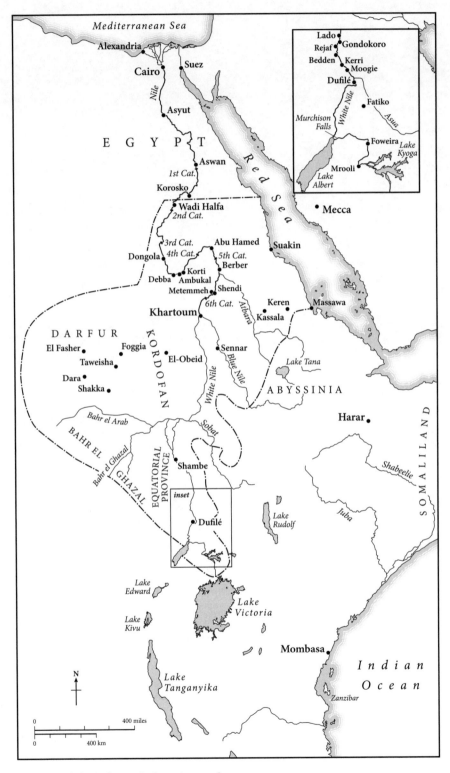

3. Egypt and the Sudan in the late nineteenth century

# INTRODUCTION

Mid-Victorian Britain was celebrating its economic pre-eminence with a 'Great Exhibition of the Works of Industry of All Nations'; it was displayed in a purpose-built 'Crystal Palace' of glass and steel on the edge of London. Louis Napoleon Bonaparte, meanwhile, was organising a coup in Paris to close down the latest of France's many revolutions and make himself dictator. The first gold rush had begun in Australia, the Taiping Rebellion was getting under way in China, and Harriet Beecher Stowe was publishing a bestseller that would stir the conscience of America and push it down the road to civil war. Karl Marx had retreated into the library to write *Das Kapital*, Charles Dickens had recently completed *David Copperfield*, and a young woman called Florence Nightingale had just discovered her vocation.

Samuel Baker, meanwhile, a restless adventurer and big-game hunter, was running a new model agricultural settlement in Ceylon. Charles Gordon, a high-spirited officer cadet, was in training for the sappers at the Royal Military College at Woolwich. Ahmad Arabi, another young man destined to be a soldier, was studying at Al-Azhar University in Cairo. Some 1,400 miles to the south, in the Sudanese town of Omdurman, a boat-builder's son called Muhammad Ahmad was also at his studies, learning to recite the Qur'an by heart. And more than 3,000 miles further south again, in one of the most remote parts of sub-Saharan Africa, an obscure missionary-doctor called David Livingstone had reached the mighty Zambesi and made a notable discovery – one destined to set the world on fire, and which would, in time, cause these men's lives, and the lives of many others, to intersect and collide.

This book is the story of how that came to be; of how, and why, and with what consequences, the lives of these men – and a good many other contemporary movers and shakers – came together during what might be called 'the Anglo-Arab Wars' of 1870–1920, or perhaps the First Modern *Jihad*.

But the book is not simply a narrative: it is an attempt at analysis. It therefore views matters not only 'from above', but also 'from below'; it explores the experiences and responses of the common people as they found themselves sucked into history's vortex, some mere victims, others agents of their own destiny, but precious few, in the nature of the events, able to find much succour, let alone salvation, as their world was torn apart. For the Anglo-Arab Wars were tragic events, where humanitarian impulse and religious piety dissolved into greed, bigotry, and violence, as two systems of oppression, the Arab slave trade and European coolie capitalism, underpinned by two forms of violence, Islamic *jihad* and modern industrialised warfare, imposed themselves on North-East Africa.

Traditional English-language accounts of the events with which this book is concerned – events in North-East Africa between 1870 and 1920, but rooted in Central African exploration up to two decades earlier – are usually sympathetic, consciously or unthinkingly, to imperialism. This is overwhelmingly true of contemporary sources – though there are some noble exceptions, like William Scawen Blunt's *Secret History of the English Occupation of Egypt* (1907) – but it is also largely true of secondary accounts written by modern historians, especially those angled towards a more popular audience. Take the case of the Egyptian Revolution of 1882 – the pivotal event in this analysis. This was a liberal, nationalist, secular movement of modernisation and reform. It was smashed by a British military invasion. The purpose of the invasion was to secure control over the Suez Canal and ensure a continuing flow of interest payments to European bankers at the expense of the native peasantry.

Philip Magnus (writing in 1958) considered the British action entirely legitimate, for Colonel Arabi, the Egyptian nationalist leader, had 'set up what was virtually a nationalist military dictatorship in opposition to the European financiers'. He thought it quite unreasonable that the Egyptian government should have mounted guns at Alexandria when a fleet of British warships arrived offshore, since these were 'evidently intended as a threat to the Royal Navy'. It does not seem to have occurred to him that Egypt was entitled to defend its national territory, nor that the subsequent British bombardment of Alexandria was an act of aggression indefensible under any imaginable framework of international law. How would the British have reacted to a hostile fleet in the Solent?

Michael Barthorp (1984), describing the situation inside Egypt, reports that 'everywhere fear and unrest grew, with the military of all ranks adopting an arrogant and overbearing attitude'. What is one to make of such a statement? What does it mean? Who was fearful? Who was restless? Towards whom were the military being 'arrogant and overbearing' (if indeed they were)? Towards the European colonial presence in Egypt, perhaps? But the implication of 'anarchy' under Arabi then allows Barthorp to argue that the whole military operation was 'to restore Egypt to stability, solvency, and security under the Khedive and his own ministers by a complete overhaul of all Egyptian institutions, guided and assisted by British advisors inspired with British standards of justice and humanity'.

Michael Asher (2005) explains that 'revolutionary forces seized their chance' to unleash 'a flood of anti-foreign sentiment', and that Arabi's supporters in Alexandria had 'slaughtered foreigners, looted the city, and threatened passage through the Suez Canal'. Asher served in the Parachute Regiment and the SAS, and one cannot help feeling that his understanding of the 1882 revolution was coloured by 'War on Terror' propaganda, much as Magnus's surely was by tabloid reactions to the Suez Crisis of 1956.

At times, the failure of critical analysis is so complete that we seem to have moved no distance at all from the reactionary jingoism of the late-Victorian yellow press. Even the better texts, both primary and secondary, usually adopt some sort of liberal-imperialist/orientalist framework. Without critical theory, nothing can be explained, and works of conservative and liberal history are, almost by definition, devoid of critical theory; they are the smug reports of an imperial (and, indeed, 'post-imperial') Establishment.

On the other hand, while recent academic research has often been far more critical of imperialism – much of it undertaken by African and Asian scholars exploring the colonial experience of their own countries – alternative narratives are sometimes informed by the 'bourgeois nationalism' of local elites engaged in modern state-building projects. The tendency is to view the coloniser critically, but to idealise the colonised; specifically, to idealise any and all forces of resistance, whatever the nature of the leadership. The tyranny, barbarism, and ignorance of native potentates have sometimes been airbrushed away in what are effectively nationalist narratives, not critical histories. Those who stand with the oppressed against the oppressor do themselves no favours by turning local tyrants into resistance heroes. We should not regard the Sudanese Mahdi or the Somali Mullah as erstwhile leaders of national liberation struggles akin to Ho Chi Minh, Che

Guevara, or Nelson Mandela. They garnered anti-imperialist forces, for sure, but not in pursuit of a progressive recasting of their countries, so much as a descent into medieval barbarism.

The story told here is a dystopian one – a conflict between coolie capitalism on the one hand, and tribalism, slave trading, and jihadism on the other.

⬛

My story unfolds in four parts. In the first, 'Black Ivory, White Nile', we follow in the tracks of a small number of mid-nineteenth-century explorers in Central Africa – Livingstone, Burton and Speke, and Stanley – and we share the shock of their discovery not only of the sources of the Nile, but also of the surging of the East African slave trade. In Part II, 'Star and Crescent', our focus shifts to the Turco-Egyptian regime in Cairo and the unfolding of a national crisis – a failed colonial/anti-slavery war, a collapse into bankruptcy, a popular-nationalist revolution, and then a full-scale British military invasion. Part III, 'The Black Flag', charts the Islamist insurgency in the Sudan – the mission of the Mahdi, the last stand of General Gordon in Khartoum, and the defeat of the Gordon Relief Expedition. Finally, in Part IV, 'The Spectre of *Jihad*', we follow the falling wave of jihadism – the degeneration of the Mahdist Caliphate, its defeat at Omdurman in 1898, the destructive insurgency in Somaliland between 1899 and 1920, and the abortive Ottoman–German efforts to trigger an Islamic holy war between 1914 and 1918. In the Conclusion, finally, I feel compelled to draw out the grim parallels with events since 2001 in our own divided and troubled world.

### Note on names

The transliteration of Arabic names is never straightforward. The contemporary English-language sources used a wide variety of approximations to Arabic pronunciation. Other versions have appeared since. The matter is further complicated by dialect, since Sudanese Arabic is different from Egyptian or Levantine Arabic, and both are very different from the Classical Arabic of the Qur'an. There are now, of course, standardised ways of transliterating Arabic into Roman script. But this, too, is problematic. The general English-speaking reader cannot be expected to know Arabic any more than she knows Serbo-Croat or Chinese. The use of formal academic transliteration known only to linguists is therefore pretentious outside the confines of specialist journals. Further problems arise in relation to derivatives and plurals. Islam and Muslim, for example, are essentially the same word, one form referring to the religion, the other to the follower. *Ashraf* is merely the plural of *sherif* (a descendant of the Prophet), but to the uninitiated English-speaking reader appears to be a different word. Problems also arise in relation to Swahili names. Buganda, for example, is the territory of the Ganda people. It is for the author to make things easy for the reader, not erect barriers. I have therefore tried to use a common rendering that approximates to a serviceable pronunciation, to avoid distracting variants, and to be consistent in my rendering of any particular name.

# Part I
# Black Ivory, White Nile

# CHAPTER ONE

# HEART OF DARKNESS

'It is the first *river* I ever saw.' So it seemed to Dr David Livingstone upon arriving at the upper reaches of the Zambesi on 4 August 1851. It was the culmination of three long journeys into the African interior from the Christian mission-station at Kolobeng in Bechuanaland, 500 miles to the south, over the previous two years. The Zambesi was indeed a river among rivers. Even now, in the dry season, it was deep flowing and up to a third of a mile wide. During the annual inundation, the explorer learned, it might rise 20 feet in height and spread its waters across 15 or 20 miles of the open plains on either bank.[1]

Reaching the Zambesi changed Livingstone's life. 'I'm going down,' he told his travelling companion after they returned to camp. 'I mean to go down.' William Oswell, a scholar and sportsman educated at Rugby in Thomas Arnold's day and afterwards employed for seven years by the East India Company, was shocked: the West Coast was 1,800 miles away through uncharted bush. Only later did he realise that Livingstone, habitually taciturn and oracular, was speaking of future intention.[2]

Behind the mask – rugged features; a countenance that seemed aloof, stern, self-contained – Livingstone's mind was racing ahead. He was thinking of the river as a giant highway, both into the interior and across the continent from east to west, an access corridor that would carry Commerce, Christianity, and Civilisation into the depths of 'Darkest Africa'. With the boundless self-assurance of a mid-Victorian gentleman – to which condition he had, by his own extraordinary efforts, raised himself from lowly origins – he felt it to be his God-given task to be the pioneer, to find and map the route, to light the way. Bored by the futility of missionary work, he had already broken free and trekked several hundred miles north of the London Missionary Society's most advanced station. Now nothing would hold him. The wanderlust became all-consuming. 'Providence seems to call me to regions beyond,' he confided. A hard-driven, hard-driving man, moody, even manic-depressive, but possessed of willpower to the outer limit of human endurance, he would, for the rest of his life, remain grimly focused on his goal in the face of every setback, regardless of hazard, and with little sympathy for the frailty of less sturdy companions.[3]

He was an exceptional man even among Victorian explorers. Most wanted to complete their journey and get out: Livingstone wanted to stay. However fraught his relationships with family and colleagues – and he would eventually leave them all behind and vanish, a lone white man, into the interior – he loved Africa and its people. It was, for sure, the love of a strict father for erring children. Livingstone was a paternalist who believed Africans were in need of an uplifting hand; and, for a man of his time and place, that meant the uplifting hand of Victorian Britain. The emerging disciplines of archaeology and anthropology seemed to substantiate such presumptions. Was it not the case that the history of civilisation revealed an evolutionary progression from lower stages of social development to higher ones? Was it not obvious that, compared with Europeans, Africans were still at an 'infantile' stage?

But at least Livingstone was free of the pseudo-scientific racism – with its skull measurements and racial typologies – that infected so many of his contemporaries. 'We have nothing to justify the notion that they are of a different "breed" or "species",' he wrote. 'The African is a man with every attribute of human kind.' Even his perception of the African as essentially child-like was tempered by idealisation of the way of life of the continent's traditional hoe-cultivators and cattle herders – and by occasional premonitions of the danger inherent in European penetration. His vision was of an Africa saved from despoliation, and elevated by industry, trade, education, and medicine – not its transformation into a colonial sweatshop.[4]

What made this urgent – the saving of a continent, which now became his life's work, his mission through the 30 years of struggle to come – was the fact that the Africa he had come to love was already dying; more precisely, it was being eviscerated. This, he and Oswell had discovered that same August of 1851 on the Zambesi.

Among the Makololo, the cattle herders of the region who had guided and sustained them on the last leg of their journey, the two explorers were celebrities, for white men had never been seen before, and curious onlookers crowded round them in the villages. But something was awry.

'Among the first who came to see us,' Livingstone recalled, 'was a gentleman who appeared in a gaudy dressing-gown of printed calico.' He was not alone: many of the Makololo came wearing 'garments of blue, green, and red baize, and also of printed cottons'. Some long tentacle of commerce had brought cloths from textile mills thousands of miles distant to this remote place in Africa where no white man had ever previously ventured – perhaps even, by some intricate chain of exchange, all the way from Blantyre Mills near Glasgow, where a young David Livingstone had once worked as a 'piecer', repairing threads at risk of breaking on the spinning frames. And not only cloths: the Makololo chief – in this realm of spears and bows – had, only the year before, taken possession of eight muskets. What had the Makololo traded in exchange? The tribesmen had expected to pay in cattle; that would have been usual. But a new kind of economy was spreading from the coast across ever more of the interior. The Mambari had been insistent: they would take payment only in boys.[5]

The Makololo had been surprised – 'they had never heard of people being bought and sold till then' – but they had relented and agreed to trade slaves, for 'the desire to possess guns prevailed'. Of course they had no wish to sell their own children. So they sold those of tribes they had subjugated. The exchange rate was one gun for one boy. Nor was that the end of the matter. The Makololo soon got a taste for this new manner of business, and agreed to join the Mambari in an attack on some tribes to the east. The Makololo later sold their share of the captives, some 30 in number, to 'some Arabs from Zanzibar', receiving in payment 'three English muskets'.[6]

When David Livingstone reached the Zambesi in August 1851, he touched the southernmost edge of a vast vortex of violence, enslavement, and profit that stretched thousands of miles across Africa and Middle Asia – to Tripoli and Cairo; to Damascus, Baghdad, and Constantinople; to Arabia, Persia, and India. Armed columns were moving through the interior of sub-Saharan Africa hunting elephants and hunting people. The demand was for ivory and slaves; and this was happy coincidence, for ivory was heavy and the only means of transport through the bush was human porters, and the fact that both could be sold when the cargo came to market doubled the profit. The slave masters were sometimes Portuguese from the Angolan and Mozambican ports, more often Arab-Swahilis from Zanzibar and the East

African coast, or Arab-Sudanese from the sultanates and caliphates along the semi-arid fringe of the Sahara. The rank and file were recruited from the lowest strata of the slave-stations, or were slaves themselves, but favoured and well armed, or African tribesmen, hiring themselves out for pay, guns, cloth, trinkets, and perhaps a chance to wage war on a neighbour. But sometimes the armed columns were all-African, for the Arabs, by supplying muskets in exchange for ivory and slaves, were turning the tribes with whom they traded into predators, setting in motion shock waves of mayhem across Central Africa.

Tribal wars had long been endemic to much of the continent. But traditional warfare in the bush had a ritualised character. The numbers engaged were few, the weapons primitive, and much of the effort went into displays of martial prowess designed to overawe the enemy without resort to killing. Armies – if that is not too strong a word for a few hundred warriors chanting, dancing, beating shields, brandishing spears – might confront each other a distance apart, neither willing to close, neither seeking a potentially lethal close-quarters mêlée. Or they might engage in a protracted campaign of raid and ambush – an occasional night attack, a skirmish in the long grass, a chase across the plain to rustle cattle. Often enough a state of war existed but nothing at all happened; sometimes inter-tribal 'wars' ended without any fatalities. Such was the way among remote communities of hoe-cultivators and cattle herders armed with clubs, spears, and primitive bows. Then the slavers came, bringing guns.

It was a fatal collision of two social orders – Iron Age tribes based on subsistence farming and pastoralism, and a predatory system of mercantile capitalism, geared to global markets, equipped by modern industry. Later, as he passed on other journeys through regions blackened and depopulated by 'the scourge of slave-war', David Livingstone would reflect on the power of the gun. The armed columns of the slavers may have been only 50 or 100, the weapons may have been Waterloo-vintage flintlocks, but they conferred 'absolute power', for 'the bow cannot stand for a moment against the musket'. He knew that Africans used to shooting arrows from the long grass had as little chance against men with guns 'as a wooden ship possessing only signal guns would before an ironclad steamer'.[7]

Greed and gunpowder were blasting open ancient tribal animosities, turning them into murderous rampages, shattering the old social structure of sub-Saharan Africa, leaving behind great swathes of wilderness. The violence was self-feeding. Tribal chiefs threatened by slave raiders armed with muskets needed guns of their own. To buy them, they needed captives to trade, so they turned slave raiders themselves. The demand for guns fuelled the demand for slaves. Guns and slaves: a vicious spiral downwards into hell. Only the slavers benefited. 'The slave-trader', Livingstone wrote, 'naturally reaps advantage from every disorder, and . . . he intensifies hatreds, and aggravates wars between tribes, because the more they fight and vanquish each other, the richer his harvest becomes.'[8]

The waves of turbulence sweeping the continent were growing stronger, reaching further. Hundreds of thousands of Africans were being sucked in and spewed out of the vortex. The slave hauls landing at Zanzibar, the island emporium on the East Coast, increased from 60,000 in the first decades of the nineteenth century to 175,000 in the 1850s. It was the same on the other routes – overland to the Red Sea, down the Nile to Cairo, along the trans-Saharan tracks to Libya, or via Timbuktu to Morocco. The trafficking of Africans soared from around 10,000 a year prior to 1800 to around five times that number by mid-century.[9]

The contrast with the situation on the Atlantic seaboard was remarkable. The British had abolished the slave trade in 1807, slavery itself in 1833. The Royal Navy's West Africa Squadron, charged with enforcement, seized 1,600 ships and freed 150,000 Africans between 1807 and 1860. The effect was to reduce transatlantic trafficking to a fraction of what it had been in its eighteenth-century heyday. But as the West African trade collapsed, the East African trade surged to unprecedented levels.

News of this, when they heard of it – and it became David Livingstone's determined intention that they should hear of it – would shock a Victorian public convinced of the virtues of 'reform', 'improvement', 'progress', and 'civilisation'; and equally convinced that Britain was the world's finest embodiment of such virtues. The matter of the East African trade would come to be viewed through an orientalist lens: a confirmation of the essential barbarism of the East, of Arabs, Turks, and Egyptians, and indeed of the Islamic faith.

But the demand for slaves in North Africa and Middle Asia – on plantations, in domestic service, as concubines – was increasing only because the sheikhs, pashas, merchants, and landlords of these regions were growing rich on the profits of trade. And trade was good because Britain had turned itself into the workshop of the world and a maritime empire. A frenetic process of capital accumulation was transforming the global economy. The slave trade was booming because of globalisation.[10]

Around the time Livingstone reached the Zambesi, Charlotte Brontë, author of *Jane Eyre*, was making her second visit to London's Great Exhibition. She stayed three hours and was even more awestruck than before. 'It is a wonderful place,' she wrote, 'vast, strange, new, and impossible to describe. Its grandeur does not consist in one thing, but in the unique assemblage of all things.' The sceptics had been confounded. They had predicted an expensive flop. But the crowds came and came, 30,000 a day, a million a month, from London of course, but also thousands a day from the provincial towns arriving on special excursion trains. Joseph Paxton's vast iron-and-glass exhibition building in Hyde Park – dubbed 'the Crystal Palace' – absorbed them all. It was itself an exhibit, a masterwork of Victorian engineering, an industrial megalith a third of a mile long, its skeleton constructed of cast-iron columns and girders prefabricated in Birmingham, its walls formed by 300,000 of the largest panes of glass ever made, these held in place by 24 miles of guttering. Displayed inside this cathedral of light were 100,000 exhibits representing every conceivable aspect of mid-nineteenth-century industrial civilisation. 'Whatever human industry has created, you find there,' reported Brontë, 'from the great compartments filled with railway engines and boilers, with mill machinery in full work, with splendid carriages of all kinds, with harness of every description, to the glass-covered and velvet-spread stands loaded with the most gorgeous work of the goldsmith and the silversmith, and the carefully guarded caskets full of real diamonds and pearls worth hundreds of thousands of pounds.'

The brainchild of Prince Albert, the royal consort, the Great Exhibition of the Works of Industry of All Nations – to give it its full title – had been 18 months in the planning and building. Despite the internationalist label, half the exhibitors were British. The real heroes of the show were British engineers like Isambard Kingdom Brunel and Robert Stephenson, and the prime exhibits were British manufactures like the 31-ton Great Western broad-gauge steam engine *Lord of the Isles*. A young Queen Victoria considered the day on which she opened the exhibition 'one of the greatest and most glorious of our lives'. It was a big, bold, brazen celebration of industrial modernity and British global leadership, apparently heralding a new age of prosperity and progress.

Civil strife had dominated the previous two decades, the era of the Great Reform Bill, the Tolpuddle Martyrs, the Corn Laws, and the Chartists. Here was the turning of the page. As Charles Dickens, another of the mid-Victorian *literati* who joined the crowds at the Crystal Palace, remarked, 'the period of revolutionary excitement has in a great measure subsided into an industrial excitement'. The 'age of revolution' (1789–1848) had passed. An 'age of capital' (1848–75) had dawned. How could one deny it amid 'these special signs and tokens of the peaceful progress of the world'? Was it not obvious that 'a good round of industrious work' could achieve so much more than 'the putting to flight of kings'?

This sense of orderly advance to a higher state of being pervaded mid-Victorian Britain. It applied equally to matters of technology and the affairs of men. 'The history of our country in the last 160 years', announced the Whig historian Thomas Macaulay in 1848, 'is eminently the history of physical, moral, and intellectual improvement.' Most informed commentators agreed. The ideal, the British way, was steady, orderly progress under monarch, parliament, and law – in contrast to the civil commotions so frequent among excitable continentals. The Great Exhibition of 1851 captured the spirit of the moment. Charlotte Brontë noticed it in the demeanour of the crowds. 'The multitude filling the great aisles seems ruled and subdued by some invisible influence. Among the 30,000 souls that peopled it the day I was there, not one loud noise was to be heard, not one irregular movement seen; the living tide rolls on quietly, with a deep hum like the sea heard from a distance.'[11]

The new age signalled by the Great Exhibition was no figment. Though British capitalism had led the world for a century or more – with a threefold increase in national income and a five-fold increase in exports during the eighteenth century – the economy had been a fitful mechanism, prone to periodic slumps that suddenly pitched millions from their merely everyday poverty into outright destitution. Early nineteenth-century Britain – run by a parliament of landlords elected on a narrow property franchise – had been shaken by a succession of mass struggles: for the vote, to build trade unions, to win wage increases or impose lower prices, for wholesale reform of a corrupt political system rigged against both the middle class and the poor. What followed this unhappy time – from the defeat of the last great Chartist demonstration in 1848 onwards – was, by contrast, a period of unprecedented economic growth and social peace. In the 20 years from 1851 to 1871, gross national income increased from £523 million to £917 million, the population of London rose from 2.7 million to 3.9 million, and the number of people earning at least £200 a year (those who might be considered 'middle class') doubled. Railway journeys increased from 67 million in 1850 to 490 million in 1875.

Chasms of inequality continued to separate rich and poor. At the top stood the aristocracy and the county families, the bankers and industrialists, the upper professionals, the £5,000 a year class, where land and money were melding into an essentially bourgeois elite, despite residual feudal trappings. At the other extreme were the one in three living at or below the poverty line, and the one in ten in utter destitution. But for a broad middle mass of skilled artisans, clerical workers, and professional men – some of them 'mechanicals', some actual or aspiring 'gentlemen', but all 'respectable', members, as it were, of 'the Bob Cratchit class' and above – the mid-Victorian ideal of 'improvement' was a matter of personal experience. Their living standards were rising, and a wider range of better-quality household goods was now within reach. With average *per capita* income in 1860 of around £33 a year in Britain (compared with £21 in France and £13 in Germany), a mass consumer society was coming into existence.

The veteran Whig politician Lord Palmerston – who served as either Home Secretary, Foreign Secretary, or Prime Minister during most of the period from 1830 to 1865 – captured the spirit of mid-Victorian Britain in a speech famous for this reason. 'We have shown the example of a nation in which every class of society accepts with cheerfulness the lot which providence has assigned to it,' he proclaimed in June 1850, 'while at the same time each individual of each class is constantly trying to raise himself in the social scale, not by violence or illegality, but by persevering good conduct and by the steady and energetic exertion of the moral and intellectual faculties with which his creator has endowed him.'[12]

The prosperity which was both the measure of British success and the underpinning of the country's social harmony depended, of course, upon a rising flow of goods from all corners of the earth. Enter a grand drawing room in the early nineteenth century and one might see chairs of rattan and lacquer-work from China, carpets and rugs from the Middle East, a table of mahogany wood imported from the West Indies and another of ebony wood from West Africa. Tea from Ceylon, coffee from Arabia, and chocolate from South America might be served in a service of Chinese porcelain and sweetened with Caribbean sugar. The hosts might be wearing clothes manufactured from imported cotton, silk, and fur, dyed with Indian indigo, madder, and saffron, buttoned with Omani mother-of-pearl, trimmed with Chinese silver. While the gentlemen smoked pipes filled with Virginia tobacco and sipped wine flavoured with Indonesian cinnamon and Zanzibari cloves, the ladies might nibble cakes made with West Indian molasses and listen to one of their number playing on a piano with keys of African ivory or reading from a book glued with African gum.[13]

⬤

Not everyone viewed the triumphs of Victorian capitalism with unalloyed enthusiasm. London – by now an urban monster ingesting people into its slums and sweatshops at the rate of a third of a million a decade – harboured its communities of discontents. All sorts and conditions of people washed up here, including numerous foreign migrants, many of them refugees from the broken continental revolutions of 1848. Among the German radicals – who spent much of their time engaged in bitter sectarian squabbles – was an obscure left-wing journalist (and squabbler-in-chief) called Karl Marx, now living in a two-room apartment on the upper floor of a terrace in a rundown part of Soho. From his vantage-point of enforced exile and shattered hopes, he observed the smug self-satisfaction of the British scene with a critical eye. Even more so his boon companion, Fred Engels, who now returned to Britain after a temporary absence fomenting revolution, alongside Marx, in the Rhineland. Engels' father had sent him to Manchester to help run the family textile mill in the early 1840s, hopeful that experience of 'the real world' would cure him of youthful idealism. It had the opposite effect. The young radical found himself staring into the Industrial Revolution's black heart. Turning sociological investigator, he ended up writing an early classic of anti-capitalist critique: *The Condition of the Working Class in England* (1845).

Engels had fallen in love with an illiterate Irish mill-worker called Mary Burns, and she, it seems, had been his guide into the nether-regions of the world's first industrial city, a nightmare realm of chimneys belching black smoke, waterways choked with chemicals and refuse, and pitted streets lined with damp, filthy, smelly hovels; a place where a third of a million people were chained to machine labour 12 or more hours a day, often crippled by industrial accidents and occupational diseases, and lived six to a room in stomach-churning squalor – all 'to fill the purses of the bourgeoisie'.

What he saw in Manchester turned Engels into a revolutionary socialist. It was not simply the wretchedness. He saw something more: the workers, massed together in factories and slums, were a potentially earth-shaking political force; an insight that would be fundamental to another publication, written jointly with Marx, three years later – the *Manifesto of the Communist Party*.

'Party' was perhaps too strong a word for the small groups of German émigrés active in London, Brussels, and Paris who had fused into the Communist League in June 1847. The main branch was in London, and the entire membership fitted easily into the White Hart Inn on Drury Lane. Marx and Engels, the leading intellectuals, had won a bitter argument to reject the slogan 'All men are brothers' in favour of 'Workers of the world, unite', and they were then commissioned to write the founding document. Published in German by a printer at Bishopsgate in the City in late February 1848, bundles were then shipped to Europe just in time to play a minor role in the German Revolution of that year. Prussian police repression had ensured that the world communist movement – essentially a German confection – had had its birth in mid-Victorian London. Perhaps this was appropriate, for here was the living heart of the emerging capitalist system.

The *Manifesto* was a rich synthesis of economics, sociology, philosophy, and radicalism. Underpinning the communist *Zeitgeist* was the perception that everything was connected with everything else, that social reality was a complex unity, and that to understand the particular it was necessary to understand the whole. Equally important was the notion that that whole was riddled with contradictions – that society was 'a unity of opposites' – and the resulting tensions gave history its motive power. Nothing was in a fixed state of being, argued the German radicals; everything was in flux, in motion, in a state of becoming.

Never had that sense of history as motion been more apposite. Capitalism had accelerated the pace of events to an unprecedented degree, hyper-charging history's chronic restlessness, packing changes that might once have taken decades, even centuries, into a matter of years. Here was a system which, powered by profit and competition, was growing exponentially, transforming the global economy in a relentless search for raw materials and markets. Nothing like this had ever been seen before. 'Constant revolu-tionising of production, uninterrupted disturbance of all social conditions, everlasting uncertainty and agitation distinguish the bourgeois epoch from all earlier ones', proclaimed the *Manifesto*. 'All fixed, fast-frozen relations, with their train of ancient and venerable prejudices and opinions are swept away, all new-formed ones become antiquated before they can ossify. All that is solid melts into air . . .'

The process knew no limits in time or space. What Marx would come to call 'the self-expansion of value' – accumulation of wealth for its own sake – was both eternal and global. 'The need of a constantly expanding market for its products chases the bourgeoisie over the whole surface of the world. It must nestle everywhere, settle everywhere, establish connections everywhere.'

The two revolutionaries – university-educated in the Teutonic subtleties of the Hegelian dialectic – delved more deeply than most into the inner meaning of such phenomena as the Great Exhibition. They shared the common sense of a world being transformed by technology and engineering, by railways, steamships, and coal power. But they saw at the same time a global system of factory exploitation and colonial oppression 'dripping from head to toe, from every pore, with blood and dirt' (as Marx would later describe it). Joseph Paxton's Crystal Palace was both an affirmation and a denial – its soaring spaces of iron and glass, enclosing wondrous machines and manufactures, amounted to a carefully constructed cocoon to exclude war, genocide, and enslavement. The achievements of bourgeois industrial civilisation were to be celebrated, for sure, but Marx and Engels wished to expose its profound malevolence, its dark alter-ego, hoping that, in the full goodness of time, it would be transcended by the revolutionary action of a class 'with nothing to lose but its chains'.[14]

For most ordinary folk going about their business, seeing such connections was hard. Take that supreme symbol of Victorian female gentility, the piano. When, after long separation, Jane Eyre's childhood nurse pays a visit to her former charge, now an accomplished young woman, she announces that she looks 'genteel enough' and 'like a lady'. Seeking confirmation, Bessie then enquires, 'Can you play on the piano?' There is one in the room, so Jane plays a waltz or two, and Bessie is delighted. Further enquiries reveal that Jane can also paint, embroider, and speak French. Her CV, it seems, is complete: 'Oh, you are quite a lady, Miss Jane!'[15]

Charlotte Brontë knew that the piano was a symbol. As well as providing musical entertainment in a domestic setting otherwise largely bereft of any, and a skilled accomplishment of women otherwise under-occupied, the Victorian piano signified rank, respectability, and refinement. It was the must-have marker of upward mobility for the fast-expanding £200-a-year class.

To meet the demand, new piano factories were opening at the rate of one a year by the middle of the century. Some 178 pianos were exhibited by 102 different manufacturers at the Great Exhibition in 1851. The industry leader alone, John Broadwood & Sons, was producing 5,000 pianos a year – 1,500 grands, 1,500 squares, and 2,000 uprights – almost half of them in a single factory in Westminster employing 575 workers. Few could afford a Broadwood, but countless workshops sprang up at the lower end of the market, and prices dropped from over 40 guineas for a cheap upright (or 'cottage') piano in the 1830s, to 25 guineas in the 1850s, and as little as 12 guineas in the 1880s and 1890s; by this time, pianos could also be hired for 10 or 15 shillings a month, or good second-hand ones purchased for £10 and upwards. Well before this, in his *Music and Morals* of 1871, the Reverend Hugh Haweis had praised the ethical excellence of the cheap piano: 'That domestic and long-suffering instrument, the cottage piano, has probably done more to sweeten existence and bring peace and happiness to families in general, and to young women in particular, than all the homilies on the domestic virtues ever yet penned.'[16]

Ladylike accomplishment, African ivory, the slave trade: here was one of those chains of connection that so few could see, or, in many cases, cared to see. But soaring demand for piano keys – and for other accoutrements of Victorian gentility such as combs, handles, fans, dress accessories, orna-ments, sculptures, and billiard balls – created soaring demand, with prices and profits to match, for the 'white gold' of the African elephant. With adult tusks averaging 5 to 8 feet long and 50 to 100 pounds in weight, the ivory of one animal could make a hundred keyboards. A pair of tusks traded in the interior for a yard or two of cloth and a handful of beads or a coil of brass wire might be worth £50 by the time it reached the coast – more than Dickens' Bob Cratchit earned in a year. The trade escalated through the century, culminating in an 'ivory frenzy' at its end, when hunters were killing 100,000 elephants a year.[17]

For ivory, read slavery: mid-century, the two were virtually inextricable. Elephants and humans shared both the equatorial forests of West Africa and the Congo (domain of the smaller forest elephant) and the savannah, the great arc of grasslands extending across North-Central, Eastern, and Southern Africa (domain of the bush elephant). Rough estimates – nothing more is possible – are that this vast region was home in 1800 to around 60 million people and 25 million elephants. Both came to be hunted on a rising industrial scale during the nineteenth century. As the interior was opened up, as Central Africa was integrated into the global market, it was penetrated by long arms of mercantile capitalism reaching in for its ivory and its labour. The imperatives of capital accumulation were predominant.

Even when, in the last quarter of the century, European colonialists displaced Arab slavers, the plundering of the continent for primary commodities meant no end to forced labour. The Europeans 'abolished' the slave trade – but still conscripted Africans to work in the mines, on the plantations, and as porters, making free use of the lash and the gun when they did so.

The ivory–slavery nexus often came down to the simple fact that ivory was heavy, the trails long, and other kinds of labour scarce. Slaves were needed as porters to transport trade goods and supplies on the outward journey, ivory and other commodities on the return; and also to serve as soldiers, guards, general labourers, domestic servants, and sex workers. But there was more to it than that. The whole Indian Ocean economy was booming on a rising global market for primary commodities. The island emporium of Zanzibar on the East African coast, for example, experienced a six-fold increase in maritime trade between the early 1830s and the mid-1850s. The Arab-Swahili merchant class was trading not just ivory, but also cloves, cowries, gum-copal, hides, sesame seeds, coconut products, beeswax, and tortoiseshell. As much as they could source, they could sell. The only way to meet demand was to expand the labour force, and that meant more slaves, for it was slaves who harvested cloves in hill plantations on the island, slaves who hacked out gum-copal from claggy pits near the sea, slaves who trawled the shorelines of the mainland for cowrie shells.

Much the same story could be told of any place on the great mercantile arc that stretched up the western shores of the Indian subcontinent, along the southern rim of Arabia, across to the Horn of Africa, down the East African coast, finally curling east again to Madagascar and the French sugar islands; an arc of commerce that included two great north-western projections, the Persian Gulf and the Red Sea, that penetrated to the heart of the Middle East. Rising demand for global commodities meant rising demand for slaves. Some for transport to the New World, in Portuguese, Cuban, Spanish, or American hulls. Some destined to labour on sugar plantations in the Indian Ocean, cotton plantations in the Nile Delta, date plantations in the Persian Gulf, or pearl fisheries on the Muscat coast, carried to these places in Indian, Omani, or Arab-Swahili dhows. Others – many others – to work as guards, domestics, concubines, and eunuchs in the households of Arab sheikhs, Turkish pashas, and Persian landlords growing rich on the profits of trade.[18]

Here, then, was another commodity of the African interior for which demand was rising and whose value rose exponentially towards the coast. And what the ivory traders had done was to open up the interior, creating the tracks, stations, and local arrangements by which commodities other than ivory might pass. 'If it had not been for the high value of ivory,' averred Dr Georg Schweinfurth, who spent the years 1868 to 1871 exploring Central Africa:

> the countries about the sources of the Nile would even now be as little unfolded to us as the equatorial centre of the great continent ... The settlements owe their original existence to the ivory trade; but ... these settlements in various ways have facilitated the operations of the regular slave-traders. Without these depots, the professional slave-traders could never have penetrated so far, whilst now they are enabled to pour themselves into the negro countries annually by thousands ...[19]

Ivory and slavery formed a predatory economic nexus that was hollowing out an entire continent. Africa's people were being killed, enslaved, and dispossessed to supply the industrial expansion and consumer societies of Europe and America. As Marx and Engels had realised, every artefact of civilisation – like a piano – was at the same time an artefact of barbarism – in the case of this example, that of the ivory trail. And the contradiction between the two – between, if you will, liberal idealism and frontier capitalism – was set to become a political storm in middle-class Britain.

The storm-maker, however, would not be either of the German revolutionaries. Both the Soho scribbler, now busy researching for his masterwork in the British Library, and the Manchester mill-manager, earning the money to keep them both, remained – for the time being at least – lost in obscurity. The age of capital was an age of social peace. Marx and Engels were destined for the long haul. Their time, for now, was devoted to theoretical groundwork. The storm-maker – the man who would re-launch the struggle against slavery – was a doctor, missionary, and explorer recently returned from Africa. And by the time he rose to address a crowded meeting of dignitaries, dons, and students in Cambridge University's Senate House on the night of 4 December 1857, he had become a national hero: Dr David Livingstone.

It was an extraordinary apotheosis. He had returned to London in December 1856, and a national lecture tour in the year since had made him headline news, the talk of the chattering classes, a man liable to find himself mobbed by people wanting to shake his hand. He was made a fellow of the Royal Geographical Society, which august body proclaimed his work 'the greatest triumph in geographical research which has been effected in our times'. He was awarded honorary doctorates by Oxford and Glasgow universities, and granted a private audience by Queen Victoria. His book, *Missionary Travels and Researches in South Africa*, published in November 1857, was destined to sell 70,000 copies. When he stood on the podium at the Senate House, therefore, it was before an audience in awe of the great man. Here, it seemed, in flesh and blood, was the living embodiment of the mid-Victorian ideal of a hero: a man of action and adventure, for sure, a man of tremendous determination and endurance, but also a man guided by Christian inspiration and noble, philanthropic purpose.

Here he was, on the stage, speaking now. The distinguished persons about him may have seemed grander. The university registrar observed the contrast: 'we saw a man of moderate height, very plainly dressed, his faced tanned to a dark brown by long exposure to sun and wind, and furrowed by deep lines that spoke of anxiety, hardship, and disease endured and overcome. I think I never saw any man whose appearance told its own tale as Livingstone's did.' A human body that was its own narrative, then: a charismatic presence, therefore; one that shone forth among the better dressed but less accomplished around him.

And what was he saying, in his Glaswegian brogue, using 'short, jerky sentences' expressive of thoughts he could not arrange in set periods', yet which, for all that, were more powerful than 'the most carefully ordered speech'? That he had gone to Africa as a missionary. That talk of this as 'sacrifice' was nonsense, for it was a privilege to do God's work. That he had discovered something monstrous: that, despite British naval patrols on the Atlantic coast, the slave trade was thriving in the interior; that 'the natives of Central Africa are very desirous of trading, but their only traffic is at present in slaves'.

This was no mere travelogue: it was a summons to crusade. 'My desire is to open a path to this district, that Civilisation, Commerce, and Christianity might find their way there.' He was going back, but he could not do all that needed to be done without help. 'I beg to direct your attention to Africa. I know that in a few years I shall be cut off in that country, which is now open. Do not let it be shut again! I go back to Africa to try to make an open path for Commerce and Christianity. Do you carry out the work which I have

begun. I leave it with you.' A moment of stunned silence. Then an explosion
of applause, everyone rising to their feet, volley after volley of cheers.[20]

It was not simply that Livingstone personified the bourgeois self-confi-
dence of Victorian Britain in the age of capital. There was something else
about his celebrity: he was working class. This made him the embodiment
of another mid-Victorian ideal: that of the self-made man, one who owed
nothing to title, money, favour, everything to effort and merit – the very
personification of 'improvement'.

He had been born the second of seven children in Blantyre, an industrial
village a short distance from Glasgow, in 1813. The entire family lived in a
single-room apartment in a company tenement block. Everything – cooking,
eating, washing, sleeping, copulating – happened in a space 14 feet by 10.
There was no piped water; slops and refuse were emptied down a communal
sluice-hole; the shared outdoor earth-closets stank. The parents were, of
course, desperately poor, and the children were sent out to work as soon as
possible. David Livingstone began work as a piecer in the local mill at the
age of 10. Work began at six in the morning and continued until eight at
night, six days a week. Many of the young piecers had to walk 20 miles in the
course of a working day. When they began to flag towards the end of a shift,
they were beaten with a leather strap or doused with cold water.

It is difficult to imagine any child worker finding time for play or study.
David Livingstone was an exception: already taught by his father to read and
write, he spent two hours in the company school after work each day
learning Latin. Education became an obsession. He would read at night
until his mother took his book away to make him sleep. He would prop up
a book on the frame of the spinning-jenny while working in the mill. On
Sundays – bar time reserved for religious observance – he would walk the
landscape teaching himself about rocks and plants. He later rejected the
grim Calvinism of his father in favour of a Congregationalist faith more
open to enquiry, science, and philanthropic activism. The middle class got
the vote in 1832, slavery was abolished in 1833, and the spirit of the age was
reform: the world beckoned. David Livingstone made the decision to
become a medical missionary in 1834. He was well enough educated, but it
took him two years to save the money for the fees. Then, in the autumn of
1836, he achieved the near impossible: the child mill-worker from a Blantyre
tenement entered Anderson's College in Glasgow to train as a doctor.[21]

Over the next four years, he qualified in medicine, was accepted for
service by the London Missionary Society, and was ordained a Congregational

minister. Then, at the age of 27, he sailed from London to Cape Town and set foot on the African continent for the first time on 15 March 1841. David Livingstone had come from the bottom; he had had no childhood; he had succeeded in elevating himself to professional status only by gruelling application. These circumstances had left their mark. He was humourless, devoid of a sense of play, lacking in every social skill, incapable of personal warmth; throughout life, to the very day of his death, he remained utterly fixated on work, pushing himself forward relentlessly, pushing aside companions who could not keep pace.

For a short while, the restless spirit was becalmed. But the desolation of Kuruman – the most remote missionary station, 500 miles upcountry, where he arrived at the end of July – was a shock. A small village and 40 Christian converts: this, he discovered, was the sum-total of two decades' work by Robert Moffat, the most celebrated missionary in Southern Africa. He had met Moffat in London in 1840 and found inspiration in his tales of 'the smoke of a thousand villages where no missionary had ever been'. Now Moffat insisted that he, Livingstone, was the man to carry the cross northwards, to establish new stations on virgin ground. Over the next several years he tried: Mabotsa in 1844, Chonuane in 1845, Kolobeng in 1847. But each failed for a different mix of reasons, and the whole achievement of Livingstone's first decade in Africa came down to one solitary convert; and he, in any case, soon lapsed, making zero.[22]

Although he never admitted as much, when he embarked on his first journeys of exploration – three of them between 1849 and 1851 that took him 500 miles north from Bechuanaland to the fringes of Central Africa – David Livingstone had, in effect, given up as a missionary and gone in search of another purpose in life. This he found with that dramatic first sighting of the Zambesi. Determined to abandon for good the sterile monotony of an established mission-station, he returned to the Cape to put his wife and children on a boat bound for England. He had married Mary Moffat, daughter of Robert, in 1845. There had been no romance, merely convenience, and Livingstone's attitude to his wife bordered on indifference. Over the next six years, much of it spent travelling in the bush, Mary gave birth to five children; her husband dubbed her 'the great Irish manufactory'. Now that he had resolved to become an explorer, she and her brood were dispatched home as so much surplus impedimenta. He then returned to the north with two aims: to establish a mission-station and trading centre – a new model settlement of Victorian civilisation – in a healthy district of the

Makololo country, one free of malaria and the tsetse fly; and to open up a route from the coast to the interior along the Zambesi.[23]

He was evolving from a doctor and a missionary into a strange hybrid: still equipped with medicine chest, still a man of deep religious conviction who yearned to bring enlightenment to the heathen, he was becoming an explorer, an anti-slavery crusader, and an advocate of trade expansion who was determined to be the first to open up new routes into the heart of Africa. Back in 1840, the same year Moffat had triggered his missionary vision, Livingstone had attended a huge public meeting in Exeter Hall on the Strand, where Thomas Buxton, a leading abolitionist, had propounded on the reforming power of capitalism. Give African chieftains who currently sell their own people in exchange for cloth, beads, and guns the chance to trade in native produce, he proclaimed, and the slave trade will wither away. *Laissez-faire* will free the slave. Commerce is civilisation incarnate. Just the message for the workshop of the world on the verge of its first great boom. The trick, though, was to open routes into the interior so that capitalism's cleansing shafts might penetrate the darkness. This was the challenge for a new generation of anti-slavery campaigners. Livingstone logged the message, stored it away, and then, ten years later, having reached the banks of a mighty river that looped and flowed through hundreds of miles of Africa's depths, he felt he had discovered his life's purpose.[24]

In the course of two further journeys – the first, between November 1853 and May 1854, north along the upper Zambesi, then west to the coast at Luanda; the second, between November 1855 and May 1856, down the Zambesi all the way to the East Coast at Quilimane – he crossed the continent and traversed a distance little short of 2,500 miles. 'I shall open a path to the interior or perish,' he had vowed; and for sure both journeys brought him close to death. He arrived in Luanda at the end of the first broken in body and soul, wracked by dysentery and fever, suffering from deep depression. Approaching the town, he had been able to remain seated on his ox for no more than ten minutes at a time; it would be two months before he was fit enough to write a letter. Two years later, he was so sick with fever when he finally reached Quilimane that he gave instructions as to what should be done in the event of his death. Yet his spirit was unconquerable. Already he was thinking ahead. 'I do not feel much elated by the prospect of accomplishing this feat,' he wrote to Sir Roderick Murchison of the Royal Geographical Society. 'Viewed in relation to my calling, the end of the geographical feat is only the beginning of the enterprise . . .'[25]

The new Zambesi expedition of 1858 set out in a warm glow of optimism, carrying the hopes of a nation. Though denied further funding by the London Missionary Society – who suspected, rightly, that Livingstone had effectively ceased to be a missionary – the celebrity explorer was now in the enthusiastic embrace of the Royal Geographical Society, whose well-connected leader soon persuaded the Foreign Office to award him £5,000 of British government money and an appointment as 'British Consul' with a roving commission for East Africa. The government grant, combined with Livingstone's book royalties and public subscriptions, made it possible to hire a team of six specialists – a naval officer, an engineer, a geologist, an artist, a combined doctor and botanist (John Kirk), and a minister cum personal assistant to the expedition leader (David's younger brother Charles) – and to ensure that the expedition lacked for nothing in equipment and provisioning. The Royal Geographical Society launched its new flagship project at a sell-out grand dinner in the Freemasons' Hall in London, where Murchison claimed that 'no expedition could have been better organised', and Livingstone reiterated his intention to 'establish a system of free labour in Africa'. For this remained the goal: to open up a route along the Zambesi so as to 'aid in the great work of supplanting by lawful commerce the odious traffic in slaves' (as Livingstone put it in a private letter to John Kirk). The fuller vision was of new agricultural settlements and new Christian communities emerging in Central Africa through integration of the interior into global markets along a great river highway. The slave trade was to be undercut by a moral economy based on *laissez-faire*.[26]

Everything that could go wrong did go wrong. The *Pearl*, a 160-foot steamship on loan from the government, was unable to get beyond the sandbanks and mudflats at the mouth of the Zambesi. The *Ma-Robert*, a 50-foot riverboat, was too small to carry the full expedition, and in any case was unable to negotiate the Kebrabasa Rapids, 400 miles upstream from the coast. Livingstone's alternative, an ascent of the Shire, a major north–south tributary of the Zambesi fed by Lake Nyasa, was only marginally more successful: the Murchison Cataracts were impassable to river traffic, and the Shire Highlands, though relatively healthy and suitable for agricultural exploitation, had already been rendered dangerous by slave raiding. Despite this, Livingstone – under pressure because of the investment of resources and expectations in the expedition – reported favourably to London and urged the dispatch of a mission. This proved disastrous: the missionaries duly arrived, became embroiled in fighting with local tribesmen, and then lost their leader, Bishop Mackenzie, to dysentery. Another new arrival also succumbed. Mary Livingstone, abandoned at home with her children for long years, had taken to the bottle and the denunciation of all missionaries. Belatedly invited to join her husband on the Shire, she soon sickened and died, leaving Livingstone guilt-ridden.

By this time, his working relationships with all of his colleagues, including his own brother, had broken down. As much as anything, it was his lack of basic leadership skills – refusal to face reality, inability to work in a collegiate way, lack of sympathy with human frailty, morose taciturnity amid all the discomfort, privation, and frustration of African exploration – that destroyed the expedition. Not least, unable to admit fault in himself, he routinely blamed others when things went wrong, often in a manner that was not only dishonest but positively malicious. As things fell apart, he withdrew inside himself, sunk in depression, harbouring a death-wish: 'Am I to be a martyr to my own cause? I begin to think I may not live to see success. Am I to experience that this cause is to be founded on my sacrifice and cemented by my suffering?' John Kirk found it 'useless making any remark to him' and eventually concluded that he was 'cracked', 'out of his mind', 'a most unsafe leader'.[27]

Six years later, in July 1864, Livingstone was back in London. *The Times* had already passed judgment on the abortive expedition in January the previous year. A damning editorial intoned: 'We were promised cotton, sugar, and indigo . . . and of course we got none. We were promised trade; and there is no trade . . . We were promised converts, and not one has been made. In a word, thousands subscribed by the universities and contributed by the government have been productive only of the most fatal results.' This was accurate, and it was the consensus: no route to the interior, no route to the Lakes, no trade, no missions, no nothing, only failures, rows, and losses. So this time there was no triumphant return of the intrepid explorer-hero; no lecture tour, no grand dinners, no handshakes in the street, no invitations from the great and the good.[28]

And yet . . . the passion of David Livingstone burned stronger than ever. His earlier narrative, *Missionary Travels and Researches in South Africa* (1857), had mentioned slavery in passing. His new book, *Narrative of an Expedition to the Zambesi and its Tributaries* (1865), was an abolitionist tirade to shake the rafters. In the very first sentence he proclaimed his intention 'to bring before my countrymen, and all others interested in the cause of humanity, the misery entailed by the slave-trade ...'. He described in detail each encounter during six long years of travel with what he called 'the curse of Africa'. The tangled corpses, bloated by the sun, victims of the latest raid. The landscapes of desolation – the smoking villages, abandoned fields, and starving fugitives in the bush. The families ripped apart; the women weeping over stolen children gone forever. The long lines of black humanity trudging on broken feet, manacled, yoked, driven forward by lash and gun. The heaps of bones, the murdered who had failed to keep up. The waste of life 'beyond description'. The human misery that 'outstrips all we ever saw'.[29]

The world was ready for this. A new wind of reform and revolution was blowing. While Livingstone was away, Europe had been exhilarated by Garibaldi, the Redshirts, and the Italian *Risorgimento* in 1860, then by a Polish national uprising against the Russian Tsar in 1863. Karl Marx, for one, had sensed the fresh current: after more than a decade in the library, he returned to political agitation, helping to launch a new socialist party, the International Working Men's Association, at a packed meeting in St Martin's Hall, Covent Garden, in September 1864. And across the Atlantic, a terrible four-year civil war was nearing its end – a war against slavery; a war that had begun as a war to reunite a nation, but had turned into a war to define what that nation was; a war that eventually put 200,000 former slaves into military uniform and transformed them into an army of liberation. 'Fondly do we hope, fervently do we pray, that this mighty scourge of war may speedily pass away,' President Lincoln said at his second inaugural address on 4 March 1865. 'Yet, if God wills that it continue until all the wealth piled by the bondsman's 250 years of unrequited toil shall be sunk, and until every drop of blood drawn with the lash shall be paid by another drawn with the sword, as was said 3,000 years ago, so still it must be said, "The judgments of the Lord are true and righteous altogether".'

David Livingstone paraphrased those words in his journal. When, barely a month later, the President was killed by an assassin's bullet, he took it hard. There were lessons to be drawn here, were there not? Perhaps he, David Livingstone, had conceived of matters back to front. He had imagined that commerce might displace slavery, when perhaps, in fact, slavery had to be displaced to give commerce a chance. As he wrote in his *Narrative*, 'The result of our observation of the actual working of the slave-trade at its source is that it must prove an insurmountable barrier to all moral and commercial progress.'

In any case, as he now knew, the Zambesi could not serve as a great conduit of civilisation into the African interior; while in the meantime, the slave trade was establishing an unlimited dominion across that interior.

Another way would have to be found, and soon. Lincoln's death had been only one among more than 600,000: that had been the cost of abolition on the North American continent. That is why the President had felt compelled to remind his people that God sometimes required a blood sacrifice in the cause of freedom. Force had been necessary against the ferocity of the slave lords of the American South. Perhaps force would be necessary also in Africa. A new vision was forming: that of armed humanitarian intervention.[30]

# CHAPTER TWO

# THE MOUNTAINS OF THE MOON

Sunrise on 7 April 1855. Berbera on the Somali coast. John Hanning Speke, a 28-year-old Indian Army officer on extended leave, woke that morning to an extraordinary spectacle, one that covered the whole breadth of the plain.

Almost 2,500 miles to the south-west, on the opposite side of Africa, David Livingstone, wracked with fever and wading through floodwater, was on his way back from Luanda to Linyanti, having completed the first half of his epic transcontinental crossing, sudden fame and subsequent failure still in the future.

Across the whole vast distance separating Livingstone and Speke at that moment, the slave trade was active. Down on the Zambesi line, it was in the hands of Portuguese traders operating out of the Mozambican ports. Up on the Horn, it was Somali warlords. A huge caravan from Harar – 250 miles away over a desiccated wilderness of sand and scrub – was arriving at Berbera bringing goods to sell to merchants working the sea lanes through the Gulf of Aden. The caravan had gathered size as it came, smaller tributaries joining along the trail, travellers and traders aggregating for safety's sake, until it had swelled into a column of 3,000 people and several thousand camels and head of cattle. They moved – 'like a busy stream of ants' – in long files, each camel's nose tied to the tail of the one in front. On the flanks were outriders armed with spears and bows, and circling about other detachments, also armed, on guard against surprise attack. In the midst of the caravan, driven along on foot by Somali camel-men, was a chain – a literal chain – of 500 or more slaves.

A great fair was in progress in and around Berbera. As many as 20,000 people had gathered, Somalis of course, but also Arabs from Yemen and Oman, and Indians from Kutch and Bombay, the visitors erecting 'mat huts as booths for carrying on their bartering trade'. The locals came to buy

American and British cloth, beads of various sorts, small bars of iron and steel, also zinc and lead, as well as dates and rice. 'In exchange for these, they exported slaves, cattle, gums of all sorts, ghee, ivory, ostrich feathers, and rhinoceros horns.'[1]

Speke was in camp near Berbera in anticipation of the departure of an expedition into the Somali interior under the leadership of Richard Burton. The intention had been that the expedition would travel under the protection of the great caravan on its return journey, but Burton had decided to wait at Berbera for final deliveries of equipment from Europe. So the fair broke up and the caravan departed, but the little encampment of explorers remained.

They had been in the region for several months, travelling and making preparations, and local suspicions had been aroused, for Europeans were known to be hostile to the slave trade. Burton had chosen to ignore the warning signs; nor had he made adequate security arrangements. The four Englishmen and their native servants were camped a short distance from the sea. Early one morning, they were awoken as some 200 Somalis invaded the camp. Assailed by volleys of stones, musket fire, and men wielding spears and swords, Stroyan was killed, Burton was stabbed in the face, and Speke was felled and pinned to the ground; only Herne was left unscathed. Burton and Herne fled the scene, finding safety on the boat that had conveyed them from Aden. Speke suffered multiple injuries at the hands of his captors, but, by some superhuman effort, finally made a run for it, outpaced all his pursuers, and was then carried to the boat by some of the expedition servants.[2]

The Somaliland expedition was over. It had been a comprehensive failure. But if it was ill-conceived and badly managed, what doomed it was the hostility of local people towards foreign interlopers. This savage little encounter had been a collision between European adventurers and Somali slave traders.

What had drawn Burton and Speke to Africa was the world's greatest geographical mystery, still, after 2,500 years, unresolved in the middle of the nineteenth century: the source of the Nile. The mystery that had once bemused the Greeks and was still bemusing the Victorians was this: how come a mighty river flowed for 1,200 miles through the desert, even at the hottest time of year, without replenishment by any tributary along this immense distance? How come its level rose and fell, on schedule, year in, year out, such that its annual floodwaters never failed to deliver the moisture and nutrients to the banks and delta that were the basis of every Egyptian civilisation that had ever existed?

The Greek historian Herodotus could obtain no reliable answers to his enquiries in the fifth century BC: 'of the sources of the Nile no-one can give any account,' he was obliged to report, 'it enters Egypt from parts beyond'. Alexander the Great fared no better the following century, getting no proper answer to his question 'What causes the Nile to rise?' when he asked it at the Temple of Ammon in Luxor. The Roman emperor Nero, equally curious, dispatched two centurions upriver in the first century AD to find the answer; but they were blocked around 2,000 miles above the mouth by the Sudd, a vast swamp, hundreds of miles wide, comprising a maze of channels choked with aquatic plants and infested with mosquitoes.

Then, from an altogether different direction, some solid information. A map drawn up in the mid-second century AD by the geographer Ptolemy incorporated the testimony of a Greek merchant called Diogenes, who had travelled inland from the East African coast for 25 days and arrived 'in the vicinity of two great lakes and the snowy range of mountains whence the Nile draws its twin sources'. Ptolemy's map duly depicted two channels converging to form the Nile, each fed by a lake lying to the south, each lake in turn fed by smaller rivers, these rising in a range of mountains which the geographer labelled 'the Mountains of the Moon'.[3]

And there, effectively, matters rested for one and a half millennia. Only then were the headwaters of the Blue Nile explored by two Jesuit priests in the early seventeenth century and by a Scottish explorer called James Bruce in the mid-eighteenth century. But the Blue Nile, which flows out of Lake Tana high up on the Ethiopian plateau, is but a tributary of the main river, dried-up for part of the year, a thousand miles shorter than its great sister. And the secret of the White Nile, despite the efforts of a succession of European adventurers and traders in the early nineteenth century, remained hidden as late as the 1850s.[4]

The matter was finally settled in the two decades between 1856, when Richard Burton and John Hanning Speke set out on the first major expedition to the Great Lakes of East Africa, and 1876, when Henry Morton Stanley completed the mapping of the Lakes before heading off into the interior to follow the Congo down to the West Coast. What drew these and other men – notably David Livingstone and Samuel Baker – deep into an Africa that was unknown, perilous, and disease-ridden? What caused them to endure the discomfort and privation, the sickness and pain, the tedium of long marches and long delays, the loneliness of the bush, the omnipresent shadow of death?

It will not do merely to describe them – and thus condemn them – as pioneers of empire. They were nationalists and colonialists, for sure, but their motives were pure, since they wholeheartedly believed that Britain was the embodiment of the Victorian ideals of improvement, progress, and civilisation. They were adventurers imbued with moral purpose – not the ruthless exploiters and mass killers of the 'age of empire' (1875–1914) to come. They drew maps and charted routes, but without knowledge of how they would be used; they blazed the trail unwittingly for a Scramble for Africa that would trample their vision of a continent lifted from poverty and ignorance, but they had little intuition of this. They were children at the dawn of capitalist civilisation, innocent of the monstrous crimes of which it was capable; they could not know, as the novelist Joseph Conrad would know a generation later, that they carried the torch for a system of 'robbery with violence' that would transform Central Africa into 'the heart of an immense darkness'. We do them an injustice, we misrepresent them, if we visit upon them the guilt of men like Cecil Rhodes, Frederick Lugard, and Evelyn Baring.[5]

The mid-Victorian explorers found in the mystery of the Nile a supreme test of manliness – of courage, endurance, and endeavour. It was a test, moreover, made virtuous by the object in view: the advancement of knowledge and science, the bringing of civilisation and progress. The explorers were embodiments of a bourgeois ideal of enterprise and achievement. They represented the optimism and absence of doubt that, in a very different way, had been symbolised by the Great Exhibition. They personified the age of capital.

They were therefore men of extremes, bordering on madness. They recoiled from the routines of commercial offices or peacetime barracks. They craved the adventure and challenge of wild places. Burton thought, 'Man wants to wander, and he must do so, or he shall die.' Speke feared being lost in 'the constant whirl of civilisation', whereas 'out in the forests of Africa you are *the* man amongst your surroundings'. Baker wanted to be 'a wandering spirit' vanishing 'into the unknown'. Stanley sought self-affirmation in a continent where the human spirit was 'not repressed by fear, nor depressed by ridicule and insults . . . [but] soars free and unrestrained'. But death waited in the bush;

and if not death, madness. As Livingstone's Zambesi expedition fell to pieces, his frantic need to be in control and never wrong drove him to near-psychotic fury. 'Still there is no change in Dr L's plans,' John Kirk confided to his journal. 'He is going on still, regardless of the return. His determination seems to amount to infatuation.' A little later he wrote starkly: 'I can come to no other conclusion than that Dr L is mad.'[6]

Their first view of Zanzibar, when it hoved into view on 20 December 1856, was of an exotic tropical island bathed in sunlight, its gentle contours carrying lush green growth right down to the water's edge, where emerald blue water lapped onto beaches of white coral. Closer, a distinctive perfume wafted on the wind, a scent of cloves and spices and the East. Burton and Speke, arriving from Bombay on the Indian Navy sloop *Elphinstone*, bringing with them a collection of scientific instruments and expeditionary equipment, were set upon a great journey to the Mountains of the Moon – 'a range white with eternal snows even in the blaze of the African summer, supposed to be the father of the mysterious Nile . . . a tract invested with all the romance of wild fable and hoar antiquity, to this day the [most] worth-while subject to which human energy could be devoted'. Thus had Lieutenant Richard Francis Burton of the 18th Regiment of Bombay Native Infantry described his intended destination in a letter to his superiors requesting a leave of absence two years beforehand.

He was a man of exceptional talent, fluent in half a dozen Indian languages, as well as Arabic, Persian, and Sanskrit, and his observations during his travels were encyclopaedic, ranging from trade statistics through physical geography and social anthropology to descriptions of plants and rocks. But people found him hard to place. He was brilliant, but also bohemian, a debauchee, a restless sensation-seeker. Though consumed by ambition, he lacked clear direction or moral purpose; his was the ambition of a dilettante; and it was capable of evolving into deranged jealousy of more successful rivals. Then, as the implosion of his relationship with Speke was soon to demonstrate, he could become sly, acerbic, and malicious – characteristics that seemed to find expression in his dark features, weather-beaten complexion, scowling countenance, and glaring, threatening eyes. Everyone remembered the eyes – they were 'large, black, flashing eyes', or 'questing panther eyes', or 'eyes like a wild beast'. Burton had the persona of a Balkan bandit.

Undercover work had been his forte in India and, later, while on leave in 1853, he had disguised himself as an Afghan Sufi and peddler of medicines and horoscopes so as to make the pilgrimage to Mecca, something forbidden to infidels on pain of death. His Nile obsession seems to have taken root later that same year. 'For unnumbered centuries, explorers have attempted the unknown source of the White River by voyaging and travelling and literally against the stream,' he wrote. 'I shall be the first to try by a more feasible line to begin with the head.' Having transferred from the East India Company's army to its political department, he had relocated to Aden, and it was from here that he had launched the shambolic Somaliland expedition. (The company, ever alert to possible commercial advantage, sometimes indulged the whims of the mavericks attracted to its service.)[7]

After a time on sick leave in England – he took several months to recover fully from the injuries received at Berbera – followed by a short period of service at the tail-end of the Crimean War with a brigade of Turkish irregular cavalry, Burton secured the backing of the Royal Geographical Society for a new expedition of African exploration. The intention this time was a direct approach from the East African coast to ascertain the limits of an 'Inland Sea or Lake' the existence of which had just been reported to the Society. The assumption, of course, was that this might be the source of the Nile.[8]

As they approached the coast of Zanzibar for the first time, the two explorers, Burton, the 36-year-old leader, and Speke, now in his 30th year, could see at anchor a distance from the harbour half a dozen square-rigged Western merchantmen. Bobbing nearer to the shore were 60 or 70 Indian Ocean dhows. Beyond lay shingle slipways and stone quays, warehouses and offices, and a little town of simple, square buildings with flat roofs and white-washed walls, mainly two-storey along the seafront, but single-storey in the narrow streets behind. The two men would have plenty of time to explore – six months gathering intelligence, assembling equipment, collecting supplies, recruiting foremen, guards, and porters, before they could set off – and Burton, a meticulous researcher interested in everything, was later to publish a two-volume description of Zanzibar.

Dominant amidst the grander merchant houses along the waterfront was the palace of the Sultan, a large two-storey house with white walls, seafront veranda, red roof, and green shutters. It was fronted by a wharf and a platform mounted with ancient cannon. Nearby stood a mosque, a mausoleum, stables, and sundry outhouses. In the square outside the palace the blood-red flag of the Sultan flew over the place of public execution and mutilation.

Next door was a low, crenellated, thin-walled fort, also mounting a handful of ancient cannon, the interior jammed with the crude huts of the household guard, and housing the only jail on the island, complete with stocks and manacles. Between the fort and the sea lay a third building no less important: the customs house. It may have lacked pretension and refinement, being little more than a long, low roof of matting supported on two dozen tree-trunks, but it was the true centre of an informal mercantile empire that stretched 1,000 miles into Africa and 3,000 miles across the Indian Ocean. 'From the sea it is conspicuous as the centre of circulation,' Burton wrote, 'the heart from and to which twin streams of blacks are ever ebbing and flowing, whilst the beach and the waters opposite it are crowded with shore-boats, big and small. Inland, it is backed by sacks and bales, baskets and packages, hillocks of hides, old ship's tanks, piles of valuable woods, heaps of ivories, and a heterogeneous mass of waifs and strays . . .'[9]

The wealth of Zanzibar was a function of its role in the Indian Ocean trading system. And this in turn was a function of the monsoon and the dhow. From November to February the prevailing winds swept down from the north-east, while from April to September they blew from the south-west. For perhaps 2,000 years, the merchant dhows of the Indian Ocean had carried Arabian spices, Persian glass, Bengali cloth, and Chinese porcelain to East Africa on the north-easters, and returned a few months later laden with gold, iron, leather, ivory, and salt on the south-westers. The dhow was a fast, sleek, coast-skimming sailing vessel, low along the sides, narrow across the beam, but with a high poop deck at the bow, and a sharply upturned stern designed to chop through water at speed. A sloping mast carried a long yard, set at a 45° angle, aligned with the keel, running the length of the ship. This supported a triangular 'lateen' sail, the lower corner of which was loose, so that it could be rigged to catch and channel the wind on either side of the vessel. Larger dhows – the deep-sea *baghlahs* – might be 100 feet in length, weigh 300 tons, carry a second mast and lateen, perhaps a 'jib' sail on the bowsprit, and require a crew of 30 or more to manage. The dhow was the supreme maritime carrier of the Indian Ocean trade. The 60 or 70 vessels at anchor off Zanzibar harbour when Burton and Speke arrived in December 1856 were waiting for the wind to shift to the south-west for the return run. When it did, the main cargo of many would be slaves.[10]

A small island barely 50 miles from north to south and 15 miles across, Zanzibar owed its importance to its close proximity to the mainland coast, just 20 miles away on the western horizon. From here a network of tracks and fortified compounds stretched away in all directions, reaching up to a thousand miles inland, a latticework of connections though which the dhows waiting at the coastal stations were supplied with the white ivory and black skin on which the wealth of Zanzibar depended. The bush trails and dhow traffic were mainly in the hands of Arab-Swahili traders, but the merchants who provided much of the capital and controlled the wholesale trade on the island were usually Omani Arabs or Indian Hindus from Kutch. The Zanzibari mercantile elite, 'active only in pursuit of gain', lived in substantial stone houses, owned large plantations, and kept 'goodly gangs of male and female slaves'. Some were fabulously rich. 'There are now Arab merchants,' Burton claimed, 'who own 80,000 clove-trees, $100,000 floating capital, a ship or two, and from 1,000 to 2,000 slaves.'

At least 100,000 people lived on Zanzibar in the middle of the nineteenth century, of whom perhaps two-thirds were African slaves. And of the 20,000 or so new slaves landed from the mainland each year, roughly one in four stayed on the island, to work in the clove plantations, the copal diggings, the grand houses, or the brothels. The rest were destined for the long passage north, anything between a handful and 500 head per dhow, packed tight beneath bamboo decks in the tropical heat, folded into tiny spaces, sitting in shit and piss, struggling to breathe in disease-ridden fug, gasping for water, gnawed by hunger. Some would not survive. Some would die where they crouched. Others, discovered to be sick, would be thrown overboard lest they contaminate the cargo. A good number would succumb to the lust and sadism of the crew. But enough would reach port – where they could be restored and fattened before going on sale – to make packing the dhows to capacity the most profitable way to traffic slaves.[11]

Burton was a bitter man and a racist. He considered slavery 'an evil necessity' and believed abolition would restore Zanzibar to 'the iguana and the turtle'. But he was an acute observer of 'the atrocities of the capture, the brutalities of the purchase, the terrors of the middle-passage, and the horrors to which the wretches are exposed when entering half-civilised lands'. He viewed Zanzibar's public slave market with the same mix of fascination and disgust as most European observers. An open square surrounded by sheds and tethering posts, it reminded many of a stock market at home. The more valuable slaves were sorted and priced by category, cleaned and groomed for display, then paraded naked for inspection. Young women destined for the harem were, according to a British naval officer who visited in 1811, prepared for sale by 'having their skins cleaned, and burnished with coconut oil, their faces painted with red and white stripes . . . and the hands, noses, ears, and feet ornamented with a profusion of bracelets of gold and silver and jewels . . .' Such prime property might be led through the principal streets of the town, the merchant shouting out qualities and prices on the way, stopping when necessary to allow potential customers closer examination. 'An Arab approaches,' reported another observer, 'and cattle-dealer like, pokes the girls in the ribs, feels their joints, examines their mouths, fingers their teeth, trots them up and down to see their paces, then, after haggling about their price, takes one and leaves the other.' Yet more intimate examination took place behind a rough awning. Since serial rape was to be the fate of such women, only the most detailed inspection would suffice.

At the other end of the scale – and there were many gradations in between – were the middle-aged, the emaciated, the sick, the broken-down, often seen standing or squatting in dejected huddles in the square, awaiting quick sale at knock-down prices. 'Lines of negroes stood like beasts,' reported Burton, '. . . All were horridly thin, with ribs protruding like circles of a cask, and not a few squatted sick on the ground.' Prices, as in all markets, reflected supply, demand, and quality. Pretty young women were the most valuable. Fit young men also fetched good prices. Children were often worth more than adults. Older people – worn out and with not long to live – were very cheap. A few could not be sold at all and would be left to die in a corner; dogs and birds of prey could sometimes be seen picking at swollen corpses floating at the water's edge.[12]

Situated sociologically between the Zanzibari ruling class – the Omani, Indian, and Arab-Swahili merchant bourgeoisie – and the African slaves from whom they drew their wealth was a large free population of Arab-Swahili farmers, traders, soldiers, and sailors. This mixed Arab and Swahili population of the East Coast, perhaps a third of a million in number in the mid-nineteenth century, had been forming for at least a millennium, ever since the first Arab trading settlements were established. The people were a creole mix of Arab and African blood. They spoke Swahili, but laced with Arabic and other loan words of the coastal lingua franca. They were formally Muslims, but spiced with local pagan superstition. They retained much African culture – matrilineal kinship, hair styles and body ornament, music and dance, alcohol – but the more prosperous aped the Arab-Islamic culture of the Omani elite. The Arab-Swahilis were the petty bourgeoisie of the Zanzibari slave empire – the dhow captains, trail-masters, musketeers, shopkeepers, and hucksters of its arterial system.[13]

At the summit of evil, the air may smell clean. The Sultan of Zanzibar received distinguished visitors – Her Majesty's Consul, Royal Navy officers, Royal Geographical Society explorers – in 'a long, bare reception-hall, ceilinged with heavy polished beams, and paved with alternative slabs of white and black marble'. Otherwise it was simple: a few dingy chandeliers, three rows of ordinary wooden chairs, but no clutter of tables, bureaux, chests, clocks, and knick-knacks such as one might see in a European drawing room. The Sultan would be dressed in traditional Omani style, in white collarless gown (*dishdasha*), dark sleeved cloak (*bisht*), both garments ankle-length, and a multicoloured turban (*massar*); the only sartorial ostentation would be the braided edges of his cloak and the bejewelled curved dagger (*khanjar*) thrust into a gaudy waist-sash. Amid exchanges of pleasantries between Sultan and guests, little trays of sweetmeats, biscuits, and glasses of sherbet would be served by well-dressed servants. The theatre of power was in the restrained manner of Arabia: a matter of gentle etiquette, carefully chosen words, delicate titbits and sips, in a setting of minimalist décor offset by occasional glitz. In this way, the greatest slave lord in the Indian Ocean met his guests. Burton found the ruler of Zanzibar to be 'shrewd and sensible, highly religious but untainted by fanaticism, affable and courteous . . . as dignified in sentiments as distinguished in presence and demeanour.' The Sultan himself never ripped a child from the arms of its mother; never severed a boy's testicles to make a castrate; never wielded the lash or the gun on defenceless people; never threw the sick over the side of a ship to drown; never nailed a proud man to a mast to break his will; never chopped off the legs of captives abandoned on the trail. All this was done by others on his behalf, and here in the palace, at the highest peak of the Zanzibari slave empire, there was only a cloud of manicured refinement.[14]

Sultan Seyyid Said, the ruler of Muscat and Oman from 1806 to 1856, had first battled and murdered his way to power, then embarked on a campaign of mercantile-colonial conquest in East Africa. By the 1830s, with the bulk of his revenue coming from the growing trade in African ivory and slaves, he was dividing his time between Oman and Zanzibar, before finally relocating his capital permanently to the island at the end of the decade. The value of both principal commodities rose exponentially as they were moved from source to final market. The basic cost at source was zero because nothing was being produced: elephants were simply shot by ivory hunters, villagers kidnapped by slave raiders. But heavy investment in soldiers, guns, porters, and supplies, in defended compounds and depots along the trails, and in securing and maintaining alliances with local chiefs was essential. Thus, by the time a captive reached the Zanzibari slave market, his or her price might be £6 or £7 for an able-bodied adult, £2 or £3 for a young child. But the price might then be ten times as much by the time a chattel reached Cairo, Mecca, or Baghdad. The Sultan owned many slaves himself. He had his own plantations and ships. He was a merchant-prince in his own right. But he also levied customs duties on all the trade moving through the ports and markets under his control. And the value of that trade – in slaves, ivory, cloves, cowries, gum-copal, hides, sesame seed, and coconut products – was rising. The increase was perhaps five-fold since the turn of the century, and the rate of increase was accelerating. The Sultan of Zanzibar had joined the international elite of the age of capital.[15]

The origins of the Arab slave trade are lost in prehistory. At the time of the Prophet, in the early seventh century AD, slavery was accepted as part of the natural order of things in Arabia, just as in the world at large. The Qur'an made reference to it, but neither advocated nor critiqued it. Muhammad was a religious leader and social reformer, not a revolutionary. His mission, so far as social institutions were concerned, was not to overturn them, but to bring about moral improvement. In this regard, slavery was a worry, for, as he put it, 'The worst of men is the seller of men.' Thus, though the Qur'an accepted the existence of chattel slavery – including concubinage – it urged kindness, condemned cruelty, and exhorted masters to free slaves in expiation of sins or as an act of simple benevolence. More than this: the Qur'an asserted the essential equality of all humankind, and insisted that freedom was the natural condition of all. The real dichotomy was that between believer and pagan; and the slave who believed was considered the superior of the idolater, and the brother (or sister) of the free Muslim. This being so, the enslavement of fellow Muslims – equals and brothers/sisters in the sight of God – was an act of impiety. The Islamic world, should it wish to acquire slaves, would perforce have to seek them among infidels.[16]

Even this was dubious. The voice of Islam – like that of Judaism and Christianity – was unable to give clear answers when it came to the morally murky questions raised by slavery. Religion – all religion – is a way of thinking about the world. It can accommodate conservative, liberal, and radical perspectives. It commonly reflects the interests of the rich and powerful, but it sometimes gives expression to the suffering of the oppressed. Because the societies in which it is embedded are riddled with contradictions, so too is religion's message. In strict logic, the Qur'an's egalitarianism was incompatible with its acceptance of slavery. If all humans were essentially equal, then none should be master over another. The contrast between ideal and real had resulted in a Qur'anic muddle. Islamic law (*shariya*) was compelled to fudge, treating the slave as both person and chattel. Theologically and legally, then, the slave was an anomaly, her/his standing in the world a matter of ambiguity. Islam, in any case, soon came to mean three quite distinct things – the original teachings, the religious tradition based on these, and the living community of believers. And there has always been a sharp contrast between what Islam says, what some Muslim theologians claim it says, and what the Muslim faithful actually do.[17]

The fact is that slavery, at root, was not a religious matter at all. The Arab slave trade was no more Islamic than the European slave trade was Christian.[18] Muslim peasants in the Nile Delta were no more complicit in it than Christian workers in Manchester. Slavery was a class question. Most Arabs owned no slaves. Most slaves were owned by members of a small minority, members of a political and social elite – the sultans, emirs, and sheikhs, the courtiers and officials, the big landowners and rich merchants. Some of the slaves, over many centuries, were enrolled as soldiers in the armies of local potentates; Mameluke, Ottoman, Sudanic, Turco-Egyptian, and Arab rulers all found use for them. Some were employed in agriculture, commerce, and industry; though, in contrast to the Atlantic trade, plantation slavery was not predominant, since the Middle Eastern economy was based largely on small-scale enterprise. A higher proportion of slaves in Arabia, Egypt, Syria, Persia, and Anatolia – compared with the Americas – were incorporated into upper-class households, serving as general labourers, domestic servants, and concubines: that is, they represented a form of luxury consumption and prestige display at the top of Middle Eastern society.[19]

Up until the eighteenth century, slaves had flowed into the Middle East from several great human reservoirs. Catholic and Orthodox Christians from Southern Europe taken in war by Ottoman armies or kidnapped by Barbary corsairs would be transported across the Mediterranean for sale in the East. The Ottoman Sultan imposed a 'slave levy' (*devshirme*) on Christian villages in his Balkan provinces. Other Slavs, people from the Ukraine and elsewhere, were conveyed across the Black Sea, while large numbers of Caucasians from the mountains west of the Caspian, and of Turks from the

Central Asian steppes to the east of it, were marched overland to the slave markets of the Middle East. For a long while, these flows from the north supplemented those from the south, from Christian Abyssinia (Ethiopia) and from pagan sub-Saharan Africa.[20]

Slavery poisoned Middle Eastern culture. Oppressive social relations spawn ignorance and prejudice. Islamic elites imagined themselves the very epicentre of world civilisation – as against the barbarians of North and South, the people they enslaved, 'who are more like beasts than men'. They proclaimed slavery a boon to humankind since it brought the backward and ignorant into contact with Islam. They came to view others – 'the Other' – through the racist lens of the slave lord.

The Qur'an said that 'the diversity of your languages and of your colours' is created by God, and that 'the noblest among you in the eyes of God is the most pious'. But a ruling class of slave lords had little use for such sentiments. When they talked about colour, a ranking was implied. Middle Eastern elites were prone to divide the world into 'whites' (themselves), 'reds' (the ruddy northerners), and 'blacks' (sub-Saharan Africans). The blacks were at the bottom of the ladder, and the blacker you were, the lower you stood. To be black was to be ugly, ignoble, and impious; it was to be a social inferior fit only for labour and service. Some drew the logical conclusion and arrived at a theory of 'natural slavery', sometimes given pseudo-religious gloss by reference to the Judaeo-Christian myth of Ham, whose descendants were cursed to live in servitude. Religion is only a way of thinking: it is social relations that decide.[21]

As commercial capitalism took off during the eighteenth century, the poisonous blend of slavery and racism was as much a feature of the Islamic East as of the Christian West. But at the same time, the tectonic plates of global politics were shifting, and as they did so, the flows of human chattels from the northern reservoirs became blocked. New powers – centralised European monarchies – had risen in the West and the North. Habsburg Spain, standing at the head of successive Christian alliances, had curtailed the power of the Ottoman fleet and the Barbary corsairs in the Mediterranean. Tsarist Russia, forged in the crucible of distant Muscovy during the sixteenth and seventeenth centuries, was advancing south – into the Balkans, the Ukraine, and the Caucasus. The absolutist rulers of these states would not allow their people to be enslaved: they had need of them as soldiers, artisans, farmers, and taxpayers.

This was one shift in the plates. There was another, starting around the same time, also reaching its peak in the eighteenth century: the colonisation of the New World. Full exploitation of these new territories by European capitalism was impeded by labour shortage. Native American populations collapsed when exposed to the diseases imported by the Europeans, while European settlers succumbed to the tropical diseases of the region. The solution to New World 'germocide' was found in West Africa, with the mass trafficking from there of black Africans relatively resistant to the diseases of both the Old World and the Tropics.

The slave trade's 'pivot to Africa' was, therefore, a global phenomenon from the sixteenth century onwards. But whereas it peaked in the Western hemisphere in the eighteenth century, and was virtually extinct by the middle of the nineteenth, it was still growing in the Eastern hemisphere as late as the 1860s. This had nothing to do with the intrinsic character of either Arab society or the Islamic faith. It reflected the law of combined and uneven development. The advanced industrial capitalism of the West was based on free labour; the traditional mercantile capitalism of the East was not. The soaring demand for manufactured goods in the metropolitan centres of the system was met by drawing upon reserves of free labour in the agricultural hinterlands of Europe; that for primary commodities in the Indian Ocean was met by the mass enslavement of Africans. Irish navvies built the canals and railways of Victorian Britain, but black slaves carried ivory down the bush trails of East Africa.

Early on the morning of 3 August 1858, John Hanning Speke ascended a long, gradual, winding slope to its summit, when 'the vast expanse of the pale-blue waters of the Nyanza burst suddenly upon my gaze'. He had marched north for 25 days from the expedition base camp at Kazeh, accompanied by 20 porters and 10 Baluchi guards. It had been a pioneering journey through uncharted and potentially dangerous territory to a lake which Arab informants had insisted was 'both broader and longer than the Tanganyika'. Burton and Speke had been aware of the greater lake to the north but had previously avoided it, deterred by reports of hostile tribes, heading instead for Lake Tanganyika to the west, which they had reached on 13 February. The journey had been gruelling, and both men had fallen sick; but whereas Speke tended to recover and remain determined, Burton became a permanent invalid and had to be carried virtually the whole 200 miles to the lake, convinced at times that he was going to die. Speke became the effective leader of the expedition, but was hamstrung by Burton's illness, fading will, and growing animosity and jealousy. A critical failure had been abandonment of an exploration of the lake by canoe when only six hours short of the River Rusizi. Though Burton considered it 'a matter of vast importance' to reach the river, after 19 miserable days afloat the pain he was suffering caused him to give up. The unresolved issue was the Rusizi's direction of flow. It was known to be connected to the northern end of the lake. But did it flow *into* the lake or *out* of it? If the former, it was ruled out as a source for the Nile. For the sake of a few hours' paddling, the matter would now remain unresolved for a dozen years.[22]

John Speke and Richard Burton were alike in their restlessness: both were in flight from the monotony of everyday life, even that – perhaps especially that – of a military camp in India. Speke was a younger son of Devon gentry who had joined the East India Company's army and seen active service in the Sikh Wars. But when not actually on campaign he got bored and would take himself off into the Himalayas to explore, hunt, and make maps. This was not enough: he craved adventure on a grand scale, and, as for so many other men of his time and caste, this meant Equatorial Africa. A chance meeting with Burton at Aden in the middle of 1854 had been that of two men with the same aim: African exploration to locate the source of the Nile.

Yet in so many other ways the two men were very different. Burton was a louche intellectual whose dark looks mirrored his ambition, cynicism, and envy; in truth, he lacked the empathy and generosity for leadership. Speke, though an acute observer and conscientious enough in making records and measurements, had little time for books; he was a thoroughbred man of action. Tall, lithe, blue-eyed, tawny-haired – 'the old Scandinavian type' according to Burton – Speke was all nervous energy and motion, knocking down barriers to race through life with ne'er a backward glance. Not that he was flighty: Speke was possessed of steely resolve.[23]

The difference between the two explorers – the mean spirit of one, the warm-heartedness of the other – was evident in their contrasting attitudes to Africans and the slave trade. Burton considered the native people 'a futile race of barbarians', the slaves awaiting purchase in the slave market at Zanzibar as having 'hideous black faces'. Civilisation was embodied in the Arab slave traders. 'Striking indeed,' he wrote, 'was the contrast between the open-handed hospitality and the hearty good-will of this truly noble race, and the niggardliness of the savage and selfish African ...'. Speke was not free of prejudice; he too saw faces 'hideously black and ugly' in the slave market. But his sympathy was with the oppressed. 'The saddest sight was the way in which some licentious-looking men began a cool, deliberate inspection of a certain divorced culprit who had been sent back to the market for inconstancy to her husband. She had learnt a sense of decency during her conjugal life, and the blushes on her face now clearly showed how her heart was mortified at this unseemly exposure . . .'[24]

Sickness and suffering, in addition to all the routine discomforts, rigours, and dangers of African exploration, were prone to put strain on the strongest of human bonds. Burton's brooding misanthropy and unfitness to lead pushed his relationship with Speke to breaking point. What would later turn this into a toxic feud, however, was Speke's decision, after the party had returned from Tanganyika to Kazeh en route back to the coast, to march to the northern lake. Burton, still debilitated by illness, did not want to go; and, fearing that his companion might make a crucial discovery on his own, tried to dissuade him. To no avail: Speke not only made the journey, but reached the lake – later to be named Victoria – and it was indeed the source of the Nile; of this, moreover, though he could not yet prove it, he became immediately convinced.

The Africans spoke of it as a vast inland sea so broad you could not see across it, so long no-one knew its length (in reality it is 160 miles by 210 miles, making it the continent's largest lake). The Arabs declared that the Mountains of the Moon lay west of it and that several large rivers flowed into it on that side (though it is also fed from the east, and the lake's catchment area extends for 70,000 square miles in all). Speke himself established – by calculating the temperature at which water boiled – that the lake lay almost 4,000 feet above sea-level (the actual figure is 3,720 feet). This last was a crucial piece of evidence, for it was known that the Nile lay just under 2,000 feet above sea-level at Juba, more than 500 miles to the north, at a latitude of 5° North. Measurements at Lake Tanganyika, on the other hand, had given its level as only 1,850 feet (though in reality it is 2,600 feet) – too low to feed the Nile. Everything seemed to fit: the size, the catchment area, and the height above sea-level of Lake Victoria all pointed to its being the source. The young explorer felt that he had arrived at the supreme moment of his life: 'the pleasure of the mere view vanished in the presence of those more intense and exciting emotions which are called up by the consideration of the commercial and geographical importance of the prospect before me.'[25]

Three weeks later, Speke's party was back at Kazeh. Over a late breakfast on the day of his return, the younger man reported enthusiastically to his superior, first describing the size of the lake, then claiming it as the source of the White Nile. Burton was taken aback and became scornful. Later, when Speke suggested a second march to the northern lake, to be undertaken jointly once fresh supplies had been brought up from the coast, Burton rejected the proposal. His health was still in a dire state, but there were probably deeper motives. He had lost the initiative and was now in the shadow of his companion. This seems to have propelled him into deep depression. The rational part of his mind admitted the probable truth. Once back in Zanzibar, he would even pen a letter to the Royal Geographical Society, enclosed with Speke's map of the northern lake, reporting 'grave reasons for believing it to be the source of the principal feeder of the White Nile'. But this was all he managed. Envy soon mastered honesty. From now on – until Speke's premature death in 1864 – Burton would conduct a malicious campaign of lying and scheming to destroy his former subordinate's reputation and rubbish his geographical reasoning. Secondary issues inflamed the bitterness. Speke preceded Burton back to London and stole the limelight. The two men subsequently clashed openly in rival published accounts of the journey. Burton accused Speke of delaying payment of his share of the expedition's debts. Speke accused Burton of denying payment due to the expedition's porters and guards. But these were symptoms rather than causes of the breakdown in personal relations. The irrational was at work. And when the Royal Geographical Society and the British government decided to back a new expedition to the northern lake with Speke as leader, Burton's cup of bitterness overflowed. The feud would fester until Speke returned, and then flare into a climactic conflagration.[26]

Like Livingstone's Zambesi expedition two years before, the Speke–Grant expedition of 1860 was launched on a wave of optimism and high hopes. Queen Victoria had graciously allowed the northern lake to take her name. Prince Albert had sent a letter wishing 'God Speed'. The explorers had the blessing of the Foreign Office and £2,500 from the Treasury, and they travelled out on the Royal Navy frigate *Forte*. Speke's companion this time was an old Bengal Army friend, Captain James Grant, and he would prove consistently amiable, loyal, and stoical, despite being crippled early on by a

poisoned leg that refused to heal. Generous government funding ensured
that a full complement of caravan masters, guards, and porters could be
hired in Zanzibar, and the expedition lacked for nothing in guns, equipment, and supplies, including ample quantities of the beads, cloth, and brass
wire that were the staples of African trade. The problem was that the
Unyamwezi region south of Lake Victoria had become a war zone. The
expedition was soon at a virtual standstill, crippled by the desertion of
guards and porters, threatened by the violence of a society in turmoil, at risk
of starvation in a country of abandoned villages.[27]

On 7 January 1861, the rebel chieftain Manwa Sera, with 30 armed
followers, arrived at Speke and Grant's camp near Kazeh. Welcomed in, he
told his story. It was the story of mid-nineteenth-century Africa in micro-
cosm: the story of a continent being shattered to pieces by the shock waves of
the slave trade. The old king had died since the departure of Burton and
Speke in 1858. Manwa Sera had succeeded to the throne, but when he
attempted to tax the Arab-Swahili slave traders active in his territory, they
had engineered a coup, overthrown him, and installed in his place a more
compliant rival, Mkisiwa, an illegitimate son of the old king. Manwa Sera was
now a fugitive waging guerrilla war against the slave traders and the client
regime. The rebel leader offered help with porters and requested in return
Speke's services as an intermediary in peace negotiations. The explorer – who
considered Manwa Sera 'as fine a young man as ever I looked upon' – agreed.[28]

But Speke's overtures were rejected. Sheikh Snay, the leading Arab trader
at Kazeh, commanded 400 slave musketeers and was confident of crushing
the rebels. Too confident: he underestimated the cunning of an artful African
bush-fighter. Falling back before the advancing enemy, Manwa fed the over-
confidence of the Arab sheikh, who, after early success, divided his force
into three columns, one to carry loot back to Kazeh, one to act as flank guard
and reserve, the third to attack the main rebel force at Mzanza. The African
chieftain continued to draw them on. The Arab force, pushing forward
against minimal resistance, scooping up loot as it went, abandoned any
concern for military security. Then, Manwa Sera, reinforced by fresh tribal
contingents, counter-attacked, achieving complete surprise and immediate
rout. The Arabs scattered in all directions and many were hunted down,
including Sheikh Snay, who could not keep pace with the other fugitives,
handed his gun to a slave, and lay down to die. He was never seen again.[29]

The war escalated. Mkisiwa sent draft officers into the countryside to
conscript men to fight the rebels; they entered villages ringing bells and

bawling out that if sufficient men did not muster the headman would be arrested and the crops confiscated. A joint Arab-African force then attacked Manwa Sera's main strong-point at Kigwe and forced him to flee again. The bush war resumed, with shootings, ambushes, and raids. Villages emptied of people, fields went untended, trade lines seized up.

The Unyamwezi country was a region of hoe-cultivators and ancient kinship networks. But the traditional social order was being dissolved by the acid of war and profit. Typical of the new order was one Sirboko, the wealthiest man in the Mininga district when Speke stayed there as his guest. He had been an ivory trader employed by Zanzibari Arabs, but had been ruined when he lost all his property in a village fire. Befriended and taken in by a local chief called Ugali, he had then defended the chief's village against a tribal raid, when a combination of his steadfastness and his muskets caused the enemy to give up their attack and disperse homewards. Ugali, in gratitude (and no doubt with future security in mind), then built Sirboko a large enclosure and gave him the use of land for the cultivation of rice. New kinds of relationship – commercial, political, military – were reconfiguring African society.[30]

From the explorers' point of view, the chaos of war either brought all forward movement to a complete halt or raised its cost to extortionate levels. Delays might last for weeks, even months, supplies would run down, porters would abscond, often having stolen valuable property, and demands for *hongo* – in beads, wire, cloth, and other valuables – from local chiefs became ever more insistent and inflationary.[31] Sometimes the explorers found themselves the effective prisoners of their hosts. Speke may not always have comprehended the complexities. It was not simply that chiefs were dissatisfied with their *hongo* and refused to grant safe passage and porters and supplies for the onward journey until more was given. They were also in awe of the power of their guests – specifically of their guns and their wealth in prestige goods – and were often reluctant to lose access to it, or, worse, see it pass within the grasp of a rival. The political fragmentation of Central Africa, exacerbated by the mayhem of slave wars, was clogging the arteries of transcontinental movement.[32]

The 500-mile journey inland from Bagamoyo on the coast to Kazeh in the Umyamwezi country had taken almost four months. Here the war imposed a delay of a month and a half. A first attempt to resume the advance then proved abortive in the face of tribal hostility and mass desertion. A second attempt was delayed for months, first by Lumeresi of Uzinza, then by

Suwarora of Uswi, the tribal chieftains who controlled neighbouring territories to the south of Lake Victoria; each proved unpredictable, grasping, and
at times aggressive.

The expedition had to reach the northern end of the lake: only there
could it be established beyond doubt whether or not Lake Victoria was the
source of the White Nile. To reach this destination, it was necessary to
climb a ladder of tribal states lying to the west of the lake, each ruled by an
autocrat. Beyond Lumeresi's Uzinza and Suwarora's Uswi lay Rumanika's
Karagwe, Mutesa's Buganda, and Kamrasi's Bunyoro. These were, in effect,
miniature military dictatorships, each chieftain claiming allegiance from a
network of sub-chiefs, each sustained by food renders and labour service,
each the pinnacle of a patriarchal and class-based hierarchy in which clan
chiefs dominated villagers, men dominated women, and the free dominated
the enslaved. As far as the explorers were concerned, everything depended
on the character of the despot. When Speke and Grant finally made it to
King Rumanika's palace in late November 1861 – by which time it had taken
them well over a year to travel less than a thousand miles – it was a great
relief to be received with warm hospitality in a country of green hills and
well-fed people. Rumanika sent messengers ahead to report that 'wherever
you stop a day, the village officers are instructed to supply you with food at
the King's expense, for there are no taxes gathered from strangers in the
Kingdom of Karagwe'.[33]

Rumanika was as good as his word. He solicited no *hongo* – though Speke
and Grant voluntarily gave him many presents – and he turned out to be a
man of dignity, a consummate host, and an intelligent companion eager to
talk and to learn. The idyll could not last long, however; the expedition had
to move on. And early in January came important news from the north.
Emissaries of Rumanika returned from the Kingdom of Bunyoro to report
the sensational news that foreigners in boats had recently arrived on the
Upper Nile. Speke and Grant – 'half wild with delight' – guessed that this
must be the Welsh explorer John Petherick, whom the Royal Geographical
Society had charged with an ascent up the Nile with boats and supplies, ready
to meet the southern expedition when it finally emerged. This was not the
only news. It was promptly followed by the report of an Indian ivory trader
that King Mutesa of Buganda had agreed to allow the explorers to march
through his territory and was sending officers to escort them. The only
disappointment in all this was Grant's health. Despite various treatments –
poultices, native medicines, even gunpowder rubbed into cuts made in the

swellings – his infected leg became more malignant. A sickness that might have been cured in a week with modern antibiotics rendered him incapable of walking or even being carried. Grant, true to character, was uncomplaining about either his suffering or the unavoidable decision to leave him behind. He would spend the next three months confined to his hut, bedridden, bored, often in agony, without news of any kind.[34]

Mutesa's cooperation was the key to unlocking the mystery of the Nile, for his kingdom straddled the land to the north of Lake Victoria. Setting out on the six-week march to the king's court, Speke confided to his journal that he was 'perfectly sure in my mind that before very long I should settle the great Nile problem forever'. In fact, he would have a very long wait, and would eventually be compelled to leave the region with questions still hanging. In the meantime he was to be tried to the limits of forbearance by the unpredictable young psychopath who had inherited the throne of one of the greatest states of Central Africa and turned it into a murderous tyranny.

'It was a magnificent sight,' wrote Speke upon his first arrival at Mutesa's palace. 'A whole hill was covered with gigantic huts, such as I had never seen in Africa before.' When Speke entered the royal compound – preceded by a Union Jack and followed by a 12-man guard of honour dressed in red cloaks and carrying sloped arms with fixed bayonets – he was received with all the pomp the Bugandan court could muster. In one enclosure musicians played on nine-stringed harps and ceremonial drums. From another he was watched by the queen-mother and Mutesa's harem of 300 or 400 wives. Further on were the king's ministers, the grand vizier, the treasurer, the commander-in-chief of the army, the admiral of the fleet of war-canoes, the chief executioner and his assistants, the governors of provinces, and such functionaries of the royal household as the commissioner of tombs, the keeper of drums, and the chief brewer.

At first, in a calculated theatre of power, the Kabaka – as the Bugandan king was known – made no appearance and Speke was left sitting on the ground waiting in the sun. But Victorian officers and gentlemen knew a thing or two about theatre of power. Speke turned about, returned to his hut, and feigned indifference to Mutesa's courtiers' entreaties to return while he smoked a pipe and drank a cup of coffee. When he finally relented, Mutesa was willing to receive him. He was sitting on his throne, a red blanket over a square platform of grass, in a huge reception hut. Tall, well-made, good-looking, in his mid-20s, he was festooned with beads and rings of brass and copper – around his neck, on arms and legs, on every finger and toe. Courtiers, guards, women, and flunkies squatted on all sides. The audience was slow and formal. Neither of the leads knew the other's language. Mutesa and Speke sat staring at each other for an hour, the former making occasional comments to his intimates, the latter in patient silence. This was the beginning of four and a half months at the Bugandan court, with Speke effectively a prisoner of Mutesa, unable to advance without the supplies, porters, and safe passage that only the Kabaka could provide; and compounding his frustration was the knowledge that all this time, chained down by the avarice, doubt, and whim of a tyrant, he was a mere 50 miles from his ultimate goal, the northern outflow of Lake Victoria.[35]

The state ruled by Mutesa from his accession in 1856 to his death in 1884 had existed since the fifteenth century and was the most powerful in Central Africa. When the army mobilised, the roads would fill with warriors, and those who witnessed such a mustering would affirm that it was the largest they had ever seen. When Speke asked the Kabaka if he knew the size of his army, he was told that he did not, with the implication it could not be known, for his warriors could not all be assembled together in a single place so as to be counted. The army was divided into regiments of 1,800 men, battalions of 600, companies of 200. A typical attack formation was in 3 single lines spaced 15 or 20 paces apart. Each warrior was equipped with two iron-tipped spears and a shield of wood and leather. Faces, arms, and legs were painted in red, blue, black, and grey. Clothing varied, either by regiment, or by individual choice. Some fought nearly naked in little more than a loin cloth of goat skin, while others wore tunics of tree-bark and cloaks of cow or antelope skin. Junior officers might be distinguished by leopard-skins and daggers, senior officers by tufts of white hair, crimson plumes, and multicoloured beads. Tattoos would culminate in vociferous chanting to the effect that the Kabaka was the greatest ruler on earth and that the lives of his warriors belonged to him forever. The literal truth of this was confirmed when Speke observed the reception of a victorious army. As each regimental commander gave his report to Mutesa, the brave were immediately rewarded with *pombe* (millet beer), but those denounced as cowards were as promptly hauled away to execution. 'When the fatal sentence was pronounced, a terrible bustle ensued, the convict wrestling and defying, whilst the other men seized, pulled, and tore the struggling wretch from the crowd, bound him hands and head together, and led, or rather tumbled, him away.'[36]

Executions – sometimes formal and ritualised, sometimes arbitrary – were almost daily events. As well as cowardice in battle, any number of other crimes were deemed capital offences in the primitive autocracy that was Buganda. But often enough there was no apparent crime at all. Perhaps a man had looked inappropriately at one of the Kabaka's wives; or perhaps one of those wives had somehow displeased or offended him; or perhaps his deceased father had appeared to him in a dream and identified someone as an enemy. Four days after Speke's arrival, during a firearms demonstration, Mutesa loaded a carbine and ordered a page to go and shoot a man in the outer court. On another occasion, he attacked a young woman who had offered him some fruit, ordering her immediate execution, whacking at her head with a cudgel; and she would surely have died but for Speke's angry intervention. Sudden death on the merest whim: the mark of deranged despotism throughout history.

The end might be swift – immediate decapitation or bludgeoning to death – or slow. Speke watched a mockery of a trial of a young woman who had fled from an abusive husband and taken refuge in the hut of an old man. Both were sentenced to death without being heard; and it was decreed that they should be kept alive as long as possible, as they were dismembered bit by bit, their severed body parts to be served daily to the vultures.[37]

Pre-colonial African society is sometimes idealised in later nationalist narratives. It should not be. The African kingdoms were oppressive class societies. Not all African kings were psychotic tyrants like Mutesa. Some were rational and moderate men like Rumanika. But the social orders over which they ruled were much alike. The kingdoms through which Grant and Speke passed on their journey were autocratic, patriarchal, and militaristic. More: they were slave states. African kings took slaves, held slaves, sold slaves. Manwa Sera, the rebel Unyamwezi chieftain, had been ousted for his attempt to tax the slave trade, not abolish it. Rumanika, the affable Karagwan ruler, had won his throne in a civil war only with the help of Arab slave-soldiers. Possessed of absolute power in their own territories, sustained by tribute and service from subject populations terrorised into obedience, commanding centralised armies for waging war against their neighbours, African rulers became instrumental in the spread of the slave trade across the continent. They sold fellow Africans for power and profit. The people of nineteenth-century sub-Saharan Africa were the victims not only of Arab-Swahili slavers and European imperialists; they were victims, too, of an African elite of despotic warlords no less malevolent.

Speke finally got away, thanks in part to the intercession of the queen-mother. By this time, Grant had been able to join him, and the two explorers now trekked towards the northern outlet of the great lake. Grant's gammy leg soon flared up again, so Speke went ahead with a reduced party. Then, in late July 1862, he struck the river which he assumed to be the Nile, and, following it south for three days, came upon the outlet itself, at a place where the channel, perhaps 500 feet wide, was broken by rocks and a 12-foot drop known locally as the 'Stones' (soon to be renamed, in honour of the President of the Royal Geographical Society, 'Ripon Falls'). Speke was certain that he had reached the Nile and confirmed Lake Victoria as its source. He watched the rush of waters at the falls for hours, mesmerised by them, then dallied three days more, savouring this supreme moment, as it seemed to him, of African exploration.[38]

But time pressed. The expedition was deep inside the African interior, its safety heavily dependent on King Kamrasi of Bunyoro, whose territory had to be crossed, and on John Petherick, with whom Speke and Grant were scheduled to rendezvous further down the Nile. Without Petherick's riverboats and supplies, they and their 20 or so remaining followers would face an overland march through territory ravaged by slave raids and deeply hostile to intruders; their chances of survival in these circumstances would be slim. Their desperation was heightened by another two-month delay, in the clutches of Kamrasi, who proved to be as unstable and unpredictable as his Bugandan neighbour. When they finally bribed their way out – promising to send back six modern carbines once they reached Petherick at Gani – they headed north on a direct trail instead of attempting to follow the river. This meant they were left with three glaring gaps in their survey of the White Nile. First, they had not actually traced along the shore of Lake Victoria and confirmed that it was indeed a single massive body of water. Second, they had not followed the northern outflow beyond the Ripon Falls down to Lake Kioga. Third, though they had explored the western end of Lake Kioga, they had not followed its outflow all the way to Lake Albert, so as to demonstrate both that it fed into this lake, and that this lake in turn fed into the White Nile. These three *lacunae* meant that they had not proved beyond all reasonable doubt that Speke's hypothesis – that Lake Victoria was the source – was correct. That they lacked the time and resources – and perhaps the energy and resolve – to fill in the gaps would leave Speke open to attack when he finally returned to Britain.[39]

On 3 December 1862, the Speke–Grant expedition reached the trading post of Faloro, about 20 miles east of the White Nile. The sun was setting as they approached what they assumed was Petherick's encampment, so they were surprised when the military procession that came out to meet them, alerted to their arrival by the customary discharge of guns into the air, was preceded not by the Union Jack but by three large red flags. The contingent, comprising about 200 Egyptians and Sudanese bearing firearms, accompanied by drummers and fifers, was led by 'a very black man named Muhammad in full Egyptian regimentals with a curved sword'. These, it turned out, were not Petherick's men, but one De Bono's. Muhammad was the latter's agent. Though Speke did not yet know this, Andrea De Bono was a Maltese slave trader. The truth emerged slowly over the next few days.

Muhammad, as well as being an army officer in the service of the Turco-Egyptian government in Cairo, was also an ivory and slave trader, and a mercenary whose miniature army was available for hire. He worked for the Khedive of Egypt, for De Bono, and for himself. He was a 'land pirate' whose 'plundering parties' – formed of both his own soldiers and African auxiliaries – brought in great hauls of cattle, ivory, and slaves. On the move, they conscripted Africans as porters by threatening to burn down their homes and murder their families. When they camped, they stole everything they needed from nearby villagers – shelter, food, even pots and pans. Muhammad's caravan of a thousand soldiers, auxiliaries, and porters – which Speke and Grant, otherwise helpless, were forced to join when it finally headed north – moved across the landscape with its booty like a horde of marauders.[40]

The two explorers had passed beyond the reach of even the longest tentacles of the Sultan of Zanzibar and the Arab-Swahili slavers of East Africa. But they had entered another slave empire: that of the Turco-Egyptian regime in Cairo and the Arab-Sudanese traders of the Sahara; an empire that funnelled its cargoes of chattels not eastwards to fill the slave dhows of the Indian Ocean, but northwards, down the Nile or across the desert, to Egypt and the Red Sea.

# CHAPTER THREE

# A RUCKLE OF BONES

The conference hall of the Mineral Water Hospital at Bath was packed on the morning of 16 September 1864. The Royal Geographical Society had organised a debate between the two leading protagonists of radically different theories concerning the sources of the Nile. Former colleagues, now bitter enemies, Richard Burton and John Hanning Speke were scheduled to go head-to-head. The debate had the feel of a clash between prize gladiators.

Since Speke's return from his second African expedition, the row between the two explorers had become highly charged. It had been fed by sneering armchair commentators – 'geographers who sip port, sit in carpet slippers, and criticise those who work in the field' – but Speke had done himself no favours, proving intemperate under pressure and making enemies. He had, for example, flung unfounded accusations of negligence, embezzlement, and slave trading at John Petherick, his intended rescuer on the Upper Nile. And he had snubbed Sir Roderick Murchison, the head of the London Royal Geographical Society – previously a firm supporter – by submitting a hopelessly inadequate report to the Society, despite the fact it had been the expedition sponsor, reserving his best work for John Blackwood, his Edinburgh-based publisher.

The denouement was beyond all expectations. On the morning of the debate, the hall was kept waiting for almost half an hour, with only Burton and his wife on the platform. Then Murchison, the Royal Geographical Society Council members, and various other geographical dignitaries, including Dr David Livingstone, trooped into the hall from a private meeting, looking sombre. When silence descended, Murchison announced that Speke was dead. An experienced sportsman, he had gone shooting on his uncle's estate the previous afternoon and been killed by an accidental discharge while climbing over a wall.[1]

'The Nile is settled', he had cabled the Royal Geographical Society from Khartoum in the spring of 1863. But no-one had been sure; and David Livingstone, for one, very much doubted it. Though he despised Burton – a bohemian, chancer, and racist who could hardly have been more different from the dour, austere Scottish evangelical and abolitionist – Livingstone was derisive of Speke's rival claims, accusing him of 'the eager pursuit of a foregone conclusion'. Livingstone argued that the northern outflow of Lake Victoria was too slight a waterway to be the Nile. Then, when he heard about Samuel Baker's exploration of Lake Albert in 1865 – immediately following the Speke–Grant expedition – he became convinced that Lake Tanganyika must be connected to it, and thus constitute the primary source, though fed by other lakes and rivers to its south, putting the ultimate sources of the Nile several hundred miles beyond Lake Victoria. In the unresolved controversy Livingstone sensed an opportunity to redeem himself and his cause. Shortly after the Bath meeting, through the good offices of Murchison and the Royal Geographical Society, the veteran explorer received British government backing – in the form of some finance and designation as a roving 'consul' – for a fresh attempt to settle the Nile question once and for all.[2]

Despite the expedition's official status, preparations and resources were inadequate. Livingstone set out from the coast into the interior in March 1866 with only 35 porters, a fraction of the number needed to carry, in addition to equipment and supplies, the trade goods on which all long-distance movement in Africa depended. Rain and mud quickly reduced this little party to misery. Equipment was lost or damaged. Supplies ran out and starvation threatened. The expedition's medicine chest was stolen. But what ensured failure was the mayhem of tribal warfare and slave raids across the region Livingstone wished to explore, triggering mass desertions that reduced the party to just 11 loyalists by September 1866. The succession of setbacks appears to have unhinged him: as during the Zambesi expedition – when John Kirk eventually concluded he was mad – the worse the prospects seemed, the more determined he became to press on. Frustrated by delay, he suddenly decided in April 1867 to resume his journey, setting out on a 200-mile march in the rainy season, through country often waist-high in water, with food almost unobtainable. Livingstone seemed propelled by some strange death-wish. All but four of his remaining men deserted.[3]

What makes this march – through swamps of black slime infested with mosquitoes and leeches – appear madder still in retrospect is the fallacious hypothesis on which it was based. Several months earlier Livingstone had established that the River Lualaba – one of Africa's two greatest waterways – flowed north out of Lake Moero. He now wished to confirm that Lake Moero in turn was fed by Lake Bangweolo, an expanse of water lying some 200 miles further south, making this the true source of the Lualaba, which he assumed to be the Nile. When he finally reached the southern lake – hugely swollen by the rains – in early July 1867, he sent a triumphant dispatch to the British Foreign Secretary announcing that 'the springs of the Nile have hitherto been searched for very much too far to the north', and that 'they arise some 400 miles south of the most southerly portion of Victoria . . . and, indeed, south of all the lakes except Bangweolo'.[4]

Livingstone considered this discovery to be his crowing glory. He believed that he had solved the 2,500-year-old mystery of the Nile, restored a reputation badly damaged by the Zambesi debacle, and gained the recognition he hoped would amplify his anti-slavery voice. For this, always, was his main purpose. 'The Nile sources', he had told a friend, 'are valuable only as a means of enabling me to open my mouth with power among men. It is this power which I hope to apply to remedy an enormous evil.'[5]

But he was wrong; doubly so. The Lualaba, the mighty river flowing northwards some 150 miles west of Lake Tanganyika, close to the very centre of continent – the river Livingstone believed had to be the Nile – was in fact the main feeder of the Congo. The Lualaba/Congo curves westwards just north of the equator, looping across hundreds of miles of Africa, finally flowing into the ocean on the West Coast. And Lake Tanganyika is not, in fact, connected to Lake Albert (and therefore to the Nile); its primary outflow, the Lukuga, is an east–west tributary of the Lualaba (and therefore of the Congo). Though Livingstone would achieve wide and enduring celebrity – he remains one of the most famous Britons of the Victorian era – it would not be as discoverer of the source of the Nile.

In the meantime, however, on the banks of the Bangweolo at the end of more than two years and a thousand miles of exploration, Livingstone was quite destitute. He had long since become wholly dependent – for supplies, porterage, and protection; for survival itself – on the benevolence of the very men whose livelihoods he had come to destroy: the Arab-Swahili slave traders. He was no longer free to determine his direction or time of travel; instead he was obliged to attach his tiny party to one or another of the trade caravans criss-crossing the region. So it was with Muhammad Bogharib, a trader he came to regard as a friend, that he first trekked back north, eventually to reach the Arab-Swahili market centre at Ujiji on the eastern shore of Tanganyika in March 1869. There, however, he discovered that the merchandise, food, medicines, and letters sent to him from the coast, which he had expected to find waiting for him upon arrival, had been plundered. His dependence on Bogharib deepened.

After several months recovering his health at Ujiji, he set out west with Bogharib's caravan, across the lake and then overland into the Manyuema country, where the ivory and slave trade was booming. Livingstone was set upon reaching the Lualaba and attempting to trace its course northwards, so as to show beyond any doubt whether it was the Congo or the Nile. But his progress was slowed by illness, the rains, and widespread fighting. Bogharib and his men eventually departed in pursuit of ivory and slaves, leaving Livingstone at Bambarre, midway between Tanganyika and the Lualaba, where he found himself trapped for seven months from July 1870 to February 1871, without supplies, down to three followers, paralysed by foot ulcers. But a party of ten men arrived from the coast in late January, carrying a small consignment of supplies, having been dispatched thence by John Kirk. Despite his grave reservations about Livingstone's leadership on the Zambesi expedition, Kirk, who served successively as vice consul, acting consul, and consul on Zanzibar, remained an essential pillar of support during Livingstone's long final period in Africa between 1866 and 1873. So it was now: Kirk's succour was just sufficient to get Livingstone, whose feet had recovered, on the move again. By the end of March he was at Nyangwe, on the banks of the great river, gazing across 2 miles of almost motionless, glassy-blue water, shimmering under the African sun.

But that was as far as he got. His friend Bogharib was away, the local Arab-Swahili were suspicious, and the native Africans refused to let him have canoes to cross the river. Thus he found himself immobilised four months on the banks of the Lualaba, about as deep in the heart of Africa, as far from any coast, as close to the continent's mid-point, as it was possible to be. He eventually offered Dugumbe, the leading trader in the town, £400 and all his merchandise at Ujiji – his stores assumed to have been replenished by Kirk in his absence – in return for the services of ten men and a canoe. Before he could receive an answer, however, his plans were wrecked by an unprecedented atrocity.[6]

Nyangwe was a riverside market town formed of little houses of timber, mud, and thatch. It would fill with up to two or three thousand people on market days, many of them travelling 20 or 25 miles to be there, all joining a great commotion of buying and selling by barter that David Livingstone much enjoyed. Knobs of iron might be exchanged for some palm cloth; a squealing pig for a quantity of grain, potatoes, or vegetables; pots filled with smoke-dried snail or catfish for some processed cassava root. Livingstone himself traded a string of beads for two gallon-sized earthenware pots, hand-thrown but of 'wonderful roundness'. While little girls rushed around selling cups of water for a handful of fish, and the men sported themselves in gaudy-coloured *lambas* (large rectangular cloths wrapped around the body), the women were the dominant presence, all working hard, the sweat beading on their faces as they humped great weights of merchandise about or engaged in the breathless banter of market haggling. 'It is a scene of the finest natural acting imaginable,' Livingstone opined as he watched sellers proclaiming the unsurpassed excellence of their wares, arguing furiously over the price by word and gesture, feigning astonishment and withering scorn when customers chose to turn away.[7]

But the market of 15 July 1871 was overcast with menace. The reports of guns could be heard on the far side of the Lualaba, and it was known that Dugumbe's men – he commanded 500 musketeers – were burning villages and shooting people or rounding them up for the slave caravans. 'He is determined to go into new fields of trade,' Livingstone recorded in his journal, 'and has all his family with him, and intends to remain six or seven years, sending regularly to Ujiji for supplies of goods.' And indeed, through the whole four months of Livingstone's enforced stay at Nyangwe, the surrounding Manyuema country was in the grip of slave war. This region, at the very heart of the continent, was now the frontier of a scourge spreading ever further westwards from Zanzibar and the East Coast. The numbers at Nyangwe's market were down, only about 1,500 on this day, for many of the villages from which the people usually came were in flames, 'and every now and then a number of shots were fired on the fugitives'.[8]

Livingstone noticed that three armed men had come into the market. As he headed away to escape the heat, he became aware of one of them haggling over a fowl and seizing hold of it. Then two guns went off. Soon all three men were volleying into the crowd from the upper end of the marketplace.

The crowd panicked, everyone scrambling away, scattering merchandise as they went. Many fled to the waterside to escape by canoe, but there, in the confusion, other men opened up with guns. Fifty or more canoes were jammed in the little creek that led out to the river, and in the fear and crush, men forgot their paddles, or canoes were swamped, or they blocked each other and could not be got out. And still the firing continued, the musket balls thumping into a shrieking mass of hundreds of men, women, and children as they hurled themselves into the water. Some crowded the handful of canoes that did succeed in paddling clear of the shore. Others had to swim, heading for an island a full mile off; but the current carried them adrift, so that those who were not shot were swept on until they drowned. One or two canoes got away, but others sank midstream. A few of the swimmers also escaped, but mostly the bobbing heads simply disappeared, one by one, beneath the water. Several hundred perished. Nor was this the end. Escaped slaves plundered the abandoned market, shooting continued on the far side of the Lualaba, and soon Livingstone saw plumes of smoke rising from burning villages.[9]

Dugumbe may not have ordered the Nyangwe massacre; according to Livingstone, he considered it 'a great error'. The frontier zone of the slave trade was a psychopathic world of murder, torture, and rape, where slave lords exercised only tenuous control over their followers. But in a wider sense, Dugumbe and his ilk were responsible for all that happened, for they were, with the sole purpose of enriching themselves, destroying African society in a whirlwind of violence, dispossession, and enslavement which left the people of the region at the mercy of gun-toting gangsters. If Livingstone – that most conscientious of mid-Victorian moral crusaders – had not grasped the hopelessness of his situation before, he grasped it now. How could he remain dependent on men like Dugumbe? How could he hitch-hike through Central Africa on slave caravans? How could he advance the cause of Commerce, Christianity, and Civilisation in this dystopian chaos?

He spent the next three months trudging back to Ujiji – arriving 'reduced to a skeleton' – only to face fresh disappointment: as before, his supplies had been stolen and sold off, leaving almost nothing of the £600 worth that had been sent from the coast by the ever-attentive John Kirk. Ujiji, 700 miles inland on the eastern side of Lake Tanganyika, was a town of about 2,000 people, dhows and caravans forever coming and going, its market a regular bustle of trade in slaves, ivory, grain, and animals. The economy was dominated by several dozen Arab-Swahili merchants. So Livingstone now found himself again at the mercy of men who were the very antithesis of his self-appointed mission. All he could do was subsist by trading his few remaining barter goods for food while awaiting further relief from the coast. Destitute, immobilised, his explorations aborted, his spirits reached 'their lowest ebb'.

But succour was at hand – far sooner than he could have expected – and from a wholly unexpected quarter. Less than week after his return to Ujiji, in early November, Susi, one of his devoted African servants, rushed up shouting, 'An Englishman! I see him!' A few moments later a great column came into view. Appearing at its head flew the Stars and Stripes of the United States of America. Advancing behind it was a man dressed immaculately in new flannel suit, chalked helmet, fresh puggaree, and oiled boots. This was none other than the 'the travelling correspondent of the *New York Herald*'. He was known (though it was not his real name) as Henry Morton Stanley.[10]

John Rowlands was only 25 when, in the winter of 1866/7, he first conceived the idea of following in the footsteps of Dr David Livingstone and taking an expedition to Africa. His plan was to do so as a correspondent of the *New York Herald* 'and thereby make a story and a sensation, and gain both fame and money'. It seemed an unlikely prospect for an illegitimate Welsh workhouse boy who was living under an assumed name, drifting from job to job, and surviving on a mix of wits and gab. Abandoned by his mother in infancy, he had been brought up by relatives for a while, and then dumped in the local workhouse – effectively a prison for the poor – for a decade. He later went to Liverpool looking for work, there took a post as a cabin boy on an American steamer, and duly arrived at New Orleans in early 1858. He found the United States liberating. Deeply scarred by his mother's rejection of him, by his loveless childhood, by the depravity of the workhouse, and by the stigma he bore in snobbish Victorian Britain, he suddenly found himself in a young, open, dynamic society-in-the-making, full of entrepreneurs and pioneers, teeming with immigrants like himself, where men were judged more for what they did than who they were. He felt that, for the first time, he was addressed 'as a reasonable being', that his person was 'sacred and inviolable'.

He worked as a cook's assistant on a Mississippi riverboat, then as a clerk in a country store at a little place called Cypress Bend in Arkansas, up to the time of the Civil War, when, because of where he was and who his friends were, he joined the Confederate Army. Captured at Shiloh, a murderous battle in April 1862, he then found himself in a disease-ridden POW camp. He got away by volunteering to serve in the Union Army, but deserted and fled the country, working a passage back to Liverpool. But there was nothing for him at home – only further humiliation at the hands of a family who disdained him – so he soon returned to the States. He joined the Union Navy in 1864, deserted for a second time early the following year, and then headed west, again making his way odd-jobbing. He was now earning some money from freelance journalism, for he turned out to have an instinct for chasing down a good story and a flair for vivid (and much embellished) reporting. He landed his first regular job in early 1867, covering the Indian Wars for the *Missouri Democrat* in St Louis, before talking his way into a foreign assignment to report on Britain's invasion of Abyssinia for James Gordon Bennett's *New York Herald* the following year.

Circumstances had turned John Rowlands into a wide-boy. Hardened by rejection, loneliness, and stigma, he had become a streetwise shifter. But he was also vulnerable and sensitive, a man in desperate need of recognition and a sense of self-worth. Work and struggle became his way of blotting out inner unhappiness and transcending humble origins. He was a coiled spring, consumed with wanderlust, insatiable for adventure, craving fame and applause. 'It is only by railway celerity that I can live,' he once said of himself. This frantic rush into the future was a flight from the past, from a childhood the memory of which was painful and shaming; so much so that, at the time of his first arrival in the United States, he had recast himself as a freshly minted person, shedding the character John Rowlands and assuming a new identity as Henry Morton Stanley. The web of lies he was obliged to weave – and other lies he would tell later, since lying became a habit, a mechanism of both self-defence and self-promotion – would one day return to haunt him.[11]

Foreign travel became an obsession. He devoured travel literature and adventure stories set in exotic places. 'He was full of aspirations for adventure,' wrote a close friend in America, 'and told marvellous tales of foreign countries . . .' During 1865 he rafted down the River Platte in Nebraska and then organised a private (and disastrous) expedition to Asia Minor. It was soon afterwards that he began to dream of African exploration – for here was to be found the supreme challenge.

A cult of muscular manliness – in a context of sharply defined and rarely transgressed gender roles – prevailed on both sides of the Atlantic during the nineteenth century. Men were expected to be active and dominant, women passive and acquiescent. Men were makers and shakers, women nest-builders. The best of men, the heroes and role models of Victorian popular culture, were soldiers, seafarers, frontiersmen, explorers. Bravery, endurance, and stoicism were supreme masculine virtues, and the greater the privation and discomfort, the more admirable the achievement. The explorers of the African interior carried this cult of manliness to near impossible extremes. Though it invariably wrecked their health and often their relationships with wives and children – or precluded any – it was an addictive drug, something they hankered to return to whenever becalmed at home, trapped, as they felt, in domestic routine and vacuous social engagements, leading what Stanley would later call 'that shallow life which thousands lead in England, where a man is not permitted to be real and natural, but is held in the stocks of conventionalism'.

Only one avenue to Africa was open to Henry Morton Stanley. He was not a gentleman of means, an army officer, a missionary doctor, or a scholar. He was a workhouse boy with a hidden past, a drifter and a deserter, a fake American, a hired hack hopping from assignment to assignment. He could never secure the backing of an august body like the Royal Geographical Society of London. Stanley's only hope of breaking into African exploration was to open a new way: media sensationalism. Having talked his way into working for James Gordon Bennett, he was soon actively canvassing a newspaper-funded expedition to 'find' Dr Livingstone. This was a novel idea in two senses: Stanley was proposing that a journey of exploration be funded by a newspaper – rather than a government, a trading company, a learned society, or a gentleman of private means – and he was implying that the newspaper might, in effect, manufacture its own journalistic scoop.[12]

Newspaper journalism was an explosive new industry. In Britain, for example, whereas in 1846 there had not been a single daily newspaper published outside London, by 1880 there would be no less than 121 provincial dailies. As for other periodicals, as early as 1864 total sales of weekly newspapers had reached 2.2 million, of other weeklies 2.4 million, and of monthlies 2.5 million. This was a communications revolution with multiple implications. Ownership of news media became, for the first time, a matter of big business, with sizeable amounts of capital to invest, and intense competition for readers. The demand for content – for news, stories, information, pictures, and much else – turned journalism into a mass profession. Cable and telegraph technology increasingly allowed copy to be dispatched at speed from distant corners of the globe, while railways and steamships facilitated rapid distribution of newspapers. The expansion of the readership from an elite of a few tens of thousands to a 'general public' numbered in millions created a new form of mass opinion and political influence. In lobbying for an African assignment, Henry Morton Stanley was pushing at the frontier of a thrusting new global industry of immense potential power.[13]

At first, however, the prospective expedition was held up by lack of any leads as to Livingstone's whereabouts, and Stanley was reassigned to cover a civil war in Spain. Then Bennett – the canny media mogul – imposed further delay to increase the potential news impact. He wanted Livingstone well and truly 'lost' – though Stanley fretted that he might, in the interim, end up dead. When the restless newsman finally set out from Bagamoyo on the East African coast on 21 March 1871, nothing had been heard of Livingstone since John Kirk had received a letter from Ujiji dated 30 May 1869. Herein the explorer had shared his intention to cross Lake Tanganyika, traverse the Manyuema country, and explore the Lualaba, in pursuit of proof of his hypothesis about the sources of the Nile. The letter had not been reassuring: the Arabs reported that the people of the region were cannibals; Livingstone expressed the hope that he would 'come out uneaten'. This missive had been followed by an inordinately long silence.

Livingstone's fate had often been a matter of press speculation. A report of his death had reached the coast in December 1866, prompting obituaries in British newspapers the following March, only for the information to be proved false by subsequent deliveries of letters. Rumours had grown again during 1868, and had again been scotched when fresh correspondence reached Zanzibar. Livingstone's last letters to Kirk had been the reason for Bennett's decision to delay: he wanted time for public speculation about the explorer's fate to rise again.[14]

For both Bennett and Stanley, the risk was high. Bennett was investing several thousand dollars of the *New York Herald*'s money in arming and supplying the expedition. Stanley was staking his health, possibly his life, and also his dignity and reputation on the outcome – for Livingstone might indeed be dead, or, whether dead or alive, untraceable; but even if alive, he might, given his reputation as a loner and a misanthropist, at least in relation to fellow white men, resent the intrusion of an American newshound in search of a story.

So the meeting with Livingstone in early November 1871 was, for Stanley, a moment of both heady exhilaration and queasy anxiety. It had taken him almost eight months to reach Ujiji. Fever contracted while crossing malarial swamps had prostrated him and reduced his weight by 25 per cent. Danger, discomfort, and sickness had frayed tempers and destroyed the cohesion of his European team. Desertion by his Wangwana – Swahili-speaking Zanzibari Africans – had at one point reduced his guards and porters to a mere 25 men. Involvement in a full-scale war between Arab-Swahili traders and a rebel African chieftain whose forces stood astride his route had brought him close to military disaster – despite the formidable arsenal he had brought with him from the coast. But he had remained doggedly determined. 'I have taken a solemn, enduring oath,' he confided in his journal on the night of 19 September, 'an oath to be kept while the least hope of life remains in me, not to be tempted to break the resolution I have formed, never to give up the search, until I find Livingstone alive, or find his dead body . . . No living man, or living men, shall stop me; only death can prevent me. But death – not even this; I shall not die, I will not die, I cannot die!'[15]

Then, after six more weeks of brutal trekking, there he was, the man he had come to find, the man who had become a living legend. Alerted by his servants, he walked from his veranda and could be seen standing in the open with a group of Arab-Swahili notables in their robes. Great crowds of Africans thronged all around. 'As I advanced slowly towards him, I noticed he was pale, looked wearied, had a grey beard, wore a bluish cap with a faded gold band around it, [and] had on a red-sleeved waistcoat and a pair of grey tweed trousers.' He looked ten years older than his 57 years. Pneumonia had weakened his lungs and slowed his walking. Dysentery had resulted in heavy anal bleeding. Fever came in frequent bouts. Ulcers on his feet, eating through muscle, tendon, and bone, had sometimes immobilised him for months. He knew that he looked awful. 'I am made very old and shaky,' he wrote to his daughter, 'my cheeks fallen in, space round the eyes, the mouth almost toothless . . .'; his smile was 'that of a hippopotamus'. Another five years in Africa had turned David Livingstone into an old man before his time – 'a mere ruckle of bones'.[16]

Stanley's fears were dissolved immediately: his reception could not have been more appreciative. Livingstone was in dire straits, and Stanley's wholly unexpected arrival meant a sudden windfall. Instead of two simple meals a day, Livingstone was soon eating four, and fast recovering his strength. His rescuer's caravan, piled high with 'bales of goods, baths of tin, huge kettles, cooking pots, tents, etc' had Livingstone reflecting ruefully on the contrast between this 'luxurious traveller' and his own desperate circumstances. He was also eager for news, hearing now for the first time of the Franco-Prussian War, the laying of a transatlantic telegraph cable, the election of General Grant to the US presidency, and the death in office of British Foreign Secretary Lord Clarendon. 'I am not of a demonstrative turn,' Livingstone wrote in his diary, '. . . but this disinterested kindness of Mr Bennett, so nobly carried into effect by Mr Stanley, was simply overwhelming. I really do feel extremely grateful, and at the same time I am a little ashamed at not being more worthy of the generosity.'[17]

This was doubly disingenuous: Livingstone cannot have been so naïve as to fail to realise that Bennett (and Stanley) were hardly disinterested; and he was far from regarding himself as a humble and undeserving soul. But mutual self-interest seems to have coincided with genuine empathy and fellowship. Livingstone the Scottish mill-worker and Stanley the Welsh workhouse boy were alike in social origin. The older man, softened by age, experience, and current circumstance, was now less judgemental and unforgiving; and perhaps, too, his new companion pricked the regret and guilt he felt about estrangement from his own children. The younger man, in awe of the great explorer, was much relieved to have been received so warmly, and impressed by an unpretentious simplicity that 'gave no token of what element of power or talent lay within'; more than that, for he was John Rowlands, the little boy who never knew his father and was rejected by his mother, a child denied love who had become a man who craved affection and esteem. So Livingstone and Stanley became like father and son. 'His manner,' Stanley wrote of his new friend, 'suits my nature better than that of any man I can remember . . . I should best describe it as benevolently paternal . . . it steals its influence on me without any effort on his part . . .' And this extraordinary friendship in the bush – 500 miles from contact with the civilisation to which both men belonged – was to be the basis of an extraordinary partnership; one destined to continue long after the death of David Livingstone, and with enormous consequence for the history of Africa. Henry Morton Stanley would soon be rich and famous, and before the end of the decade would emerge as the greatest African explorer of them all. But of still greater significance was this: inspired by the missionary-doctor's life-long abolitionist passion, Stanley would turn Livingstone into a secular saint – and thereby fan the flames of the Victorian anti-slavery movement into a firestorm.[18]

The four months that Stanley stayed with Livingstone were laden with future import. They became confidants and spent long hours talking. They travelled together, drawing upon Stanley's ample resources to explore Lake Tanganyika, fixing in place another piece of East Africa's geographical jigsaw by establishing that the river at the northern end flowed into the lake, not out of it, and that Tanganyika was therefore not linked with Albert. When the time for parting came, it was an emotional wrench for both men. Stanley had wanted Livingstone to go home with him – not to give up his work, but with the intention of returning to Africa when his health was fully restored, his recurring bowel problem cured, a set of artificial teeth procured, perhaps at the head of a joint expedition. But Livingstone would not leave. He may have sensed that he was too old and broken down ever to return if once he left. He remained grimly determined to complete his search for the sources of the Nile. He was eager to march on 'four full-grown gushing fountains' far to the south, each of which became 'a large river'; they might or might not be Herodotus' fountains, but they were unquestionably worthy of discovery, for they were 'the last 100 of the 700 miles of the watershed, from which nearly all the Nile springs do unquestionably arise'.[19]

Stanley could not join him on this journey: he was a newsman with the scoop of the century. So they parted, on the morning of 14 March 1872, Livingstone walking some way on the trail with Stanley's caravan, delaying the moment of final leave-taking. The old missionary-doctor in his sun-bleached cap was losing a close friend, a soulmate, a substitute son. He sensed that his simple African home would now look 'as if a death has taken place'. He knew, as he walked back into the loneliness of his exile, that he might never see another white man.

Stanley stared down from a ridge as he went: 'I looked back and watched his grey figure, fading in the distance . . . I gulped down my great grief and turned away to follow the receding caravan.' He was convinced that the parting was final, that the great journey of exploration Livingstone was set upon would almost certainly kill him, and that he was losing a personal relationship of an intensity and significance he had never before experienced; he wrote of 'the utter loneliness of myself, the void that has been created, the pang at parting, the bleak aspect of the future'.[20]

Livingstone set out from Unyanyembe in August 1872, heading south-west to Tanganyika, then south along the eastern shore, before striking out south and west for Bangweolo and the region of 'four full-grown gushing fountains' which he took to be the watershed of the Nile. It was, thanks to the provisions left by Stanley, the best equipped and supplied of all his expeditions. But grave miscalculations made during his journeys through the south-western lakes in 1867 and 1868 – due to a damaged chronometer and rain-swollen waters – now caused him to become hopelessly lost. And then the rains came again, turning the landscape into leech-infested swamp that sometimes left only heads showing above water, often slowing progress to an energy-sapping wade through mud and slime of barely a mile a day.

Livingstone was afflicted with severe bleeding which gradually wasted his strength; and this proved to be the onset of his body's terminal crisis. His phenomenal willpower remained unbroken to the end. Amid agonies of internal haemorrhaging, short of food, without warmth, soaked through, he remained determined to go forward. 'I am pale, bloodless, and weak from bleeding . . . an artery gives off a copious stream and takes away my strength. Oh! How I long to be permitted by the Over Power to finish my work.'

By the end of April 1873, Livingstone was desperately sick and unable to continue further. His followers endeavoured to make him as comfortable as possible. When, in the early hours of 1 May, the faithful Susi entered his master's hut, he was surprised to find him kneeling beside his bed in prayer. He was cold to the touch. Dr David Livingstone had been dead for several hours.[21]

*LIVINGSTONE. Herald Special from Central Africa. Finding the Great Explorer. Exciting History of the Successful Herald Expedition.* So ran the breathless headlines in the *New York Herald* on 2 July 1872. Below them was printed a long dispatch from London, sent, readers learned, by 'Mr Stanley, Chief of the *Herald* Exploring Expedition to Central Africa'. A full page of close type described the epic journey and meeting, illustrated by a large map showing lakes and routes, and was followed by a précis of Livingstone's career. Readers were informed of the explorer's decision to remain in Africa, but the *Herald* was able to publish exclusive letters entrusted to the care of its intrepid reporter.[22]

It was only seven years since the guns of the Civil War had fallen silent and 4 million American slaves been liberated. Now the people of the United States heard a call from the heart of another continent to renew the struggle, this time against the East African trade.

The abolitionist cause had remained paramount for Livingstone, even during his final years of frantic searching for the sources of the Nile. 'What I have seen of this horrid system,' he wrote to a friend before setting out on what proved to be his final journey, 'makes me feel that its suppression would be of infinitely more importance than all the fountains together.' Now 100,000 readers of the *Herald* heard the same clarion voice ring out:

> In now trying to make the East African slave trade better known to Americans, I indulge the hope I am aiding on, though in a small degree, the good time coming yet when slavery . . . will be chased from the world . . . It would be better to lessen this great human woe than to discover the sources of the Nile . . . May Heaven's rich blessing come down on every one . . . who will help to heal this open sore of the world.[23]

There was no 'small degree' about it. Though he would never know it, David Livingstone was being transformed into an international superstar and the patron saint of abolitionism. The architect of this work of cultural construction was, of course, his new protégé, Henry Morton Stanley. As well as publishing his own dispatches and Livingstone's letters – world news that immediately went viral – he churned out a 700-page manuscript during six weeks holed up in an apartment in London's West End in the late summer of 1872; this was published under the title *How I Found Livingstone* before the year was out. It was flawed, for sure, by haste and sensationalism, and by exaggerated descriptions of floggings and shootings that did much damage to Stanley's reputation, but it became a runaway bestseller – and it canonised David Livingstone.

Stanley was well aware of some of the explorer's flaws – he was too much a man of the world to be blinded by his friendship – but these found no place in the book. They would not have served his own purpose – fame, recognition, applause – nor Livingstone's, whose moral crusade would have suffered from any darkening of his reputation. It was necessary that David Livingstone should become a saint, and Stanley duly made him so. 'God grant that if ever you take to travelling in Africa,' he wrote, 'you will get as noble and true a man for your companion as David Livingstone! For four months and four days I lived with him in the same house, or in the same boat, or in the same tent, and I never found fault in him . . . with Livingstone I never had cause for resentment, but each day's life with him added to my admiration for him.'[24]

British public opinion was soon in uproar. American commentators, warmed by self-righteousness, denounced the hypocrisy of Britain's official anti-slavery stance. 'It would be unjust to charge the government of Great Britain with intentional criminality . . ', boomed one:

> But it stands proved, by the failure of English expeditions to find Dr Livingstone, and by his own positive, earnest testimony, now that an American expedition has succeeded in discovering him, that it is the subjects of the British monarchy who are responsible for the existence of the slave trade of Zanzibar and all the nameless horrors of the interior resulting therefrom. The moral culpability . . . is therefore made manifest; and of this great national turpitude that government must stand convicted before the bar of Christendom.[25]

Under mounting pressure to act, the British government announced new measures in August 1872, and Sir Henry Bartle Frere, a senior diplomat with previous East Africa experience, duly sailed into Zanzibar harbour in January the following year, charged with negotiating a new treaty with the Sultan. Back home, while news of Frere's mission was pending, the agitation continued. Not one, but two British rescue expeditions were launched, one by the Royal Geographical Society, the other by James Young, the Scottish paraffin magnate, both intended to bring relief to the explorer-saint, who was again 'lost', his whereabouts unknown in the absence of any further communication since Stanley's return. The official Royal Geographical Society expedition carried a letter from the new president of the Society, Sir Henry Rawlinson, informing Livingstone that Frere's mission meant that 'there is now a definite prospect of the infamous East African slave trade being suppressed'. Sir Henry was in no doubt about the reason for this optimistic state of affairs: 'For this great end, if it be achieved, we shall be mainly indebted to your recent letters, which had a powerful effect on the public mind in England, and have thus stimulated the action of the government.'[26]

Four years before – in fact in the very month that John Kirk received his last letter from Livingstone before the explorer set out on the journey that would end with the Nyangwe massacre – HMS *Forte*, waiting off the southern Arabian coast, was about to spring a trap. It was May 1869. The *Forte* was a

Royal Navy frigate powered by steam and sail, crewed by 500 men, mounting 28 guns. It was commanded by Commodore Leopold Heath, a big-set man with round face, bald pate, and luxurious sideburns. Also under command he had three of the navy's new Amazon-class vessels, the *Daphne*, the *Dryad*, and the *Nymphe*, each a fast, iron-framed, steam-and-sail sloop, with a crew of 140 men, and armament comprising two 7-inch rifled muzzle-loaders at the bow and two 64-pdr rifled muzzle-loaders amidships, all mounted on tracks for pivoting. He had frigate and sloops deployed in a wide-spaced 'spider's web' designed to snare Arab trading dhows as they made the run from the East African coast to the Persian Gulf.

Whenever a dhow hoved into view, the *Forte* kept as close to the coast as she dared: the danger otherwise was that the Arab would make a dash for the shore before she was overhauled. On this occasion, as the distance closed, the *Forte*'s gunners fired a blank warning round, then another, then two signal rockets. The master of the dhow lowered his sail, and the *Forte*'s cutter was launched to carry out an inspection. It was a slaver: 10 young men, 2 women, 40 boys, and 28 girls had been jammed into the tiny spaces beneath the bamboo deck of the 40-foot dhow. Folded and squashed, packed tight in sweltering heat, mired in their own filth, they now emerged from the hold naked, stiff, attenuated, wilting. Each had a story. Kiada's village had been attacked, her brother killed, and she and another brother had been kidnapped and marched to the coast. Masumambe, Masuk, and Aminha – teenagers like Kiada – had also been abducted from their villages, but had then worked for a while on Zanzibar before being seized or sold for transport overseas. Bakaat had been kidnapped from his father when he was only 11 years old. Mabluk, also 11, had been sold by his own brothers, because they were starving, reduced to eating grass. Each of the 80 human beings now brought back into the light had their story of violence, abduction, families lost, former lives suddenly terminated.[27]

Commodore Heath's squadron had taken station the year before. He had slowly worked out a strategy of interception for enforcing the ban on overseas trafficking of slaves agreed with the Sultan of Zanzibar in 1845. The difficulties were numerous: how to patrol the vastness of the Indian Ocean with one frigate and three sloops; how to distinguish dhows moving slaves within the Sultan's territory (legally) from those moving them beyond (illegally); how to prevent relatively small, sleek sailing vessels from escaping interception by a dash to shore; how to ensure that cargoes of slaves were not thrown overboard and drowned to avoid detection. But once the 'spider's web' system was operational, the results were spectacular. In April and May 1869, the squadron rescued 970 people from 13 slave dhows – twice as many as the average *annual* total over the preceding decade of Royal Navy patrolling. Heath later estimated that his ships were netting roughly half the slave dhows making the run for the Arabian and Persian ports. His thousand or so officers and men, which included a good proportion of Kroomen – West Africans, many of them former slaves or their descendants, who made anti-slavery work a profession – became deeply committed to their mission. Hardened sea-salts would become mother-hens, working with solicitude and sympathy to revive the victims they had rescued.[28]

This was not supposed to have happened, and the British authorities were soon inundated with complaints. Heath and his men, with the ingenuousness of professional service personnel, had assumed that when they were dispatched to the Indian Ocean to enforce an anti-slavery treaty that their job was to intercept slavers, release the captives, and destroy the vessels. This was naïve: an unfortunate conflation of public image and practical action. Opposition came from merchant interests, colonial administrators, and native potentates. Major General Sir Edward Russell, the British Resident at Aden, for example feared 'a great injustice' and informed Heath and the imperial administration in Bombay of his opinion that 'if the wholesale destruction of dhows is permitted, the British name will be abhorred, and the minds of the chiefs and natives will be turned decidedly against us'. Thus was the view from Arabia; and the Bombay Resident concurred, writing to Heath to inform him that he was referring the matter to the India Office in London.

Meanwhile, another man on the spot, Dr John Kirk, now the British Consul on Zanzibar, was equally alarmed. In his role as a vice-admiralty judge, with the job of ruling on the legality of interceptions, he began passing judgments against the naval officers. The squadron was being overzealous. They looked like pirates. Britain was getting a bad name. The Sultan was angry. The captives themselves were not to be considered reliable witnesses. Captured dhows should not be destroyed on the spot, but towed to port for proper adjudication. Kirk even ordered released captives returned to slave traders and payment of compensation for burnt slave dhows. His judgments were laced with racism. Kirk was outraged when a white slave entered the Sultan of Zanzibar's household and made strong representations for his release, but wrote that 'this traffic in Europeans and Asiatic slaves is to us much more revolting than the negro slave trade'.

The Foreign Office got involved. A high-level meeting chaired by Foreign Secretary Lord Clarendon decided to send out new instructions. Heath's squadron, it turned out, was interrupting the free flow of trade and stirring up trouble. It was engendering the distrust of local rulers and making it likely they would look to the French for protection. It was undermining the Zanzibari economy and ran the risk that important industries would be ruined. Burning ships on suspicion was unacceptable. The word of an African child could not be accepted against that of an Arab captain. Runaways who were the 'lawful property' of their owners were to be returned.[29]

But the mandarins of imperial power were no longer in control of events. For one thing, Heath's officers were contemptuous. Captain George Sulivan of the *Daphne* was moved to write: 'I have been led to conclude by many circumstances that the suppression of the slave trade and the interests of the Indian Government do not coincide. And there is a tendency to sacrifice the slave to the political advantage gained in relation to the chiefs and others of the slave-holding tribe.' Captain Edward Meara of the *Nymphe* was of the same mind; he refused point-blank Kirk's order to re-enslave liberated Africans and to pay compensation to slave traders for their dhows. Both captains, along with their colleague, Captain Philip Colomb of the *Dryad*, considered their ships British territory, where slavery was illegal, such that any runaway taken on board became, by virtue of that fact alone, a free person.[30]

The defiance of Heath's officers might have been quashed, but for the furore at home. The same Victorian public that was speculating on the whereabouts of Dr Livingstone and endorsing his abolitionist convictions was enthralled to read of these naval action-heroes performing deeds of derring-do thousands of miles from home, advancing the cause of civilisation, freeing slaves from bondage – and facing wilful obstruction from cynical politicians. The popular press carried dramatic pictures of the clashes at sea under captions like 'The cutter of HMS *Daphne* capturing a slave dhow off Brora'. The *Penny Illustrated* reported that 'Our Jack Tars . . . have this year struck more than one good blow against the inhuman slavers . . .' The *Anti-Slavery Reporter* denounced the authorities under the headline 'Britain a participant in the slave trade'. What, asked the *Pall Mall Gazette*, would Britain's lost explorer and leading anti-slavery campaigner make of this official hypocrisy? The steady stream of stories, many of them re-run by provincial newspapers, totalled 60 in the three years 1868 to 1871. Then came the sensational news that Livingstone was alive and was renewing his call for action against the East African trade.[31]

The Gladstone government found itself on the back foot. William Ewart Gladstone was a *laissez-faire* liberal, a strict non-interventionist, an opportunist political operator, and, if truth be told, a serial hypocrite. He wrote privately from his estate in North Wales to his Foreign Secretary in Westminster in November 1872 that he could not understand what all the fuss was about. The 'negrophilists' (as he called them) would sacrifice white lives to save black ones. Yet the blacks were a less developed race. And it all cost money, taxpayers' money, government money, for ships and crews – when, in the full goodness of time, Commerce could be relied upon to suppress the slave trade.

But the political pressure from the 'Anti Slave Trade People' (another Gladstone epithet) had already forced the government to act. A parliamentary select committee had begun taking evidence on the East African slave trade the year before – including evidence from Heath and his officers – and it had already reached its momentous decision when Gladstone penned his whinging note to the Foreign Secretary: a new treaty was to be negotiated with the Sultan of Zanzibar. Not that the anti-slavery uproar died down. On the contrary, it reached a new peak in the autumn of 1873, just before the British government's special envoy, Sir Henry Bartle Frere, set out for Zanzibar. The Stanley circus was on tour from August to November, with a heavy schedule of lectures, banquets, and civic receptions. Tens of thousands packed into the lecture-halls; hundreds of thousands read the newspaper reports. By the time Frere sailed, the first edition of How I Found Livingstone had become a sell-out and the publishers were planning to reprint before the year was out. Interest in the outcome of the Frere mission was intense. Expectations were high.[32]

The upsurge in the Victorian anti-slavery movement coincided with an upsurge in the slave trade: an exquisite contradiction. A cholera epidemic had killed swathes and the demand for replacements had seen 14,000 slaves shipped from Kilwa and landed at Zanzibar between May and December 1871. The boom continued through the whole of the following year – John Kirk thought Zanzibar harbour more crowded with slave dhows in May than ever before – and prices hit record levels in September, with slaves selling for as much as $40. In the very month of Frere's arrival, January 1873, dealers on the waterfront were bragging about how good business was that season. Unsurprisingly, the increasingly assertive British presence – on the island, in the interior, and on the open sea – was viewed with growing suspicion by the Zanzibari elite.[33]

The Sultan's dilemma was acute. He was menaced by British military power. Frere – who arrived in a steam yacht with an escort of three warships – may have posed as an anti-slavery crusader, but he saw abolitionism as merely one expression of a wider 'Civilisation' that it was his duty to enforce. He had entered the Bombay civil service in 1834 at the age of 19, and then worked his way up the ranks of the service, becoming Chief Commissioner of Sindh in 1850, Governor of Bombay in 1862. Embodying the top-down technocratic ideals of Indian Civil Service officials, he laboured hard for land reform, infrastructure projects, and the advancement of education and health care. Native rule he considered corrupt, brutal, backward; the rule of men like himself, by contrast, implied order, improvement, justice. Later, as High Commissioner for Southern Africa, he would engineer the destruction of the Zulu Kingdom in 1879, and thereby, unwittingly, clear the way for the white domination that would culminate in Apartheid. His purpose was beneficent, but his vision blurred, his assumptions arrogant, his methods manipulative and domineering. Frere, in short, was an empire-expansionist, a man of the new age of empire now dawning, a pioneer of the Scramble for Africa. Lord Acton, a Gladstonian Liberal, considered him 'a dangerous agent', his strength 'akin to obstinacy and self-will', a man who would 'gain his ends by crooked paths when he has tried the straight in vain'. In Acton's view, 'Indians [civil servants and officers who had served mainly in India] are not generally a healthy element in the body politic, and he [Frere] has the constant vice of Indians: belief in force.'[34]

Frere, the Victorian public, and British warships formed one side of the Sultan's dilemma. Zanzibar's existence as an international slave emporium formed the other. The island economy and the informal mercantile empire over which the Sultan presided were based on slavery. Vast profits were accumulated by the Omani, Indian, and Arab-Swahili ruling class through the employment of slaves and the trading of slaves. The Sultan's own wealth was derived from slave plantations, and his government was financed by customs duties levied on the trafficking of slaves. Barghash bin Said, moreover, who had succeeded his brother upon the latter's death in 1870, was a canny political operator and a zealous defender of Zanzibari independence and the slave economy. And he was supported in his resistance by an influential Islamic-fundamentalist movement with pronounced anti-Western views: the Mutawas.

Frere – and Kirk, who henceforward functioned as Frere's right-hand man – were contending in Zanzibar not only with vested interests, but with protagonists who were as much men of conviction as themselves. The Mutawas, like some British empire-builders, were visionaries who dealt in certainties and moral absolutes: only they came to very different conclusions. Based in Oman, where they had become dominant in government, the Mutawas were a politico-religious movement dominated by imams, committed to *shariya* law, and hostile not only to European colonialism but to any kind of Western-style reform and modernisation. Henry Churchill, the former British Consul on Zanzibar, described them as 'the concentrated essence of fanaticism'. Before he was felled by ill-health and replaced by John Kirk, Churchill had fought a rearguard action against Mutawa influence, promising British support for Barghash's succession in return for reassurance that 'he would be friendly towards England and would not revert to bigotry or *mutawa* principles with which HM Government could have no sympathy'. Reassurance was given, but it was duplicitous, for Barghash, unwilling to play the role of British client, included Mutawas among his close advisors. Though they seem to have had little popular support, working very much in the shadows, John Kirk was able to list the names of six leading members of the group in his journal. And as pressure mounted on Barghash following Frere's arrival on Zanzibar in January 1873, the Sultan came to rely ever more heavily on this cohort of advisors steeled by intractable religious conviction.[35]

Frere's steam yacht bore an ominous name: *Enchantress*. Two months of negotiations between the British delegation and the Zanzibari court failed to enchant anyone, and Frere sailed away in the middle of March, leaving matters in the hands of John Kirk. The Zanzibari slave trade was not to be negotiated away. As Frere reported to London, 'For Zanzibar Arabs, even of the highest class, the speculation in slaves seems to have the same sort of attraction which horse-dealing has for the ordinary Yorkshireman . . . To the lower classes in Zanzibar, a slave is a safe, easy, and profitable investment . . .' Only force would work, and this would now be applied. As he explained to a meeting of Indian dignitaries, 'It is, I believe, the fixed determination of the Her Majesty's Government and of the people of England to spare no exertion or expense till the trade in human beings has ceased on every sea to which the influence of England extends . . .' When he spoke these words, in May 1873, British warships of Admiral Arthur Cumming's East India Station had already deployed to the waters off Zanzibar. Kilwa, the principal slave port on the mainland, and Zanzibar were blockaded. HMS *Daphne*, now in company with HMS *Briton*, rode at anchor off Kilwa, where thousands of slaves were penned awaiting transportation. Between them, the two British warships mounted 14 guns, any of which was capable of sinking a dhow with a single round. By late May, delegations of Arab, Indian, and Swahili traders, men who cared nothing for politics or religion, only for making money, were lobbying Barghash to cut a deal and save the rest of the island's commerce.

The capitulation came on the night of 3/4 June. Kirk hurried to the palace in response to Barghash's request for an emergency meeting. The Sultan was there with his council and three leading Mutawa advisors. British Consul and Zanzibari Mutawas were face to face for the first time. Kirk brushed aside attempts to have the blockade called off pending further negotiation: there had to be immediate agreement. A new treaty was duly drawn up and signed on 6 June. The Sultan's soldiers shut down the Zanzibari slave market, and a notice was posted at the customs house informing the people that the slave trade was now illegal in all harbours and markets within the Sultan's domain. British military power, mobilised by a combination of public outrage and imperial calculation, had ended the 1,000-year-old slave trade in the Indian Ocean.

▄

The Royal Navy, by its campaign of interception and blockade between 1868 and 1873, had closed down the maritime routes by which slaves were transported from East Africa to the Red Sea and the Persian Gulf. But there were other routes. They ran from Equatorial Africa down the River Nile and its tributaries, or overland across the arid wastes of the Sudan, to the same rich markets in Egypt, Arabia, Syria, Persia, and Turkey. As the liberal-leaning *Manchester Guardian* commented on 11 July 1873, 'the slave trade at sea has been suppressed, but both slavery and the slave trade by land still continue'. The paper's correspondent on Zanzibar reported that 5,000 slaves were being held at Kilwa, their onward transportation by sea now permanently blocked by the new treaty and naval enforcement patrols, with the implication that this valuable cargo would now be moved another way.[36]

Henceforth the dismal caravans of the doomed would all flow northwards. The remaining routes would soon be flooded with unprecedented numbers of slaves. The great struggle between Victorian 'moral' capitalism and the Arab-Islamic slave trade had only just begun. The little drama played out on the island of Zanzibar in the spring of 1873 was but the prologue to an epic confrontation destined to engulf much of North-East Africa for a generation. It would not, in the manner of a Greek tragedy, be a conflict between two rights. It would, in the manner of some other kind of tragedy, be a conflict between two wrongs; two forms of exploitation and oppression, based on two different modes of economic and political domination. British imperialism, wearing a mantle of Civilisation and Progress, would seek to turn the native people into coolies, dark-skinned proletarians managed by colonial policemen, for the benefit of white plantation-owners, big trading companies, and City of London banks. Islamism, wearing a mantle of Piety and Tradition, would uphold the power and wealth of an Arab ruling class of sheikhs, landlords, and slave traders. The former would look forward to a new world order based on steamships, railways, and commodity markets. The latter would look back to a medieval world of dhows, medinas, and slave markets. Neither would offer any kind of redemption to the common people of the region, the hoe-cultivators and riverside farmers, the pastoralists and petty traders, the plantation workers and general labourers, the women and the poor. And the collision between them, between imperialist and Islamist, between two rival dystopias, would plunge the region into full-scale war.

# Part II
# Star and Crescent

# CHAPTER FOUR

# BAKER PASHA

In November 1873, John Kirk, the British Consul on Zanzibar, dispatched his number two, Captain Frederick Elton, to the mainland on a fact-finding mission. He wanted to know what Indian traders – technically British subjects – were up to following the closure of the slave market on the island. Elton's reports were alarming. He attempted to monitor movement up the three main coast roads for a month, from 21 December to 20 January, despite threats of shooting and tense encounters with slave traders. He counted one caravan after another: no less than six during the first week, totalling 1,280 slaves in all. The condition of many was wretched:

> One gang of lads and women, chained together with iron neck-rings, was in a horrible state, their lower extremities coated with dry mud and their own excrement, and torn with thorns, their bodies mere frameworks, and their skeleton limbs tightly stretched with wrinkled, parchment-like skin. One wretched women had been flung against a tree for slipping her rope, and came screaming up to us for protection, with one eye half-out, and the side of her face and bosom streaming with blood.

Elton estimated that in the 30 days he kept watch more than 4,000 slaves passed down the roads heading north. The implication was that the annual total might be 50,000. His conclusion was grim: 'a brisker slave trade has seldom been known'.[1]

Equally disturbing reports were soon reaching the British authorities from other parts of Africa. Lord Derby, the new Foreign Secretary, learned from his vice consul in Benghazi, in a letter dated 24 December 1875, that large slave caravans were regularly making the gruelling Sahara crossing, the captives who survived arriving in appalling condition. 'They were emaciated skeletons,' he wrote of some he had seen at an oasis stop, 'their long thin legs and arms and the apparently unnatural size and prominence of their knees and elbows and hands and feet giving them a most repulsive and shocking appearance ...' It was hardly surprising: they had endured a ten-week march across the desert on a cup of water and a handful of maize every 12 hours. Many, of course, having collapsed of thirst, hunger, and exhaustion, had been left behind 'to die a frightful death in the desert'. Some succumbed because their bare feet became so chapped and swollen traversing the hot sand that they could not keep up. For every one of the estimated 20,000 a year who survived the crossing, one, two, or three more may have died on the way. No-one knows. No-one was counting. It did not matter. When those who made it had been given time to recover, learned a few phrases of Arabic, and been dressed in cotton shirt and skullcap, they could be sold for export to Egypt for between 300 and 500 per cent of their sub-Saharan value.[2]

The interruption of the Indian Ocean traffic had certainly been inconvenient. But demand remained buoyant, prices high, and the men who dealt in human chattels soon adjusted. One of these – among the greatest of the slave lords – was Tippu Tip. In the six or seven years since leaving Zanzibar, Hamid bin Muhammad (his real name) had built up a very substantial business in ivory and slaves. Early in his career, in 1867, gloating over the spoils of victory over a native African chieftain, he had proclaimed himself Tippu Tip – 'the gatherer of wealth'. So it proved. A tall man of somewhat swarthy appearance, with round features and black beard, he looked typically Arab-Swahili. Strong, energetic, intelligent, bright-eyed, with gleaming teeth, he nowadays received visitors in the style of the great man he had become, wearing spotless white dishdasha, clean fez or turban, rich waistband, and dagger decorated with silver filigree. When he appeared in public, attended by a retinue of a dozen or so dependants, his immaculate costume, combined with his courtesy and dignity, elicited a buzz of admiration from onlookers.

Though he had acquired the manners of an oriental courtier, Tippu Tip remained essentially a businessman. He was a merchant-prince, a latter-day

Medici, and the informal empire he ruled – for such it was becoming, eventually to span tens of thousands of miles of the Upper Congo basin – was not so much a realm to be governed as a territory to be plundered. He had the instincts of an accountant. He expressed open scorn for explorers who wasted their lives searching for 'rivers and lakes and mountains'. The Arabs, he explained, 'travel little by little to get ivory and slaves, and are years about it'. The human cost did not figure; only economic cost – the investment made against the profit earned. 'Slaves cost nothing,' he proclaimed. 'They have only to be gathered.' Once, having seen a boatload of women and children swept over a waterfall and drowned, his only remark was, 'What a pity! It was a fine canoe.'

Tippu Tip had emerged supreme from the chaos of slave war. In a disintegrating world dominated by gangs and guns, political power is fragile and unstable. The usual laws of economic competition, which tend to work incrementally over decades, do not apply. The gun imposes a different dynamic, a high-velocity process of politico-military accumulation, where killing, or at least the power to kill, causes territories to change hands, armies to form and dissolve, fortunes to be made and lost, in a fraction of the time. The power of Tippu Tip was reducible to his army, around a thousand men in the mid-1870s, but destined to grow still larger in the succeeding two decades, until its leader could be ranked among the greatest potentates in Central Africa.

Its core was formed of 'household' contingents of Arabs, Arab-Swahilis, and Wangwana, armed with flintlock muskets. Its second-line troops might be slaves, freedmen, or free-born mercenaries, some with muskets, others with spears and shields. These were supported by African tribal allies, equipped with traditional weapons. What was decisive was not numbers – for the bush was inhabited by tens of thousands of potentially hostile warriors – but centralised command and control, and firepower. As early as 1859, 23,000 muskets were being imported annually into Zanzibar, most of them destined for the interior. Each advance, each operation, was carefully measured; for Tippu Tip ruled an empire of profit, to be expanded, as he said, 'little by little', with minimum risk and maximum gain. But when the moment came to move into virgin territory, and force was needed, it took the form of concentrated firepower at the point of decision.[3]

The business model was simple enough. Slaves were rounded up in raids carried out either by Tippu Tip's men themselves, or by other slave-trading gangs operating effectively as contractors, or by native warriors whose tribal chiefs had become suppliers. Older villagers were usually killed, along with younger men who resisted, but the rest were likely to be seized as chattels. Occasionally all the men were killed, presumably because the women were easier (and therefore cheaper) to control on a long march, and their market value was that much higher. One European observer recorded a raid in which 170 able-bodied men, their legs severed, were left to bleed to death, while between 500 and 1,000 women and children were seized for the caravans. Captives would be held in pens inside trading-posts that were stockaded and guarded. The pens were often crowded and devoid of cover, and the captives often remained shackled. When a sufficient number had been assembled – usually several hundred – a caravan would be organised, the slaves moving on foot, yoked at the neck with ropes, iron rings, or wooden forks. Some, especially the more intractable men, would also be bound at the wrists, but many, especially women and children, would serve as porters, carrying ivory, trade goods, supplies, or water. All would be driven by guards armed with guns, whips, and clubs.

Sickness and disease were endemic. Food was meagre, water insufficient, medical care non-existent, and the captives, naked and barefoot, faced weeks of marching under the African sun. Those who fell by the wayside were routinely killed. Some were battered to death with clubs, others killed with axes or daggers, a good number garrotted. Babies considered a burden were sometimes torn from their mothers' arms and tossed into the bush. Resistance and attempts at escape were dealt with in the same way: by summary killing. The main slave trails were easily followed, since they were marked by the bones of the dead, scattered and picked clean by scavenging animals.

Another fate awaited many of the young boys on the trail. They were especially valuable because of the Middle Eastern demand for eunuchs – to serve in harems, but also as administrators, family stewards, and attendants at mosques and other holy places. As the demand for eunuchs rose during the nineteenth century, specialist centres for operating to remove the testicles were established on the slave routes. Medical skills and hygiene standards were basic, the wastage rate high; though estimates of mortality varied widely, the fact that the prices of castrated boys were about three times those of uncastrated boys tells its own story.

The female counterpart of the male eunuch was, of course, the concubine. If some boys were mutilated (and sometimes sodomised), girls and younger women were subject to serial rape. This was routine on the trail –

one of the perks of the trafficking business – but it was also the fate of so many African women after their sale into household service. Whereas in the Western trade the numbers of male and female slaves had been roughly equal, and the price of a male had been on average higher, in the Eastern trade females seem to have outnumbered males by about three to one, and a teenage girl might be worth twice as much as a mature man. This reflected the predominance of domestic service over plantation labour in the East; great numbers of young women were required for sexual service in the harems of rich Arabs, Turks, and Persians. The harem of the Ottoman Sultan Abdul Hamid II in 1908, for example, contained 370 women and 127 eunuchs.

Livingstone had estimated that only one in five, perhaps as few as one in ten, of the Africans displaced by the slave trade actually reached market. Far more perished in the endemic warfare, in the cull of the unwanted, on the long marches to the north, or, having fled into the bush when their homes were destroyed, because they simply starved to death. Perhaps as many as half a million people a year were being sucked into the vortex of the slave trade. This was the horror masked by Tippu Tip's veneer of culture.[4]

Two battalions of Turco-Egyptian soldiers lined the shore. The guns fired a salute. And finally, after a year's delay, the flotilla was under way, 2 steamers, 31 sailing vessels, 800 men, departing Khartoum and heading up the Nile. Leading the expedition was an English gentleman, Sir Samuel White Baker, who now gloried in the rank of Major General of the Ottoman Army and Governor General of Equatoria. His mission was to take possession of his province on behalf of the Khedive Ismail of Egypt – who ruled in Cairo in the name of the Ottoman Sultan in Constantinople – and to suppress the slave trade, open navigation to the Great Lakes, establish a chain of military posts, impose government authority, and facilitate legitimate commerce; which, his official instructions stated, would be 'a great stride towards future civilisation'.

The flotilla departing 8 February 1870 was the advanced contingent of a somewhat larger force. Baker's army, 1,645 soldiers in all, comprised a regiment of Egyptian infantry, another of Sudanese infantry, some 200 irregular cavalry, 2 batteries of rifled mountain guns, and 200 rockets. Most of the infantry were armed with muzzle-loading rifles of Crimean War vintage, but Baker had used 50 modern breech-loading Sniders supplied by the royal arsenal at Woolwich to equip an elite of picked men dubbed 'the Forty Thieves' (though in fact they numbered 46). The Governor General's fleet was planned to comprise 9 steamers, the largest a specially constructed 250-ton paddle steamer, 55 sailing vessels averaging 50 tons a piece, and two steel lifeboats of 10 tons – though in the event he was never able to assemble so many, and was forced to operate with less than optimum river-power.

Baker's principal officers were his nephew, Lieutenant Julian Alleyne Baker RN, who functioned as chief of staff, Colonel Raouf Bey, his Turco-Egyptian second-in-command, and Lieutenant Colonel Abd el-Kader, another Turco-Egyptian officer who acted as aide-de-camp and commander of the Forty Thieves. The other Europeans in the party included a secretary, a doctor, a civil engineer, a chief engineer of steamers, a chief shipwright, and a combined quartermaster and interpreter. They were supported by a small team of servants, clerks, and artisans. As well as investing in steamers, artillery, rifles, and munitions, Baker had spent lavishly on supplies – expected to last four years – including industrial machinery, engineering materials, spare parts, tools of every conceivable type, and an abundance of trade goods, mainly textiles. Most of this had to be transported by boat and camel a distance of about 3,000 miles – from Alexandria on the Mediterranean coast to Gondokoro on the Upper Nile – including the heavy metal sections of river steamers, saw mills, and boilers.[5]

Baker knew what he was about: he had spent his whole life in the outdoors, and had already clocked up several years exploring in the Sudan. Though now almost 50, he had an iron constitution and was still in the peak of condition. Tall, burly, with broad shoulders and deep chest, he was powerfully built yet agile and fast on his feet. His heavyweight form combined with rugged features and black bushy beard to convey a raw masculinity. Born into a prosperous bourgeois family of merchants, colonial planters, and navy men in 1821, he had from an early age been fascinated by geography, travel, and adventure. After a spell on a family sugar plantation in Mauritius, where he soon grew restless, he spent many years in Ceylon, attracted at first by the prospect of elephant hunting, then devoting himself to creating, with the help of his family, a new model estate. His passion for big-game hunting remained with him throughout life. He was drawn to the wilderness, the physical challenge, the thrill of the chase, the stalk, the kill; by his own admission, he killed several hundred elephants during his early adulthood.[6]

The Ceylon settlement was only a modest success, and the personal cost was high: he lost some of his much-loved children to sickness in Ceylon, he nearly died of fever himself, and he became concerned about his wife's well-being. So the decision was made, after seven years on the island, to return to Britain. But the death of his wife the very same year left him psychologically crippled; he lost his zest for life, drifting without clear purpose, becoming the despair of a family that feared he would fail to live up to his early promise. A second marriage – to a Hungarian woman 20 years his junior – seems to have restored his mental balance. It was both love match and work partnership, for henceforward Sam and Florence Baker would travel everywhere together. And it was around the same time that he was first drawn to African exploration. The trigger seems to have been the Burton/Speke controversy about the sources of the Nile which had erupted in the British press in the spring of 1859.[7]

Learning of Speke's planned second expedition to tackle the sources from the south, he conceived the idea of a separate, privately funded expedition of his own to approach them from the north. The mystery of the Nile had acquired another disciple. 'I commenced an expedition to discover the sources of the Nile,' he wrote, 'with the hope of meeting the East African expedition of Captains Speke and Grant, that had been sent by the English government from the south, via Zanzibar, for that object.' But this was heady ambition indeed, and Baker was reticent about his plans before setting off, giving out that all he had in mind was a grand hunting expedition. 'I had not the presumption to publish my intention,' he confessed, 'as the sources of the Nile had hitherto defied all explorers, but I had inwardly determined to accomplish this difficult task or die in the attempt.'[8]

Die he almost did. His preparations were thorough. Before heading up the White Nile, he spent a year exploring the Blue Nile river system in the south-eastern borderland between Sudan and Abyssinia, getting acclimatised and learning the language. He then passed another six months in Khartoum, hiring 3 riverboats, 30 transport animals, 45 soldiers, and 40 sailors, and assembling all the equipment, supplies, and trade goods he needed. But the challenges he faced were prodigious: a long, tedious river passage through vegetation-choked, mosquito-infested swamps; equally gruelling treks through grasslands populated by hostile tribesmen armed with poisoned arrows; violent opposition from slave traders, and lack of supply in regions depopulated by slave raids; a succession of mutinies by his own men; and eventually becoming marooned without porters or supplies, wholly at the mercy of a capricious African tyrant called Kamrasi. 'We were in perfect despair,' he later admitted in his account of the expedition, 'as we were completely worn out with fever and fatigue, and certain death seemed to stare us in the face . . .'[9]

Yet there had been triumph amid the tribulation. Baker had indeed met Speke and Grant on their way north, and it was with their encouragement that he had pressed on to Lake Albert (as he named it), there making his own exhilarating contribution to geographical knowledge. Standing on a 1,500-foot granite cliff, he had looked down 'upon those welcome waters, upon that vast reservoir which nourished Egypt and brought fertility where all was wilderness, upon that great source for so long hidden from mankind, that source of bounty and blessings to millions of human beings . . .' Baker's assessment of his discovery was overblown: he had in fact seen very little of the lake, and claimed too much when he announced that 'the Victoria and the Albert lakes are the two sources of the Nile'. It would be another decade before Stanley finally demonstrated the predominance of Lake Victoria in supplying the waters of the White Nile. But it was heady achievement nonetheless, a large piece of the jigsaw fixed in place, and news of it would transform Samuel White Baker into a celebrity explorer with the prominence to secure his appointment in 1869 to a senior post in the Turco-Egyptian service.[10]

Baker has been described as 'the perfect Victorian hero'. Perhaps it would be more accurate to say 'the perfect *late*-Victorian hero'. For, with the exception of determination and powers of endurance, Baker had little in common with a man like Livingstone. He was not self-made: he had been born to privilege and opportunity. He had no real sense of duty and obligation: his approach to life was self-indulgent. And he was largely devoid of social conscience or anything beyond routine religious conviction. His amoral hedonism seems to have been more typical of the Georgian era than the Victorian. His politics reflected this. A Tory, a jingo, a racist, and an unashamed imperialist, he had none of Livingstone's sympathy with either working-class Britons or native Africans. He was contemptuous of missionaries, mocking of liberals and radicals who believed in 'the brotherhood of man', and gave free expression to his irritation at the power wielded by 'almighty niggers'.

While he subscribed to the Livingstonian vision of transformation through Commerce, Christianity, and Civilisation, the emphasis was very much on the former, and he assumed that compulsion would be necessary.

The philanthropist and the missionary will expend their noble energies in vain struggling against the obtuseness of savage hordes, until the first steps towards their enlightenment shall have been made by commerce. The savage must learn to want; he must learn to be ambitious; and to covet more than mere animal necessities of food and drink. This can alone be taught by a communication with civilised beings . . .

His views on slavery were no less reactionary. He considered the 1833 Slavery Abolition Act to have shown 'a lack not only of statesmanship but of common sense in the sudden emancipation of a vast body of inferior human beings, who, thus released from long bondage, were unfitted for sudden liberty'. So how was Africa to be redeemed? 'The explorer is the precursor of the colonist; and the colonist is the human instrument by which the great work must be constructed . . . the civilisation of the world.' In the vanguard of this movement were the British. 'England, the great chief of the commercial world, possesses a power that enforces a grave responsibility. She has the force to civilise. She is the natural coloniser of the world.'[11]

Men of Livingstone's era had spoken with conviction laced with sympathy and good intent. Baker spoke with the arrogance of the age of empire. And in February 1870, heading up the Nile to establish a modern administration, he cast himself in the role of standard-bearer of Civilisation. Had he been a representative of the British Empire, this would have been delusional enough; but at least the British were taking action against the slave trade. Baker, on the other hand, was the armed proconsul of a Turco-Egyptian regime intent on expanding its Sudanese slave empire.

The Middle Ages had ended for Egypt in 1798, when the most modern army in the world, that of the new French republic, had used artillery and massed musketry to destroy an army of medieval cavalry armed with lances and sabres at the Battle of the Pyramids and thereby terminated the 500-year rule of the Mamluks. The French did not stay long – their fleet was destroyed by Nelson that same year, their commander, Napoleon Bonaparte, went home to organise a military coup, and the army left behind was evicted by the British in 1801 (who themselves departed two years later). But the political shock waves were not stilled by the rapid withdrawal of foreign troops. Egypt had been served three sharp lessons: that it was threatened by

European colonial powers; that the country's Ottoman overlord was impotent; that it needed cannon, musketeers, and military discipline to defend itself.[12]

Throughout its 5,000-year history of civilisation, Egypt has oscillated between being itself a centre of imperial power and being the colonial dependency of another. This history is inherent in the country's geography. The delta and the Lower Nile represent one of the world's richest agricultural territories, and taxes raised from its tens of thousands of riverbank villages have been the basis of many powerful polities. 'There is no country in the world,' Napoleon observed, 'where the government controls more closely, by means of the Nile, the life of the people. Under a good administration, the Nile gains on the desert; under a bad one, the desert gains on the Nile.' The relationship between the desert and the sown, between nomad and farmer – more precisely, the balance between the two – has been a crucial one throughout Egyptian and wider Middle Eastern history. Traditionally, Egyptian rulers have sought to control the desert, to draw upon its resources, and to use it as a protective mantle. And when they have been strong enough, to further secure their power, they have sometimes attempted to project their *imperium* beyond the desert mantle – eastwards, via the Mediterranean, Sinai, and the Red Sea, to Syria and Arabia, or southwards, across the Sudan, up the Blue Nile into the Abyssinian highlands, or up the White Nile to the grasslands and forests of sub-Saharan Africa. So it was in the wake of the Napoleonic invasion.

The self-appointed saviour of Egypt was a Turkish soldier called Muhammad Ali who had first-hand experience of French and British military power in the campaigns of 1798–1801. Amid the chaos following British withdrawal in 1803, he obtained command of a force of 10,000 Ottoman Albanian soldiers. A few years later, in 1807, he was strong enough to defeat a second British expedition, thereby establishing himself as the new strongman of Turco-Egyptian politics. Acting with the authority of the Ottoman Sultan, and support from a broad swathe of the Egyptian people, he raised taxes, conscripted a large army, and smashed residual Mamluk resistance to his rule by a mix of treachery and massacre. A military dictator, he was also a moderniser and a reformer. He regretted the necessity for brutal force, but he saw no alternative if he was to rouse 'this land from the sleep of ages'. Yet, in aspiring to transform Egypt into a modern state, he straddled a contradiction between national ambition and economic backwardness. Egypt was far behind Europe in the struggle for global power, and only a ruthless programme of centralised state-driven development could hope to close the gap. A nineteenth-century nation-state was, perforce, to be constructed using thirteenth-century methods. An army of cannon and musketeers was to be created by violence, plunder, and enslavement.[13]

This was the context for the Turco-Egyptian conquest of the Sudan between 1820 and 1823. Muhammad Ali sent his son Ismail up the Nile with a force of 4,000 regulars. They were reinforced by thousands of irregulars, recruited on a promise of loot and payment of 50 piastres for every human ear taken in battle. The disintegrating Kingdom of Sennar collapsed at first contact with Turco-Egyptian imperialism, and thereafter Ismail's army moved across the Sudan against minimal resistance, cutting a swathe of devastation and displacement as it went. Ismail's soldiers lived off plunder, and Muhammad Ali had demanded 10,000 strong male slaves of military age and as much gold and other precious metal as could be taken. 'You are well aware,' the dictator wrote to his son, 'that your mission in those parts has no other aim than to gather negroes.' The invasion of Sudan was a gigantic raid to secure slave-soldiers for Muhammad Ali's army. Tens of thousands were taken in the regions beyond Khartoum, from among the Dinka, Shilluk, Nuer, and other negro peoples; and of those taken, such was their maltreatment, barely one in eight made it to Egypt. Meanwhile, the Arab-Islamic Sudanese north of Khartoum were driven by the ravages of the soldiery to desperate, doomed revolts. These were met with horrific reprisals: men were emasculated, women had their breasts cut off, and wounds were filled with boiling pitch to slow the death agony. When the fighting finally ended, the Sudanese having been terrorised into submission, an estimated 50,000 had been killed and at least as many enslaved.[14]

The Sudan then became a tributary of Cairo. For the next 60 years it would be subject to violent expropriation by Turco-Egyptian officers. The wealth extracted was expected to cover the full cost of the occupation and deliver a return to Cairo; and, on every possible occasion, corrupt officials, backed by soldiers, would also take their cut. Land and poll taxes were imposed on riverbank farmers, and payment, often in kind, in corn, cloth, or whatever, was enforced by armed detachments and use of the *bastinado*.[15] Around 85 per cent of the tribute raised was spent on the army of occupation. A crude cyclical mechanism was at work here: a subsistence economy was being ransacked to support around 15,000 foreign soldiers, and these soldiers were chiefly necessary to enforce this flow of tribute. As one French observer explained in the mid-1860s:

Musa Pasha [the Governor General] was operating in a vicious circle which, to the extent he expanded it, was enveloping the Sudan in ever-growing wretchedness and had ended by ruining it completely. His method seems to have consisted in expanding the Sudan army excessively in order to secure the revenue collection and thereby to augment the revenues to pay his army.

The result was economic decline and the impoverishment of society: the Turco-Egyptian colonial infrastructure consumed its own productive base. Samuel Baker was witness to this. Passing down the Nile in 1870, he was shocked by the change since his visit only five years before.

The rich soil on the banks of the river, which had a few years since been highly cultivated, was abandoned. Now and then a tuft of neglected date-palms might be seen, but the river's banks, formerly verdant with heavy crops, had become a wilderness. Villages once crowded had entirely disappeared; the population was gone. Irrigation had ceased.

Baker guessed that many of the people had abandoned farming to take up slave trading. He may have been right. Cairo was interested above all in slaves, and government soldiers, when not otherwise employed, were active in the trade. A complex relationship had developed between Turco-Egyptian officers, Arab-Sudanese sheikhs, and private slave traders active on the Abyssinian border, along the Upper Nile, and in the Kordofan region. The main concern of Cairo was that it receive its annual tithe of African humanity. How this was achieved by the officers on the ground was a secondary matter. Sometimes they strove to establish a state monopoly. On the river, for example, private slavers were sometimes intercepted and their captives confiscated. Baker was one of many observers to bear witness to this process. 'Two vessels had been seized and brought to Khartoum,' he had reported in May 1865:

containing 850 human beings, packed like anchovies, the living and dying festering together, and the dead lying beneath them . . . The slaves were in a state of semi-starvation, having had nothing to eat for several days . . . the dead and many of the dying were tied by the ankles and dragged along the ground by donkeys through the streets . . . the women were divided by the Egyptian authorities among the soldiers.

Other methods were also employed. Tribute was levied in the form of slaves. Nomadic pastoralists in the desert and semi-desert regions of the west, for example, sometimes had their cattle impounded until they delivered prescribed quotas of slaves. Alternatively, army units or their contractors organised their own slave raids. Alongside this 'official' slave trade – by confiscation, tribute, and raid – the 'private' slave trade continued. Taxes were levied on this where possible, though sometimes army officers were simply paid off, or even recruited as agents in the enterprises of powerful private traders. What is clear is that the slave trade, official and private, boomed across the Sudan under Turco-Egyptian rule, creating a complex nexus of connections and interests, and that the only real question was the distribution of profit between the different parties.[16]

The appointment of Baker as Governor General of Equatoria in 1869 was controversial. His own appreciation of the matter seems disingenuous and self-interested. Against all evidence, he maintained that the Khedive Ismail was determined to eradicate the slave trade in the Sudan, and that he, Samuel Baker, was his chosen instrument. In truth, Baker was employed primarily to provide cover for a new advance of Turco-Egyptian imperialism in North-East Africa. A British invasion of Abyssinia in 1867 had broken the power of Emperor Theodore and upset the balance of power in the region. The Khedive Ismail, the grandson of Muhammad Ali, had inherited the latter's ambition to build Egypt into a great power and make it semi-independent of Constantinople. Territorial gains in Sudan would increase his resource base. So multiple expeditions were mounted between 1868 and 1873 – east to the Red Sea littoral, south-west to the Abyssinian borderlands, south to Equatoria and Bahr al-Ghazal, and west to Darfur. This military surge was liable to alarm the imperial powers, in particular the British, and its presentation as a 'civilising mission' might prove useful. As Nubar Pasha, the Khedive's chief minister, observed, compliance with expansion into new territories would be more likely if Ismail 'appeared preoccupied in the eyes of Europe with their well-being and with the slave trade'. How better to package a land-grab than to appoint a celebrated Victorian explorer as one of the military commanders? Thus, a Turco-Egyptian exercise in window-dressing began a process which – despite the Gladstone government's refusal to accept any responsibility for Baker in 1869 – would culminate in a full-scale British invasion of the Sudan within 15 years.[17]

Many local villagers had assembled to watch the little ceremony. None had ever seen anything like it. A remote river-station on the Upper Nile was being proclaimed the capital of the newly created province of Equatoria. Henceforward Gondokoro would be ruled by the Khedive of Egypt, 2,500 miles away in Cairo, and the settlement would shortly be renamed 'Ismailia' in his honour. The soldiers of the Governor General had been given two days' rest to wash their clothes and burnish their equipment. Then, on 26 May 1871, 1,200 strong, they marched down to the parade ground in white uniforms and keffiyehs, bayonets glittering, led by their band, to form up on three sides of a newly erected 80-foot flagstaff. Ten mountain guns were lined up on the fourth side. The proclamation of annexation was read out, the red banner of the Ottoman Empire was raised, officers and men stood to attention, swords drawn, muskets presented, and the guns fired a royal salute. The main ceremony over, the soldiers took part in a noisy mock charge – 10,000 blanks were fired – and then dispersed to prepare a celebratory dinner.[18]

By the standards of Gondokoro, it had been a most impressive spectacle – as, of course, it was intended to be. But theatre of power is not substance of power. And the simple truth was that the authority of the Governor General of Equatoria extended only about as far as his little mountain guns could fire. It was questionable, indeed, whether he even controlled Gondokoro. Though once a mission-station, the church was ruinous, and no town as such existed, merely some 'miserable grass huts'; for the place had been until now only a staging-post for the ivory and slave trade. Baker had considered it 'a perfect hell' when he visited in 1863, 'a colony of cut-throats', where some 600 traders passed their time 'drinking, quarrelling, and ill-treating the slaves'.[19] Corruption had been all-pervasive; his own men were suborned within days, and he had to face down a mutiny.[20] Eight years later, all that had changed was the further increase of the slave power. Everyone was implicated; and everyone looked upon Baker with the jaundiced eye of the racketeer. Arab merchants, African chiefs, and Turco-Egyptian soldiers were all involved in the slave trade, and if any had entered the region with good intent – an honest official, a professional soldier – they were soon drained of it, either becoming profiteer themselves, or sinking into indifference. Even the victims of the slave system were hostile to the white intruder. How could they not be, when Baker carried the flag for Turco-Egyptian domination? Not only was the colonial regime a byword for taxation, requisitioning, plunder, corruption, and violence; it was itself the paramount slave trader in the Sudan.

Baker's plan was sound enough: to establish a series of military posts in the Upper Nile region. Each garrison was to be responsible for monitoring traffic on the rivers and for policing part of the hinterland. They were to be supplied, reinforced, and backed up by a flotilla of river steamers and *nuggars* (sailing boats). The idea was to choke the slave trade's primary arteries. The problem was not the plan: it was that the means to execute it did not exist. The further south Baker pushed, the more his spearhead was diminished by the placing of garrisons behind him; and these garrisons – small, isolated, easily worked upon – soon ceased to be remote arms of the Governor General, and became instead local adjuncts of the slave power. Officials were cutting deals with slave traders at the highest levels – in Khartoum – and at the same time depriving Baker of the soldiers, steamers, and supplies he needed to prosecute his campaign in Equatoria. This covert policy – collusion on the one hand, obstruction on the other – infected the entire administration, so Baker's own officers would take bribes to allow slave shipments pass, take up trading in slaves themselves, and even employ their own soldiers on slave raids.

Despite the omens, Baker – whether brave or just bludgeon-headed – pressed on, deeper into the interior, eventually reaching Masindi, about 35 miles east of Lake Albert. A settlement of about a thousand beehive huts surrounded by long grass, Masindi was the capital of the Bunyoro, a cattle people ruled by King Kabba Rega. Here, in the midst of the northern Great Lakes, Baker wanted to create a new centre of commerce, one whose flourishing, underpinned by colonial power, would, he convinced himself, squeeze out the slave traders. 'I was anxious to establish a new and legitimate system of trade in this country which would be the first step towards a higher civilisation.'[21] Intent on annexation, he built himself a grandly styled 'government house' – complete with wall coverings, floor mats, gilt-framed oval mirrors, sofa beds, gun rack, and various pictures, including a near life-size coloured print of the Princess of Wales placed on the far wall, and a photograph of Queen Victoria on the toilet table. 'It would have been vulgar if in England,' Baker explained, 'but . . . it shortly became the wonder of Central Africa.'[22] A flagstaff was affixed to one end of the building, and a formal ceremony of annexation duly announced for 14 May 1872. On the appointed day, Baker's little army – he now had barely a hundred regulars – formed hollow square and the Ottoman flag was raised as volleys were fired. Kabba Rega and the people of Masindi looked on. The King of the Bunyoro – the master of some tens of thousands of African warriors – was duly informed that his country was now under the 'protection' of Egypt, and that he himself was now 'representative of the government'.

The farce could not long continue. Kabba Rega, as ruler of a militarist state, was interested in Baker's store of prestige goods – potentially valuable tokens in tribal power-play – and his relatively disciplined and well-equipped musketeers – a potentially decisive force on any Central African battlefield. Baker and Kabba Rega – slowly getting each other's measure – were on a collision course. On 31 May, Baker's men, engaged in a regular military drill, found themselves suddenly under threat. 'In less than ten minutes,' he recalled:

> horns were blowing and drums were beating in all directions, and with extraordinary rapidity, some five or six thousand men came pouring down from every quarter, fully armed with spears and shields, in a state of frantic excitement, and at once surrounded the troops. Fresh bands of natives, all of whom were in their costume of war, continued to concentrate from every side. The crowd of warriors leapt and gesticulated around my little company of men as though about to attack.[23]

The danger was acute. Most of Baker's men were armed with old muzzle-loaders. Had they been rushed, they could easily have been overwhelmed while reloading. But the Africans, it seemed, were still too much in awe of Turco-Egyptian firepower to attempt it. With the immediate danger passed, Baker set about constructing a fort. A circular construction of earth and timber, it comprised ditch and bank enclosing a small court and three fire-proof rooms for accommodation, stores, and munitions; just four days was sufficient to provide 'an impregnable protection'.[24] Impregnable, perhaps, but of little use when Baker was isolated and surrounded, with supplies running down, in the middle of a hostile country mobilised against him. The storm broke on the morning of 8 June. Thousands of Bunyoro warriors massed against the Turco-Egypian station, answering the summons of horns and drums, some firing muskets from the long grass, the majority, armed with spears and shields, preparing to overwhelm the little contingent of regulars in a great charge.

Baker was at his best in a military crisis. He ordered his Forty Thieves to counter-attack. One platoon of 16 men under Colonel Abd el-Kader and Lieutenant Baker was dispatched to flush out the snipers in the long grass on the right flank and then push on into the town. A second group of 15 men under Lieutenant Ferritch Agha was sent forward on the left. While

some soldiers delivered covering fire with their breech-loading Snider rifles –
capable of ten rounds a minute – others advanced with 'blue lights' to ignite
the grass huts and start a conflagration.[25] The Bunyoro fell back through the
town, amid a rattle of Sniders and a roar of flames that reached 70 or 80 feet
into the air. Wherever they tried to make a stand, the rapid fire of the thin
Turco-Egyptian skirmish line broke them up. Soon they were beyond the
town, seeking refuge in the long grass, and here the one-sided battle
continued a while longer; 'but a steady fire of Snider rifles soon purged the
covert upon which the enemy had relied'. After an hour and a quarter, the
Battle of Masindi was over. The Bunyoro had fled and their capital was a
smoking ruin. Four Turco-Egyptian soldiers had been killed; no count was
made of the African dead.[26]

But this tactical triumph was both strategic disaster and political trav-
esty. Baker's micro army of 120 men was now embroiled in a full-scale war
in the heart of Africa almost 3,000 miles from Cairo and 1,500 miles from
Khartoum. And this eruption of violence, so far from being a war against
slavery, was the very opposite. Samuel White Baker, the Victorian hunter
turned Ottoman general, instead of waging an abolitionist war on behalf of
civilisation, was actually waging a colonial war against native tribesmen to
expand a slave empire. Masindi represented the decisive defeat of that
project. Baker's position was now untenable: the entire countryside was in
arms against him. But the nearest friendly garrison was 80 miles away to the
north-east, at Foweira (80 men), and the next beyond that another 80 miles
further north, at Fatiko (100 men); and much of the terrain through which
Baker's force would have to march to reach these posts comprised dense
grass taller than a man, where musketeers could see only a few yards, and
spearmen could lie in wait at lethal range, for a Bunyoro tribesman could
cast 50 yards with sure aim. Moreover, as the column of retreat set out, at
9.30 a.m. on 14 June, having fired the small Turco-Egyptian settlement with
its 'government house', it started to rain, threatening to render muzzle-
loading muskets useless. Two contingents of 15 Snider men each formed the
advance and rear guards; 10 marched with the ammunition; the remaining
few were distributed along the length of the column to protect porters and
cattle. The Bakers – Samuel, Florence, and Julian – marched together,
heavily armed, two trusted servants armed with breech-loading elephant
rifles alongside them. Communication was by bugle.

They had gone barely a mile when the sound of drums and horns was
heard. The first ambush was sprung in the early afternoon, and one man

was mortally wounded by a spear cast. The following night was spent behind the protection of a log-wall. Baker, reflecting on the day's march, decided to abandon the cattle. The following day, as the column approached a stream and swamp via a narrow path through 9-foot grass, a full-scale attack was launched:

> The advance-guard was not more than a hundred yards from the bottom, and the line was descending the hill in close order, when a sudden uproar broke out, as though all the demons of hell were let loose. Yells, screams, drums, horns, whistles from many thousands of concealed enemies for an instant startled the troops. A tremendous rush in the grass gave notice of a general attack from an immensely powerful ambuscade.[27]

A ferocious exchange of breechloaders and spears at point-blank range continued for some time before the Africans were driven off. Baker then ordered most of the heavy baggage burnt, prior to resuming the march. The running fight was soon resumed. So it continued, day after day. Though the soldiers made themselves secure overnight in improvised forts of logs and thorn bush, each day, whenever they passed through sufficiently dense terrain, the Africans would spring an ambush. Fresh tribesmen would join the action as Baker's column passed successive Bunyoro villages along the line of march; whereas the soldiers grew more weary, and fewer in number, losing one or two killed or wounded in every attack; and, most serious, they began to exhaust their precious supply of ammunition.

Some of the advance-guard fired 80 rounds on the morning of 16 June alone; many fired 50. Even the musketeers, with their slow muzzle-loaders, were wasting ammunition. 'The men had come to the conclusion that the only plan of marching in safety through the high grass, which was full of unseen enemies, was to constitute themselves into a sort of infernal machine that would be perpetually emitting fire and bullets on all sides.' This was unsustainable. Baker inventoried the remaining ammunition at the end of the third day's march and established that he was down to about 100 rounds per man. Strict fire-discipline was essential. Each soldier was limited to 40 rounds, and firm instructions were given 'that in future not a shot should be fired without orders, unless spears actually were thrown, on which occasions the troops would fire a few shots exactly into the spot from which the weapons had arrived; but on no account was a bullet to be fired at random'.[28]

After a pause of several days, tending the wounded and resting his men in a defended camp at Kisuna, about 20 miles short of Foweira, Baker set off again on 23 June. On the following day, the eleventh since leaving Masindi, a final march of 7 miles – the first to be wholly free of attack – brought Baker's column to its destination. Though he found the Turco-Egyptian post abandoned and reduced to 'blackened ashes', he was relatively safe, having reached the territory of Chief Rionga, a Bunyoro rebel eager to forge an alliance with the Governor General against his arch-rival Kabba Rega.

But Baker could not dally. There was fire in his rear. During his absence in the far south, with rumour rife that his force had been destroyed, Abu Saoud, the greatest slave lord in Equatoria, had reasserted his power. He and Kabba Rega were now planning the liquidation of the Turco-Egyptian presence in the province. Baker moved fast. He built a new log stockade at Foweira and posted there 65 men under Colonel Abd el-Kader, charged with supporting Rionga and raising fresh native forces, with which to renew the war in the south. He, with 40 Snider-armed 'Thieves' and 50 native porters, set out north for Fatiko on 27 July, marching to the relief of Major Abdullah, whose small detachment of 100 was now in danger of being over-whelmed by the gathering forces of the slave power.[29]

News of Baker's imminent return had reached Fatiko before his arrival on 2 August. Not only were Major Abdullah's 100 men paraded, in scarlet and white uniforms, to meet his 40, but a third force was approaching the post, 270 strong, its intentions unclear. Seven large crimson banners, the staffs ornamented with lance heads and black ostrich feathers, flew above them. Two officers, one clad in bright yellow garments, the other wearing a snow-white robe and black trousers, dressed their ranks. They came on in a skirmish line, advancing with confidence over the open ground, musket-armed: a very different enemy from the spear-throwers of the Bunyoro bush. Baker, eager to avoid a clash, ordered his men back into camp and sought to open negotiations. Suddenly a volley of musketry crashed out. Abu Saoud's men, about 90 yards distant, were kneeling and firing, then darting behind cover to reload.

Pushing through the entrance to the palisaded enclosure around the government post at the head of the Forty Thieves, Baker formed his men into line and led a charge with fixed bayonets.

Although the slave-hunters had primed themselves well with *araki* [Sudanese liquor] and *merissa* [Sudanese beer] before they had screwed up courage to attack the troops, they were not quite up to standing before a bayonet charge. The Forty Thieves were awkward customers, and in a quarter of a minute they were amongst them. The enemy were regularly crumpled up, and had they not taken to flight, they would have been bayoneted to a man.

Baker ordered a general advance, though few of Abdullah's men heeded the order; it was left to the Forty Thieves to harry the retreating slave traders, firing as they went, for upwards of 4 miles, killing, in Baker's estimation, more than half of them.[30]

The shock and awe of a bayonet charge by a compact disciplined body, coupled with the grim execution of the breechloader, had been sufficient to destroy a skirmish line of musket-armed snipers. But the Battle of Fatiko, like the Battle of Masindi, was a momentary tactical triumph amid strategic stalemate. It was like shooting into a lake: however spectacular, it had no lasting effects. For sure, the immediate threat of an armed insurgency of slave traders had been extinguished. Abu Saoud had fled and would soon be arrested and detained at Khartoum. Some of his former agents jumped ship and offered their services to the government. Baker's three outposts – at Gondokoro, Fatiko, and Foweira – were consolidated. But his governorship was at an end – he departed his province in May 1873, reaching Khartoum in June, Cairo in August, England in October – and this was to remove the sheet anchor of abolitionism from Equatoria. Even Baker, eulogising his governor-generalship in his memoir *Ismailia* (1879), was uneasy. The slave trade on the White Nile could be eradicated, he opined, 'so long as the government is determined'. But it would continue 'so long as the so-called traders of Khartoum should be permitted to establish themselves as independent piratical societies in the Nile Basin'. Even if the river route were closed, he prophesied, 'the road through Darfur and Kordofan would be adopted in place of the tabooed White Nile'.[31]

※

A few months after Baker's return to England, on the morning of 28 January 1874, the London papers carried the news that David Livingstone was dead.

His lonely fate signalled the failure of an idea and the end of an era. The mid-Victorians, believing fervently in the redemptive power of Commerce, Christianity, and Civilisation, had imagined that men armed with nothing more than moral purpose and a holy book could somehow 'save' Africa. Their political leaders – awed by the power of the new industrialism, steeped in the fantasies of *laissez-faire*, wedded to the doctrine of small government – were only too willing to endorse such low-cost virtue.

But it had been the guns of Commodore Heath's squadron – not David Livingstone's preaching – that had closed the Zanzibari slave market. And while the Royal Navy had the capacity to terminate the Indian Ocean traffic in human cargo, it could do nothing about the overland routes of the African interior. Here, the power of slave lords like Tippu Tip and Abu Saoud was advancing. They were a new class of men, the rulers of informal mini-empires based on slave raiding, ivory hunting, and cattle rustling, each with his army of several hundred gunmen and some thousands of tribal auxiliaries. The social order of the African interior was being hollowed out by violence and displacement. The new *mores* infected all who came in contact with them, especially the officers and men of the Turco-Egyptian Army, for whom slavery was a social norm and who had the guns to secure their share of the spoils. In any case, as everyone with eyes open could see, the Khedive's policy was not abolition but nationalisation; in so far as the Turco-Egyptian authorities sought to curb the activities of the private traders, it was to establish a state monopoly. Baker Pasha's defeat on the Upper Nile between 1871 and 1873 – despite having his own miniature army of 1,600 Turco-Egyptian soldiers equipped with modern rifles – was testimony to the corruption of the regime, the power of the slave lords, and the rule of gun and spear.

Baker, so different from Livingstone, heralded the late-Victorian era. A rich English gentleman, a big-game hunter, an adventurer and man of action, he was also an imperial proconsul backed by gunboats and artillery. Moral power was being displaced by violence. 'War is inseparable from annexation,' he wrote in *Ismailia*, 'and the law of force, resorted to in self-defence, was absolutely indispensable to prove the superiority of the power that was eventually to govern. The end justified the means.'[32] That he could not prevail alerted the world to the need for greater force. And this – for reasons far removed from events in Equatorial Africa – was something the world was increasingly willing to contemplate.

As it happened, on the very day that news of Livingstone's death was published in London, a man who, in some respects at least, seemed the embodiment of this new age was setting out to replace Samuel Baker as Governor General of Equatoria. Whereas Baker had been an adventurer and an amateur, the new man was a professional soldier, whose appointment implied a more serious application of force to the intractable social complexities of Central Africa. Yet, strangely, in his inner life, he had far more in common with David Livingstone than with Samuel Baker. An obsessively religious man animated by a deep sense of moral purpose, he was, in this respect, a creature of the more idealistic age now passing; yet, during his decade-long relationship with the Sudan, he would display all the qualities of an excellent professional officer, and would achieve his apotheosis as a late-Victorian hero through his doomed defence of Khartoum against an Islamist uprising. His name was Charles George Gordon.

# CHAPTER FIVE

# GORDON PASHA

It was an accidental meeting that lifted Charles Gordon, a middle-aged British Army officer, from the obscurity of a career that had been almost a decade in the doldrums. Successive applications to join one or another of the empire's frequent 'small wars' had been turned down. After six years at Gravesend supervising the construction of forts to guard the Thames Estuary that he considered entirely useless, he had accepted a posting to Galatz on the Danube as part of an international boundary commission. But this had meant leaving behind valued friends and a routine of charitable and evangelical work in Gravesend for a remote Balkan town and a job that made few demands on his time. He was soon bored, homesick, and melancholy.

Returning from a visit to the Crimean battlefields – he was a veteran of the war – he had a chance meeting with Nubar Pasha at the British embassy in Constantinople towards the end of September 1872. The two men had a long conversation. The British officer was a slight, wiry man of medium height, with brown hair, full moustache, and piercing blue-grey eyes. His manner was dignified, simple, even humble. He listened intently now as Nubar Pasha spoke. A tall, heavy, fleshy-featured Armenian Christian who wore the red fez of Ottoman officialdom, Nubar was a leading minister in the administration of the Khedive Ismail of Egypt. The appointment of the English adventurer Samuel Baker as Governor General of Equatoria had proved astute: convenient cover for a war of colonial expansion. But Baker's term of service would shortly expire, his mission unfinished, and a replacement was needed. Who better than Charles Gordon? For here was a most excellent British officer with a unique reputation as a highly successful leader of foreign soldiers; so much so that he had been lauded as 'Chinese Gordon' by the London press when he returned laurel-crowned from the Far East in 1865.[1]

Gordon was interested. A man of restless energy and moral passion, here was an escape from the *ennui* of Galatz. The Sudan offered a wide field of action and a cause – the abolition of slavery – that Victorian Britain had come to regard as the supreme task of Christian civilisation on earth. But he had to wait a year. Then, in October 1873, following Baker's departure from Egypt, he received a telegram from Cairo offering him the post. He accepted, subject to War Office permission, and there was a further delay of a month before this came through. While waiting, he confided to his sister his sense of mission: 'God has allowed slavery to go on for many years; born in the people, it needs more than an expedition to eradicate it; open out the country, and it will fall of itself.' It was Livingstone's vision again: Commerce, Christianity, and Civilisation. A week later, he explained his plan: 'I believe if the Sudan was settled, the Khedive would prevent the slave trade; but he does not see his way to do so till he can move about the country. My ideas are to open it out by getting the steamers on to the lakes, by which time I should know the promoters of the slave trade and could ask the Khedive to seize them.' Baker's strategy: a line of government posts to impose a *Pax Ottomana* and open trade routes into the African interior. An alliance of Turco-Egyptian authority and Victorian capitalism was to suffocate the slave trade.[2]

Though his mother was the daughter of a ship-owner, Charles Gordon was descended on his father's side from a line of Highland army officers. He followed in the family tradition, attending the Royal Military Academy at Woolwich, passing out as a second lieutenant of the Royal Engineers in 1852 at the age of 19. He was boisterous, mischievous, rebellious, and hot-tempered, but his early career continued conventionally enough: in-service training at Chatham was followed by a short period working on fortifications at Pembroke, and then he shipped out to the Crimea, arriving at Sebastopol on New Year's Day 1855. The Crimean War – the only major war Britain fought against a rival great power between 1815 and 1914 – was the principal combat training-ground for a whole generation of later Victorian officers. Even so, Gordon stood out, displaying qualities of personal leadership and a willingness to share the hardships and dangers of the rank and file that was rare in the class-ridden Victorian army. The indolence and incompetence of fellow officers earned his derision.

After the fall of Sebastopol, Gordon returned to routine military duties, serving 18 months with the boundary commissioners charged with delimiting the borders of the Ottoman Empire, then a further 18 months at Chatham. It was not enough. He had acquired a yearning for the wilderness and a life of adventure. 'I do not feel at all inclined to settle in England and be employed in any sedentary way', he wrote. Nor did career success, and the recognition and honours it might bring, interest him. Though promoted captain and marked for rapid advancement, he had no wish to become what one superior described as 'an ornament to the service'. Instead, he volunteered to fight in China.[3]

Gordon spent four years there. Initially he was engaged in fairly routine garrison and survey work, but in March 1863 he accepted appointment to the command of a small force of Europeans and Chinese based at Shanghai – a force named by its previous commander, without the least justification, 'the Ever-Victorious Army'. It was an extraordinary position. Barely 30, a British officer and gentleman, a Royal Engineer whose career so far had been largely a matter of compasses, pedometers, and technical drawings, Gordon now found himself in independent command of an army of about 3,500 men, a mix of European adventurers and Chinese workers and peasants. 'You never did see such a rabble', Gordon wrote to a military friend. His achievement over the next 18 months was astonishing by any measure. Instilling discipline and pride, always leading from the front, advancing under heavy fire carrying nothing but a cane (which became his 'wand of victory'), Gordon led the Ever-Victorious Army to a succession of spectacular victories against the odds over the Taiping rebels. Bold in conception, rapid in action, tireless in execution, his campaigns were models of strategy and tactics. In his 18 months at the head of the Ever-Victorious Army, he played a central role in the suppression of the Taiping Rebellion.[4]

But there was a dark side, and Gordon emerged tainted. The Ever-Victorious Army had been funded by Chinese merchants, equipped with European weapons, and used to crush a popular uprising of peasants, labourers, and dissident intellectuals led by a Christian mystic. The imperial powers had become involved following their invasion of China in 1858 – an invasion which culminated in the occupation of Beijing by 18,000 foreign troops and the looting and burning of the imperial summer palaces. The main purpose of the incursion was to defend the drugs trade. Chinese consumption of opium increased a hundred-fold during the nineteenth century, and a quarter of adult males became addicts. The trade was controlled by European profiteers based in coastal enclaves or mini-colonies known as 'concessions'. The Taiping Rebellion was a revolt against corrupt imperial officials, a parasitic landlord class, and foreign drug barons. Its suppression involved the unleashing of brutal counter-revolutionary violence. Massacres of captured rebels, sometimes of entire communities, were widespread. It is estimated that as many as 20 million Chinese may have died as a direct or indirect consequence of a civil war that lasted from 1850 to 1864. The horror eventually caught up with Gordon following his capture of Soochow. Imperialist troops looted the city, and rebel captives were beheaded. Gordon's promises of good treatment had been betrayed, and he was hysterical with rage and remorse.[5]

When the war ended a year later, Gordon refused all honours and payments, and deprecated his lionisation by the British media when he arrived home early in 1865. The applause, anyway, was far from universal. He had been accused of participation in the Soochow massacre, or at least of failing to take effective action to prevent it, and these charges would pursue him to the end.[6] Perhaps the hint of scandal was one reason for his being denied further combat assignments; though it seems likely, too, that Gordon was considered too odd, too eccentric, too much his own man, to find favour in the socially closed world of the Victorian army, with its regimental system, its officer caste, its clubbish exclusivity. Whatever the reason, he found himself marooned in the Thames Estuary.

During his time in command at Gravesend, Gordon underwent a 'born-again' religious experience. Though always conventionally Christian, his faith had not thus far been central to his life. Now he was struck with great force by a passage in the Bible he happened upon by accident: 'Whosoever shall confess that Jesus is the Son of God, God dwelleth in him, and he in God.' This triggered a conversion experience. 'Suddenly,' wrote a close friend, one who shared his religious sensitivity, 'it flashed upon him that he had found a jewel of priceless value. He had found what alone could satisfy him: nearness to God; oneness with God. Henceforth that was the key to his whole life.' For Gordon, his sense of the 'indwelling' of God became paramount. He felt that God was inside him, acting as mentor and master, elevating him above the depravities of earthly existence. He acquired an almost messianic sense of himself as an instrument of God's will; as he later put it, 'I am a chisel which cuts the wood; the Carpenter directs it.'

He had a brooding awareness of two elements in human experience, the body and the spirit, the former evil and doomed, the latter divine; and henceforward he understood 'spirit' to be nothing less than the immanence of God. It was the doctrine of a mystic, and it transformed him into an evangelical who henceforward spent much of his time distributing tracts and seeking converts. He became especially obsessive about the moral redemption of teenage boys – whom he called 'scuttlers' – inviting them to his home, making provision for their education, seeking suitable positions for them, taking an interest in their later careers. The inner soul remained troubled, however, as his letters to family and friends often, to the modern eye at any rate, reveal. Can there be any doubt that he was tormented by forbidden desire? Is this not the meaning when a man avers that 'all are lepers in the flesh'; when he confides, 'I wished I was a eunuch at 14'; when he states, 'I died long ago'? Charles Gordon was compelled to renounce his sexuality or face social extinction, finding solace in religion, becoming a melancholy soldier-saint, sublimating his libido in missionary work among working-class youths whose bodies he dared not touch.[7]

Gordon shared many traits with Samuel Baker – iron constitution, grim determination, unflinching courage. But in one critical respect he was different. For Baker, the 'civilising mission' of Victorian colonial pioneers was mainly a matter of form; it was the adventure that drew him. For Gordon, a deeply religious and conscientious man, the 'civilising mission' was a moral imperative. The corollary was a radically different approach to the relationship between authority and native people. Where Baker was bull-headed, tackling obstacles by threat and force, Gordon was a diplomat with a keen sense of human suffering; however we judge the *effects* of his actions, his *intentions* were noble. Baker embodied one dimension of 'the perfect Victorian hero' – he was a fearless man of action – but not at all the other dimension – he lacked the ethical integrity, the sense of mission, that animated men like Livingstone and now Gordon. Victorian Britain was in the forefront of bourgeois civilisation in its heyday, and its ideal of manhood expressed a surging confidence in this civilisation's capacity to 'lift up' humanity and 'improve' the world. The reality was otherwise: European imperialism was an exercise in violence, exploitation, and oppression. But this only made the need for 'heroes' like Livingstone and Gordon more urgent – 'heroes' who were the personification of bourgeois individualism, but imbued with moral purpose.

That he was the authentic article was clear from the beginning of his Egyptian service. He declined his full salary, accepting only a fifth of the proffered amount, on the grounds that the money was extracted from the impoverished Egyptian *fellaheen* (the peasantry). When he arrived at Gondokoro, the administrative capital of his embryonic province, he immediately ended the pernicious practice whereby the Turco-Egyptian authorities paid their soldiers in consignments of spirits and slave women. He made great efforts to ensure sufficient supply from Khartoum, so as to obviate the need to requisition *durra* (sorghum) and cattle from local villages. He moved about with a small escort, avoiding excessive displays of force, endeavouring to negotiate his way to peaceful relations between the new administration and the native tribes. He made an example of soldiers who plundered the African population. He exercised justice with the intention of spreading goodwill. It was the paternalism of the liberal imperialist; but it was tangible enough, and it carried Gordon far.[8]

His plan was to use the Nile as the central spine of the new Turco-Egyptian occupation. Whereas Baker had attempted to establish inland routes and stations, Gordon was convinced that riverine communication was essential to effective government control. His stations, moreover, were to be closely spaced, ideally only a day's march apart, and thus mutually supporting. A dozen were constructed, each with its stockade and small garrison. The plan was to extend this system of stations all the way to the Great Lakes, with steamers providing the primary transport system, moving information, supplies, equipment, munitions, and manpower between the stations. In particular, Gordon wanted to establish stations and steamers on lakes Albert and Victoria. The slave traders would continue to find a way through – if not down the Nile, then on overland routes to the west, via Bahr al-Ghazal to Kordofan and Darfur – unless their supply was choked off at source, in the region of the Great Lakes. Gordon had proclaimed a government monopoly over the ivory trade, and his hope was to promote other forms of legitimate commerce; but the success of his mission depended on government control of the routes north from the Lakes.[9]

The project crashed against two barriers, both beyond Gordon's power to alter, one natural, the other human. On 17 October 1875, on a personal reconnaissance in the vicinity of Dufilé, about 100 miles north of Lake Albert, he reached the Fola Falls. 'I fancied I heard a voice like thunder, which increased as we approached the river,' he recorded.

At last we stood above it on a rocky bank covered with vegetation, which descended abruptly to the stream, and there it was appalling to look at, far less to think of getting anything up or down, except in splinters. It was more a rush down a slope of one-in-six than a fall. Above it the water was smooth, and 80 to 150 yards side; and here it was suddenly contracted to two passages of 15 and 20 yards wide; for a rocky isle stood in the centre. It boiled down, twisting into all sorts of eddies, while the banks, steep and precipitous, prevented a great length of view. These shoots last for two miles.[10]

This was the seventh of the Nile's cataracts, the most distant from the sea, the last to be discovered, and a place impassable to any river vessel. Another plan would be needed. The *Khedive*, his 108-ton steamer, could never be transported overland to Lake Albert. The best he might manage would be to dismantle the 38-ton *Nyanza* and employ porters to convey it to the lake in hand-carts; he would need a contingent of 1,000 men for this, and it would take time to assemble them.[11]

The second, human barrier to the success of Gordon's mission proved more intractable. At first, things seemed to go well: Gordon's advance parties reported that the King of Buganda had made his submission and the King of Bunyoro had fled; new government stations were established at Magungo, Mrooli, and Niamyongo; an effusive dispatch announcing the annexation was duly sent to Cairo. Too soon: Gordon's officers, eager to please, had exaggerated. So far from submitting, the King of Buganda had, in fact, put 160 Turco-Egyptian soldiers under siege. 'Mutesa has annexed my soldiers,' lamented Gordon, 'he has not been annexed himself.' Emin Pasha, a German doctor who had converted to Islam and was now on Gordon's staff, was sent to negotiate their release. As for the King of Bunyoro, his 'flight' – with the sacred stool that symbolised his power – turned out to be a tactical withdrawal into the bush. Gordon was on his way to Masindi when he learned the truth, coming under attack from Bunyoro spearmen concealed in long grass on the very track down which Baker had been forced to retreat three years before.[12]

Gordon's attempted conquest of the northern Great Lakes region thus unravelled as surely as Baker's had done. The military power necessary to overawe and subjugate Central African states like Bunyoro and Buganda could not be projected so far south. Contingents of 100 or so men armed with rifle-muskets could not prevail against thousands of tribal spearmen waging guerrilla war in dense bush. The small numbers that could be brought to bear at the end of such long and tenuous supply lines were just not enough.

This was not the only problem. Gordon's administration was riven with cross-currents that rendered the accomplishment of his mission – stable colonial rule, agricultural development, new trade routes, abolition of the slave trade – well nigh impossible. Perhaps Gordon's complex personality was not the least of the difficulties. It had something of the manic-depressive, combining a yearning for adventure and action, a craving 'to board the tram of the world', with an aversion to wealth, honours, and fame that could give rise to profound feelings of guilt about his high-profile career. The greater the achievement, the more insistent the doubts; he had a sometimes para-lysing anxiety about self-glorification. As he told one of his intimates, 'some of my letters are written by one nature, others by the other nature'. His belief in predestination – the notion that all human affairs are preordained by God – and his sense that he was a providential instrument of an 'indwelling' God for the purpose of eradicating slavery enabled him to mediate the contradiction. But the inner anguish endured, and the persona Gordon presented to the world was marked by frenetic activity, obsessive micro-man-agement, and not infrequent impatience, intolerance, and bad temper in his relations with subordinates.[13]

Few could match his exacting standards. His judgement, in any case, was often poor – a reflection, perhaps, of his own introspection – and he was betrayed by some of his appointees, notably the Arab slave trader Abu Saoud, whom he had released from prison in Khartoum, and the American officer Charles Chaillié-Long, who had been appointed Gordon's chief of staff. The former, restored to his slave-hunting domain, repaid his saviour with open defiance and had to be returned to prison. The latter fell out with Gordon, became a bitter enemy, and went on to launch a widely publicised slander that Gordon was a drunkard given to bouts of sodden seclusion. (Gordon was, in fact, only a moderate drinker; his real vice was chain smoking.) Other subordinates – those who survived: many succumbed to malaria and other tropical diseases – found Gordon's lack of trust and endless interference tiresome. And when they failed, or were considered to have failed, this merely confirmed Gordon in his fussiness. 'I act for myself and judge for myself', he had written to his mother from China; 'this I have found to be the best way of getting on.' So it had been ever since, and while this might have been fine had the task been such as a single man might

manage on his own, it was hopeless where the aim was the colonisation of
Equatoria's 100,000 square miles of swamp, forest, and grassland. This
required a team, a 'band of brothers', and Gordon was too much a loner, an
oddball, a fusspot, to build one.[14]

Of far greater significance, however, was the sheer intractability of
Equatoria's slave-based social order. What he saw as the lethargy, dishon-
esty, and corruption of his Egyptian and Sudanese soldiers could evoke in
the frustrated Governor General racist tirades. They were 'cowardly, lying,
effeminate brutes' and 'totally devoid of patriotism'. They lacked any 'regen-
erating quality, either a commercial, military, religious, or patriotic spirit'.
And the most bitter outburst: 'I hate them! There! A twopenny-halfpenny
nation, for whom it is not worthwhile to stay a day in these countries.' A gulf
of orientalist misunderstanding separated Gordon from the officers and
men of the Turco-Egyptian Army under his command; a gulf deepened by
his own ingenuousness with regard to the khedivial regime, for which the
appointment of British governors charged with the eradication of slavery
was mere spin. Charles Wilson, a senior British officer then at the War
Office, took a more realistic view:

> The slave trade cry is one got up by Baker to make matters go smooth.
> No man can in a moment change an institution in an oriental country
> which has existed for thousands of years, and any reform of that kind
> must begin at home. As long as there is a demand for slaves in Lower
> Egypt and Palestine, so long will there be a slave trade ... When the
> Khedive frees his own slaves, I shall believe something is being done ...[15]

Here was the root of the problem. Demand for slaves was rising in the
Middle East. Supplies of slaves were plentiful in Central Africa. The Indian
Ocean routes had succumbed to the guns of the Royal Navy. The Nile route
was increasingly clogged with government stations, river steamers, and rapa-
cious officials demanding payoffs. But there was another way: the overland
route through Bahr al-Ghazal, Darfur, and the 'Forty Day Road' to Upper
Egypt. And here, in the far west, even as Gordon planted his stations and
launched his steamers on the equatorial Nile, a new slave power was rising:
that of Al-Zubeir Rahma Mansour Pasha. On 25 October 1874, the army of
Zubeir, equipped with modern rifles, shattered the medieval army of the Sultan
of Darfur in a battle fought not far from the capital at Al-Fasher. The Sultan
was left dead on the field, and Zubeir the slave lord became master of Darfur.[16]

How was this all-pervading power to be resisted when Khartoum was 'headquarters of the system' (Gordon's words). Again and again, Gordon had been thwarted in Equatoria by the Governor General of Sudan, Ismail Ayoub Pasha, protector and patron of the slave dealers of Khartoum, whose tentacles reached across the whole of Turco-Egyptian Africa. Frustrated, Gordon returned to Cairo at the beginning of December 1876, resigned from the Khedive's service, and was home before the end of the month.

No sooner had he decided than he wavered. He had yearned for the comforts of home in Africa; but homesickness soon gave way to *ennui* once there. He had come to believe that the corrupt colonial regime in Khartoum was beyond redemption; yet he still felt the pull of 'the tram of the world' and wondered whether he might yet prevail. In a private audience at the Abdin Palace prior to his departure for England, the Khedive – a master of manipulation and dissimulation – had extracted a promise to return. This was followed by a letter reminding Gordon of the promise, expressing the Khedive's refusal to believe that 'when Gordon has once given his word as a gentleman, anything will induce him to go back on it'. By the end of January, Gordon had decided to return – but armed with a firm resolve that he would demand, as a condition of continued service, control of the whole of Sudan. Only thus empowered, he reasoned, could he root out the scourge of slavery.

His demand was duly granted. So Charles George Gordon was appointed Governor General of the Sudan, the colonial overlord of a million square miles of North-East Africa. 'I am astounded at the power he [the Khedive] has placed in my hands,' he wrote. 'With the Governor-Generalship of the Sudan, it will be my fault if slavery does not cease, and if those vast countries are not open to the world. So there is an end of slavery, if God wills it; for the whole secret of the matter is in the government of the Sudan, and, if the man who holds that government is against it, it must cease.'[17]

Thus was the stage set for the first great military confrontation between armed abolitionism and the Arab slave trade.

 

The Sudan was a pitiless country. It ranged from burning desert through sub-tropical grassland to disease-infested swamp. G.W. Steevens, the embedded *Daily Mail* reporter who accompanied the British military expedition of 1898, hated it.

People talk of the Sudan as the East; it is not the East. The East has age and colour; the Sudan has no colour and no age – just a monotone of squalid barbarism ... Nothing grows green. Only yellow halfa-grass to make you stumble, and sapless mimosa to tear your eyes; dom-palms that mock with wooden fruit, and Sodom apples that lure with flatulent poison. For beasts it has tarantulas and scorpions and serpents, devouring white ants, and every kind of loathsome bug that flies and crawls. Its people are naked and dirty, ignorant and besotted. It is a quarter of a continent of sheer squalor. Overhead, the pitiless furnace of the sun, underfoot the never-ceasing treadmill of the sand, dust in the throat, tuneless singing in the ears, searing flame in the eye – the Sudan is a god-accursed wilderness, an empty limbo of torment for ever and ever.[18]

The Sudanese did not entirely disagree. 'When Allah made the Sudan,' they said, 'he laughed.'[19] The land was indeed unforgiving, and life was hard; but people had adapted, found ways to survive, even thrive, and, in doing so, become tough, enduring, and independent. Yet Sudan was not really a country, let alone a nation; it was a new construct of Turco-Egyptian colonialism, reaching its greatest extent only in 1875, a glueing together by administrative fiat of some 600 tribes, speaking 100 different languages, spread across thousands of miles of North-East Africa. The 'immense command' over which Charles Gordon assumed responsibility in the spring of 1877 comprised four broad regions. Along the Middle Nile, the historic core of the ancient Kingdom of Sennar, Nubian tribes of mixed Arab and African ancestry inhabited mud villages and palm groves on the banks of the river, working as subsistence farmers, growing grains, beans, and vegetables, irrigating their fields with the aid of creaking wheels. To the east, for between 200 and 400 miles, from the Nile banks to the Red Sea coast, was the desert and scrub inhabited by the Beja, an ancient tribal people, older than the pharaohs, living as farmers where they could, more often as herders, sometimes hunters. To the west, stretching much further, 600 or 700 miles, were the provinces of Kordofan and Darfur, the domain of Bedouin tribes like the Baggara and the Fur, again a 'Sudanic' mix of Arab and African, people who herded cattle, rode horses, and used camels, oxen, and asses to ferry cargo across the wilderness. All these regions – the whole of the north – were predominantly Arab in culture and Islamic in religion.[20]

The south – the provinces of Equatoria and Bahr al-Ghazal – were quite different. The former, 500 miles from north to south, 200 miles from east to west, extended either side of the White Nile between the River Sobat in the north and the vicinity of the Great Lakes in the south. The latter stretched westward from here for up to 500 miles, bounded in the north by the Bahr al-Arab, and dissected by half a dozen major tributaries. These were regions of sub-tropical grassland and forest, of vegetation-choked rivers and malarial swamps, inhabited by African tribes – Nuer, Dinka, Shilluk, Bari, and many others – people who cultivated garden plots with the hoe, measured wealth in head of cattle, and still performed ancient pagan rituals.[21] In contrast to the desiccated north, the land here was green and well-watered, the flora and fauna plentiful, and it supported a relatively numerous population settled in large villages. Because of this, the south was preyed upon by the north, the African tribesmen by the Arab slave traders of Khartoum and Kordofan and the Turco-Egyptian officers of the colonial administration. After Gordon's departure from Equatoria, his stations had fallen into ruin, his officers had resumed trading in slaves, his soldiers had sold their guns, and the riverside villages had been abandoned.[22]

But whereas Gordon in Equatoria had found himself lopping off stems only for them to re-grow, was he not now in a position to destroy the canker at root? For the Khedive had united all of Sudan's 17 governorates in 'one great governor-generalship' centred on Khartoum, charging its new viceroy with 'the suppression of slavery and the improvement of the means of communication' across the whole of this vast north-east African empire.[23] Gordon had at his disposal an army of 21,000 Turco-Egyptian regulars, equipped with modern Remington rifles, and they could be supplemented by locally raised native irregulars – Bashi-Bazouks as they were generally known in the Ottoman service, *bazingars* in local parlance. He also had a small flotilla of river gunboats and a modest array of field guns. He refused to forward revenues to Cairo, reserving local income for local expenditure, enabling him to pay his soldiers regularly and improve their discipline, as well as creating a fund to develop infrastructure and relieve distress.[24] Not the least asset was his own extraordinary personality, a dynamo of physical energy and idealist passion, symbolised by his epic camel rides, taking him to distant reaches of his vast domain, as he clocked up 7,500 miles over three years. 'The solitary grandeur of the desert makes one feel how vain is the effort of man,' he wrote. 'It is only my firm conviction that I am only an instrument put in use for a time that makes me bear up; and in my present state, during my long, long, hot, weary rides, I think my thoughts better and clearer than I should with a companion.'[25] He would appear out of the haze, fast approaching on loping camel, heading towards some sleepy garrison post, arriving long before the men could be paraded and the salute fired, the Governor General himself, coated in dust, drenched in sweat, yet resplendent on his mount in the £150 blue-serge and gold-lace uniform of an Ottoman marshal. If one man could wield moral power – if one man could change the world by mere act of will – that man was Charles Gordon.[26]

He tried. He made enemies of the powerful and the corrupt as he sought to relieve the suffering of the oppressed. The privileges of the *ulema*, the men learned in Islamic theology, were restored. A box for the posting of petitions was placed at the door of the Governor's Palace; all received attention. Public flogging was abolished; and an official who had mutilated a poor man's feet by imposing 1,200 strokes of the *kourbash*, the hippopotamus-hide whip, was sacked. Alms were distributed to the poor of Khartoum. Above all, this strange man, this liberal reformer in a military uniform, this Christian missionary in an Islamic land, was an anti-slavery crusader. 'I declare solemnly that I would give my life willingly to save the sufferings of these people,' he wrote from Dara, in distant Darfur, the heart of the slave-running country. He was instrumental in the adoption of the Slave Trade Convention by Britain and Egypt in August 1877. This branded slave hunting 'robbery and murder', and stipulated that the trade should be outlawed in Egypt within 7 years and in Sudan within 12. It was less than he had hoped for, but it was a clear step forward, and on this basis, the Governor General issued a decree to the effect that all Europeans living in the Sudan were to issue papers of enfranchisement to their slaves (to be redeemed after 12 years). Soon he was at work in the field, monitoring river traffic, seizing overland caravans, arresting slave traders, dismissing corrupt officials; some of his own appointees, like Tayib Bey, the Governor of Fashoda, and Ibrahim Fawzi Bey, the Governor of Equatoria, ended up in chains. 'I am striking deadly blows against the slave trade,' he proclaimed, 'and am establishing a sort of Government of Terror about it.' His supporters thought so too. Bishop Comboni, head of the Roman Catholic Mission at Khartoum, detecting a sharp drop in the numbers of slaves being trafficked, had no doubt that this was down to Gordon, who had 'singlehanded, by sheer force of willpower, succeeded in striking a blow at the slave trade and slavery'.[27]

But the task was impossible for one man and a mere handful of willing associates. The Turco-Egyptian Sudan was a gimcrack edifice no sooner constructed than crumbling. The dispatch of predatory expeditionary forces into the mountainous borderland between eastern Sudan and Abyssinia had triggered full-scale war. The Khedive's forces had suffered three successive defeats, the last, at Gura in March 1876, when a thousand dead were left on the field, a decisive one, marking the definitive failure of any attempt to push the boundary of the Turco-Egyptian Empire into the Abyssinian high-lands. Stabilising the frontier and negotiating peace with King Johannes was an immediate priority for the new Governor General.[28]

Problematic in a different way was the extension of governmental power towards the Great Lakes. Though Gordon sent Dr Emin Pasha to reopen contact with King Kabba Rega of Bunyoro and King Mutesa of Buganda – and even ordered four new steamers from Britain for service on Lake Victoria – he later changed his mind, realising that the resources to sustain colonial outposts a thousand miles south of Khartoum did not exist. Retrenchment also affected planned infrastructure projects, notably a railway-and-steamer transport line from Wadi Halfa southwards down the Nile.[29] These econo-mies reflected a growing crisis of state indebtedness in Cairo: the Sudan would receive no subsidies from the north during Gordon's governorship. Gordon was much agitated by the crisis; he was summoned to Cairo for consultations, but his advice was rejected, in deference to the interests of Anglo-French finance.[30]

A bankrupt state, a stalled development programme, a corrupt adminis-tration, a mosaic of ethnicities, a vast, backward, resource-poor domain: this was the context for Charles Gordon's war on slavery. Then, in late June 1878, shocking news reached Khartoum. Earlier rumours of a slave traders' revolt in distant Bahr al-Ghazal were dramatically confirmed. A govern-ment outpost at Deim Idris had been overwhelmed, the entire garrison of 200 men massacred, and all cannon, rifles, and ammunition captured. The province was now under the effective control of Suleiman Zubeir Pasha (son of Al-Zubeir Rahma Mansour Pasha), the greatest slave lord in the Sudan.[31]

Sudanese slavery was not a marginal phenomenon, something belonging to a shadowy underworld, to be dealt with by police action. Sudan was a slave society in the same sense as the state of Mississippi had been a slave society in the 1850s or the sugar islands of the British West Indies in the 1820s. Slavery was woven into the social fabric, creating a complex mesh of vested interests. And the economic centre of gravity was the province of Bahr al-Ghazal, where the Arab north interpenetrated the African south. Here was a veritable 'heart of darkness'. Romolo Gessi, the Italian officer charged by Gordon with suppression of the revolt in 1878, bore witness to the devastation: 'there is no need for a guide, as it is only necessary to follow for 12 days the track of the skeletons of the negroes scattered along the way . . . while crossing the country, not a village was to be found; nothing was to be met with but the ruins of huts, and the posts to which the natives used to attach their cattle at night, the only signs of former habitation.'[32]

Dr Georg Schweinfurth, a German botanist, explorer, and ethnographer who travelled the region between 1869 and 1871, observed the workings of the slave economy. In the region of Bahr al-Ghazal dominated by the 'Khartoumers' – the slave traders from the Arab north – he estimated the population at a quarter of a million. Around 190,000 of these were African tribespeople, and a further 40,000 were slaves belonging to Arab settlers based in *zaribas* (fortified compounds). This subject population was controlled by an army of 10,000 men, half of them free Nubians from the north, the other half *bazingars*, black slave-soldiers; though these might be supplemented by African auxiliaries recruited from the subject tribes according to need. The ruling class was formed of the great slave lords (the *khabirs*), some of them resident, most based in Khartoum or one of the slave-trading emporia of Kordofan or Darfur. The managers of the slave system on the ground were the *jallaba*, a petty bourgeoisie of local settlers, small traders, gang masters, militia officers, and agents of the *khabirs*, estimated to number 4,000 in the Bahr al-Ghazal, but perhaps 20,000 across the western Sudan as a whole. As well as policing the compounds and convoys on behalf of the big operators, many *jallaba* traded on their own account, so the slave trade comprised both large caravans of several hundred slaves and many smaller transports – perhaps a modest Nubian huckster riding an ox or an ass, with two or three soldiers and half a dozen captives in leather neck-ropes or wooden yokes, making the hazardous journey across the wilderness. Why did they do it? Because, Schweinfurth averred, it was more profitable than growing corn, raising cattle, and paying taxes.

Slave raids were highly organised military operations. Resistance by tribesmen armed with spears was crushed by massed gunfire, and the slavers pushed ever deeper into Central Africa. And while most captives were for sale in the Sudan or the wider Middle East, a good number were turned into auxiliaries of the *jallaba*, men serving as soldiers, boys as porters, women as domestic servants. Others were put to work in garden plots at trading-posts in the bush. Slave-soldiers might have slaves of their own, so there was a hierarchy in which slave exploited slave, a pecking order of petty privilege that fragmented solidarity.

The oppression of women – in the fields, in domestic labour, in sexual service – was hard-wired into the system. 'The single slave of the poorer soldiers,' reported Schweinfurth:

> is a regular drudge, or maid-of-all-work: she has to bring water from the well in great pitchers, which she carries on her head; she does all the washing, if there is anything to wash; she grinds the corn . . . makes the dough . . . roasts the [bread] . . . and finally prepares the [stew] . . . Not only has she to do the sweeping of the whole house, but she has to get wood from the wilderness, and, when on a journey, to supply the want of any other bearer by carrying all the lumber of her lord and master.

The primitive technology of grinding corn was one reason for the high demand for female slaves. Women were sometimes yoked at the *murhaga*. 'The very laborious process is performed by pounding the grain on a larger stone, called a *murhaga*, by means of a smaller stone held in the hand; it is the only method of grinding corn known to the majority of African nations, and is so slow that by the day's hardest work a woman is able to prepare only a sufficient quantity of meal for five or six men.'

This slave-based social order was not restricted to Bahr al-Ghazal: it extended northwards, especially to Darfur, Kordofan, and Khartoum, and to some degree to the rest of the Sudan as well. Perhaps as many as 100,000 slaves a year were transported from the south, and of these, perhaps half were traded in the northern provinces, where they were exchanged for calico, copper, firearms, or Maria Theresa thalers, typically fetching at least six times their original cost, the price varying according to 'quality', with teenage eunuchs and pretty young women most highly valued. 'Strong adult women, who are ugly,' reported Schweinfurth, 'are rather cheaper than the young girls, whilst old women are worth next to nothing, and can be bought for a mere bagatelle. Full-grown men are rarely purchased as slaves, being troublesome to control and difficult of transport.' The high value-added of slave merchandise made the business of trafficking exceptionally brutal: if the price in Khartoum was six times the price at source, even allowing for the cost of transportation, the *jallaba* would realise a handsome profit even if only half his slaves reached market. Thus the lines of emaciated victims, yoked at the neck, trudging across the desert, driven forward by the *kourbash*; and the skeletons, the fallen of earlier convoys, marking the trail.[33]

Many, of course, perhaps 50,000 a year, were destined for the more distant markets of Egypt, Arabia, Turkey, and Persia, where slaves were valued primarily as *objets de luxe* in the households of the rich. By the 1870s, with the Nile route subject to police interference – involving the added cost of bribes and a risk of confiscation – most slaves were passing down the western overland route through Darfur, the 'Forty Days Road'. This was controlled by the Sultan of Darfur, the ruler of a state founded in the early seventeenth century, whose capital was at Al-Fasher, and whose principal emporium was Kobbei, at the southern end of the Forty Days Road. Kobbei was a 2-mile straggle of mud houses, garden plots, and wells situated in a wadi, flanked by smaller villages on either side. It was home to several thousand people, but its chief significance derived from the perpetual motion of long-distance trade caravans. The Fur elite supplemented income from land, herds, and people by engaging in slave raids (to the south) and slave trading (to north, west, and east). Slaves were the sultanate's staple export, exchanged for the arms, horses, and consumer goods that were the basis of aristocratic power and display. Big slave raids were state-sanctioned military operations led by Fur nobles. The largest caravans might number 2,000 camels and 1,000 chattels. The slave raid was the Sudanic state in motion.[34]

A measure of mafia-type stability seems to have endured for 250 years in Darfur. But the surge in slave trading that David Livingstone had first noticed on the Zambesi in 1851, and that Richard Burton, John Speke, Samuel Baker, and Henry Stanley had borne witness to in the quarter century following, powered by rising global demand in the booming markets of nineteenth-century capitalism, had unsettled the fragile frameworks of remote desert-edge polities like the Sultanate of Darfur. Here was the new powerbase of the man now emerging as Sudan's greatest slave lord: Al-Zubeir Rahma Mansour.

Zubeir, a Nubian of the Ja'alin tribe of northern Sudan, had been 26 when he left Khartoum with a small private army to set up a trading empire based on ivory and slaves in Bahr al-Ghazal. When Schweinfurth visited him in 1871, he had already made himself master of the province, having killed or incorporated all rivals.[35] Holding court in a large *zariba* – Deim Zubeir – he received visitors in a suite of large, square huts, enclosed by tall hedges, which formed his private residence. Guests waited in special rooms provided with carpeted divans, where they were served coffee, sherbet, and tobacco pipes by richly dressed slaves. Chained lions contributed a 'regal aspect to these halls of state'. Behind a curtain, in the innermost hut, was the couch of Zubeir. 'Attendants were close at hand to attend to his wants, and a company of *fakis* [holy men] sat on the divan outside the curtain and murmured their never-ending prayers.'[36]

Though the slave lord had already acquired a veneer of courtly manners and piety, his power had not yet reached its zenith. When the Khedive attempted to assert government control over Bahr al-Ghazal by dispatching a military expedition to the province under Sheikh Hilali, the Turco-Egyptians were decisively defeated and their leader killed (May 1872). When the Rizeiqat tribe, whose territory straddled southern Kordofan and Darfur, threatened the caravan routes to the north, Zubeir defeated them in battle and occupied the trading emporium of Shakka (August 1873). Unable to curb his rising power militarily, the Khedive now attempted to co-opt the slave lord, making him Governor of Shakka and Bahr al-Ghazal (December 1873).[37] This gave Zubeir semi-official status when he embarked on a full-scale war against the Sultan of Darfur the following year.

The contest was a mismatch, a collision between an essentially medieval state and a battle-tested warlord militia equipped with modern weapons. New military units formed of *bazingars* – black slave-riflemen – had become decisive. At the Battle of Shatta (January or February 1874), Zubeir's *bazingars* fought a defensive battle and shattered the charges of their enemies. After a lull – moving armies across hundreds of miles of near-waterless waste was the main challenge – Zubeir, reinforced to 7,000 riflemen, went onto the offensive. His mission, he proclaimed, was an Islamic one. The Sultan had not only failed to protect the caravan routes; he had violated *shariya* law; whereas, he, Zubeir, in the Bahr al-Ghazal, had fought against polytheism and idol-worship and made many coverts to the community of Islam. Thus, in 1874, in distant Darfur, was the germ of an idea implanted – of a slave traders' *jihad* – an idea destined to set the whole Sudan aflame within ten years. Right now, though, it was Zubeir's legions of *bazingars* that mattered. On 16 October 1874 at Dara, and again on 25 October at Manawashi, the chivalry of Darfur was destroyed by massed rifle fire. The Sultan was killed and his sacred drum captured. Zubeir had destroyed an independent Sudanic state three centuries old and blown a gaping hole in the geopolitical map of north-eastern Africa.[38]

But the forces of the Governor General of Sudan, Ismail Ayoub Pasha, were soon on the scene; indeed, Ismail made a triumphal entry into Al-Fasher, to the salute of 100 guns, only a week after Zubeir. And for the next year, even while joint campaigning against renegade rebel forces continued, the *bazingar* warlord and the Ottoman governor struggled for control of the newly conquered province. Finally, Zubeir resolved to put his case to the Khedive in person. Leaving his southern powerbase in the hands of his son Suleiman, he set out from Kordofan on 13 December 1875, bound for Cairo via Khartoum. This was the wily old fox's greatest mistake: he would never be allowed to return.[39]

Yet his influence endured. Cairo, where Zubeir found himself under effective house arrest, became the distant head office of the family firm, its operations on the ground now in the hands of the son, with whom the father was in regular correspondence. When Gordon returned as Governor General in early 1877, the situation in Darfur had deteriorated sharply. A three-cornered struggle was under way. The 16,000 Turco-Egyptian troops in the province were holed up in Al-Fasher and other towns, demoralised and inert, under threat from rebel forces commanded by the Emir Haroun al-Rashid, the nephew of the former Sultan, whose appeal for resistance had met a willing response from a native population already smarting under the exactions and corruption of the new colonial administration. Meanwhile, Suleiman, with 3,000 men at Shakka, the slave-dealing emporium in southern Kordofan, was contemplating his options, which certainly included throwing in his lot with Haroun's rebels.

Gordon's intervention – he set out from Khartoum on 19 May at the head of 300 men – averted immediate disaster. In a whirlwind of fast camel rides, he galvanised the Turco-Egyptian garrisons into action and drove the rebels into the Jebel Marra mountains. He then entered the den of the slave traders at Shakka to confront and overawe Suleiman in person. He might easily have been killed. 'I am running a great risk in going into the slavers' nest with only four companies,' he confided, 'but I will trust God to help me, and the best policy with these people is a bold one.' In the event, boldness paid off. It is easy to understand why. Gordon's presence had activated the local garrisons; he had behind him the full power of the Turco-Egyptian state; and perhaps, given his nationality, the British state as well. Suleiman could not calculate the consequences of violence with any confidence; so he succumbed to Gordon's moral authority, agreeing to withdraw to Bahr al-Ghazal, and there to accept subordinate rank under a newly appointed provincial governor.[40]

Gordon later regretted that he had allowed Suleiman to get away. At the time, he convinced himself that the young slave lord had been won over, that he lacked courage and resolution, that 'the cub' had become 'very friendly'. Naïvety was an intrinsic feature of Gordon's essentially humane personality. He saw goodness in others where none existed. He saw sincerity where there was dissembling. Often, in his assessments of people, hope triumphed over experience.[41]

A short while after his meeting with Gordon at Shakka, Suleiman received a letter from his father. 'Free Bahr al-Ghazal from the Egyptian troops,' it ordered. 'Attack and make yourself master of Shakka.'[42] This was the trigger for the first great revolt of the Sudanese slave traders.

On 15 July 1878, Romolo Gessi departed Khartoum in the river steamer *Bordein*. He had two *nuggars* in tow, bearing his escort of 40 soldiers and supplies of ammunition, and he was waved off by friends on the quay and, as he passed Government House, by the Governor General from his balcony. Gessi was heading south, charged with suppressing the revolt in Bahr al-Ghazal, an event which threatened to unravel all Gordon's work since his first arrival in Sudan back in 1874. The Governor General's wider responsibilities precluded his taking personal command of the expedition; so he had persuaded his most trusted subordinate to undertake the mission. A small, trim, energetic man in his late 40s, with brown hair, pointed features, and bushy beard, Gessi had been born in Constantinople to an expatriate Italian mother and father, and had spent most of his early life in the Ottoman Empire. He had served as a staff officer during the Crimean War, and it was here that he had first met Gordon and the two had became friends. When Gordon became Governor of Equatoria, Gessi had joined him, undertaking a hazardous exploration of the upper reaches of the Nile. When Gordon returned as Governor General, Gessi was again at his side. But plans for new explorations were interrupted by news of the massacre of the garrison at Deim Idris and Gordon's insistence that his friend should accept command.[43]

The odds were forbidding. The intention had been that Gessi should assemble an expeditionary force from the government posts along the river, but he found garrisons run down and officers in league with the slave traders. Few wished the expedition any success. Few thought it would succeed. Gessi was so shaken by the 'labyrinth' of obstruction that he repented having accepted the mission, at one point retreating to his quarters leaving orders not to be disturbed. 'Gordon Pasha found himself in a bottomless pit in everything relating to the slave trade. All, without exception, were interested in not betraying their friends. The very officials and officers near his person took the greatest care that none of this should reach his ears. They had, in fact, persuaded themselves that, with the abolition of slavery, misery would be the fate of all.'[44]

In the event, Gessi's little army amounted to four companies of regulars (400 men), a larger contingent of under-motivated irregulars (1,000 men), along with two cannon, a *mitrailleuse* (machine gun), and a rocket launcher. As he pushed inland from the river post of Shambé, he was joined by another 1,000 well-armed men under Abu Muri – African tribesmen prepared to fight alongside the Turco-Egyptians to rid themselves of the slave traders – bringing his force up to 2,400 in total. But these were perilously few compared with Suleiman's army – estimated to comprise 10,000 modern riflemen backed by four cannon and their own rocket launchers. 'The old traders and slavers,' reported Gessi, 'with millions of *jallaba* and Arabs, who knew Zubeir senior and his valorous troops well, were firm in their conviction that all attempts to make Suleiman yield to my inferior force were ridiculous, and that the Governor-General of the Sudan could not possibly cope with Suleiman's well-trained and well-organised army.'[45]

⬤

When Gessi departed Shambé on 25 August 1878 to begin his march from the river into the heart of Bahr al-Ghazal, he became lost to the world. The whole anti-slavery war that would rage across southern and western Sudan over the next two years would pass largely unnoticed in Europe. Readers of *The Times* and the *Illustrated London News* would soon be preoccupied by events in Afghanistan and South Africa. They would, in due course, hear of the spectacular British victory at Ulundi, where a square formed of 4,000 modern riflemen would shatter the attacks of up to 15,000 African tribesmen armed with spears and clubs, one in ten of whom would fall, none of whom would get closer than 30 yards, in a battle lasting barely half an hour. Thus would the British Empire destroy the most powerful black kingdom in Southern Africa and clear the ground for a century of mining capitalism and white supremacy.[46]

The Battle of Ulundi would be typical of colonial 'small wars': an asymmetrical collision between European drill, firepower, and logistics – the warfare of the machine age – and a tribal society of traditional warriors employing an Iron Age weapons system. It was an accident of journalism that Ulundi echoed across the English-speaking world – the *Illustrated London News* had their own man inside the British square – while hardly anyone ever heard of Deim Idris, fought the year before. For no war correspondent accompanied Romolo Gessi's little field force. Yet the Battle of Deim Idris, fought in a remote tract of African bush, beyond the gaze of history, turned into an apocalyptic three-month struggle between abolitionism and the Arab slave trade. 'The air was poisoned by the thousands of corpses left in the field,' Gessi would afterwards report, 'and vultures and hyenas hovered and prowled continually around us.'

What made it so was that it was a wholly modern battle, a stalemate of firing lines, more like the trenches of Sebastopol in 1855 or of Petersburg in 1865 than an open-field slaughter pen like Ulundi. For the *bazingar* of Suleiman's army, though almost naked and a slave, but elevated above other slaves to a position of trust and privilege, was a trained professional soldier with *esprit de corps* and a modern rifle. Many carried the same weapon as the Turco-Egyptian regulars, the Remington single-shot breechloader, which had a maximum range of about 1,000 yards and could deliver six shots a minute. Even those equipped with more primitive muzzle-loading rifle-muskets had a weapon effective at about 500 yards and capable of two or three rounds a minute; more, if possessed of a spare gun and assisted by a loader. When *both* sides deployed this kind of firepower, it became virtually impossible to carry entrenched positions in direct assault. Battles turned into firefights. Tactical success came to depend on winning fire superiority at the decisive point.[47]

But first it was necessary to get to grips with the enemy, and Gessi's march was to be a military triumph in itself. The route lay along paths barely wide enough for a man to pass between 10-foot-tall stands of grass, across neck-high swollen waters choked with foot-dragging weed, through swamps filled with glue-like mud, and in the face of electric storms that blackened the sky and poured down torrents of rain. Forward units of Suleiman's forces contested the advance, but were driven back with relative ease. The terrain was the real enemy: it took almost four months for Gessi to cover the 250 miles to Suleiman's main position, building a succession of fortified posts along the way. But this slow advance, so determined and implacable, upset the balance of forces in Bahr al-Ghazal. Africans terrorised by the slave power hailed Gessi as an emancipator. 'A report spread amongst us that the government troops were arrived,' explained one of three black chiefs who held conference with Gessi at Bisellia. 'We are the sheikhs of the villages of Bisellia, Bongo, and Gonfora. Suleiman has taken our wives and children captive. He has destroyed all our substance, and for months we lived like wild beasts amongst the high grass. We have come to tell you that we are ready to help you with all our men, as much as we are able. Command and we will obey.'[48]

The moment of decision was approaching. Suleiman's army was near, concentrated at the *zariba* of Deim Idris. A frontal assault on a fixed position held by modern riflemen who outnumbered the government forces four to one was out of the question. So the wily old bush-fighter had recourse to subterfuge. He had a captured scout write a dispatch for Suleiman, reporting that he was marching on his main *zariba* at Deim Suleiman. The ruse worked: Suleiman redeployed his entire army to defend his capital, and Gessi 'without striking a blow, took possession of the fine position of Deim Idris'. This he immediately prepared for defence, working his men through the night to demolish all the huts and use them to build a great rampart of earth and timber. He then deployed most of his men around the perimeter and stationed a tactical reserve in the centre of the compound. At 6.45 that morning, 28 December 1878, Gessi's pickets fell back on the *zariba* to announce that Suleiman's army was approaching. By means of deception, Gessi had contrived an advantageous defensive battle at the end of his four-month strategic offensive.

The enemy advanced in long lines against two sides of the improvised fort, led by their standard-bearers, before halting at about 25 yards distance and opening fire. But the ensuing firefight was unequal, for the government forces were well-entrenched, and the attackers were driven back by musketry and grapeshot. The firing continued at greater range, but periodically the enemy would surge forward, only to be thrown back again by weight of fire. The battle raged in this way for three and a half hours. Then the rebels broke and ran, pursued a short distance by Gessi's men, before they fell back on their ramparts. Gessi had 93 killed and wounded, but the rebels had lost a thousand, including a hundred Nubians, among them several chiefs, along with ten standards. The moral effect was greater still: around 3,000 Niam-Niam tribesmen deserted Suleiman's camp and returned to their villages, shrinking his force to little more than half of what it had been before the battle.[49]

This first violent collision might have decided the war had Gessi had the force for vigorous pursuit and an immediate assault on Deim Suleiman. But he did not, and the defensive posture forced upon him by military weakness allowed the rebels to rebuild their forces. The whole slave power of the Bahr al-Ghazal perceived a mortal threat in the little government outpost at Deim Idris, and within a week Suleiman's losses had been made good. Learning lessons from the first battle, Suleiman now avoided frontal assaults – made more perilous by reinforcements that had increased Gessi's strength to 4,000 men. Instead, the rebels deployed cannon around the government *zariba* and commenced a bombardment on 3 January – though with little effect – and set in train a plan to cut off the garrison's food and water supplies – a potentially far more dangerous development.

Warned of this by a deserter, however, Gessi laid an ambush, deploying 1,800 men armed with Remingtons in long grass on the line of the antici-pated rebel operation. A second full-scale battle then erupted on 13 and 14 January. On the first day, government troops opened fire at 200 yards, but the rebels fought back for half an hour, then mounted two further attacks in the afternoon, before finally fading away under the weight of rifle, machine gun, and artillery fire. On the following day, the battle raged for a full eight hours, though with the same outcome; this time, the victorious government troops pursued the defeated rebels back to their own fortified camp at Deim Jallaba. Gessi now constructed an outwork manned by 500 men and two cannon to prevent the enemy making another attempt on the garrison's water supply.[50]

The struggle continued in this manner for two months. The government and rebel *zaribas* were a mere two hours apart, but each was too strong to be taken in frontal assault. Reinforcements continued to arrive, along with fresh supplies of munitions, feeding the vortex of violence. Hunger and pestilence – smallpox and dysentery – stalked the government post. The ground around was littered with dead. Most days there was sniping, bombardment, skir-mishes. Supply columns and foraging parties were ambushed. Fugitive slaves inhabited the woods. Sometimes the fighting flared into full-scale battle. A chance shot set fire to the government camp on 2 February, and the rebels took the opportunity to attack *en masse*; but they were beaten off. A firefight erupted all along the line on 28 February, lasting two and a half hours; then, when the rebels fell back, the government men, 'blinded by their success', rushed the enemy's ramparts, suffered heavy loss, and came close to panic flight as they withdrew.[51]

The struggle at Deim Idris finally ended on 16 March. Gessi conceived a plan to cut off the rebels' water supply by building a barricade to block the approach to it about 300 yards from their camp. In the course of two hours, while some men provided covering fire, others constructed a rampart of earth and timber. Cannon and rockets were also deployed, and late in the morning these started a fire among the huts in the enemy camp. This spread during the afternoon to the defences around the camp.

> The despair of the slave traders was great. Suffering from thirst, surrounded by fire, smoke, and suffocating heat, they tried to make a sortie *en masse*, but were repulsed at least five times. Seeing all their efforts were vain, they finally withdrew to their position. It was six in the evening. The spectacle of the immense burning palisades was indescribable ... During the night, the rebels fled in all directions, abandoning their dead and killing their wounded so that they might not fall into our hands. Suleiman, the famous chief, almost naked, mounted his horse, and with a few faithful comrades, fled towards the north, forsaking his routed troops.[52]

The war was not over, but the victory at Deim Idris changed its character. Gessi's strategic mobility was constrained by lack of men, shortage of ammunition, and the hostility of the *jallaba*, who faced ruin, and the *faki*, who were preaching an anti-government *jihad*. The slave power proved many-headed. 'The warfare we were engaged in,' reported Gessi, 'was of the guerrilla sort, and it was necessary to attack or to stand on the defensive everywhere. When the revolt had been subdued in one place, it raised its head in another as soon as we had gone away. But all this did not deprive me of the hope of mastering it, and pacifying the whole country, vast though it be ...'[53]

In fact, there were two guerrilla wars: that of *jallaba* against the government; and that of Africans against *jallaba*. As Suleiman trekked away from the smouldering wreckage of Deim Jallaba, the oppressed rose in his rear to exact vengeance on their persecutors. In countless little clashes unrecorded by history, 'the *jallaba* of Bahr al-Ghazal fell by hundreds under the lances of the natives, who largely revenged themselves for the excesses to which they had fallen victim when their families were captured and sold in the markets of Shakka and Kalaka'. The hunters became the hunted. Those who had spread terror through African villages now fled as their *zaribas* were torched.[54]

But Suleiman was still at large, heading for Shakka, rallying fresh support as he went among the thousands of *jallaba* whose livelihoods were imperilled. Perhaps he would form an alliance with Emir Haroun and the Darfur rebels? Perhaps the whole of Kordofan and Darfur would join the slave traders' revolt? Perhaps an army of 20,000 would rise from the sands of the western provinces? This possibility had brought the Governor General into the field. He had left Khartoum even before the fall of Suleiman's stronghold in Bahr al-Ghazal, riding west, creating a northern pincer to reinforce Gessi's advance from the south. What he saw – an unprecedented flood of emaciated, parched, exhausted slaves being driven across the scorching desert – filled him with anger and renewed resolution. 'The *jallaba* have lost all right to pity,' he wrote to Gessi. 'These barbarians do not merit the least regard or consideration. As we are at work, let us finish it, and destroy their infamous commerce in human flesh. If we lose this opportunity, dear Gessi, you must know that all your labour will have been in vain.' A couple of months later, on 25 June, the two leaders held a conference in Gordon's tent at Taweisha, 80 miles north of Shakka. Suleiman had already broken away into Darfur; the priority was to hunt him down before he could unite with Haroun, raise a new army, and stir the whole region into revolt. Gessi's main forces had been left far behind: he now commanded only a small flying column of 250 picked men. Suleiman was at the head of ten times that number. But again, in the face of daunting odds, Gessi set forth.[55]

He caught up with Suleiman on 13 July. The fleeing rebel force had been degraded by hunger, exhaustion, desertion, and the hostility of local villagers, who had hidden their grain, leaving Suleiman's *jallaba* and *bazingars* to subsist on leaves and roots. The supply crisis had forced Suleiman to divide his force into three columns, and this dispersal was Gessi's opportunity, for he had followed circuitous paths and approached undetected. Even so, Suleiman had 800 men in his column, encamped at Gara, and these were too many to be rushed by a mere 250. So Gessi pitched camp about four hours' distance from the enemy and gave orders that no fires were to be lit and strict silence observed. At 2.30 the following morning, he commenced a night march on the enemy camp, arriving at dawn. No sentries had been posted and the camp was surrounded by man-high scrub. Gessi deployed his men in a ring, concealed by the thickets. He then sent a message to Suleiman which read: 'I give you five minutes to surrender. That time passed, I shall attack you from all sides. Remember that you are surrounded.'

Pandemonium broke out in the rebel camp, the women and children screaming, the black troops rushing to escape. The rebel leaders were unable to restore order, and before Gessi's five minutes had expired, Suleiman and ten others walked out of the camp and surrendered. The bluff had worked. Suleiman was appalled when he learned how few men Gessi had, but by then the captured rebels had all been disarmed. Overnight, however, under guard in the camp, Suleiman and his confederates planned to suborn Gessi's men and break out. When Gessi got news of this, horses had already been saddled and food and arms packed. The conspiracy alerted the Italian officer to the grave risk that Suleiman might yet get away. Hundreds of his men were still at large nearby. Thousands of his supporters infested the region. Gessi's little command of 250 men had triumphed momentarily by nothing more than a well-executed ruse. On the morning after the surrender, therefore, he had Suleiman and nine other rebel leaders executed by firing squad.[56]

Gordon and Gessi thought the war over and the slave trade eradicated. So, for a moment, it may have seemed. Gessi issued a proclamation to that effect:

> The war against the rebels is terminated and order restored. The govern-ment intends to take active measures in order to ensure discipline and protect the natives. All Arabs, without exception, must aid the authori-ties against any individual who commits a crime. Those will be punished with death who are convicted of the following crimes: carrying on the slave trade; abducting boy, woman, or girl; premeditated murder; burning or robbing a village with the intention of robbery or destruction.

Across Kordofan and Darfur, the slave caravans were interrupted, *bazingars* deserted, *jallaba* found themselves on the run. Government manhunts resulted in mass arrests and summary executions. In the Bahr al-Ghazal, the Africans had looted many guns in the mayhem of the war and were now meeting slave raiders with massed musketry.[57]

But in Khartoum a different narrative prevailed: that of economic disaster. The big merchants, the *khabirs*, faced a loss of almost 3 million thalers a year. They accused Gessi of ruining the Sudan. His measures against the slave trade had crippled agriculture and prevented people paying their taxes. He was promoting Africans, excluding Arabs, and 'propagating the idea of emancipation'. The *khabirs* dominated the politics and culture of the city. The *ulema* – the clerics and men of religious learning who were the northern Sudan's ideologues of reaction – parroted the pro-slavery line. The Turco-Egyptian administration – preoccupied with revenue, riddled with corruption – was sympathetic. For Gordon had gone: his health broken, believing that his work was done, alarmed by news that the Khedive Ismail, his patron, had been deposed in an Anglo-French coup, he had decided to return home. The new regime in Cairo, a client of foreign finance-capital, then installed a pro-slavery governor general to replace Gordon, and under Raouf Pasha the slave trade surged again. When Gessi himself set out for home – his own health broken in the swamps of the south – he knew that his mission had failed, for 'the slave traders have recommenced their infamous commerce with renewed courage'. Romolo Gessi – adventurer, abolitionist, master of bush warfare – died of sickness and despair at Suez on 30 April 1881, *en route* for home.[58]

Long before, in late 1879, while campaigning in Bahr al-Ghazal, he had interviewed an old ivory and slave merchant whose firm conviction it had been that all abolitionist effort was a waste. Cairo issued orders, but they were not carried out. Khartoum was far away. The Nile route was blocked, but the slaves were moved overland. Too much profit was at stake. In any case, slaves were necessary to cultivate the fields and grind the corn; who else could do this under such an ardent sun? As for Gordon, how long would he remain, and after him, would another Gordon come? 'This conversation,' Gessi had written, '. . . shows what hopes are nourished by the Arabs as to a possible change of things after Gordon's departure. They hope that the departure will soon take place, and that an Arab is destined to succeed Gordon, and the slave trade will once more flourish as before.'[59] So it came to pass.

# CHAPTER SIX

# EGYPT FOR THE EGYPTIANS?

A month before Romolo Gessi executed Suleiman and extinguished the Sudanese slave traders' revolt, a very different kind of political crisis had come to a head in Cairo, where the Khedive Ismail had been overthrown by an Anglo-French conspiracy.

The crisis had begun three years before, in 1876, when it became apparent that the Egyptian state was bankrupt, and it would end three years later, in 1882, with a full-scale invasion and the occupation of the country by British military forces.

The Khedive Ismail, who had come to power in 1863, was a man of vanity, greed, and ambition. Of mixed Albanian-Circassian descent and the grandson of Muhammad Ali, the strongman who had ruled Egypt in the early nineteenth century, he was a dark, corpulent, middle-aged man, with fluent French, the style of a merchant-prince, and a character that combined beguiling charm with absolute insincerity.[1] 'By nature a speculator and inordinately greedy of wealth,' wrote the English radical Wilfrid Scawen Blunt, 'he seems to have looked upon his inheritance and the absolute power now suddenly placed in his hands, not as a public trust, but as the means above all things else of aggrandising his private fortune.' Blunt, a diplomat, traveller, writer, critic of imperialism, and friend of the Arabs and Islam, was on intimate terms with many of Egypt's leaders as the crisis unfolded. His *Secret History of the English Occupation of Egypt* (1907) is a detailed insider's account that fully justifies its title.

Blunt records the way in which Egypt was converted into a private fiefdom of the Khedive, who concentrated no less than a fifth of the country's cultivable land in his own hands, built himself vast French-style palaces, and hosted lavish entertainments for the Turco-Circassian court elite and the European diplomatic and commercial community.[2] At the same time, aspiring to cut a figure as a modern ruler, he sponsored gargantuan infrastructure projects: 112 canals were dug, totalling 8,400 miles in length; the railway system was quadruped to 1,200 miles; 430 bridges were built; and 1.5 million acres of new agricultural land was brought into use. Dwarfing all these, however, was the Suez Canal, which opened in 1869, having cost £16 million, of which shareholders contributed £4.5 million, the Egyptian government the rest.[3]

The economic development of Egypt provided the platform for a yet greater project, one of truly pharaonic ambition: the construction of a vast African empire extending 3,000 miles from the Mediterranean to the Great Lakes. Expeditionary forces were sent west into Darfur, south into Equatoria, east into Abyssinia. This, of course, had been the context for the military mission of Charles Gordon, who, with saintly naïvety, had assumed the mantle of abolitionism while advancing Ismail's scheme of colonial conquest.

These expenditures were paid for by raising loans with British and French banks. So ruinous were the terms that only 60 per cent of the capital raised actually reached Egypt: the rest was 'discounted', held as 'security', or paid in 'commission' (hallowed euphemisms by which bankers seek to dignify their profiteering). By 1876, the Egyptian government had foreign loans amounting to £68 million, internal loans of £14 million, and a floating debt of £16 million. Interest payments on these consumed the bulk of state revenues. The budget for 1877, for example, would show £9.5 million in revenue, of which more than £8 million went, one way or another, to the bondholders, leaving only £1.4 million to cover all government expenditure. Bankruptcy had been avoided in 1873 only by contracting a new loan of £32 million from Rothschilds. It was averted again, in 1875, only by selling Egypt's shares in the Suez Canal to the British government at the rock-bottom price of £4 million. The whole tottering financial edifice – extortionate loan piled upon extortionate loan to cover soaring interest payments – finally collapsed in 1876, when Ismail announced that he was postponing payment of the 'coupon' (the interest due to bondholders).[4]

The imperial powers acted immediately to defend the interests of European finance-capital. The British and French governments imposed an International Commission of Debt on Egypt, each appointing a controller-general of finance – a system of colonial debt-bondage that came to be known as 'Dual Control'. The new arrangement was essentially a mechanism for leeching wealth from the *fellahin* – the Egyptian peasantry – to the metropolitan elite of London and Paris. This was now, under the bankers' dictatorship, more or less the sole function of the Cairo government.

The *fellahin* had been the beasts of burden on whose backs 'civilisation' had rested for 5,000 years. Exploited by pharaohs, Greeks, Romans, Arabs, Mamluks, and Ottomans in their turn, so now they were exploited by Anglo-French bankers. Throughout these five millennia, tax collection in the villages of the Nile and the delta had been a paramilitary operation, enforced by the *bastinado*. In the years of Ismail's rule, the land tax had been quadrupled in a series of stages. The big landowners, often Turks or Circassians, used their influence to evade taxes, so that the burden fell disproportionately on the poor. The Egyptians viewed their ruling class much as the English-speaking peasantry viewed their Norman-descended lords in the Middle Ages. Ottoman Turks had arrived in the early sixteenth century to reinforce an existing Mamluk (or Circassian) elite dating back to the thirteenth century; this Turco-Circassian ruling class had maintained a distinct cultural identity ever since. To pay their dues, peasants were encouraged to mortgage their land to moneylenders, often Armenians, Greeks, Jews, or Maltese; these would sometimes attend the tax-gatherers on their rounds. *Corvée* labour – state conscription of local peasants – was used to dig canals, lay railways, and build bridges. The Suez Canal was a monument to both modern industrialism and medieval barbarism, for the peasantry was fleeced to pay for it and dragooned to build it. Conscripts were seized from their villages by military press-gangs and many would never be seen again. Young men would mutilate themselves, often by putting out one of their eyes, to avoid military service. Many peasants, of course, were also tenants, who paid rent to landowners, while others were forced to hire out their labour on the large estates. Corruption added further distress: it was endemic throughout the administration, so in addition to tax, rent, interest, and conscript labour, the *fellahin* were often milked by local officials.[5]

The Anglo-French coup of 1879 was designed to strengthen the whole rotten system of exploitation by Turco-Circassian lords and Anglo-French bankers. When Ismail made tentative moves to reduce the tutelage of the controllers-general, he was quickly struck down by his foreign overlords, who induced his nominal sovereign, the Ottoman Sultan, to depose him and replace him with his son, the more compliant Tewfik. The new Khedive was a weak, vacillating, two-faced schemer of whom it was said 'that he was never sincere, and that no-one ever trusted him who was not betrayed'. This puppet prince would have played the role of willing collaborator – as was the intention – had not powerful forces emerged from deep within Egyptian society to challenge the nation's growing humiliation. The British and

French consulates, the controllers-general, the Khedive and his court, and a new ministry led by arch-conservative Riaz Pasha formed a tight nexus of power: but it rested on a void. 'The *fellahin* were still governed mainly by the *kourbash*, the courts of justice were abominably corrupt, the landed classes were universally in debt and were losing their lands to their creditors, and the alien caste of Turks and Circassians still lorded it over the whole country.' Thus did Blunt describe the state of the country on the eve of the Egyptian Nationalist Revolution of 1881.[6]

Most Western accounts of events in Egypt between the Anglo-French coup of June 1879, when Ismail was deposed, and the bombardment of Alexandria in July 1882, when Britain commenced military operations to bring about regime change, are unreliable. From February 1881 onwards, and especially from September 1881, the British press was filled with grotesque distortions of the truth (a pattern of media disinformation in relation to events in the Middle East which has continued ever since). British diplomats, acting with malevolent counter-revolutionary intent, fed stories to the press in a deliberate effort to whip up jingoism and militarism. These stories were repeated uncritically in leading organs like the *The Times* and *The Pall Mall Gazette*. The impression was given of a moderate, popular, benevolent regime threatened by a military conspiracy; of a slide into disorder, lawlessness, and tyranny. Behind the scenes, the hawks were pressing for military intervention, and the orchestrated press campaign intensified pressure on the Liberal government of William Ewart Gladstone to take action; 'all the jingoism of the Empire,' reported Blunt, 'asleep since Disraeli's parliamentary defeat in 1880, was suddenly awake and crying for blood'.[7] Far too many English-speaking historians have followed faithfully these tainted sources; far too many have been willing to exonerate the Liberal regime in London.[8]

The truth, as so often in history, was rich in irony. In attacking Egypt in 1882, the British Liberal Party was waging war on liberalism. The Egyptian Revolution was one of a type that would become familiar during the twentieth century, similar in many ways to the Young Turk Revolution of 1908 (in the Ottoman Empire), the Free Officers Revolution of 1952 (again in Egypt), the Bolivarian Revolution of 1998 (in Venezuela), and many others. It was not first and foremost a revolution of workers or peasants, though all the indications are that the Egyptian masses were enthusiastic supporters of the revolutionary movement. It was a revolution of the middle class, especially of army officers, clerics, and intellectuals. Many of its leaders were teachers or former students of Al-Azhar University, where, though religious studies formed the core curriculum, 'Islamic Modernism' was the dominant paradigm. The Islamic Modernists argued that Islam was wholly compatible with nationalism, democracy, equality, civil rights, and economic progress; indeed, they were outspoken advocates of these very things, being described by Blunt as 'the Liberal Party of Reform'.[9] These were the ideas of the moment, for Egyptians, ruled by the Ottoman Turks since 1517, and a prey to the European imperial powers since Napoleon's expedition in 1798, were acutely aware of their national weakness. Cairo lay in the shadow of the Pyramids, a constant reminder of the country's former greatness; and the black earth of the Nile, which had made pharaonic civilisation possible, meant that Egypt was still blessed with some of the most productive farmland in the world. During the American Civil War, when global cotton supplies had been disrupted, demand for Egyptian cotton had soared, creating what some had called 'the Klondike of the Nile'. With world demand for primary commodities rising exponentially, Egyptian agriculture had experienced a boom in the 1860s and 1870s, its 4 million acres of farmland in 1862 rising to 5.5 million acres by 1879.[10] And yet: Egypt was ruled by foreigners, by Turks, Circassians, and Europeans, the administration was riddled with corruption, and the Egyptian *fellahin* were ground down by taxes, debts, and the *kourbash*.

Among the people who experienced this national humiliation most acutely were army officers of Egyptian origin. There were immediate professional grievances. Careers were often blocked by the preferment of Turks, Circassians, and other regime loyalists. Military defeat in the Egyptian-Abyssinian War of 1874–6 could be attributed in large part to the incompetence and corruption of the high command. Soldiers often went unpaid. And as the crisis intensified, the cleavage of class and culture that ran through the service – between the 80 or so Turco-Circassian senior officers and the mass of Egyptian junior officers and conscript soldiers – widened into a chasm. The court continued to live lavishly; the positions and perquisites of the ruling caste were sacrosanct. As for the 90,000 Europeans resident in the country, they paid no tax. The grotesquely inflated salaries of the 1,300 Europeans employed by the Egyptian state consumed a full 5 per cent of government revenues. The £9,000 subsidy to the European Opera House was deemed essential. But 'economies' were necessary to pay the bondholders' coupon, so the army was to be reduced in size by dismissing 2,500 Egyptian officers, many of them with pay months in arrears.[11] What made this proposal exceptionally dangerous for the court, the consulates, and the controllers-general who effectively ran the country after 1879 was the special place of the army in the state. The army – a highly centralised body of armed men – is often the only effective expression of what might be described as 'the national spirit'. In the absence of strong civil-society institutions – parliament, political parties, trade unions – the army may become the most effective representative of a national movement. And where that national movement is led by the middle class, especially a middle class subject to colonial domination and racial oppression, it may readily find its leaders among army officers. So it was in Egypt in 1881.

Colonel Ahmad Arabi Pasha was an archetype. Born in 1840, he was the son of the sheikh of a small village near Zagazig in the delta, the owner of eight and a half acres of land; he belonged, then, to the rich peasant class. He studied for two years at Al-Azhar, but, being tall and strong, was taken by the army for a soldier at the age of 14. He enjoyed rapid advancement, with promotion from the ranks, becoming lieutenant at 17, captain at 18, major at 19, and lieutenant colonel at 20 – an extraordinary achievement for a *fellah* officer in the caste-ridden Turco-Egyptian Army. But with the death of the old Khedive in 1863, and the succession of his son Ismail, the policy of encouraging Egyptian officers ended, and Arabi's career, until this time meteoric, henceforward stagnated.

Arabi's outlook became more radical as the national crisis deepened. Since he was one of the relatively few *fellah* officers of senior rank, he soon came under suspicion, and the experience of attempted political repression, directed at him and other radical officers – 'the three colonels' – pushed him into active opposition. Heavily built, somewhat slow of movement, endowed with classic Egyptian features, he seemed the very embodiment of the *fellahin*, the time-worn class of native peasants who had, for 5,000 years, performed agricultural labour to sustain their masters in wealth and power. When the London yellow press later described him as a military dictator or a Muslim fanatic, the characterisation could not have been more wrong, for he was a man of the people imbued with liberal values. His aim, like that of the European revolutionaries of 1848, was a modern parliamentary constitution, national independence, political freedom, and social reform; accordingly, though a devout Muslim, he advocated complete freedom of worship.[12] No-one reading the London press in 1882 would have had the slightest notion of this.

Some nationalists had welcomed the overthrow of Ismail and his replacement by Tewfik in June 1879. This was naïve: Tewfik had been installed in
the interests of Anglo-French finance, and he promptly appointed a conservative Turco-Circassian ministry, with Riaz Pasha as Prime Minister and
Osman Rifki as War Minister. Rifki was described by Blunt as 'an extreme
representative of the class which for centuries had looked upon Egypt as
their property and the *fellahin* as their slaves and servants'. The new regime,
accordingly, was determined to crush the nationalist opposition. A succession of repressive measures culminated in a decision, at the end of 1880, to
dismiss Arabi and another leading radical officer, Colonel Abd al-Aal.
Supported by a third radical officer, Colonel Ali Fehmi, they responded by
delivering a petition to Riaz Pasha demanding the dismissal of the War
Minister. Summoned to a meeting in the Kasr el-Nil barracks on 1 February
1881, the three officers anticipated an attempt to arrest them and put their
men on stand-by. When they failed to reappear, their soldiers burst into the
meeting room, overturning tables and chairs, pelting senior officers with
inkpots, causing the War Minister to escape through a window. The three
colonels then led their men to the Abdin Palace, the official residence of the
Khedive, and successfully demanded Osman Rifki's dismissal.[13]

This semi-coup failed to resolve matters. It elevated Arabi to the effective
leadership of the national movement, and it shifted the balance of the
ministry somewhat in favour of reform; but the foreign powers and the
Turco-Circassian conservatives continued to scheme; and both sides vied
for the support of the ever-slippery Khedive. A new crisis point was reached
in September 1881, following the appointment of another Circassian reactionary, Daoud Pasha, as War Minister. Daoud issued orders for the departure of Arabi's and Abd al-Aal's regiments from Cairo – another transparent
attempt to break up the nationalist caucus inside the army. This time, the
officers, supported by the civilian opposition, issued a programme of three
radical demands – dismissal of Riaz Pasha, the convocation of an Assembly
of Notables, and the increasing of the army to 18,000 men – and then
marched on the Abdin Palace. The Khedive attempted to enlist loyalist regiments to crush the revolt, but there were none to be had. When he arrived
at the palace, the square was occupied by infantry, cavalry, and artillery.
Behind them stood great crowds of ordinary citizens. Presented with the
officers' demands, Tewfik attempted to bluster, insisting that Arabi dismount

and surrender his sword, announcing, 'I am the Khedive of the country, and I shall do as I please.' Arabi's voice came back: 'We are not slaves, and shall never from this day forth be passed from one master to another.' Tewfik disappeared into the palace. Then the mask slipped, for Sir Arthur Cookson, the British Consul at Alexandria, continued the negotiation, scurrying in and out of the palace half a dozen times, threatening on one occasion, 'but we will bring a British army'; and the essence of the question in hand, in that tense confrontation on 9 September 1881 – who ruled Egypt: the Anglo-French bankers or the Egyptian people? – was transparent to all who cared to notice.

The Khedive capitulated. Riaz Pasha was dismissed and a new ministry was formed under the reformer Sherif Pasha. 'All Egypt woke next morning,' wrote Blunt:

> to learn that not merely a revolt but a revolution had been effected, and that the long reign of arbitrary rule was, as it hoped, forever at an end. The Khedive had promised to assemble the Notables and grant a consti-tution, and henceforth the land of the Pharaohs, Mamluks, and Ottomans was to be ruled according to the laws of justice and administered not by aliens but by representatives of the Egyptian people themselves.[14]

Arabi became known as *Al-Wahid*, 'The Only One'. Vast crowds cheered him in the streets, and great numbers flocked to his house bringing their griev-ances. Blunt, an eyewitness, gives a vivid description of the euphoric mood.

> Throughout Egypt a cry of jubilation arose such as for hundreds of years had not been heard upon the Nile, and it is literally true that in the streets of Cairo men stopped each other, though strangers, to embrace and rejoice together at the astonishing new reign of liberty which had suddenly begun for them, like the dawn of day after a long night of fear. The press . . . freed more than ever from its old trammels, spread the news rapidly, and men at last could meet and speak fearlessly everywhere in the provinces without the dread of spies or of police interference. All classes were infected with the same happy spirit, Muslims, Christians, Jews, men of all religions and all races . . .[15]

The new administration rolled out a programme of radical reform. There was to be a new parliamentary constitution, an overhaul of the courts, an end to censorship and repression. Investment in the education of both men and women was promised. *Corvée* labour was to be abolished, along with the landlords' monopoly of water at high Nile, and measures would be taken to protect the *fellahin* from exploitation by moneylenders. A state bank was to be established to make loans at affordable rates for agricultural improvements. What of slavery? The Europeans scheming against the nationalist government claimed that 'the Muhammadan revival would mean a revival of the slave trade'. Yet most Egyptians had no interest in the slave trade. Arabi told Blunt 'that the only persons in Egypt who still had slaves or wished to have slaves were just the khedivial princes and rich pashas, against whose tyranny the *fellah* movement was directed; that according to the principles of liberal reform all men were to be henceforth equal, without distinction of race, or colour, or religion.' In short: 'The last thing compatible with these was the revival of slavery.'[16]

This was the mass movement for national independence, economic development, social reform, and the abolition of slavery that the government of William Ewart Gladstone now set out to destroy.

Gladstone, by then a 69-year-old veteran of British politics, fought a much-celebrated election campaign – the 'Midlothian campaign' – in late 1879, speaking at 27 meetings to more than 80,000 people during a two-week period. 'People's William' was at his oratorical best, blasting the Tory administration of Benjamin Disraeli for its bellicose imperialism, in violation of the freedom of Boers, Zulus, Afghans, and Egyptians, for its 'false phantoms of glory', for its 'series of theatrical expedients, calculated to excite, calculated to alarm, calculated to stir pride and passion'.[17] To this jingoism Gladstone counterposed calm reason and liberal precept; but he advanced the argument with such charisma, voice, and passion that he moved deep emotions. 'His dominant theme,' Churchill later wrote, 'was that conscience and moral law must govern political decisions'; 'the spirit of the preacher breathed in Gladstone's speeches'.[18] The result was a landslide in the general election of April 1880, with 351 Liberals returned and only 239 Tories.

Two years later, the Gladstone government ordered a full-scale invasion of Egypt, and two years after that, a full-scale invasion of the Sudan. Speaking in Glasgow on 5 December 1879, he had proclaimed his intention to administer the Empire 'by the strict application of the principles of justice and goodwill, of benevolence and mercy'. Blunt was one of many who took these promises at face-value, urging his Egyptian friends to trust Gladstone, the friend of liberty, to support their efforts to end autocratic rule, establish a liberal constitution, and achieve national independence. He was to rue this advice when he came to understand that Gladstone was, in fact, 'two person-ages'. One, Blunt insisted, was a man of charm, sympathy, and enthusiasm; a man of principles and ideals. The other, however, was the public figure, the parliamentarian, in whom 'the insincerities of debate were ingrained', the man who looked upon 'the Vote of the House as the supreme criterion of right and wrong in public things'. This way of thinking became so much second-nature that 'his own personal impulses of good had assumed the character of tastes rather than principles. They were like his taste for music, his taste for china, his taste for *bric-à-brac*, feelings he would like to indulge, but was restrained from by a higher duty, that of securing a parliamentary majority'. Long habit in the game bred 'a tendency to self-deception', such that 'if he had a new distasteful policy to pursue, his first object was to persuade himself into a belief that it was really the most congenial to him, and at this he worked until he made himself his own convert, by the inven-tion of a phrase or an argument that might win his approbation. Thus he was always saved the too close consciousness of his insincerities . . .'[19]

Gladstone's hypocrisy was an inevitable consequence of his position, for he was both a liberal politician and the first minister of the world's greatest imperial power. Liberal ideals were incompatible with the interests of finance-capital. In relation to Egypt, the choice was between supporting a popular revolution which might default on its debts and propping up a client autocrat who could be relied upon to squeeze the peasants to pay the bondholders. Stripped to its essentials, the war of 1882 – Gladstone's war – was a bankers' war.

That the idealism of Midlothian was so quickly subsumed is not to be explained simply by personal failure. Gladstone's sanctimoniousness – the *leitmotif* of his entire political career – merely made him a fitting symbol of what would later be called 'the strange death of Liberal England'. The mid-Victorian period – Eric Hobsbawm's 'age of capital' (1848–75) – had been the heyday of British liberalism. Commitment to *laissez-faire* economics, a small state, low taxation, constitutional government, political liberty, and individualism reflected the interests of the industrial bourgeoisie of the new manufacturing towns. Most firms were relatively small, often operating only one factory, and the competition between them spurred constant innovation and rapid growth. All the key indices soared upwards: cotton goods exported; railway mileage laid; steamship tonnage carried; coal, iron, and steel produced. After mid-century, a majority of the population were living in towns and cities, and the workforce in mining, engineering, textiles, and transport, the dominant industries, numbered several million. The mid-Victorian bourgeoisie was confident, enterprising, buoyant; liberalism was the ideology of an age of 'progress' and 'improvement'; an age whose optimism was epitomised by the Great Exhibition of 1851.[20]

Gladstone's first administration (1868–74), in its reforming zeal, had captured the spirit of the age. The *ancien régime* of encrusted class privilege represented by Court, Church, Tory Party, and 'the landed interest' found itself assailed by bourgeois ministers intent on throwing open public service to talent and industry. The civil service, the army, the universities, and the law were all subject to radical reform. Disraeli accused the Liberal ministers of attacking 'every institution and every interest, every class and calling in the country'.[21]

But Gladstone lost power in 1874 and returned to office only in 1880; and by then the world had changed. During the boom years from 1850 to 1870, world trade, which had barely doubled between 1800 and 1840, had increased by more than 250 per cent. The crash, when it came, was a shock. It started in the Vienna stock market in May 1873. It spread quickly to Germany, then the United States, where it brought down 98 banks, 89 rail companies, 18,000 other businesses, and eventually put one in seven Americans out of work. Prices and profits plunged everywhere, and growth rates dropped sharply. There had been financial crashes before – in 1825, 1837, 1847, 1857, and 1866 – but this time it was different. Before, there had been a quick bounce-back, as weaker firms were bankrupted, markets cleared, and new investment opportunities opened up. Not this time: world capitalism settled into what the liberal economist John Maynard Keynes would later call 'an underemployment equilibrium'. The veteran revolutionary Frederick Engels, surveying the scene from London in 1886, concluded that the world was 'in the slough of despond of a permanent and chronic depression'.[22]

The root of the problem was the changing structure of capital. The frenetic competition of the boom years had seen the rise of the first modern corporate giants. The shock of deflation was no longer absorbed by a plethora of small firms, the weak giving way, the strong filling the space. Instead, the collapse of major banks and industrial companies shook down the whole system, leaving it prostrate. Britain faced an additional problem. Having built the world's greatest empire and become 'the workshop of the world', Britain's global supremacy was coming to an end by the 1870s, as rival states forged ahead with their own industrial revolutions. The Long Depression (1873–96) presented Britain's rulers with a double-edged challenge: contracting global markets and rising economic rivals.

States and businesses responded to the crisis in three ways. First, the centralisation and concentration of capital accelerated. Small and medium firms went to the wall, markets became dominated by a small number of giant corporations, and these organised themselves into 'trusts' or 'cartels' as a way of managing competition to protect prices and profits. The resulting industrial giants relied heavily on government contracts and bank loans, creating a tight nexus between the state, finance-capital, and industrial capital. 'Classical capitalism' gave way to what contemporary Marxist commentators called 'monopoly capitalism', 'state capitalism', or 'finance capitalism' – though it was, in fact, all three at once. The process was most advanced in Germany and the US – the two countries that now pulled ahead of Britain to become the world's leading economic superpowers.

Second, in pursuit of cheap raw materials, captive markets, and new investment outlets, the great powers turned much of the 'underdeveloped' world into a geopolitical battleground. Colonial rivalries erupted in the Far East, Central Asia, the Middle East, Africa, and the Balkans. In 1876, only 10 per cent of Africa was under European rule. By 1900, more than 90 per cent had been colonised. Railways, the great infrastructure projects of the epoch, were at the centre of events. With the market glutted in Europe, new railways were constructed across the globe. The 'Berlin-to-Baghdad' railway, designed to link Germany, Austria-Hungary, the Balkans, and the Ottoman Empire, is a famous example. It was a direct challenge to British and French interests in the increasingly important Middle East.

Colonialism was competitive, especially when markets were squeezed and profits down. The consequent intensification of corporate and great-power rivalries gave rise to a third development: rising arms expenditure. About £10 million a year between 1830 and 1850, British military spending averaged £20 million between 1850 and 1880, more than £30 million in 1890, and around £60 million between 1903 and 1913. State arms contracts turned firms like Armstrong-Whitworth of Newcastle into giant corporations. By 1914, the firm employed 40 per cent of all the engineering workers on Tyneside. The multiplier effect was huge. Some 1,500 small firms worked as direct subcontractors of Armstrong-Whitworth, while uncounted thousands more supplied the goods and services required by a growing industrial city of 200,000 people. [23]

The Long Depression was ended (like the Great Depression of the 1930s) by arms expenditure and imperialist war. The period between 1896 and 1914, known in Europe as *la belle époque*, in America as 'the progressive era' – a period of faster growth, rising living standards, and renewed optimism – was based on colonies and guns. Behind the glamour were dark forces. A new ideological discourse permeated public consciousness: nationalism, jingoism, militarism – laced, of course, with racism. This conservative cocktail – which would eventually give rise to inter-war fascism – represented a regression to a pre-Enlightenment *mentalité*. The 'imagined community' of the European nation-state, with its 'invented traditions', became the embodiment of a superior 'civilisation'; whereas 'the Orient' was depicted as a realm of backwardness, squalor, and barbarism, in need of redemption, becoming 'the White Man's Burden'.

That this discourse became so pervasive in the age of empire was not simply because it legitimised colonial violence and exploitation; it was also a reaction to the rise of organised labour, socialist parties, and the spectre of revolution at home. Jingoism was an ideology of spectacles to distract attention from 'the social question' – or, as Gladstone had put it in the Midlothian campaign, an ideology of 'theatrical expedients' designed to stir 'pride and passion'. Liberalism, on the other hand, was a product of the Enlightenment, an ideology of 'improvement' and 'progress' – represented, in different ways, by people like Isambard Kingdom Brunel, Florence Nightingale, David Livingstone, and, of course, Gladstone himself – but it could not remain true to itself in a world of ironclads, rifled artillery, and colonial policemen. The Liberal Party remained – since human organisation is sustained by its own inertia – but only by ceasing to be liberal. When the guns of the Royal Navy opened fire on Alexandria on 11 July 1882, they sounded not only the end of Egypt's revolutionary experiment, but also the end of mid-century Gladstonian liberalism.

How could it be otherwise? The 'Eastern Question' – which revolved around Russian designs on Constantinople and British and French desire to keep the Tsar out of the Eastern Mediterranean – had just been rekindled by the Russo-Turkish War (1877–8). A 'Great Game' was being played in Central Asia, again pitting Russia against Britain, where Tsarist probing towards the North-West Frontier seemed to threaten the security of India, and the British had just fought the Second Afghan War (1878–80) in an effort to keep the stopper in the bottle. A 'Scramble for Africa' was beginning, with Britain and France the leading protagonists, rivals for influence in the northern part of the continent since Napoleon's expedition. The French had conquered Tunisia in 1881, and hawkish politicians in Paris, and colonial freebooters in Africa, harboured an ambition to build an empire spanning the continent from the Atlantic to the Indian Ocean; Suez, after all, had been a French project, and French banks were as heavily committed in Egypt as British. The British were duly alarmed; more so following a string of recent defeats in colonial 'small wars' – at the hands of Zulus at Isandlwana in 1879, Afghans at Maiwand in 1880, and Boers at Majuba Hill in 1881. Empire was largely a matter of bluff. A known willingness to deploy effective military force kept colonial rivals at bay. The ability of relatively small numbers of soldiers, administrators, and white colonists to retain control over large Asian and African native populations depended on fear. Defeat set a bad example: it made the imperial power look vulnerable. More immediately, stocks were down on the London market, the bondholders in uproar, the jingo media baying for blood. The Gladstone government was swept into a military attack on Egypt as a demonstration of British power.

The 'honeymoon' of the revolution – the period of unity and euphoria that usually follows the overthrow of a hated dictatorship – lasted four months. It was terminated abruptly by publication of the Anglo-French 'Joint Note' on 6 January 1882. The Assembly of Notables, meeting for the first time only two weeks earlier, had immediately claimed authority over the state budget. What had been conceived as a purely consultative body had thereby revealed its ambition to become a national legislature – much as the Estates-General had transformed itself into the National Assembly at the beginning of the French Revolution in 1789. This deepening of the revolution represented a direct threat to the autocracy of the Khedive, the privileges of the Turco-Circassian elite, and the profits of Anglo-French bankers. The Joint Note proclaimed British and French support for the Khedive and 'the order of things established in Egypt'. The two great powers were, in effect, announcing their support for the dictatorship and their opposition to parliamentary government and any programme of reform that damaged the interests of European bondholders.

The impact was dramatic. It immediately drove a wedge between conservative 'constitutionalists' like Sherif Pasha, the new Prime Minister, and the radical nationalists around Arabi. Sherif was 'a Europeanised Turk of good breeding and excellent manners, but with all that arrogant contempt of the *fellahin* which distinguished his class in Egypt'. He told Blunt: 'The Egyptians are children and must be treated like children. I have offered them a Constitution which is good enough for them, and if they are not content with it, they must do without one. It was I who created the National Party, and they will find that they cannot get on without me. These peasants want guidance.'[24]

A fortnight later, the Egyptians dispensed with Sherif Pasha's 'guidance'. The Assembly of Notables forced his resignation and imposed a new ministry, with Mahmoud Pasha as Prime Minister, Arabi as War Minister. This ministry was committed to the defence of Egypt against foreign aggression, and, as the crisis escalated over the next few months, Arabi's stature rose and he became the dominant voice in government. The nationalist leader told Blunt that the Joint Note had been written 'in the language of menace', and this was confirmed when, on 20 May, a combined Anglo-French fleet of ironclads anchored off Alexandria. A few days later, the consulates issued an ultimatum demanding the dissolution of the Mahmoud ministry and Arabi's exile from Egypt. When the Khedive capitulated and attempted to dismiss the ministry, Cairo exploded in mass demonstrations, forcing the immediate reinstatement of Arabi as War Minister, now with emergency powers. 'I will never yield to either Europe or Turkey', he told Blunt. 'Let them send European, Turkish, or Indian troops, as long as I breathe I will defend my country. And when we are all dead, they will possess a ruined country, and we shall have the glory of having died for our native land. Nor is this all. A religious war will succeed the political one, and the responsibility for this will fall on those who provoke it.'

Popular support for the nationalist regime was overwhelming. Arabi had the backing of a large majority of the Notables, of the Muslim and Coptic religious leaders, and of 90,000 signatories to a petition defending Egyptian independence. The Khedive and the great powers were denounced at a 10,000-strong meeting in Alexandria. The streets resounded with the chant 'The Note. The Note. Reject it! Reject it!' Arabi's cause – 'Egypt for the Egyptians' – was that of a popular mass movement. The whole country faced the central question of revolution: which of two rival powers – the Western-backed client monarchy of Tewfik or Arabi's nationalist government – should be obeyed? The internal balance of forces is evident in the powerlessness of the Khedive. None of his orders could be carried out: there was no mechanism. The nationalists controlled the country.

The Egyptians now moved onto a war footing. Old soldiers were recalled to the colours. Horses were requisitioned. Arms were distributed. Trenches were dug and ramparts strengthened. Supplies were accumulated in forward depots. Soldiers were deployed to front-line positions. Guns were hauled into position. In response, on 3 July, Admiral Beauchamp Seymour, in command of the British fleet at Alexandria, received the following telegraph from London: 'Prevent any attempt to bar channel into port. If work is resumed on earthworks or fresh guns mounted, inform military commander that you have orders to prevent it; and if not immediately discontinued, destroy earthworks and silence batteries if they open fire.' A week later, Seymour issued a final ultimatum: the Egyptians were to surrender the forts guarding Alexandria or face bombardment. Blunt called this 'an act of piracy'. The war began early the following morning.[25]

Alexandria has been one of the Mediterranean's greatest emporia for 2,300 years. The historic port-city was squeezed onto a coastal reef of limestone and sand barely a mile wide, with the Mediterranean to the north-west, the wide brackish expanse of Lake Mareotis to the south-east. A curving loop of reef, extended by a mile-long breakwater terminating in a lighthouse, enclosed the harbour, divided by a mole into inner and outer areas. In the late nineteenth century, Alexandria was home to some 200,000 people, a cosmopolitan mix of Muslims, Copts, Greeks, Armenians, Jews, Maltese, Syrians, and, of course, Europeans, virtually all of them dependent for their livelihoods on the rich commerce of the port. The crowded native town, built of two- and three-storey tenements overlooking narrow alleys and centred on bazaar and mosque, contrasted with the official town, with its khedivial palace, foreign consulates, commercial offices, and numerous elegant villas. The 50,000-strong European community was served by a choice of coffee-houses, two small theatres, a book club, and a French newspaper. 'Other amusements adapted to the taste of civilised nations are likewise obtainable: music parties, *conversazioni*, *soirées*, balls, routs, dinners, wine, and dancing girls, etc.' So ran one enthusiastic report. 'As a place of residence, it is undoubtedly preferable to any other city in Egypt; indeed, it would in many respects bear a comparison with some of the seaport towns of Italy or France.'[26]

The calm of this expatriate enclave was shattered on Sunday 11 June 1882. The full truth of what happened on that day will never be known. The events of the afternoon and evening quickly became the basis for a torrent of fake news from London's jingo press. The events matter less than the *reportage*. News of a local squabble seems to have spread through the streets of a city already in a state of hyper-tension due to the presence of foreign warships, rumours of war, and the defensive military preparations in hand. The European community, widely perceived to be an 'enemy within', became the principal (though not exclusive) target of looting and violence. The Europeans were well armed and defended themselves. The anger and the killing intensified. The local authorities seem to have made little or no attempt to control the streets. Indeed, with paramilitary police sometimes participating in the riot, it seems likely, as Blunt believed, that the local governor – a conservative opposed to the nationalist movement – was operating as an *agent provocateur*, intent upon discrediting the ministry through a breakdown of order and a massacre of Europeans. What is certain is that, as soon as Arabi received news of the rioting, he dispatched troops from outside the city to suppress it, and order was restored on the streets during the evening, a few hours after the disturbances began. But 50 Europeans had been killed – and many more uncounted Egyptians – and the tales grew in the telling as a flood of panic-stricken refugees made their way to the safety of Seymour's ships and reported atrocity stories to the newsmen of the yellow press. London was soon in uproar. Charles Dilke, one of the more rational members of the Gladstone government, wrote in his diary: 'Our side in the Commons are very jingo about Egypt. They badly want to kill somebody. They don't know who.'[27]

This was the political context for the bombardment of Alexandria a month later. Needless to say, the British government's claim that the Egyptian coastal forts were a threat to Seymour's fleet was a lie – the fleet was free to move wherever it wished – unless, of course, the intention was to violate Egyptian sovereignty by mounting an attack on Alexandria. Lord Northbrook, the First Lord of the Admiralty, had reported that the navy did not 'entertain the slightest apprehension with regard to them [the forts]'. But he also opined, 'If we want to bring on a fight, we can instruct Seymour to require the guns to be dismantled.' This was precisely what the Liberal ministers did want: to bring on a fight. In this they were supported by the

Khedive, who urged the British to shell his own subjects. The hated Turco-Circassian elite's hold on power had become a matter of foreign ironclads.[28]

At 7 o'clock on the morning of 11 July 1882, the ironclad *Alexandra* fired a signal shot. This was answered by an explosion of broadside and turret-mounted cannon. The eight battleships of the British fleet carried 84 rifled heavy guns in total, including 12-inch, 11-inch, and 10-inch monsters weighing up to 25 tons. The most modern ship in the fleet, the *Inflexible*, was armed with four 80-ton guns of 16-inch calibre, mounted in two giant revolving turrets, placed at diagonally opposite corners of a central armour-plated citadel, so as to fire ahead and astern; these guns took five minutes to load after each discharge. In addition to main armament, each vessel carried between six and eight 20-pdr guns, perhaps four torpedo-tubes, and a dozen or more machine guns. Additional firepower was provided by seven smaller gunboats attached to the fleet. The morning calm was shattered by noise – the drum tapping of the Nordenfelt machine guns, the constant crashing of 20-pdr broadsides, the occasional deep boom of giant turret guns. The air filled with white smoke, forming a slowly rising and thickening fog in the absence of wind, such that targets and ships disappeared from view, and midshipmen climbed aloft to direct the fire.

Onshore, ranged along 4 miles of rock and sand, posted in a dozen coastal forts built of rubble, earth, and cement, were some 260 Egyptian guns guarding the approaches to Alexandria. Most of the guns were old smoothbores. It had been thought that Egypt's military leaders might accede to Admiral Seymour's ultimatum to cease work on strengthening the forti-fications and to surrender those nearest the harbour entrance. They had not. It had then been thought that the Egyptian soldiers manning the guns might slink away to avoid an unequal fight. They did not. And now, as huge shells howled down and smashed ramparts to fragments, they stood by their guns though a day of unequal battle.[29]

But the Egyptian fire was poorly directed and lacked the weight to pene-trate ironclad armour a foot thick. No British ship was seriously damaged, and British casualties were just 5 killed and 28 wounded. One by one, the Egyptian batteries were silenced. Masonry was shattered and hurled in all directions. Most of the guns were dismounted and their carriages smashed. Numbers of dead, ripped apart by shellfire or riddled by machine guns, lay about.

The British fire was often misdirected. Numerous overshoots landed in the city, smashing into the bazaars, mosques, and mud-walled homes of the inhabitants, pushing total Egyptian casualties, soldiers and civilians, to perhaps 2,000. Fires broke out in various parts of the town; a great pall of smoke lingered over it in daytime, and it was illuminated by flames during the night.

The Egyptian Army was ordered to withdraw inland on 12 July, and two days later Seymour landed a force of marines and bluejackets to occupy the abandoned city. British officers were stunned by the evidence of a new kind of war: the bombardment of a civilian community by modern artillery. 'Our gunnery during the bombardment had not been very good,' reported one. 'Considerable damage had been done to the town of Alexandria by the bombardment, and the fire which followed it,' reported another. 'The huge shells flew wide and high, some of them reaching ... two miles inland,' reported a third.[30]

The British Empire was at war with the Egyptian people. This had nothing to do with slavery. On the contrary: the British military intervention was directed at the overthrow of a revolutionary nationalist regime committed to its abolition. Seymour's ironclads had started a war to defend the old order.

But bombardment alone cannot win a war, let alone conquer a country. Seymour's landing parties, sent in after the white flags went up, could do little more than occupy the city under cover of the warships' guns. Even when reinforcements arrived – South Staffordshires and King's Royal Rifle Corps sent from Cyprus, plus an armoured train mounting artillery and machine guns manned by bluejackets – General Archibald Alison, who assumed command onshore, was unable to advance beyond a coastal bridgehead. Arabi's men had retreated 14 miles down the Alexandria–Cairo railway to a place called Kafr el-Daur and were strongly entrenched. An advance on Cairo, the revolutionary capital, more than 120 miles away at the apex of the delta, was going to require a full-scale invasion. The nationalist leader's political position, moreover, was stronger than ever: another attempt by the Khedive to dismiss him was brushed aside by the Notables, who now established a Military Committee to run the war, with Arabi as commander-in-chief.[31]

War radicalises revolution. The British attack turned political chaos into national emergency. The 'dual power' regime – with authority divided between the Khedive's court and the Egyptian Army – was ended. The Assembly of Notables published a proclamation that made this explicit:

In consequence of the occupation of Alexandria by foreign troops, of the presence of the English squadron in Egyptian waters, and finally of the attitude taken up by Arabi Pasha for the purpose of repulsing the enemy, Arabi Pasha was to be upheld as Minister of War and Marine, instructed with the general command of the Egyptian Army, and full authority in all that concerned military operations, and the orders of the Khedive and his ministers will be null and void.

The Military Committee immediately set to work. It took control of the Treasury, recalled all reservists to the colours, ordered the construction of defence-works around Cairo, and appointed a new governor and corps commander for the Suez Canal district. Orders were then issued for one in six men in every province to be conscripted for service and to make their way to the main military camp at Kafr el-Daur. Arabi subsequently issued a general appeal to all Muslims to rise against the aggressors. Arms were freely distributed to all comers. There were soon at least 15,000 men confronting Alison's expeditionary force at Alexandria.[32]

Imperialism had conjured its radical antithesis: nationalist revolution. The *laissez-faire* foreign policy of the mid-Victorian era had been based on trade and soft power. Wherever possible, the expense and entanglements of military action, let alone full-fledged occupation and direct rule, were to be avoided. In 1859, towards the end of his career, Viscount Henry Palmerston, the dominant British political figure of the preceding half century, had disclaimed any annexationist ambition with regard to Egypt. 'Our interests require that Egypt should remain what it is, an integral part of the Turkish Empire. We do not want it or wish it for ourselves, any more than any rational man with an estate in the North of England and a residence in the South would have wished to possess the inns on the North Road. All he could want would have been that the inns should be well kept.'[33] Here was the authentic voice of liberal capitalism and mercantile empire. So long as access was guaranteed, possession was a quite unnecessary complication. But what if access was in question? What if others – Russian autocrats, French statesmen, Egyptian nationalists – should threaten access? What then? It was becoming clear that a new age was dawning, an age of imperial rivalries and insurgent nationalisms, when British global supremacy could no longer be taken for granted. So it was that William Ewart Gladstone – a man who in every other respect might be considered Palmerston's successor – reluctantly agreed, on 20 July 1882, to sanction a British invasion of Egypt. A week later, the House of Commons voted a war credit of £2,300,000, sufficient to dispatch an invasion force of 21,000 men. Despite this, Gladstone informed the honourable members that 'the country was not at war', apparently on the basis that the planned expedition was essentially a police operation, to rescue Egypt from what he called 'lawless military violence aggravated by wanton and cruel crime'.[34] Later, it turned out that it was a war after all, but not a war in the usual sense: 'We have carried out this war from a love of peace, and, I may say, on the principle of peace.'[35] The Prime Minister remained a self-deluding hypocrite even as he presided over the biggest British military invasion since the Crimean War.

# CHAPTER SEVEN

# ALL SIR GARNET

The man chosen to lead the expeditionary force was already in place; indeed, he had been working on plans for the operation for some time. Of moderate height, light build, clean-cut features, curly brown hair, and piercing blue eyes, he was vain, arrogant, and opinionated – Disraeli described him as 'an egoist and a braggart' – but also hard-working and, when it came to complex military operations, brilliantly efficient. He was, moreover, an ambitious military reformer, in the forefront of a long internal battle to modernise the British Army. His career, in fact, had combined a succession of combat commands in which he had demonstrated both organisational efficiency and battlefield flair, and a series of top-level administrative posts in which he had pushed forward reform in the face of entrenched conservative opposition. Contemptuous of 'spit and polish' and parade-ground drill, his aspiration was to build an army fit for modern war through musketry practice, realistic field exercises, and training in new tactics based on skirmishing, fire and movement, and individual initiative. By 1882, Lieutenant General Sir Garnet Wolseley was a famous public figure, dubbed 'Our Only General' in the popular press. His renowned obsession with efficiency had even given rise to a popular expression, 'All Sir Garnet', meaning 'everything in good order'.[1] His appointment to the Egyptian command was a measure of the seriousness with which the Liberal government viewed the military challenge.

Though born into the Anglo-Irish Protestant gentry from which so many Victorian officers were recruited, Wolseley's family was relatively impoverished. This might have been a fatal impediment to a career in an officer corps still based on the purchase system. Wolseley started work in a land surveyor's office after an education truncated by lack of means. But in 1852, when he was 19, successive applications to Horse Guards (the war ministry) for an officer's commission were finally rewarded. For this he had to thank the aged Duke of Wellington. There was irony in this: Wellington had blocked all reform for 35 years; Wolseley was destined to become the leading moderniser. Conversion to the cause of reform was the fruit of experience. Wolseley was ambitious, and without money his only chance of advancement was through active service. 'There is only one way for a young man to get on in the Army', he averred. 'He must try to get killed in every way he possibly can'. He therefore joined the Indian Army, with its greater prospects of field experience, serving with distinction in the Second Anglo-Burmese War of 1852–3, where he was wounded for the first time, suffering permanent damage to his left leg. As for so many officers of his generation, however, the Crimea was the formative experience. Again volunteering for hazardous employment – as an engineering officer at the Siege of Sebastopol – he was twice more wounded and lost the sight of his right eye. Here, moreover, he witnessed first-hand the rotten condition of the military infrastructure, the incompetence of superannuated senior officers, and the ignorance, negligence, and snobbery of most of his fellow juniors. Like Charles George Gordon, who became a friend, Garnet Wolseley sympathised with the rank and file and chose to share the dangers of the front line.[2]

From the American Revolution onwards, the British Army's military tradition had been anachronistic. The 'nation-at-arms' – mass citizen armies inspired by a national, even a democratic, ideal – had proved a formidable challenge to Britain's small professional army of highly drilled redcoats in both the American War of Independence and in the French Revolutionary and Napoleonic Wars. But victory in the Peninsular War and then at Waterloo bred complacency. The conservative tradition – a present paralysed by the past – was strengthened by several other factors. First was the global dominance Britain achieved with the defeat of Napoleonic France and the post-war settlement of Continental Europe. In marked contrast to the preceding 150 years, Britain faced no major European military challenges between 1815 and 1914. Second, in so far as Britain had security concerns, they were adequately met by the Royal Navy. If the lesson of Waterloo had been a false one – that the British Army ruled the battlefield – that of Trafalgar most certainly was not: the Royal Navy had indeed achieved a maritime supremacy that it was to retain for well over a century. The island-fortress, its vital trade lines, and its distant colonies were all secure so long as the strength of the navy was maintained.

From this followed another factor in the army's relative decline: the parsimony of a parliament of taxpaying gentlemen whose primary interest was economy. The post-1815 'peace dividend' meant radical cuts in military expenditure, bringing the size of the army down sharply from 234,000 in 1815 to 103,000 in 1828 and just 88,000 in 1838. Such fighting as the army was required to do, moreover, rarely tested its true mettle. About half was stationed overseas, where it engaged in colonial small wars, usually against vastly inferior opponents, often armed with nothing more than spears and swords. The other half was stationed in Britain and Ireland, where its primary role was suppressing popular protests against unemployment, land hunger, and lack of democracy.

The army's role in defending a corrupt governing elite did it no favours. Soldiers became social pariahs and recruitment slumped. The morale of men whose only military employment was to attack unarmed crowds of their own countrymen (and, often enough, women and children) was bound to be dismal. The authorities contributed to the malaise by accommodating soldiers in overcrowded slum barracks from which most books were banned. A particular concern, of course, was Jacobin or Chartist literature; the regular use of the army against demonstrators made it inadvisable that soldiers have access to radical tracts – better the bottle than books. Ridiculous, impractical, pompous uniforms; the tedious, pointless routines and drills of a peacetime army; rotten food and barren, squalid, disease-infested accommodation; brutal discipline, with the use of the lash diminishing only slowly towards its final abolition in 1881; the virtual impossibility of any man of talent rising from the ranks to a commission; a vast chasm of class difference and privilege separating officers and men; the sullen hatred of the common people: these things made army service in the first half of the nineteenth century so dire a prospect that even most of the unemployed preferred poverty to enlistment. Little wonder that around 1830 it was reported that 42 per cent of soldiers were Irish, 14 per cent Scottish, and that desertion was an epidemic, several thousand men absconding from the home force every year.

The architect of this decline was none other than Arthur Wellesley, Duke of Wellington, the victor of Waterloo. Arch-Tory in politics, hard-nosed opponent of electoral reform, establishment bulwark against Jacobins, Luddites, Fenians, and Chartists alike, he had maintained an iron grip on the army, and in his hands it remained a thoroughly eighteenth-century institution as the world around it entered the industrial age. Wellington died in 1852, two years before the Crimean War laid bare the shocking decay of the British Army under his long supremacy at Horse Guards. And laid bare it was: by the new phenomena of war journalism, fast communications, and mass-circulation newspapers. During the Napoleonic Wars, the circulation of *The Times* had been 5,000; during the Crimean War, it was over 40,000. Moreover, the mail coach and sailing vessel had been replaced by the railway and steamship. Newspaper correspondents had accompanied the army in the Peninsula, but the 'news' they reported was hardly that by the time it was read in the drawing rooms of grand houses in the Home Counties. Modern war journalism was pioneered in the Crimea, primarily by William Howard Russell of *The Times*, who penned vivid eyewitness descriptions of both the fighting and the conditions endured by the troops, laced with raw first-hand testimony. Read at the breakfast tables of the Victorian middle class, his reports conjured a storm over the heads of the politicians and generals in whose hands the fate of British soldiers on active service rested.

'Let the reader imagine,' wrote Russell at the start of the campaign:

old generals and young gentlemen exposed to the violence of pitiless storms, with no bed but the reeking puddle under the saturated blankets, or bits of useless waterproof wrappers, and the twenty-odd thousand poor fellows who could not get 'dry bits' of ground, and had to sleep or try to sleep, in little lochs and watercourses – no fires to cheer them, no hot grog, and prospect of no breakfast; let him imagine this, and add to it that the nice 'change of linen' had become a wet abomination, which weighed the poor men's kits down, and he will admit that this 'seasoning' was of rather a violent character – particularly as it came after all the luxuries of a dry ship stowage.[3]

Nothing had been prepared: no tents, no food, no comforts of any kind. And so it went on. The soldiers were to spend the bitter Crimean winter camped out on the hills around Sebastopol, and between 1 October 1854 and 30 April 1855, mortality soared to 35 per cent of the army's strength. 'This excessive mortality,' intoned the subsequent report of an official commission of enquiry, 'is not to be attributed to anything peculiarly unfavourable in the climate, but to overwork, exposure to wet and cold, improper food, insufficient clothing during part of the winter, and insufficient shelter from inclement weather.'[4]

The bulk of the troops might have been accommodated in timber barracks at the main British base at Balaclava. But they were not. The single road between Balaclava and Sebastopol became a bog. Plentiful ship-borne supplies rotted at the base while men starved on hilltops a few miles away. Fuel and cooking equipment were not issued because the commissary-general (a Treasury civil servant) was not obliged to supply these to men on active service, only to those in home garrisons: a cock-up which can therefore be attributed to the labyrinthine bureaucracy and criss-crossing of departmental responsibilities characteristic of army administration at the time. Nothing was right. Not even what soldiers were wearing. British Army uniforms – tight breeches, scarlet coatees, bearskins and shakos, useless bits of braiding – were wholly impractical and soon turned to rags. The Highlanders were in kilts. Winter clothing was in desperately short supply. Men died in the Crimea for lack of a greatcoat or a new pair of boots.

Disease and sickness were the great killers. The British lost 25 per cent of the men deployed to the Crimea – a higher casualty rate than in the Great War – but of these, four in every five died from illness. Conditions in the camps were part of the problem, but these were mirrored by the insanitary squalor of army hospitals. The scandal has since become known to every British schoolchild because of the work of the one truly great figure to emerge from the Crimean debacle: Florence Nightingale. Idolised by wounded soldiers, who would kiss her shadow as she passed on her rounds, dubbed by the press 'the lady with the lamp', she was the epitome of no-nonsense Victorian philanthropy. With open contempt for negligent authority, a willingness to interfere in any matter pertaining to health and welfare, and a dynamic determination to make things happen, she became the sharp cutting-edge of outraged middle-class opinion back home. She was fortunate in her supporters. Reforming War Minister Sidney Herbert had first dispatched her, and he continued to back 'Miss Nightingale and her ladies' against complaints from army top brass. She also carried the endorsement of none other than Queen Victoria. The pressure for military reform was getting a head of steam.[5]

Even so, the forces of reaction were strong. Prince George, the Duke of Cambridge, who was Queen Victoria's cousin, was installed at Horse Guards as the new commander-in-chief in 1856. He would remain in post until 1895. Like Wellington before him – but with less justification – he opposed all reform. The Crimean War, the American Civil War, and the Franco-Prussian War demonstrated that war was changing profoundly, as the firepower of long-range precision weapons came to dominate the battlefield, as factories churned out munitions in unprecedented quantity, and as modern nation-states created mass armies of citizen conscripts. The crisis came to a head during Gladstone's first administration.

That the late-Victorian army was an efficient fighting force was largely due to the reforms of Viscount Edward Cardwell, the Liberal Secretary of State for War from 1868 to 1874. As with all great programmes of reform, that of Cardwell was informed by a coherent vision: the need to create a large, modern, professional army that matched the demands of the military revolution which had taken place in the middle of the nineteenth century.[6] Wolseley was brought into the War Office to help drive through the changes, and it was he who produced the blueprint of reform.

Since the Crimea, Wolseley had served in India (against the Mutineers), in China (during the taking of the Taku Forts and the looting of the Imperial Summer Palace), and then, after 18 months leave, had commenced a long involvement with Canada. A visit, in September 1862, to the camp of General Robert E. Lee's Army of Northern Virginia immediately following the Battle of Antietam, had been formative. Wolseley became a life-long admirer of Lee and a dedicated student of the Civil War. At first shocked by the sight of an army of half-starved men in rags, he never forgot the essential lesson: they belonged to one of the hardest fighting armies the world had ever seen. The citizen-soldier became central to Wolseley's thinking about the future of the military. He set up a militia training college in Canada, organised local defence against cross-border raids by Irish-American Fenians, then led a mixed force of regulars and militia deep into the interior to suppress a revolt by French Canadians and Native Americans. This 'Red River Expedition' of 1869–70 involved no actual fighting – the rebel leader Louis Riel simply fled at the British approach – but it was Wolseley's first independent command and it involved a 1,200-mile journey through river rapids and forested wilderness that represented a major logistical achievement. Equally challenging was his second independent command, against the Ashanti of West Africa in 1873–4, when he led a small column of regulars and local levies through disease-infested jungle to defeat a tribal army ten times as numerous and burn down the enemy capital. Subsequent service in India and South Africa did not involve comparable military campaigning – 'I feel like an eagle that has had his wings clipped,' he lamented when denied the command in Afghanistan in 1878 – but he played a central role throughout the decade in driving through the Cardwell reforms.[7] The first edition of his *Soldier's Pocket-Book for Field Service*, published in 1869, was virtually the reformers' bible. The language was characteristically forthright and uncompromising. 'Let us sink as far as possible the respective titles of officers, sergeants, and privates,' he wrote, 'merging them into one great professional cognomen of soldier ... Let us give up the phrase "officer and gentleman", substituting that of "soldier" ... Let the word officer be used as seldom as possible ...'[8] The vision was of a new model army based on comradeship-in-arms, professional pride, and promotion on merit; a bourgeois vision for a modern nineteenth-century army, as against the caste-based anachronism that Wolseley had joined.

For the British Army in the Crimea had had more in common with that of Waterloo than with the armies of either the American Civil War or the Franco-Prussian War. Industrialisation meant that far larger numbers of men could be equipped and supplied, and this in turn meant that a higher proportion of men of military age needed to be trained in the use of arms. Modern firepower was making old-fashioned drill and discipline redundant; increasingly, what the battlefield demanded was men who were highly motivated and capable of initiative and flexibility in combat.

New weapons technology was a key factor. The old Brown Bess, a flintlock musket, had had a maximum range of about 300 yards and a rate of fire of two rounds a minute. The Martini-Henry, with which the British Army fought the Zulu War, the Second Afghan War, and the First Boer War, was a percussion-fired, single-shot, breech-loading rifle with a maximum range of 1,400 yards and a rate of fire of about six rounds a minute. It was also far more accurate at any range. Mid-nineteenth-century tests showed that rifling doubled the accuracy of small arms at 200 yards and trebled it at 300 yards. If infantry firepower is increased by a factor of 30 or more – with comparable increases for artillery – you have a military revolution. Short-range musket volleys have to be delivered *en masse* to be effective, and even so they may fail to stop a charge by equally close-packed ranks of enemy. The lethal sweep of accurate long-range rifle fire, on the other hand, puts a premium on individual fieldcraft and marksmanship. Ideally, attackers should move forward in rushes, supported by suppressive fire, gradually building up a firing line close to the enemy.

The flintlock musket had meant a battlefield as closed-up as a medieval one. The breech-loading rifle opened it out. Parade-ground drill, slow and steady movement, officers attempting 'to keep their men well in hand' belonged to the past. 'This rigidity of movement,' explained Wolseley, 'looks very pretty in Hyde Park, but is unsuited for war: it was copied from the Prussians, who used it, as we did also, to excellent purpose where the effective and destructive range of musketry did not extend beyond what a soldier could run over in charging, and when not more than one, and at most two rounds could be delivered by the defenders during the time occupied by such a charge.' Long-range, rapid action, precision small arms had changed everything.[9]

Modernisation hinged on a series of closely interwoven measures. The Army Enlistment Act of 1870 abolished the old long-service soldier (who was expected to sign on for 22 years) and replaced him with the short-service soldier who spent six years with the colours and six in the reserve. Linked with marked improvements in pay and conditions, this was transformative. Previously, recruiting sergeants had preyed mainly on the most destitute and desperate (with varying degrees of subtlety) in order to fill the ranks with men who were then condemned to a life sentence of disease-ridden squalor and draconian discipline. The army was now to be rejuvenated with willing recruits from the 'respectable' labouring class. It was, moreover, through short service, to become the training institution for a much larger pool of reserve manpower available for immediate call-up in the event of war.

Equally important was the linking and localisation of regiments. The old system had been based on numbered line regiments and a ragbag of militia, yeomanry, and 'fencibles'. Cardwell created new regiments by linking a home battalion with an overseas one, and then anchored these on a fixed regional base, where, moreover, they were formally associated with existing local militia and volunteer units. Britain was divided into 66 districts (usually counties), each managed by a lieutenant colonel and his depot staff, each with its own brigade formed of two regular battalions, two militia battalions, and the volunteers. The army was thus 'territorialised', creating a basis for local identity and affiliations, with further benefits to recruitment. This geographical fixing of the army also provided a ready-made framework for rapid wartime expansion.

A third measure was the attempt to professionalise the officer corps by abolishing purchase. This utterly pernicious system – where advancement depended almost entirely upon means – had meant that a military career 'open to talent' was closed off by class-based vested interests which, in effect, privatised military commands and turned regiments into commodities to be bought and sold. Blue-blooded privilege (and stupidity) was thereby institutionalised, with talented men of the middle class frozen out. Unsurprisingly, Cardwell faced fierce resistance in his attempt to abolish purchase. But legislation was not required: purchase, it turned out, had no statutory basis. So Cardwell took the matter to the Queen and persuaded her to issue a royal warrant abolishing the purchase of commissions in her armed forces. The ground was laid for the conversion of the British Army officer corps from an aristocratic caste into a professional service.[10]

The reforms took time to bed down, and traditionalist resistance continued. The effect of the abolition of purchase, for example, was checked by two factors. One was the fact that promotion by seniority became the rule. Wolseley railed against the consequences: 'splendid battalions kept in the rear ... whilst others of inferior quality were sent to the front, because the general commanding did not dare to employ against the enemy a corps whose commanding officer was manifestly incompetent . . .'[11] No less delim-iting were the mess and social expenses required of a late-Victorian officer. At the end of the nineteenth century, the pay of a second lieutenant in the British Army stood at 5 shillings 3 pence per day, while obligatory mess expenses ranged from 6 shillings to 8 shillings 6 pence, depending on regi-ment.[12] Men from poor backgrounds faced social ostracism and a stalled career. Needless to say, among officers elevated by birth rather than ability, mess-room tradition continued to matter more than professional expertise or the welfare of the men in their charge. The British class system, with all its snobbery and stupidity, repeatedly reasserted itself against the efforts of the military reformers, up to and beyond the First World War. Even so, by 1882, the British Army had come a long way since the Crimea. A large modern European army of the industrial age was about to be pitted against a colonial revolt.

Mission creep may arise at any stage of an operation. Often it arises during the planning. Gladstone's moral collapse had not come all at once; it proceeded in several steps, making possible what could not have been done in a single leap. At first, the hope had been that the Ottoman Sultan might bring his unruly Egyptian subject to order: an appropriately Muslim policeman to act on behalf of what statesmen liked to call 'the Concert of Europe'. The Sultan proved a disappointment: though concerned, he remained immovably cautious. Then it was felt that joint Anglo-French action might be an option, reducing the risks, spreading the blame, endowing colonial coercion with a more international feel. Until as late as 29 July 1882, this looked like a runner. The French, after all, had designs of their own on Egypt – they had built the canal, Paris bankers held half the Egyptian debt,

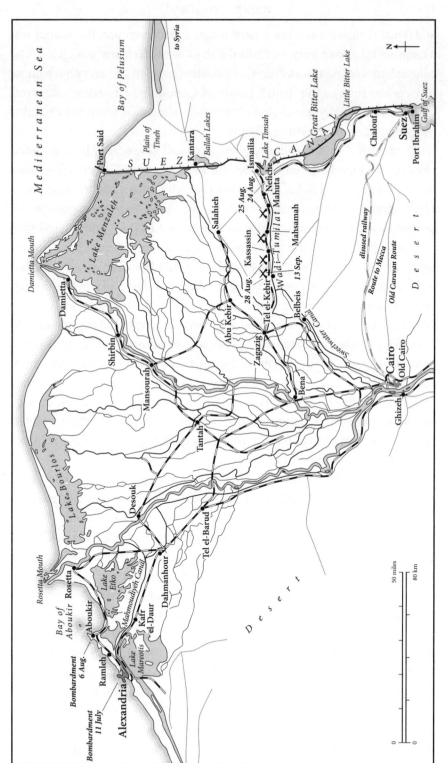

4. The Nile Delta, illustrating the Anglo-Egyptian War of 1882

and 'Dual Control' had been a joint Anglo-French venture. But France was a continental power, very much in the shadow of Germany since 1870, and colonial adventurism was even more controversial in the French Chamber of Deputies than in the British House of Commons. The French dithered, retreated, and finally repudiated intervention altogether when the Chamber overthrew the government on 29 July.

By this time, British military plans were well advanced. The Alexandria riots on 11 June had emboldened the new breed of 'Liberal Imperialist' hawks – represented in Cabinet by Joseph Chamberlain and the Marquis of Hartington – to demand military retaliation. They were soon pressing for unilateral action and all-out intervention against Egypt – nothing less than a British invasion to crush the revolution and occupy the country. Planning for this began as early as 21 June. To the eleventh hour, however, Gladstone argued for a limited operation to secure the canal. The Duke of Cambridge, commander-in-chief of the army, and Wolseley, then serving as Adjutant General, ruled this out: a landing anywhere in Egypt would provoke full-scale war, so the only realistic option was to commit sufficient force to achieve regime change; anything short of this 'would be not only most hazardous but really quite unjustifiable by all the rules of war'. When Wolseley boarded his transport at the Albert Docks on 2 August, his mission was to overthrow the nationalist government. War Minister Hugh Childers had assured him of his 'absolute confidence', adding that he did not 'much care to know your intentions'.[13]

Not only had he planned the operation and been given a free hand in its conduct, but Wolseley had also been able to staff it with members of his 'Ring', a group of officers who had served with him in the Ashanti War and proved themselves both competent and loyal. These included Major General Evelyn Wood (4th Brigade), Colonel Baker Russell (1st Cavalry Brigade), Lieutenant Colonel William Butler (Assistant Adjutant and Quartermaster General), Major John Maurice (Deputy Assistant Adjutant and Quartermaster General), and Colonel Redvers Buller (Intelligence); other members of the Ring served in more minor posts. Wolseley's control did not extend to the three principal divisional commands, however, and while his relations with the Major General Drury-Lowe (Cavalry Division) were good, they became strained with both Lieutenant General Willis (1st Infantry Division) and especially Lieutenant General Hamley (2nd Infantry Division). The force comprised 16,000 men from Britain, 7,500 from various Mediterranean stations, and 7,000 from India. The British component was formed of four cavalry regiments (2,400 men), ten infantry battalions (8,000 men), eight batteries of artillery (54 guns), and supporting engineers, commissariat, and transport troops. By the time the force was fully assembled in theatre, Wolseley stood at the head of nearly 35,000 troops.[14]

Throughout, as with his Red River and Ashanti campaigns, Wolseley considered transport and supply to be decisive. His aim was to bring the main Egyptian force to pitched battle, confident that it would easily be crushed; the challenge was to concentrate a sufficient mass on the battlefield. The problem was the peculiar geography of the Nile Delta. It comprised a vast network of artificial canals devoid of serviceable roads, where movement was by boat, cart, or pack-animal, usually on a slow meandering course. The time of year, moreover, August to October, was that of the high Nile, when the whole delta was flooded by the irrigation works. In practice, there were two viable routes to Cairo, both of them served by railways, the longer 120-mile route from Alexandria, and the shorter 75-mile route from Ismailia on the Suez Canal. But only the latter consisted almost entirely of hard gravel desert with occasional sandy patches – ground suitable for the rapid movement of large numbers of men, horses, and guns. An eastern approach would also have the great advantage that the Suez Canal could be put under immediate military protection, whereas a western campaign would afford time for the Egyptians to sabotage the waterway. A third consideration was the ease with which the British and Indian components – the first via Port Said on the Mediterranean, the latter via Suez on the Red Sea – could effect a junction.[15]

Even so, the logistical challenges were immense. A monument to nineteenth-century engineering it may have been, but the canal was narrow and shallow. Large vessels were in danger of grounding, and British naval officers lacked experience of its navigation. Nor could large vessels pass one another, so northbound vessels would have to be moored in the various 'stations' at the sides of the canal as the expeditionary force headed down from Port Said to Ismailia. Here were further problems. Ismailia, the main port on the canal, roughly midway between Port Said and Suez, had one small pier for disembarkation and unloading; it could handle only one vessel at a time. The canal, in short, was a giant bottleneck, with Ismailia its narrowest point. Everything would take time, and the worry was that the Egyptians would seize the opportunity to sabotage the entire operation. This might be done in several ways. They might sink block-ships in the canal. They might wreck the railway line running west from Ismailia. Perhaps most worrying of all, they might dam the Sweetwater Canal, the vital channel which supplied Ismailia and the Suez Canal with freshwater from the River Nile, access to which was another military imperative.[16]

All these problems were anticipated in the planning. Five locomotives, 100 goods wagons, and 10 miles of track, along with repair wagons, heavy tools, and specialist engineers, were provided. Mules were transported from Britain, other parts of the Mediterranean, and as far away as South Africa and the Americas; as many as 10,000 were purchased, while the Indian contingent brought its own, another 2,500. Numerous light vessels were supplied and others commandeered in theatre, these to enable the rapid landing of men, animals, and kit. A small army of sappers was to construct new bridges, landing stages, and storage facilities. Everything was done to enable the British expeditionary force to land, march, and fight as quickly as possible.[17] But it was clear that it would take around a month between the time when the army arrived off Port Said and the time when it might fight a major battle on the road to Cairo. This was the reason for an elaborate deception plan designed to convince Arabi that, in this two-front war, the British would make their main effort on the Alexandria–Cairo route.

Well before the main force arrived in theatre, General Alison at Alexandria received orders 'to keep Arabi constantly alarmed'.[18] He had already occupied Ramleh, a long straggle of European villas a few miles east of Alexandria, turning the waterworks there into a fort, thereby establishing a blocking position on the approach to the port.[19] Ramleh lay at the northern end of a causeway of land that ran between two lagoons, Lake Mareotis to the west, Lake Aboukir to the east. The Egyptian position at Kafr el-Daur was located at the southern end of the causeway, about 10 miles to the south-east. This narrow neck of land now became the scene of skirmishing, raiding, and the occasional reconnaissance in force. It was a high-tech war. Naval searchlights swept the sand in front of the British lines at night. On one occasion, they illuminated an Egyptian cavalry patrol, which attracted a fusillade from pickets of the Guards Brigade: 'could the outpost have given notice on the instant to the operators of the electric light,' reported one fascinated newsman, 'its rays would have been concentrated on the spot, and the enemy would assuredly have suffered'.[20]

Another innovation was an armoured train, improvised in Alexandria and manned by marines and bluejackets under the command of one Captain Fisher. This was used to support probing attacks towards the Egyptian lines. The locomotive was placed in the middle of the train, with armoured trucks on either side, and several ordinary flat-bed trucks were placed at the front to detonate any mines.[21] On 5 August, when the train was deployed in support of a full-scale probe to Mehalla Junction, it carried a 40-pdr cannon, two 9-pdrs, a Nordenfeldt (multi-barrel) machine gun, and two Gatling (rotating-cylinder) machine guns. The armoured train, followed by an ordinary train carrying a battalion of 1,000 marines, formed the right flank of the British advance. The left was formed of 1,400 infantry drawn from the Duke of Cornwall's Regiment, the South Staffs, and the King's Royal Rifle Corps, supported by some mounted infantry and a couple of 9-pdrs; these were to advance astride the Mahmoudiyeh Canal. Beyond Mehalla were the enemy's outposts, set amid houses, gardens, and irrigation ditches. The enemy, about 2,000 strong, were driven back in an unequal firefight that cost the British 4 dead and 27 wounded, the Egyptians 79 killed and many more wounded.[22]

The wide discrepancy in casualties would be typical of the campaign. The Egyptians were capable of building strong entrenchments, but their musketry was second-rate. One British officer reported that the enemy lines were 'strong in front [affording] no cover for about 1,000 yards . . . but the Arabs can't see well and shoot very badly, though they fight fairly well'.[23] A typical mistake was for rifles to be wrongly sighted and for Egyptian fire to go high, which is probably what this officer meant by 'can't see well'. This was a critical matter when rifles had maximum ranges of almost a mile. Because of the ballistic curve, at ranges above 100 yards they had to be aimed over the heads of the approaching enemy, the precise elevation depending upon distance. The trained marksman would repeatedly adjust the rear site on the rifle according to his estimate of range.[24] He was also trained to couch the butt of his weapon against the right shoulder, to keep the left arm steady, to aim carefully, and to pull the trigger slowly. Ideally, he also needed a cool head, but regular practice could often make good musketry an automatic reflex. Men might go into battle with near identical weapons: there was little to choose between the British Martini-Henry and the Egyptian Remington. It was training that turned men so armed into effective killers. Drill more than technology decided the outcome of the Anglo-Egyptian War of 1882.[25]

A week after the Battle of Mehalla, the main force from England began disembarking at Alexandria. Wolseley himself arrived on 15 August and promptly gave orders to Hamley, now in command at Alexandria, to work out plans, with Alison and his other brigadier, Evelyn Wood, for a full-scale frontal assault on the Kafr el-Daur position. Hamley was informed that the rest of the army would be shipped to Aboukir Bay, 15 miles to the east, so as to effect a turning movement. Everyone, above all the press correspondents, who had been filing enthusiastic reports about the fighting around Alexandria, was given to believe that this was to be the main effort. On the 18th, to strengthen the deception, many of the troops were re-embarked and the fleet sailed round the coast to Aboukir, arriving in the late afternoon and dropping anchor. This grand display of naval power – 20 ironclads of the line in front, 30 transports following behind, filling miles of sea – had the intended effect. Suspecting a grand assault was pending, Egyptian infantry were sent forward to probe the British lines. These were met with fire and driven back when Evelyn Wood deployed a skirmish line of the Berkshire Regiment. But as the Berkshires advanced to within 600 yards of the Egyptian lines, they came under fire from a strongly held redoubt at Kindji Osman. Several 18-pdr and 9-pdr cannon opened up, along with two rocket tubes, supported by a battalion or more of riflemen. Then two heavy siege guns joined the barrage, while three battalions of infantry and a strong force of cavalry began deploying on the right to flank the British skirmish line. Wood gave the order to retire.[26]

The action was resumed the following afternoon, the British this time advancing in force, the Berkshires now joined by the South Staffs and the Cameron and Gordon Highlanders. But the demonstration had largely served its purpose, for the British fleet had weighed anchor the previous night and sailed for Port Said.[27] Early on 20 August, Hamley opened a sealed letter from Wolseley to be told by his commander-in-chief that 'the whole thing is a humbug' because 'I do not mean to land at Aboukir; my real destination is Ismailia'. Hamley felt hoodwinked and humiliated by a superior who had been unwilling to trust him; it was as well that he did not know how amusing Wolseley had found Hamley's 'fond conviction'. A somewhat choleric personality, Hamley harboured deep dislike of his commander from then on. The latter's promise to 'bring you on as soon as I can, as I shall want every available man I can get for my fight near Tel el-Kebir, if Arabi will in kindness stay to fight me there' cannot have helped. In the meantime, Hamley was to tell no-one of the real plan and continue the campaign of distraction in front of Kafr el-Daur.[28]

On the same day, naval forces commanded by Admiral Hoskins executed a plan to take control of the Suez Canal from Port Said to Ismailia by a series of *coups de main*. A commando of six marines landed in the early hours from an open boat to surprise and seize the sentries at Port Said. Companies of marines from HMS *Monarch* and HMS *Iris* under Captain

Fairfax then captured the sleeping garrison in its barracks and took possession of the town. A second force, of marines and bluejackets from *Orion*, *Northumberland*, *Coquette*, and *Nyanza*, commanded by Captain Fitzroy, took control of Ismailia with equal ease in an hour-long operation. A party under Commander Edwards of HMS *Ready* occupied all the barges and dredgers in the canal and forced all shipping into one or other of the stations, clearing the way for the main fleet's descent to Ismailia. The telegraph station at Kantara was also captured. Meanwhile, Admiral Hewett, on station off Suez at the southern end of the canal, dispatched a task force under Captain Hastings of the *Euryalus* to capture Shalouf. The enemy post was stormed by Seaforth Highlanders, supported by cannon and machine-gun fire from naval gunboats *Mosquito* and *Seagull*. The only slight hitch was Hewett's delay in capturing Serapeum until the following day. Otherwise the entire operation had been a masterpiece of planning, timing, and what British officers liked to call 'pluck'. An Egyptian council of war at Kafr el-Daur, meeting on the same day, had in fact decided on the destruction of the canal. Too late: before action could be taken, the waterway was under British control and Wolseley's transports had begun their 40-mile descent to Ismailia. By midday on the 21st, thousands of British soldiers had already disembarked. The war had suddenly changed shape.[29]

The Royal Navy's seizure of the Suez Canal on 20 August 1882 has been overshadowed by the army's subsequent victory at Tel el-Kebir on 13 September. Yet it is no less emblematic of what might be described as a distinctively 'British way of war'. Continental European warfare traditionally involved clashes of mass armies in pitched battle. Only occasionally – mainly during the two world wars of the twentieth century – have the British fought in this way. Britain is a medium-sized island on the north-western edge of the Eurasian land mass. This, combined with its heavily indented coastline and abundance of natural harbours, has ensured a rich maritime and colonial history. British grand strategy, in consequence, has typically involved maritime power, expeditionary forces, and amphibious operations. It has made maximum use of the mobility afforded by maritime supremacy to project elite strike-forces across the globe. Mobility, technology, and training have been used to compensate for relative lack of mass. This strategy goes back a long way. The number of British soldiers who fought on the Continent in the War of the Spanish Succession, the Seven Years War, or the Napoleonic Wars was small compared with the number of French, Austrians, Prussians, and Russians. While the British were sending out expeditions to the Americas, the Indies, and Africa to create a worldwide colonial empire, the Europeans – hapless occupants of a 'continent of warring states' – were engaged in successive rounds of mutually destructive bloodletting. There could hardly be a better illustration of the British way of war than the Egyptian campaign of 1882.

Ismailia was quickly transformed, becoming at once a vast tented encampment, industrial park, and construction site as the railway was repaired, additional landing piers erected, and new roads laid down. Even so, the congestion was immense: though most of the troops were disembarked in the first three days, the landing of equipment and supplies remained heavily backed up in the canal. In the event, it would be three weeks before Wolseley was ready to bring on a decisive battle. Meanwhile, the enemy was active. The level of fresh water in the Sweetwater Canal was soon seen to be falling. The Egyptians had constructed a dam at Magfar, about 6 miles west of Ismailia, and another at Tel el-Mahuta, a further 6 miles inland. Wolseley's response was immediate. A small battle-group of cavalry, infantry, and marines, supported by light gunboats on the Sweetwater Canal, made a dawn attack on Magfar on 24 August, easily dispersing enemy skirmishers and capturing the solidly constructed dam. Reconnaissance then revealed a strong enemy presence at Tel el-Mahuta, estimated at over 8,000. Wolseley ordered the existing force to push forward and keep the enemy in play, pending the arrival of reinforcements from Ismailia sufficient to storm the position. But the British advance faltered under long-range artillery fire and the debilitating effects of the crushing summer heat.[30]

Wolseley had already complained to the War Minister about the inappropriateness of traditional uniforms – red serge jackets and blue woollen trousers – for summer campaigning in hot climates. Now were felt the full effects of Old Army 'spit and polish'. Many men collapsed, including one divisional commander, and all were tortured by temperatures in the 30s as they humped across clogging sand weighed down by rifle, bayonet, backpack, bottle, and 100 rounds of ammunition. The total weight – including clothing, armament, and equipment – was probably in excess of 50lb, around one-third of the soldier's body weight, which is what medical opinion considers the maximum safe load. New 'valise' equipment introduced in 1871 had reduced the weight carried by infantry – part of an incremental decrease since a crippling high of around 75lb in Wellington's army – but it was still at the upper limit of comfort, and well above what Wolseley considered ideal. The combination of heat, sand, and weight was gruelling. Private Macauley of the Scots Guards recalled 'a long stretch of shifting sand on which our feet slipped backwards at every step. The hot wind that was blowing made us terribly thirsty, and soon the pint and a half which each of our bottles held was exhausted.'[31]

The advance, now reinforced, was resumed early the following morning, 25 August, but the Egyptians were found to have abandoned the trenches at Tel el-Mahuta. The cavalry and horse artillery were ordered forward to try and cut off the enemy's retreat, but the animals were out of condition and the effort failed against an effective rearguard. Even so, the way was now open for a further push westwards, as far as Kassassin, which Wolseley had identified as the ideal jumping-off point for his planned attack on the main Egyptian line at Tel el-Kebir. The place was occupied on 26 August without resistance, and Wolseley was able to record that he now held a forward position 'far in advance of what I expected to have occupied for at least a week hence.'[32]

Ahead of schedule in one regard, but not in another, for his forward elements were now far in advance of the rest of the army, which could not be moved up until the logistical bottleneck in the rear had been cleared. Wolseley reckoned on up to two weeks before the advance could be resumed. Large working parties were needed to clear the dams across the Sweetwater Canal, both to guarantee fresh water supplies to Ismailia and to free the navigation for Wolseley's boats, and others to clear an embankment across the railway, repair stretches of track, and thus get traffic moving on the line. Additional problems were the need to filter and boil water because of pollution from dead bodies, and the inadequacy of wheeled transport, partly because the regimental carts were too weak, partly because, despite every effort, there were still not enough mules. Some units were left without tents under the blazing sun, others went without adequate provisions. The London press complained about the delays, The Times making explicit reference to the transport arrangements. Wolseley wrote to his wife that 'despair seems to come over me at times.'[33]

The Egyptian high command sensed the lack of readiness and sent a strong sortie against General Graham's forward battle-group at Kassassin on 28 August. Graham, with only 2,000 men, immediately requested support from the Guards Brigade and the Cavalry Division, both stationed further back due to the supply problem. The main Egyptian attack came in the late afternoon, when a mile-long line of skirmishers in white tunics and red tarbooshes moved towards the British line, perhaps 8,000 in all, supported by about 1,000 cavalry and perhaps 2,000 Bedouin, with covering fire from well-served guns. But the attack was not pressed, degenerating into a long-range exchange of fire, and the situation altered radically when a brigade of Drury-Lowe's cavalry arrived at dusk. Coming up on the open desert flank north of canal and railway, 7th Dragoon Guards in front, Royal Horse Artillery behind, Household Cavalry in the rear, the brigade advanced to attack the exposed Egyptian left. Receiving heavy fire, Drury-Lowe ordered the 7th Dragoons to clear the front to allow the Royal Horse Artillery's four 13-pdrs to fire. The Household Cavalry, riding up to the right of the guns, were ordered to charge.

Darkness had descended and the charge was made in moonlight. This added to the awesome spectacle of a thundering charge by yelling men in scarlet and blue, riding big black horses, brandishing steel sabres. The 'moral effect' of cavalry, Wolseley had explained in the *Pocket-Book*, was far greater than its material effect.

> All reasoning soldiers know that a single man on foot is better than a single mounted man, both being armed alike . . . [But] a large proportion of men on foot get flurried when they see a man on horseback charging down upon them with a bright sabre flashing in the sun, and the moral effect of a large number of such men charging in a formed body is much greater in proportion; the very noise of the horses galloping has a terrifying effect that frequently goes home to the heart of infantry, particularly if it has been at all shaken previously by artillery fire.

For the Egyptian peasant-soldiers facing the charge of heavy horse at Kassassin, however, there was no time and no place to run. The menace was upon them too soon, the horsemen hacking and slashing in a frenzy of killing in the midst of a terrified mob, cutting down 200, tearing the Egyptian line to shreds. By 8 o'clock the battle was over, the enemy in flight across the sand. The British cavalry had lost 9 killed and 17 wounded.[34]

The Egyptians tried again two weeks later, on 9 September, coming on in three massed columns, perhaps as many as 15,000 men in all, again a mix of infantry, cavalry, guns, and irregulars. While the central column fixed the British front, the other columns, from north and south, attempted to lap round the flanks. But the attack seems to have been based on false intelligence – a gross underestimation of British strength – and the British reinforced their line, dominated the firefight, and then mounted a general counter-attack which routed the enemy and brought the British to within 5,000 yards of the main position at Tel el-Kebir. This might have been taken on the rush, but Wolseley called off the pursuit and ordered a return to camp. His reasoning was sound: losses would have been considerable and the attack might have failed; even if it had succeeded, with only half the army on hand, the reserves for a pursuit to destruction would not have been available. Wolseley was determined to destroy Arabi's main army in the field and then advance rapidly on Cairo and end the war.[35] This was to be a 'method' war.

Ahmad Arabi Pasha had arrived to take command at Tel el-Kebir at the end of August. It was the Egyptian leader himself who had commanded the two great attacks on the British lines at Kassassin. The centre of gravity of the Egyptian national defence – the main army position – had shifted from Kafr el-Daur to Tel el-Kebir as soon as it was known that the bulk of Wolseley's army was on the Sweetwater Canal. Arabi had about 20,000 regulars in the line, 20 battalions in all, 14 of which were in the main position, 3 in a forward position south of the canal, 3 more in reserve. They were armed with good, single-shot, breech-loading Remington rifles, and supported by 75 cannon, mainly 9-pdr and 14-pdr Krupp field guns, well served by artillerymen whom Wolseley considered 'the only good branch of the Egyptian Army'. Egypt's peasant-soldiers had proved reluctant to press attacks in the face of superior firepower. Concentrated in defence of strong fortifications, backed by plentiful artillery, they might prove more formidable. If they stood their ground, they might exact a heavy toll.

The fortifications were indeed strong: the British commander considered them 'a hard nut to crack'. They comprised a continuous line of sand-and-gravel earthworks running northwards into the desert from the canal and the railway. The works, located on a plateau about 120 feet high, were fronted by a ditch, 10 feet wide and 5 deep, with the upcast used to form an embankment of similar dimensions, behind which was the Egyptian fire-step. The sides were revetted with mud and reeds. Along the length were ten projecting artillery redoubts of varying size, with the strongest defences on the right, closest to the canal and railway. Also on the right, some 1,000 yards in advance of the main line, was a forward redoubt with eight guns and supporting infantry. These artillery redoubts were more substantially constructed, the main ditch wider and deeper, with secondary ditch and rampart in front. The obstacle to attacking infantry was substantial: even poor marksmen might achieve fearful execution firing at point-blank range into a backed-up mass of men struggling to climb out of the ditch. A second, shorter line, running at an angle for about 2 miles and facing north-west, lay behind the first; this was designed to protect the rear of the Egyptian position against any attempt at a flanking movement through the open desert to the north. A third trench, facing south, ran between the first and the second, so as to enclose the Egyptian camp, located in the centre of the position. Behind each of the two main trenches lay a support line formed of short lengths of trench, where defenders might rally if their forward line was lost. The ground facing east towards the British position at Kassassin was gently shelving and completely devoid of cover. 'To have marched upon the enemy's position in daylight,' Wolseley reported after detailed reconnaissance, 'our troops would have had to advance over a *glacis*-like slope in full view of the enemy, and under the fire of his well-served artillery for about five miles. Such an operation would have entailed enormous losses from an enemy with men and guns well protected by entrenchments from any artillery fire we could have brought to bear upon them.'[36]

Nor was this the only problem confronting the invaders. In addition to the main concentration at Tel el-Kebir, around 30,000 regulars and 80 guns were distributed across half a dozen other posts in the delta. Operating on internal lines and served by telegraph lines and a rail network, these separate garrisons were capable of mutual support. Each, moreover, was assisted by a large contingent of Bedouin irregulars. The latter were waging a low-intensity guerrilla war, harassing outposts, attacking vessels on the Suez Canal, tearing down telegraph lines, looting where they could. The main effect was a considerable diversion of British military strength in guarding the line of communications, such that, as Wolseley lamented, 'I could place in line only about 11,000 bayonets, 2,000 sabres, and 60 field guns.' The Bedouin also supplied Arabi's officers with abundant (though not always accurate) intelligence, while their presence on the edges of successive battlefields was a constant source of British anxiety. Also encouraging was news from the Sudan, where Osman Bey, the Governor General, had renounced his allegiance to the Khedive and declared for Arabi. His army of 22,000 regulars included large numbers of Sudanese – the best troops in the Egyptian Army. The insurgency seemed to be gaining momentum, the military resistance thickening.[37]

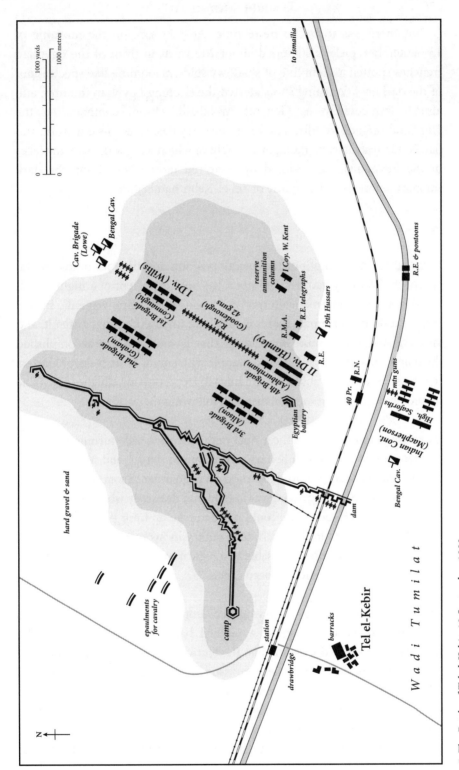

5. The Battle of Tel el-Kebir, 13 September 1882

But there was to be no more time. At 4.50 a.m. on the morning of 13 September, pickets stationed about 200 yards in front of the Egyptian trenches spotted a silent line of shadowy soldiers looming like spectres out of the darkness. Warning shots alerted the sleeping Egyptian infantry, and almost immediately, as General Archibald Alison, commanding the Highland Brigade, recalls, 'a blaze of musketry flashed across our front, and passed far away to each flank, by the light of which we saw the swarthy faces of the Egyptians, surmounted by their red tarbooshes, lining the dark rampart before us.'[38] The Battle of Tel el-Kebir had begun.

Daunted by the strength of the enemy position and the forbidding frontal approach, Wolseley had decided upon the bold expedient of a night march and dawn attack. The main alternative – a wide flanking movement – he had ruled out on two grounds: that it would have involved 'a long, difficult, and fatiguing march', and, more importantly, that 'it would not have accomplished the object I had in view, namely to grapple with enemy at such close-quarters that he should not be able to shake himself free from our clutches . . .' As he further explained in an official dispatch following the battle:

> I wished to make the battle a final one; whereas a wide turning move-
> ment would probably only have forced him to retreat, and would have
> left him free to have moved his troops in good order to some other posi-
> tion further back. My desire was to fight him decisively where he was, in
> the open desert, before he could retire to take up fresh positions more
> difficult of access in the cultivated country in his rear. That cultivated
> country is practically impassable to a regular army, being irrigated and
> cut up in every direction by deep canals.[39]

The risk of a night march – always an accident-prone operation of war – was taken to achieve the ultimate: a pitched battle that would destroy the Egyptian Army and the Nationalist Revolution in a single hammer-blow.

Orders to prepare for battle were issued at 3 o'clock on the afternoon of 12 September. One hundred rounds and two days' rations were issued to every man. The troops were told to maintain strict silence on the march; orders were to be given in whispers and rifles would be unloaded to avoid chance shots. No lights were to be shown; smoking was banned. Tents were left standing until dusk, campfires burning thereafter, so as not to alert the enemy to the fact that the British were on the move. By 11.00 p.m. the men were assembled in their jumping-off position, and Wolseley inspected the lines. South of the canal was General Macpherson's Indian Infantry Brigade (1st Seaforth Highlanders, 7th Bengalis, 20th Punjabis, and 29th Baluchis), supported by some 13th Bengal Cavalry, a mountain-gun battery, and a 250-strong Naval Brigade with 6 Gatling guns and a 40-pdr cannon mounted on an armoured train. Their job, starting an hour after the main advance so as not to alert local residents, was to clear the area of houses, garden plots, date palms, and irrigation ditches around the village of Tel el-Kebir. General Hamley's 2nd Division was deployed about 2,000 yards north of canal and railway, General Alison's Highland Brigade leading (Black Watch, 1st Cameron Highlanders, 2nd Gordon Highlanders, and 2nd Highland Light Infantry), Colonel Ashburnham's Composite Brigade forming the reserve (2nd Duke of Cornwall's Light Infantry and 3rd King's Royal Rifle Corps). General Willis's 1st Division was deployed on the right, General Graham's brigade leading (Royal Marine Light Infantry, 1st Royal Irish Fusiliers, 2nd Yorks and Lancs, and 2nd Royal Irish), the Duke of Connaught's Guards Brigade forming the reserve (1st Scots Guards, 2nd Coldstream Guards, and 2nd Grenadier Guards). Each division formed on a front of about 1,000 yards, with an interval of about 1,000 yards between the forward and reserve lines. Between the respective inner flanks of the two infantry divisions lay a gap of 1,200 yards, and here was deployed a grand battery of 42 field guns commanded by Brigadier General Goodenough, with orders to keep pace with the rear brigades and provide close fire support as the attack developed. Finally, on the outer desert flank was Drury-Lowe's Cavalry Division (Household Cavalry, 4th Dragoon Guards, 7th Dragoon Guards, 2nd Bengal Cavalry, 6th Bengal Cavalry, and two batteries of Royal Horse Artillery), its mission to flank the Egyptian line, cut off retreat, and mount an aggressive pursuit.[40]

The advance began at 1.30 a.m. – timed to ensure a dawn attack on the assumption of a 1-mile-per-hour average speed – and was guided by the stars. Halts to check direction and alignment were frequent. On one occasion, the wings of Alison's Brigade wheeled inwards to form a crescent during a poorly communicated halt. At the same time, Graham's Brigade was compelled to halt to alter its formation. Despite these upsets, the advance proceeded to schedule – much time had been allowed for the inevitable stops and starts of a night march – and the Egyptians were taken totally by surprise. The Bedouin, on whom they relied for long-range scouting, did not operate at night. The first warning of the British onset was that given by the forward picket line. This was quickly followed by bugles sounding the alarm and an eruption of musketry from the Egyptian parapet. The Highlanders fixed bayonets and charged the enemy works 'with pipes playing and one long continued howl'. The 'howl' was what Wolseley expected. 'A ringing cheer is inseparable from charging,' he had written in the *Pocket-Book*. 'It encourages, lends nerve and confidence to an assailant; its very clamour makes men feel their strength as they realise the numbers that are charging with them. Nothing serves more to strike terror into a force that is charged than a loud ringing cheer . . .' Spencer Ewart, a young lieutenant with the Camerons, was in the thick of it: 'We all ran cheering as hard as we could towards the earthworks, stumbling into holes in the darkness. It was a distance of 400 yards, and I was dead beat when I fell into their trench, a great deep place.'[41]

The sudden shock to men only just aroused from sleep might have triggered immediate panic. It did not. The Egyptian infantry delivered a fierce close-range fire into the crowded mass of Highlanders struggling to get out of the ditch and up the scarp. Some Camerons and Gordons eventually mounted the summit and broke into the enemy position, but others recoiled before the fire and had to be rallied by Hamley himself, the divisional commander, coming up behind.

The situation was still more perilous on the flanks. The Black Watch on the right was held up for 25 minutes by a big five-gun redoubt with a double ditch in front and a 14-foot embankment beyond. Only when a sergeant and some others cut steps with their bayonets and clambered up did the regiment gain a footing on the summit. 'Then up they came in swarms,' recalled one participant, 'wheeling to right and left, bayoneting or shooting every man.'

The Highland Light Infantry on the left had an even harder time against a four-gun redoubt protected by an exceptionally wide and deep ditch defended by determined Sudanese infantry. 'The enemy soon put a heavy fire on us,' remembered one traumatised private, 'both from big guns and rifles; shot and shell were flying over our heads and on both sides of us. The shouting of our men as they got wounded was something heart-rending. I thought every moment I would be launched into eternity. I can't write about it any more.' Only after three-quarters of an hour, with help from the Duke of Cornwall's Light Infantry, was the position taken.

Even when the British crossed the first line of entrenchments, Egyptian resistance continued along the second line. 'I never saw men fight more steadily,' recalled the Highland commander. 'Retiring up a line of works which we had taken in flank, they rallied at every re-entering angle, at every battery, at every redoubt, and renewed the fight. Four or five times we had to close upon them with bayonet, and I saw these men fighting hard when their officers were flying.' The casualties are a measure of the ferocity of the resistance: the Highland Brigade took 231 casualties at Tel el-Kebir; of these, the Black Watch suffered 56, the Highland Light Infantry 74.[42]

The Highlanders were in advance of Graham's Brigade on the right, and for 10 minutes fought alone in the enemy trenches. Then the right-hand division joined the fight, the Royal Irish charging with 'unearthly yells', followed by the Irish Fusiliers and the Yorks and Lancs. Though the main trench was taken quickly in the first rush, the Egyptian infantry rallied on their second line, pouring fire on their assailants, who advanced in rushes, before closing to a frenzied *mêlée* with bayonet and clubbed rifle. The Royal Marine Light Infantry, on Graham's left front, had a still harder time, under fire from the same redoubt that had halted the attack of the Black Watch, taking 86 casualties in the course of their desperate struggle to reach the summit of the embankment. 'The whole line of ramparts seemed in a blaze,' reported Colonel Jones, 'but, nothing daunted, our men gave a cheer and dashed into the ditch and scrambled up the parapet. Heaven knows how. I managed to dig my sword into the sand, and made a lever of it, by which I pulled myself up.'[43]

By now, as well, some of Goodenough's field guns had been hauled over the entrenchments and were in action in support of the infantry firefight inside the works. As Viscount Fielding, serving with N/2 Battery, Royal Artillery, explained to his parents:

> We found the enemy bolting in every direction across the plain, but they were pegging away hard at us from lines to our left front. After giving them a few rounds, they began to run, so we galloped after them, coming into action every 300 or 400 yards . . . We drove the enemy out of two or three redoubts, where they tried to stand . . . and got so close to the Egyptians sometimes that we fired several rounds of case-shot at about 200 yards, with great effect.[44]

On the outer flank, Drury-Lowe's cavalry and horse-guns had flanked the enemy position and were riding down the rear, cutting off the line of retreat. Panic spread down the Egyptian line from left to right, and soon thousands of *fellahin* soldiers were in flight, heading south-westwards, some towards the bridge over the canal at Tel el-Kebir, others with no particular plan except escape. For the killing was not yet over: the enemy were to be cut down, traumatised, scattered in panic; they were not to be given a chance to rally. 'I had not the heart to cut dozens down that I might have done,' wrote one trooper of the 7th Dragoons:

> for they fell on their knees and held up their rifles for mercy. But I could not help cutting some down, because they fired on us to the last. One of the enemy was laid on his face, and as a man of the 4th Dragoon Guards rode past him he rose up and fired at him, and I just caught him as he galloped by and cut him from his shoulder to the middle of his back. But the best fellows for fighting are the Indian troops. They cut heads off as if they were cabbages, and the head fell in many cases eight foot away from the body. The battle only lasted two hours, and the whole time we were butchering them on the flanks as they tried to run away.[45]

In truth, the battle proper was over in barely an hour; it was only one-sided killing that continued longer. When it did finally end, around 7 o'clock that morning, while British casualties were 57 killed and 412 wounded, Egyptian casualties were around 2,000 killed, with an unknown number wounded. The correspondent for *The Standard* penned a graphic description of the carnage: 'The sufferings of the Egyptian wounded – as many were dying from bayonet stabs and lacerations by exploded shells that set their cotton clothing on fire – were awful. Their cries for aid and water loaded the morning air, and many were seen to tear off their scarlet tarbooshes and bury their bare heads frantically in the sand for coolness.' Many corpses were headless or had been disembowelled. Amputated arms and legs piled up around the British field hospitals where the wounded were brought in by stretcher-bearers. 'Words cannot describe the horrors in the lines,' wrote a Royal Engineer officer:

> the fearful stench, the corpses of the Egyptians all unburied and covered with masses of flies, which flew up into your face the moment you approached, even two of the Marines not yet buried, and one or two wounded Egyptians still living under the broiling sun (over 115° in the shade), the dead horses, mules, and camels, the wreck of camp tents, arms, etc abandoned by the Egyptians, the returned fugitives and Bedouin robbers prowling about all through the ruin, and even stripping the

corpses of their clothes. It was necessary to keep a revolver ready for these fellows.[46]

It had been a highly professional butchery; a matter of organisation, technology, and precision; an industrial operation. It had been carried out by thoroughly trained men, many of them grizzled combat veterans. The soldiers of the Highland Light Infantry averaged eight years' service. The Camerons had 460 men above 24 years of age, the Gordons 370. The Black Watch had left all soldiers under 20 at home. Armed with the best weapons that Victorian industry could supply, trained for years in their use until every action became a reflex, the men of Wolseley's army operated like small moving parts of a well-oiled machine. South of the canal that terrible day, after Captain Fitzroy's Gatling guns had broken up an Egyptian cavalry attack, firing first in one direction, then another, the Seaforth Highlanders had smashed the Egyptian infantry defending Tel el-Kebir with fire. *The Times* correspondent described the operation: 'The leading company was commanded by an ex-musketry instructor, who cautioned his men not to fire save by the word of command, and himself successively named the ranges. The consequence was that their fire was so deadly that not an Egyptian dared to show his head above the parapet.'[47]

Colonel Arabi had sent a letter to Prime Minister Gladstone on 2 July 1882. He explained that Egypt wanted peace, but that she would fight if her territory was violated. He added something more: a prediction of pan-Islamic religious war in the event of British aggression. 'Egypt is held by Muhammadans as the key of Mecca and Medina,' he wrote:

and all are bound by their religious law to defend these holy places and the ways leading to them. Sermons on this subject have already been preached in the Mosque of Damascus, and an agreement has been come to with the religious leaders of every land throughout the Muhammadan world. I repeat it again and again, that the first blow struck at Egypt by England or her allies will cause blood to flow through the breadth of Asia and Africa, the responsibility of which will be on the head of England.[48]

Arabi – driven against a wall by British hostility – had indeed made efforts to summon an Islamic *jihad*. He had made professions of allegiance to the Ottoman Sultan as Caliph and leader of the pan-Islamic cause. He had appealed to all Muslims to rally to the defence of Egypt. He had dispatched emissaries to Muslim rulers elsewhere in the Middle East. He was in close contact with Sheikh Muhammad al-Senussi, the leader of a radical Islamic sect based in the Western Desert.[49]

But Arabi was defeated by time. 'Ask anything of me but time,' Napoleon is supposed to have said, and he might have been referring to the Egyptian National Revolution of 1882. Arabi was crushed in a *Blitzkrieg* of 'shock and awe' before he could build a revolutionary army and a pan-Islamic front. In 1793, an army of republican *sansculottes* had saved the French Revolution. In 1919, an army of socialist proletarians would save the Russian Revolution. Both armies took time to build amid the chaos of social upheaval. The Egyptians were not granted such time in 1882. So the Egyptian Revolution and the Islamic Enlightenment were destroyed in the trenches of Tel el-Kebir. The first attempt at a modern Middle East based on nationalism, citizenship, liberal precept, and religious tolerance was bulldozed by an imperial war-machine.

Thus were the decks cleared for a different kind of revolution – an atavistic and reactionary revolution, more counter-revolution in fact, involving an Islamic-fundamentalist regression to a darker world of ignorance, oppression, and enslavement. This was to be the bitter fruit of Gladstone's 'liberal' interventionism.

Barely a month after the restoration of the *ancien regime* in Cairo – the Khedive was returned on 25 September – came news from the Governor General of Sudan. Government garrisons at Bara and Obeid in the distant western province of Darfur were under siege. A relief force sent from Khartoum had been annihilated. The insurrection was spreading to other parts of Sudan. An army of 10,000 men should be sent immediately; otherwise things were liable to spiral out of control, and it would then require an army at least four times the size to restore government authority.[50]

The leader of this insurrection was one Muhammad Ahmad bin Abdullah. A Nile boat-builder who had become a religious scholar and teacher, he had, in June 1881, announced that his mission was to restore the true faith of Islam and prepare the way for the Second Coming of the Prophet Isa. He was, in short, the long-awaited 'Guided One' – a special religious leader whose arrival heralded an apocalyptic transformation of the world at the end of time: *Al Mahdi*. Accordingly, he had summoned the Muslim people to holy war.

# Part III
# The Black Flag

# CHAPTER EIGHT

# A MUSLIM PROPHET

The myth of the Mahdi is older than Islam. It is part of a Judaeo-Christian-Islamic tradition that extends back to at least the sixth century BC. All three of the great Semitic monotheisms have spawned countless 'orthodoxies' and 'heresies', and among them is the radical millenarian notion of a Messiah or Mahdi.

The unity of Islam was shattered in the first generation, and has been shattered in every generation since. If there is a single thread running through the knotted skein of Islam's sectarian histories, now 14 centuries old, it has been the collision between the *realpolitik* and grand living of Muslim elites and the eternal poverty of the Muslim masses.[1] The Islam of princes and muftis has been repeatedly challenged by another Islam, that of itinerant preachers, local saints, and Sufi mystics. In some measure, this difference is ever-present, a pervasive undercurrent in all Islamic societies, for religion, being unable to eliminate class divisions, is perforce obliged to reflect them. Most times, the difference is managed; the contradiction between the glaring injustices of social existence and the egalitarian ethos of Islamic teaching fails to achieve traction through long epochs of torpor. Until a moment comes when social tensions acquire a critical, explosive mass; a moment when Islam reaches deep inside itself, drawing upon half-forgotten traditions, to re-erect an old totem and trigger a revolution.

Though the Qur'an is silent about the Mahdi, the *hadiths* – the collected sayings of the Prophet – include one that reads as follows: 'If there were to remain in the life of the world but one day, God would prolong that day until He sends in it a man from my community and my household. His name will be the same as my name. He will fill the earth with equity and justice, as it was filled with oppression and tyranny.' Other *hadiths* amplify the message, and seem to chime with Qur'anic references to the hour of the resurrection, expected to arrive suddenly, following a time of religious 'ignorance' and 'much killing'. Belief in a special prophet for this 'end of time' upheaval, a religious leader capable of guiding the people back to righteousness and the true faith, is common to the entire Judaeo-Christian-Islamic tradition; indeed, in one form or another, messianic millenarianism appears to be a near-universal undercurrent in pre-modern religion.[2]

Through most of history, the millenarians were few, isolated, and without influence. Their conceptions – of an essentially dichotomous world divided into righteous and unrighteous, of an imminent mass uprising to cleanse the world of evil, of divine intervention to lift up the wretched of the earth and enable them to defeat God's enemies – seemed too wacky. Their appeal was mainly to the marginal and rootless, especially in times of unsettling social change. But the idea of a radical redemption, a recasting of the world to rid it of ungodliness and oppression, an idea that in normal times was nothing but a murmur, might, in a moment of social crisis, attract a mass audience and flare into revolution.

At such moments, a Messiah or Mahdi was called for. Most men were busy with their lives and less than holy; they were everyday people, and everyday people could hardly be expected to have a direct line to God. Nor could everyday people, caught up in the parochial minutiae of family, village, and tribe, be expected to conjure heady visions of holy war, the world transformed, the end of time. To lift people's minds to the heavens and bind them into a unitary movement was the work of a charismatic leader. For the myths of messianic millenarism to rise from the recesses of the social order to the realm of historic action required a magician, a mystic, a patriarch.[3]

Nothing about Islam is inherently mystical or 'fundamentalist'. Like other great religions, it can accommodate to modernity, rationalism, and science; its adherents can be democrats, liberals, and socialists. The long history of Islam leaves no doubt about its dynamic eclecticism. Between the eighth and sixteenth centuries, the Arabs stood in the vanguard of world cultural development, the humanism of Arab intellectuals far in advance of their contemporaries in priest-ridden medieval Europe. Relative stagnation between the sixteenth and eighteenth centuries had ended abruptly in 1798, when Napoleon Bonaparte invaded Egypt and, at the Battle of the Pyramids, destroyed the medieval order of the Mamluks in an hour of musketry and grapeshot. What followed was nothing less an 'Islamic Enlightenment', which saw the Middle East changing fast in an effort to meet the existential threat of Western imperialism, a process of reform and modernisation driven forward by strongman regimes like that of Muhammad Ali in Egypt. Late nineteenth-century Cairo and Constantinople were cities of steamships, railways, and telegraph lines, no less than of mosques and madrasas.[4]

But here was the rub: catch-up modernisation provoked strong traditionalist reaction. Reduced to questions like land improvement, public sanitation, and printed books, the value of modernity could not easily be gainsaid. But closing the gap between East and West demanded rapid action which could not wait upon the consent of the governed. Muhammad Ali, who ruled Egypt from 1805 to 1848, was typical of a new generation of autocratic modernisers. He transformed Alexandria into a modern port, imported industrial machinery, nationalised land held in religious endowment, launched a public health programme, and set up a printing press to churn out translations of foreign books. But taxes went up, the slave trade boomed, Sudan was ransacked by soldiers, and the *fellahin* were press-ganged and plundered. Muhammad Ali was a moderniser, but also a tyrant. State-driven capital accumulation was underpinned by medieval barbarism. Egypt was to be bastinadoed into the nineteenth century.[5] It was the continuation of this lopsided nation-building project by the Khedive Ismail between 1863 and 1879 – funded by foreign loans – that had toppled Egypt into a popular revolution. But the Egyptian revolutionary movement of 1879–82 – a true flowering of the Islamic Enlightenment – had then been destroyed by British artillery. So what did modernity mean? The yoking of the Egyptian *fellahin* to Anglo-French finance-capital? In the encounter with the West, with world capitalism, liberal reformers had argued that Islam should embrace the new and create a synthesis of machines and mosques. The village saw only armed tax collectors.

Liberalism and nationalism were ideologies of the city. They were discussed in the coffee-houses of Constantinople, Cairo, Beirut, Damascus, and Baghdad, much less in the mud-brick villages, small towns, and caravan-stations where most Muslims lived. In the countryside and the desert, the old ideas, the received wisdom of the ages, still provided the main framework of people's worldview. But the orthodoxies preached by government-approved *ulema* (as the Islamic clerical class was collectively known) were rendered less certain by changing times; and other types of holy men, once marginal, now gained a hearing. Unlike the argument between modernisers and traditionalists, between secular liberals and Qur'anic scholars, this was an argument between moderate and radical forms of Islam. Was it not the case, people asked themselves, that the year 1300 was nigh (as indeed it was by the reckoning of the Islamic calendar)? Was the dawn of a new century not the very time when a Mahdi might be expected? Did the current state of the world – afflicted with the oppression, corruption, and irreligion of the 'Turks' – not herald the great cleansing? 'One would hear nothing but curses on the rulers and on everyone who controlled one of the government departments,' wrote Yusuf Mikhail, a religious student resident in the western desert town of El-Obeid. 'Indeed, by the will of God most high, most people, both men and women, began to ask: "Isn't there a Mahdi for us? Isn't it said that this is the right time for the appearance of the Mahdi?" '[6]

Mainstream Shia Islam had professed belief in the Mahdi since the late seventh century, and even more so its radical Ismaili offshoot. In Shia myth, the Mahdi was imagined to be a sleeping imam, a divinely inspired religious teacher who had disappeared from the world and would one day return to inaugurate an apocalyptic struggle to restore righteousness. The Sunni tradition was more muted in this matter, but the conservative *ulema* had never wholly succeeded in extinguishing an undercurrent of Mahdist expectation. Ibn Khaldun, the great fourteenth-century Arab historian and social scientist, was in no doubt that belief in 'the Guided One' was deep-rooted in popular religion: 'Know that it has been commonly accepted among the masses of the people of Islam throughout the ages that there must be at the End of Time the appearance of a man from the People of the House who will help the Faith and make Justice triumphant, whom the Muslims will follow, who will gain control over the Islamic lands, and who will be called the Mahdi.' One Sunni version of the myth had Jesus as the Mahdi, envisioning a Second Coming similar to that of Christian millenarians. Other versions – anxious, perhaps, to distinguish true from false claims – were specific about the hallmarks of an authentic Mahdi. He would be descended from the Prophet's family, would bear the Prophet's name, and his father would bear the Prophet's father's name. He would have various physical identifiers – a broad forehead, a prominent nose, a gap between the teeth, a mole on the cheek. In June 1881, on an island in the White Nile about a day's passage by steamer south of Khartoum, a man answering to that description, a Sufi mystic and religious teacher of local repute, announced to the world that he was, in fact, the Expected One.[7]

It was visceral experience of the real world, of course, that caused the murmur of messianic expectations to rise in the Sudan of the 1870s. The

Turco-Egyptian colonial regime imposed taxes on everything from bean fields to date palms, from livestock to wheels. Its corrupt officials demanded bribes and payoffs. Its requisition squads seized agricultural produce and stole camels, horses, mules, and donkeys. Appropriation was carried out by armed detachments, either Turco-Egyptian regulars or Bashi-Bazouks, the ubiquitous Ottoman irregulars that one official report described as 'swaggering bullies, robbing, plundering, and ill-treating the people with impunity'. Payment was enforced by the *kourbash* and the gun. These paramilitary tax-collecting operations – a fleecing of the poor in the interests of the Ottoman ruling class and its financial backers in London and Paris – filled a well with bitterness in ten thousand villages. 'The people assure us that over and beyond the lawful rates they are obliged to pay', wrote the British traveller Cornelia Mary Speedy, 'almost every farthing they can make is demanded of them, and seized by force. They have no incentive consequently to cultivate their land, and thence arises their wretched state of poverty, and the degraded condition of deceit engendered by oppression, in which they habitually live.'[8]

Was there no hope? Or were the rumours true, rumours that ran down the camel tracks and sea lanes from Arabia, Libya, and West Africa, rumours of mahdis and holy wars elsewhere?

An Islamic revivalist movement had been founded in the Nejd region of Central Arabia in the middle of the eighteenth century by Muhammad Ibn Abd al-Wahhab. The Wahhabi faith had been adopted by the desert warlord dynasty of Ibn Saud, and early the following century, in 1805, the men of Nejd had stormed into Mecca and Medina, smashed every shrine and image they could find, and turned away pilgrims from Egypt and Syria on the grounds they were 'idolaters'. The Islamic Enlightenment had struck back – the fanatics had been evicted from the Holy Cities by Muhammad Ali, the Egyptian strongman, in 1812 – but the Wahhabis, having retreated into their desert fastness, had endured; and, though none knew it yet, the power of the House of Saud was poised to rise again.[9]

Another Islamist movement – on the western border of Egypt and the Sudan – had been founded in the middle of the nineteenth century by Muhammad Ibn Ali al-Senussi. Centred on the remote Saharan oasis town of Kufra, the Senussi, with their web of local *zawiyas* ('lodges'), dominated some 1,500 miles of northern Africa, extending from the central Sahara to Cyrenaica in western Libya. Though fundamentalist in advocating a return to the true Islamic *tariqa* or 'way', the Senussi were loosely structured across their widely scattered oasis-settlements, where they cultivated garden plots, serviced the caravan trade, and organised themselves as an armed religious brotherhood (*ikhwan*).[10]

On the far side of the Islamic world, around 1,500 miles west of Khartoum, beyond Lake Chad, across a great swathe of semi-arid grasslands inhabited by cattle herders and scratch farmers, another Islamic revivalist movement held sway. A Fulani religious leader, Sheikh Usman dan Fodio, had proclaimed a holy war in 1804, and, within a few years, at the head of an army of horsemen, had created an Islamic-fundamentalist super-state, the Sultanate of Sokoto, centred on Hausaland (northern Nigeria). Usman, a Sufi mystic, had castigated the orthodox *ulema* for their breaches of Islamic stricture, and denounced the predatory taxation of Hausa rulers. His message, a combination of religious renewal and social emancipation, laid the foundation for a Central African state that would be ruled by his son and still be in existence in the 1890s. Further west, other Islamist leaders triggered more localised *jihads*, creating a handful of smaller theocracies on the borders of the European colonies on the West African coast; states which, again, would endure until overwhelmed by British and French military expeditions in the last two decades of the nineteenth century.[11]

While it would be wrong to imagine some sort of pan-Islamic 'conspiracy', these movements were connected. Leaders exchanged letters and emissaries, and occasionally made personal visits. More importantly, news and ideas jumped across the desert from town to village to caravan-station, like firecrackers, propelled by the numerous travellers ever on the move in a region of nomads, traders, and pilgrims. So there was an informal 'international', a current of Islamist subversion extending across 5,000 miles of Afro-Asia, growing in strength at each success, slowly burning out allegiances to the potentates and *ulema* of the *ancien régime*. It was a current of reactionary holy war, not liberal revolution. It sought return to an imagined past that had never existed, not advance to a new world yet to be created. It was the dark alter-ego of the Islamic Enlightenment extinguished by British cannon on the slopes of Tel el-Kebir.

⬛

It was easy to miss, buried at the bottom of page three. But the more persistent readers of the London *Times* on 23 August 1881, perusing the Foreign and Colonial News that day, would have learned of an 'affray' in a distant corner of North-East Africa. 'Intelligence from the Sudan reports an affray between the population and the military, caused by the preaching of a false prophet. One hundred and twenty Egyptian soldiers were killed. The rise of the Nile is satisfactory.'[12]

The Battle of Aba on 12 August 1881 was indeed a small affair; but viewed in retrospect, it assumes portentous significance. A Sufi mystic, theologian, and teacher called Muhammad Ahmad bin Abdullah had been running a mosque and religious school on Aba Island since 1868. The island, a strip of palm groves, bean fields, and mud houses about 30 miles long and 3 miles wide, was located in the middle of the White Nile, a day's journey south of Khartoum.[13] Muhammad Ahmad, now in his mid-30s, had a well-deserved reputation for asceticism, piety, and, not least, outspoken criticism of the moral corruption and religious backsliding he observed in the Turks and those Sudanese, sheikhs and imams, who consorted with them. Sometimes, beginning his evening prayers around nine o'clock, he would stand in a secluded spot reciting the Qur'an, from memory, through the night until four in the morning, the time of the pre-dawn prayers. Other times, he would retreat to a cave and pray for hours in solitude, abstaining from food and all worldly things, waiting for a divine revelation to come 'like the break of day'. Alternatively, he would travel around, an itinerant preacher, carrying his message of Islamic renewal to all who would listen; and, over the years, the number who did so steadily increased. He was an impressive man, tall and well-built, with a handsome face and a winning smile that revealed a tell-tale gap between his top front teeth; but also, it seemed, a humble man, for he wore an old cotton tunic or *jibba*, repaired with dyed woollen patches, baggy calf-length drawers, and a wide turban of twisted white cloth; and he was notable for his calm, polite, and respectful manners.[14]

But Muhammad Ahmad was no simple man of the people. He had been born in 1844 on a small island 10 miles south of Dongola, in the far north of Sudan, the son of a prosperous boat-builder and one of four brothers. The family was of some standing, and it claimed a proud lineage, descent from the Prophet himself. The family had moved to Omdurman in 1849, to be near Khartoum, where the boat business was booming, and here he had commenced his formal education, learning the Qur'an by heart, a relentless routine of repetition, with errors punished by beatings, punctuated by inter-vals for communal prayers, menial chores, and basic meals. Muhammad Ahmad thrived, earning the plaudits and patronage of his masters, and he might have progressed to higher studies in Islamic theology and law, perhaps at Al-Azhar University in Egypt, a pathway to the highest ranks of the Sunni *ulema*. But he chose not to; instead, he entered a lodge of the Sammaniya order, committing himself to a seven-year novitiate at the feet of a Sufi master who demanded total obedience of his students. Again, Muhammad Ahmad thrived, and when finally he graduated, his life's course was set: he would found his own religious community and commence a mission to return the world to the *tariqa*, the true way, of Islam.[15]

Muhammad Ahmad was a priggish, sanctimonious, humourless young man; a benighted bigot ignorant of almost everything in the world except the contents of a medieval holy book; a reactionary zealot intent on Armageddon. But he was also a charismatic mass leader, a preacher able to speak the everyday language of villagers and tribesmen, and, at the same time, a man of immense learning able to hold his own with the most elevated Islamic scholars of the age. It was these two complementary aspects of Muhammad Ahmad that enabled him to play his historic role as the person-ification of an Islamist counter-revolution that was set to surge across the Sudan and sweep away the rotten edifice of Turco-Egyptian colonial rule.

Seclusion, starvation, and sleeplessness, combined with long hours of monotonous recitation, can induce a trance – a state of hysteria in which 'voices' are heard and 'revelations' imagined. There is no reason to believe that Muhammad Ahmad was a charlatan; it seems far more likely that he believed in the literal truth of his claim that he had been chosen by God to be a new messenger. Early in 1881, he confided to his closest companions that he had experienced a *hadhra*, an audience with the Prophet himself, an event which implied a divine mandate superior to that of any other living Islamic authority. Then, on 29 June 1881, four days after his thirty-eighth birthday, came the declaration that he was indeed, as his intimates had guessed, the Mahdi.[16]

The news was immediately transmitted – by that most modern of devices, the telegraph – to the authorities in Khartoum. 'Whoever does not believe in my Mahdiya,' he threatened, 'will be purified by the sword.' And he signed no longer as plain Muhammad Ahmad, but as 'the Servant of the Lord, Muhammad al-Mahdi'.

The Turco-Egyptian Governor General, Raouf Pasha, responded with a summons to Khartoum, to face a delegation of senior *ulema*, men qualified to judge the claim. The Mahdi delivered an uncompromising rebuff: it was not for Raouf Pasha to summon him, for 'who can be set above the Mahdi, personally selected by the Prophet? It is Raouf who is duty bound to obey

me, along with the rest of the Community of the Faithful.' The Governor
General then dispatched a company of 200 soldiers, commanded by one
Abu al-Saoud, to arrest the recalcitrant holy man and bring him by force
to the capital. They arrived at Aba Island on the steamer *Ismailia* late on
11 August. They moored the boat, disembarked, and advanced in heavy rain
towards the residence of the Mahdi.

That should have been the end of the matter. For sure, anticipating force,
the Mahdi had sent urgent messages to his supporters to rally to his defence,
and some 300 men from tribal communities along the river had answered
the call. But the Turks were armed with breech-loading rifles, the Mahdists
with spears, swords, clubs, and farm tools. Dispersing the crowd and
arresting the leader ought to have been a minor police operation.

The soldiers advanced on the Mahdi's village in two groups. By now,
darkness had fallen, and it was still raining. Suddenly, on all sides, men
concealed in undergrowth, howling as they came, hurled themselves at the
soldiery. The Turks fired a ragged volley, then, as they struggled to reload, the
Mahdists were among them, hacking, stabbing, clubbing. The entire company
broke and ran for the steamer. Losing their way in the dark, impeded by
scrub, slipping in mud, many were cut down. Abu al-Saoud rallied some of
his men at the water's edge, turning the steamer into a miniature fortress to
hold the Mahdists at bay. Now it became a firefight, for many of the Mahdists
had picked up the discarded rifles of their enemies. Though it dragged on
until sunrise, it was clear the mission was abortive. Abu al-Saoud steamed
away with what remained of his command, leaving 120 dead on the island,
ten times the losses of the Mahdists.[17]

However other-worldly he was, the Mahdi knew that Aba Island was not
safe, being too accessible by steamer from the capital, so would now have to
be evacuated. In any case, for a Muslim leader, flight from one's enemies
enjoyed the best of precedents: the Prophet's *hijra* from Mecca to Medina in
AD 622. The Mahdi's *hijra* took him to Jebel Gadir in the Nuba Mountains of
southern Kordofan, a region dominated by Baggara cattle-nomads and slave
traders. The Mahdi himself was sprung from the riverbank peasantry, but
his closest companion, Abdullahi Ibn Muhammad, was a holy man of the
Baggara, and years of proselytising had established a network of supporters
across this region. The journey of 79 days was therefore accomplished

with ease. Those who made the trek became the Mahdi's *muhajiroun* ('companions'), while those who afterwards joined the movement would be his *ansar* ('helpers'): further echoes from the time of the Prophet. At Jebel Gadir, the Mahdists were welcomed by Sheikh Mek Nasir, a supporter who had been primed for their arrival. Work began immediately on a new religious settlement.[18]

The Mahdists made a virtue of poverty and were embedded in Sudanese society; they flowed through the landscape like water. Not so the Turco-Egyptian Army. The government response was cumbersome and sluggish, a matter of mobilisation orders and musters, equipment inventories and steamboats, supply lines and depots. To these logistical difficulties were added errors in calibrating an appropriate level of response; in this regard, facing an insurgency that fast acquired tremendous momentum, the army high command found itself permanently behind the curve, its reactions invariably piecemeal and underpowered. On 8 December 1881, a government column of 400 regulars, supported by some Shilluk tribesmen, attempted to storm the Mahdi's stronghold on Jebel Gadir. The Ansar waited until the approaching soldiers opened fire, then launched a single fanatic charge and destroyed them. 'Serious troubles have again broken out in the Sudan,' intoned *The Times*. 'The false prophet, to whom attention was called some time ago, at head of 1500 men, has totally annihilated a force of 350 Egyptian troops, whom the Governor of Fashoda was leading against him. The Governor himself was among the killed.'[19]

Raouf Pasha was sacked, his place taken, pending the arrival of a replacement from Cairo, by Acting Governor General Carl Giegler. The first phase of the government counter-insurgency operation was over. The effect of the twin Mahdist victories at Aba Island and Jebel Gadir had been to trigger a mushroom growth of local insurrections across much of Kordofan and the Jazira (the region between the White and Blue Niles south of Khartoum). A more serious response was required than a single column of a few hundred men.

So Giegler dispatched small columns to tackle the various Jazira outbreaks and a large column against Jebel Gadir. The former had considerable success, winning two battles, inflicting heavy casualties on the rebels, and restoring the allegiance of many tribal sheikhs. But at Massa in distant Kordofan, there was disaster. In the dim light of dawn on 30 May 1882, the Ansar of the Mahdi's main field army stormed the *zariba* of the government column, 6,000 strong, under Brigadier Yusuf Hassan al-Shallali Pasha. It was over in minutes, the *zariba* penetrated, the soldiers split into separate groups and pressed back against their own thorn-hedge, the Ansar howling and hacking everywhere, thousands more piling in behind. Many soldiers fled, but only to be hunted down and slaughtered. Hardly any got away: another battle of annihilation, but on an altogether bigger scale.[20]

Massa seemed to confirm God's judgment. Surely this must be the true Mahdi, when the faithful, armed only with spears and swords, prevail over so many Turks? Is he, as reported, no mere mortal, but a divine figure endowed with supernatural powers able to turn bullets to water? Victory, anyway, is its own propaganda. The Mahdists offered booty in abundance and an end to the occupation. Their success implied that loyalists were backing the wrong side; that now was the time to switch. So the insurgency swelled across southern Kordofan and beyond, and the government retreated into the bigger towns. Its heaviest column had been defeated, so active counter-insurgency was now given up, in favour of the defence of fixed positions, pending the arrival of reinforcements from Cairo, and, perhaps, through some mix of propaganda and bribery, a shift in the balance of forces, rebel versus loyalist, among the tribal sheikhs of the Sudan.[21]

The Mahdists, on the other hand, now went over to the offensive. Their initial aim was the total subjugation of Kordofan, to be accomplished with the capture of the provincial capital at El-Obeid.

An ancient caravan-station and now a Turco-Egyptian provincial capital, El-Obeid in 1882 comprised an outer sprawl of mud-and-thatch roundhouses, an inner suburb of merchant houses, and a core of more substantial official buildings, including a gatehouse, a governor's residence, and a barracks. Two watercourses ran through the town, dry in summer but cascading floodwater in winter, and these sustained a rich growth of trees, scrub, and grass. El-Obeid was home to a large community of foreign merchants, including Egyptians, Syrians, Greeks, and Jews, as well as many rich Sudanese who traded in camels, cattle, gum arabic, and slaves. Some thousands of artisans and shopkeepers made a living in the local markets. The town was now swollen with fugitives, whose stories of Mahdist atrocities had grown in the telling, spreading alarm among many, especially the better-off. Others, though, perhaps with less to lose, were rooting for the Mahdi, either out of hatred of the Turks, or simply to be on the winning side.[22]

Unlike many senior Turco-Egyptian officers, the Governor of Kordofan, Muhammad Said Pasha, proved to be calm and efficient. The town was surrounded by a wide defensive circuit comprising thorn-hedge, ditch, and earth rampart. But this perimeter – about 4 miles in total – was too long to be defended effectively by the fewer than 10,000 or so armed men at Muhammad Said's disposal. These comprised a core garrison of about 6,000 regulars, another thousand or so military fugitives, various contingents of Bashi-Bazouks, and loyalist townsmen to whom firearms had been issued. Allowing for reserves – essential to plug breaches – this would have allowed for only one man per yard: far too few to deal with such classic Ansar tactics as the night approach and the sudden dawn charge. So Muhammad Said created a strong inner work. An earth rampart, with loopholes along the top, protected by a thorn-thicket in front, was laced around government buildings converted into blockhouses; this allowed for tiers of concentrated fire to be directed down the surrounding streets.[23]

In the Ansar camp at Kaba, 6 miles from El-Obeid, the Mahdi addressed his followers, promising easy victory over a meagre garrison, a wealth of treasure in the town, and, for those who fell as martyrs, immediate entry to paradise. Few of them had firearms, but, he assured them, God and his Prophet had decreed that the faithful should annihilate their enemies with the weapons of their ancestors. After dawn prayers on Friday 8 September 1882 – just a week before a very different battle, that of Tel el-Kebir, 1,300 miles to the north – the Ansar advanced to launch a full-frontal assault on the government lines. The outer defence was penetrated, but hidden reserves sprang a lethal fire trap, unleashing a storm of converging close-range musketry into the dense masses of Ansar spearmen. Other intruders, funnelled down the streets of the town, racing forward in thick columns, ran into sheets of fire from the inner defence, where Muhammad Said's regulars were packed shoulder to shoulder. Blocked in front but with ever more men rushing up behind, the Ansar formations concertinaed into a heaving mass of thousands, almost immobile, choking the streets, while the Turks fired rockets, canister, and bullets into them until weapons became too hot to handle. 'We killed hundreds and thousands of them,' recalled Yusuf Mikhail, the religious student, 'though they continued to fall upon us, fearless and dauntless. We answered them with bullets . . . one could see nothing but dead people heaped everywhere.' Father Joseph Ohrwalder, an Austrian missionary, already a prisoner of the Mahdi, a man destined to spend a further ten years in captivity, was nearby. 'It was impossible not to admire the reckless bravery of these fanatics,' he later wrote, 'who, dancing and shouting, rushed up to the very muzzles of the rifles with nothing but a knotty stick in their hands, only to fall dead one over the other.'

The killing continued throughout the day. Only at sunset did the last of the Ansar finally withdraw. They had suffered 10,000 casualties. Among them were the Mahdi's two remaining brothers (the other having been killed in May). The garrison had lost only 288 men. The shattered Ansar regiments fell back on their encampment at Kaba. The Mahdi blamed his followers for the disaster: they had been ordered 'to enter the city in an orderly manner from the eastern direction', but instead had broken discipline intent on 'seizing booty'. In the private conclaves of the Mahdist leadership, however, the real lesson of the defeat was heeded. Mysticism could not defeat firepower. Men armed with 'knotty sticks' could not overwhelm entrenched riflemen. Frontal daylight charges against lines of modern regulars were slaughter-pens. Never again would the Ansar be advised to eschew firearms; henceforward re-equipment with captured enemy weapons would be a priority. But, in the short run, too few were available; so El-Obeid was to be invested and starved into submission.[24]

Provisions in the town lasted well for the first two months, supplemented by armed sorties to snatch cattle and sheep from enemy lines, searches for grain in homes abandoned by deserters, and smuggling by entrepreneurs tempted by fast-rising prices inside the town and willing to risk losing their hands if caught by the Ansar.

Then the food began to run out, and, as Yusuf Mikhail recalled, 'we had to eat camels, horses, dogs, cats, etc.' It got worse: 'A month before the town fell, we were reduced to eating the fibre of palm tree, gum, skins, and even the leather of our *angaribs* [native couches/beds].' From the enemy lines came harassing fire – the Mahdi had ordered up more firearms from Jebel Gadir – as well as taunts and appeals to defect. 'We lost a number of men daily from the enemy's fire, but towards the end of the siege, 30 or 40 used to die of starvation at their posts. The men fought well, but we were all heartbroken from want of food.' Defectors now fighting as Ansar shouted appeals to the defenders to give up.[25] Contrary to much hostile propaganda – sometimes repeated uncritically by modern historians – it was not usually Mahdist practice to massacre prisoners. On the contrary: the religious mission was to win converts, trained soldiers were welcome recruits, and it made no strategic sense to leave enemy soldiers with no alternative but a fight to the death.

Prices had skyrocketed in the beleaguered town early in the siege, and the poor had been the first to die. But soon there was little food to be had at any price, and, according to Ohrwalder, once all the camels and cattle had been eaten, 'donkeys, dogs, mice, and even crickets were consumed, as well as cockroaches, which were considered quite tit-bits; white ants, too, were eaten'.

> And now the deaths by starvation had reached an appalling figure. The dead and dying filled the streets; the space within the fortifications being so limited, there was not room for all the people, and in consequence, many lay about in the streets and open spaces. The air was poisoned by the numbers of dead bodies lying unburied, while the ditch was half full of mortifying corpses. Scurvy and dysentery were rife; the air was black with the scores of carrion-kites, which feasted on the dead bodies; these ugly birds became so distended by constant gorging that they could not even fly away, and were killed in numbers by the soldiers, who devoured them with avidity.
>
> Later on, gum became the only food; there was a quantity of this, but it brought on diarrhoea, and caused the bodies to distend – indeed, numbers died from eating it. The ground was dug up in all directions in search of the white ants' nests; and the food which they had collected for the winter was greedily consumed. Some poor sufferers eked out a miserable existence by living on the undigested food found in the excrement of animals. All sorts of leather, shoes, and sandals were boiled and eaten. It was a terrible sight to see these human skeletons – their eyes sunk into the backs of their heads, wandering about in search off food.[26]

The end came on 19 January 1883, after 133 days. The hoped-for relief had never arrived. The town of Bara, 30 miles away, had also been under siege. A relief column of 2,500 men sent out in September had been cut to pieces, and the survivors, about half the total, had then staggered into the town only to join the besieged. Bara, also reduced to eating domestic animals, had surrendered a fortnight before El-Obeid.

The whole of Kordofan was now controlled by the Mahdi. But the reverberations were felt far further afield. The three provinces of Darfur, where the Austrian military adventurer Rudolf Slatin was governor, Bahr al-Ghazal, where the British merchant seaman Frank Lupton was governor, and Equatoria, where the German-Jewish naturalist now known as Mehmed Emin was governor, were effectively cut off from Khartoum with a sea of Islamist insurgency rising around them. All three men had served under Gordon, forming part of his anti-slavery administration: this was now fast unravelling. The Mahdi had become the dominant power in western Sudan, his authority underpinned by a spectacular military victory, his power enhanced by the capture at of 6,000 rifles, 5 cannon, and £100,000 in bullion at El-Obeid. Waverers now rushed to recognise his claim and offer allegiance. His ranks swelled with new recruits – deserters, prisoners, new tribal contingents.[27]

A pause was necessary, however, to reorganise and make ready for an anticipated government counter-offensive. The Mahdi's spies were everywhere; secrets flowed through the Sudan like flour through a sieve. He knew that Abd el-Kader, the newly installed Governor General of Sudan, had issued yet another appeal to Cairo for reinforcements, and he soon had confirmation that these were preparing. This was not yet the moment for a lunge at Khartoum itself. Better that the enemy should be lured from his bases on the Nile, deep into the interior, to be confronted and destroyed in the heartland of the insurrection. So the Mahdi preached holy war to the assembled multitudes in his new capital, and dispatched letters far and wide to the emirs and sheikhs of his domain, calling upon them to rally with their followers to his banner. In the meantime, the administration of the embryonic Mahdist state was expanded, the army enlarged and remodelled, and a new moral order based on *shariya* law imposed.

The Mahdi had already appointed three *khalifas* (the word means 'successor' and therefore 'leader'). These formed his inner cabinet and also commanded the three great divisions of the army. Pre-eminent was Khalifa Abdullahi, effectively the field marshal of the Ansar army, whose division bore the Black Flag of the Mahdi himself, while Khalifa Ali Wad Helu led the division of the Green Flag, Khalifa Muhammad al-Sharif that of the Red. As well as a banner, each division carried a great war drum of deep sound, a *nogara*, made of beaten brass and leather. Under each *khalifa* were ranged the military sheikhs, known as *umara*, who acted as senior officers, each in command of his own tribal contingent; though some of these, like Osman Digna in eastern Sudan, would become major commanders in their own right, in control of military regions.[28] In addition, following the lesson learned from the massacre of Ansar regiments at El-Obeid on 8 September

– and with the grand total of captured rifles estimated at some 20,000 – new units of black 'holy warriors' were formed. These *Jihadiya* – like the *bazingar* contingents of the slave traders – were recruited from black slaves and placed under the command of Hamdan Abu Anja, a former follower of the slave lord Zubeir Rahma Mansour Pasha. Equipped with captured breech-loaders, they became the Mahdi's personal rifle corps.

So the Mahdist army, which had begun as a few hundred religious fanatics armed with spears, swords, and clubs, was evolving into a complex, multi-ethnic, combined-arms force of tens of thousands. Nubian tribesmen of mixed Arab and African ancestry from mud villages along the banks of the Nile provided units of infantry spearmen. The cattle-herding Baggara nomads of southern Kordofan provided first-class cavalry. Other tribes of western Sudan, from the more arid regions, supplied contingents of camel-men. Among all these, some men, the sheikhs, the better-off, carried firearms – hunting weapons, antiquated muzzle-loaders, captured breech-loaders – because the Sudan was full of guns, having long broiled with the violence of the slave trade and tribal warfare; and some of the slave traders brought entire contingents of *bazingars* to Mahdist musters. While the new *Jihadiya*, who would soon number many thousands, provided concentrated firepower for the first time. Elsewhere in Africa, tribesmen sometimes acquired firearms, but, knowing little of their maintenance and operation, made poor use of them. Not so in the Sudan. Not only were many Arabs and their *bazingars* familiar with modern weapons, but large numbers of Turco-Egyptian soldiers, often enough Sudanese conscripts, joined the Ansar after deserting or being taken prisoner, bringing their military skills with them. There was nothing amateur about Mahdist musketry; and this would be a factor in the fighting to come.[29]

The army was the core of the Mahdist state, the civil administration little more than a mechanism for recruiting, arming, and supplying holy warriors. Centralisation of power was essential. The Sudanese were diverse: 600 tribes, 100 different languages, a dozen distinct lifeways. The Turco-Egyptian invasion of 1820 had been the first attempt in modern times to weld the Sudan into a single polity; but then, of course, it had been a colony of foreign overlords. Now it was to be united under its own authority. But common interest in fighting the Turks was not sufficient to overcome an endemic centrifugalism, liable to reassert itself as soon as the colonial power was overturned. The need was for leadership, ideology, and organisation capable of transcending the parochialism of tribal life. This was the historic function of the Mahdi, the theocratic dictator who stood above Sudan's social mosaic, and of Islam, the universal religion that proclaimed the brotherhood of all Muslims. Centralisation – of power, wealth, justice, culture, morals, the whole of social experience – now proceeded apace. The Mahdist regime was constructed as a totalitarian state.

Shocked by a rampage of less-than-ascetic looting when the Ansar tribesmen entered El-Obeid, the Mahdi set up a state treasury, the *Beit al-Maal* ('House of Money'), headed by Ahmad Suleiman, one of his most loyal companions, and ordered that all booty in private possession be handed over. He also established a new system of taxation, the *zakat*, fixed at 10 per cent; ostensibly a voluntary donation, it was effectively compulsory, though with various exemptions and dispensations.[30]

Another appointment was Ahmad Ali as *Qadi al-Islam*, supreme Islamic judge, the head, in effect, of the Mahdist justice department, responsible for the administration of the law. The orthodox Sunni legal systems were set aside in favour of a mixture of traditional tribal law and primeval *shariya*. The various Sufi sects were also abolished. The aspiration was nothing less than a return to the primal Islam of the time of the Prophet, pre-dating the Sunni-Shia schism, a reuniting of all Muslims in a single *umma* ('community'). Books representing alternative traditions were burned. Music and dance were banned. Regulations covered dress codes, wedding expenditure, and personal deportment. Dissent and deviance of all kinds were savagely punished. Thieves had their right hands amputated for a first offence, their left foot for a second. Women caught having sex outside marriage were executed by being buried up to their necks and then battered to death by stones or horses' hooves. Men caught drinking alcohol, smoking tobacco, taking snuff, or using abusive or obscene language received 80 lashes (which, under the blows of the *kourbash*, could be a death sentence). Good citizens were expected to inform on their neighbours. Men were ordered to beat wives, children, and slaves who refused to perform the mandatory five prayers a day. Women were to remain at home, obey their husbands, speak in whispers; women who shouted or uncovered their hair in public risked 27 lashes.[31]

The Mahdist state also facilitated a wholesale resumption of the slave trade. 'It was to the slave-dealers that Muhammad [Ahmad] appeared in the light of a saviour,' wrote Father Ohrwalder, 'and it was to them that he owed his subsequent success.' Numerous slave traders had complained to the Austrian missionary of their ruin since the anti-slavery war in the Bahr al-Ghazal. 'These men were all warriors, accustomed to every description of hardship, well trained in the use of firearms, and from their constant slave fights well accustomed to war; they flocked in numbers to the Dervish, and he gave them elaborate promises of quantities of booty and a complete resumption of the slave trade.' Francis Reginald Wingate came to the same conclusion. A British officer destined to have an exceptionally long involvement with the Sudan between 1883 and 1919, his early work as an intelligence officer provided the opportunity to acquire documents and first-hand testimony concerning the Mahdist movement. Gordon had been 'a scourge' to the slave dealers, Wingate affirmed, and whenever and wherever he was present, the trade had been suppressed. But when he left, the Turco-Egyptian administration had lapsed into indifference, and the slave dealers had again raised their heads. 'He [Gordon] set the house on fire, and Raouf and Abd el-Kader Pashas, who succeeded him, could do nothing but watch the flames.'[32]

The Mahdist state was devoid of any programme of economic development, social reform, or cultural enlightenment; it was a reactionary regime of sheikhs, slave traders, and wife beaters. Gordon and Gessi's campaign against the slave trade, culminating in the defeat, pursuit, capture, and execution of Suleiman Zubeir Pasha, had ruined many powerful men in western Sudan. These now become one of the two foundation blocks of Mahdist power. The movement was an alliance of villagers and nomads, of people who cultivated beans and dates in riverside garden plots, and people who herded cattle, bred camels, and worked the long-distance caravan routes. Taxes were the main issue for peasant villagers, but mattered less to the sheikhs and slave traders of Kordofan and Darfur. The warlike nomadic tribes of the west were not easily taxed; what mattered to them was the slave trade. If Gordon and Gessi had represented an abortive anti-slavery revolution from above, the Mahdi represented a pro-slavery counter-revolution from below.

'Some men are born great, others achieve greatness, some have it thrust upon them. I am to be of the last!' So wrote Colonel William Hicks to his wife Sophia before setting out from Cairo to take up his new post as Chief of Staff of the Army of Sudan. Tall, handsome, grey-bearded, a 53-year-old retired Indian Army officer, Hicks had served with distinction in both the Indian Mutiny and the Abyssinian Expedition, but had never achieved high rank or directed large-scale operations. He had drifted into the Egyptian service – where Evelyn Wood was building a new Anglo-Egyptian Army from scratch following the defeat of Arabi Pasha – and he was recommended when the newly restored Khedive made it known that he was seeking British officers for the Sudanese service. Offered the highest of responsibilities and the rank of major general, Hicks seized his opportunity. His modest career to date may have had something to do with certain deficiencies. He appears to have been somewhat irascible, old school, and lacking in imagination. He was subject to mood swings. The day before his 'greatness' letter, he had confessed to 'feeling anxious as to my ability to conduct all this ... it is rather formidable'. Perhaps he was bipolar.[33]

If he had doubts, they were well founded. The dominant view among senior British officers was that the western Sudan should be given up, and no soldiers of the new Anglo-Egyptian Army – firmly under British control – would be sent there. The restored Khedive – still the nominal ruler of Egypt – had other ideas. His forebears over the previous half century had poured blood and treasure into the Sudan to build an empire. So Tewfik, instead of proceeding with the demobilisation of Arabi's captive soldiers, had them chained, loaded onto cattle-trucks, taken by railway from Cairo to Suez, herded onto steamers and taken down the Red Sea to Suakin, and then marched across the desert to a military encampment at Omdurman. This most unpromising of military material – defeated revolutionaries conscripted to fight a colonial war 1,500 miles from home, some so demoralised they had tried to avoid service in the south by cutting off their trigger fingers or rubbing lime in their eyes to ruin their sight – was to form the core of Hick's army of reconquest. That worthy officer, used to the stern discipline of *sepoy* regiments, had no illusions about the quality of his soldiers. 'The Egyptian is the most hopeless man to make a soldier out of: he has no patriotism, no loyalty, no courage; there is no discipline among them, and neither officer or man has any feeling of honour. It is simply heartbreaking to try to do anything with them – there is nothing to work upon. I cannot tell you how disgusted I am with everything in this place.' Most junior officers proved indifferent and negligent. The senior officers bickered and wrangled. 'I am surrounded by intrigue, deception, and liars,' Hicks complained. Though coloured by the orientalism prevalent among British colonial officers, Hicks was not blind to the invidiousness of his conscripts' situation: 'Here I have 4,000 of Wolseley's *enemies* under my command. He got great kudos for breaking them – my great anxiety is lest they should run away when I take them before the rebels ...'[34]

Nonetheless, things began reasonably well. More recruits and some modern equipment arrived. Hicks imposed a regime of regular drill and musketry practice. His agents scoured the eastern Sudan and secured 4,000 transport camels. He led a large expeditionary force into the Jazira and, on 29 April 1883, fought a major battle at Marabieh, where his riflemen, tight-packed in a dense square, the ground in front sown with iron spikes, machine guns, mountain guns, and rocket launchers at the corners, smashed the charges of up to 5,000 local Ansar. It was all over in half an hour. The enemy lost 500 men, Hicks a mere handful, and the rebellion on the Jazira collapsed as rebel sheikhs arrived in great numbers to make their submission. Victory is a tonic. The soldiers' morale soared, and the small coterie of British officers around Hicks was briefly popular. His enhanced prestige – reinforced by a threat of resignation – enabled Hicks to insist that he be given sole command of the intended advance into Kordofan.[35]

But if victory is a tonic, it is also a drug. Wiser counsels – to the effect that an attempted reconquest of the western Sudan with an army of the size and composition of that commanded by Colonel Hicks was doomed – were set aside. The army marched out of Omdurman on 9 September 1883 on the great expedition. It comprised: 7,000 Turco-Egyptian regular infantry; 1,000 cavalry, mainly Bashi-Bazouks, Shaigiya tribal irregulars, and 100 'Cuirassiers' in chainmail; ten 7-pdr mountain guns, four Krupp field guns, and six Nordenfelt machine guns; 5,500 transport camels and some 2,000 handlers and camp servants.[36] Though only a preliminary march of about 110 miles upriver to the expedition's forward base at Dueim, the problems were immediate. It took place in searing heat, with temperatures rising to 50°C, and after 12 days marching the men were exhausted, many sick, and 150 camels had died from neglect. Six days later, on 27 September, Hicks moved out west, heading into the interior. The mood was sombre. Rumours were rife of the size, fanaticism, and brutality of the Mahdi's forces. Few had any wish to die for the Khedive; most wanted to go home. Many, indeed, were in sympathy with the rebels; not only the Sudanese, but many of the Egyptians, for were the Mahdists not pious Muslims fighting the very same enemies they had themselves faced the year before? Thousands of men trudged west with sinking hearts. 'We plunged into the desert,' wrote a slave boy in the service of an Egyptian officer, 'having turned our backs on the Nile, which the greater part of our soldiers was to see no more. They had commenced their last march, the march from which there was to be no returning. No more would they greet the rising sun, with backs turned to the east; every step they traced on the sand led to the sunset – the sunset of their lives.'[37]

Two strategic dilemmas sealed the fate of Hicks' army. The first involved the choice of route. There were two options: a more direct, northerly route to El-Obeid (the ultimate objective) of about 165 miles; or a more circuitous, southerly route of about 250 miles. Hicks had originally intended to take the former, but his guides persuaded him to divert to the more southerly route, partly because water was more plentiful there, close to the watershed of the Nuba Mountains, and also because the track ran close to the territory of Chief Adam of the Tagalli, a tribe of black highlanders and ironworkers who had successfully defied Mahdist forces for months and were promising to reinforce the government army if it came that way. The northerly route may well have been impossible: the wadis were dry in late summer, and the residual water in the wells and cisterns probably inadequate. But the northerly route was shorter and through open desert, whereas the southerly took the army through a region of forest, dense with acacia and mimosa trees, tangled thickets of thorn scrub, and impenetrable stands of tall grass. This difference would determine the outcome of the battle.

The second dilemma concerned the line of communications. Hicks had planned to establish a series of fortified depots along the line of march in the rear of the advancing army; these were to have secured his supply-line. But senior officers persuaded him that the garrisons would be too small either to defend the posts themselves or to escort transports between them: the enemy was too numerous and active in the territory through which they were to advance. These officers were surely correct: but the implications were ominous. 'So I have now to cut myself adrift from communication with the outer world, and from my supplies,' Hicks wrote. Thousands of tons of provisions had to be left at Dueim, for, without depots along the road, the army could take only what its own baggage-train could manage. This – a huge swaying mass of pack-camels – proved a tremendous impediment. Nor was the column able to resupply itself from the land. Hoped-for support from tribal allies along the track never materialised. Local cattle and food stores were spirited away ahead of the army as it advanced. Thousands of prowling enemies made attempts to forage lethal. So the camels were fed on grain and became sick, or, when this ran out, on the straw pads of their saddles, leaving bare wood to rub great sores on their backs, until they broke down and died, leaving the survivors to bear additional loads. 'The ill-fated army scarcely met a living soul,' reported Father Ohrwalder, 'but flocks of vultures followed them as if waiting for their prey.'[38]

Muhammad Ahmad received regular reports of Hicks' progress. The landscape was saturated with Mahdist spies and scouts; the enemy column itself harboured many sympathisers. All was unfolding according to plan. The southerly route was the preferred one, for the forests offered concealment and protection for the Ansar; it is possible that the choice had been influenced by false intelligence planted by Mahdist agents, for the water was less abundant, and harder to get at, than Hicks had been led to believe. Wells often remained hidden, or were blocked up, or access to them was denied by swarms of enemy skirmishers. The very last dispatch received from any of the Europeans with the column, Edmund O'Donovan of the *Irish Daily News*, reported:

> We have halted for the past three days owing to the uncertainty of the water supply in front. Here we are entirely dependent on surface pools. A reconnaissance of 30 miles forward yesterday by Colonel Farquhar ascertained that the pools were barely sufficient for a rapid march to the village of Serakna, now deserted, where there are a few wells. The enemy is still retiring, and sweeping the country bare of cattle.[39]

A great strategic wisdom had been born at El-Obeid. When some of his followers expressed anxiety about the outcome of the struggle, the Mahdi spat into the palm of his hand and asked them what it was. They answered spittle, and he said, 'We are like the ground and the Turks are like the spittle.' Then he asked where a bird in flight would descend. They answered to the ground, and he said, 'The Turks are like birds and we are like the ground.'[40] This was the nightmare vision of Hicks' officers told in simple parables: the army adrift in a landscape drained of water and stripped of food, yet teeming with hidden enemies in all directions, falling back in front, hovering on the flanks, lapping at the rear. The Mahdi had in fact dispatched 3,000 men under the emirs Abd al-Halim and Abu Girja with orders to rouse the local tribes, harass the enemy, pick off stragglers, and send back regular reports; but under no circumstances were they to attack, for the enemy was to be drawn deeper into the trap, and slowly worn down.[41]

The Mahdi had ordered his army outside the walls of El-Obeid as early as 29 September, forming a great camp of *tukhuls* (huts of mud and thatch) that slowly spread across the plain as fresh contingents arrived in answer to his summons. The fleshpots of El-Obeid, with their harems of women, were now forsaken in favour of holy war, and there were daily manoeuvres and reviews, sermons and prayers, in preparation for battle. The Mahdi had issued a jihadist proclamation as soon as he heard of Hicks' departure from Omdurman on 9 September. In this, he reiterated his identity as the Mahdi, sent by God to defeat the Turks, who were the enemies of God and the Prophet. He announced his mission to conquer the world for Islam. And he extolled the virtues of holy war and promised the joys of paradise to all who fell fighting. He repeated this message to the multitudes as they assembled, eventually 50,000 strong, telling *Jihadiya* riflemen, Baggara nomads, Kordofani camel-men, Nubian spearmen, tribal contingents from the most distant corners of western Sudan, that this was God's holy battle, and that they would be joined by thousands of His angels. On 1 November, as Hicks' column advanced from Rahad through the Forest of Shaykan towards Kashgil, the great Ansar army began its advance to battle. It was an awesome sight, like a scene from the Crusades, a surging mass of Muslim warriors beneath a forest of spear-blades and banners gilded with Qur'anic verses, the air ringing with the old battle-cry, *Allahu akbar!* 'Anyone who saw the enormous hordes of savages which were brought together must have trembled for the fate of Hicks' (Ohrwalder).[42]

First the horses had died. Then the camels. By the end of October, as men stumbled forward in the heat and dust, they did so with mouths dried-out, lips cracked-open. Shadowed by 3,000 Ansar all the way, now, as Hicks' army entered the Shaykan, trying to reach the next watering-place, the enemy mass concentrated for the endgame. The forest, formed of acacia trees and thorn scrub, was so dense that it was impossible for Hicks' square to keep order, while it provided ideal cover for Ansar riflemen, and, in due course, for Ansar shock-troops massing for a charge. The advantage shifted from regulars trained to deliver massed volleys of long-range fire to irregulars who moulded themselves to the ground, moving with its contours and covets, to kill at close quarters.

The fighting began in earnest on Saturday 3 November. Throughout the day, thousands of Hamdan Abu Anja's *Jihadiya* riflemen were deployed as a great swarm of skirmishers in the thickets around the Turkish column. 'So fierce was the fire,' one of them later recalled, 'that all the bark was stripped from the trees and they gleamed white as if washed by soap.' This fire fell upon a close-range target of exceptional density. Hicks had organised his men into a single massive square, a battalion of regular infantry on each face, the camels, stores, and servants sheltering inside, the cavalry on the flanks. This was a textbook formation in colonial 'small wars' when fighting numerically superior and more mobile masses of spearmen like the Zulus. It was designed to prevent the enemy lapping around the flanks to attack the rear and the baggage-train. It was, in effect, a mobile *laager*. But the problems were many. The interior of the square was liable to be heavily congested by the sheer mass of impedimenta. The formation was slow, hard to manoeuvre, and frequent stops were necessary to sort jams and close gaps. It was especially difficult to manage in broken ground. The arrangement in four faces reduced firepower, since attacks tended to come from only one direction at a time, whereas the square offered enemy riflemen a target akin to a football crowd. Ten thousand men, 5,000 camels, shuffling shoulder to shoulder, stumbling through thickets. 'The huge square crawled forwards like a tortoise' (Slatin). All the time, bullets whizzed and thudded. The Egyptian officer's slave boy was terrified: 'Presently, all around, we saw Arabs innumerable; the whole world surrounded us, and [flags] were waving and spears gleaming in the sunshine above the bush. Our square was halted, and we opened fire, killing a great many, but we too lost many. There were too many bushes for the Krupps to do execution, but the machine guns were at work day and night.'[43]

As darkness fell, Hicks ordered a *zariba* constructed, for it was clear that the enemy were now present in vast numbers. But he could not stay put the following day, for his army was dying of thirst. During the chaos of the day, many of the water-carrying camels had been lost outside the square, and the risks had been too great to recover the waterskins; and there was no water to be had where the camp was pitched. They had to reach the wells at Kashgil, still 8 miles distant. Nor did the ammunition situation permit delay. The men were down to 240 rounds each, and it was clear they were going to have to fight their way to El-Obeid, still 30 miles off. To fire off scarce ammunition in static defence was not an option. The camp, in any case, was of limited value. By dawn, the Mahdi's riflemen had crept through the scrub and taken position close to the Turkish lines. Whether Hicks moved or stood, he faced a steady stream of close-range fire. So next morning, the tortoise resumed its advance. And still the Mahdi restrained his men, denying permission for the final all-out assault, determined to grind down the enemy with another day of skirmishing.[44]

'These are bad times,' confided Major Arthur Herlth, the Austrian commander of the Bashi-Bazouks, to his diary.

> We are in a forest, and everyone is very depressed. The general orders the band to play, hoping that the music may enliven us a little; but the band soon stops, for the bullets are flying from all directions, and camels, mules, and men keep dropping down; we are all cramped up together, so the bullets cannot fail to strike. We are faint and weary, and have no idea what to do. The general gives the order to halt and make a *zariba*. It is Sunday, and my dear brother's birthday. Would to God that I could sit down and talk to him for an hour! The bullets are falling thicker . . .

At that point, the diary broke off: Major Herlth had made his final entry.[45]

The third day of battle, Monday 5 November, began like the previous two, only Hicks now deployed his infantry in three squares, set 300 yards apart in a triangular arrangement. The main advantages were that smaller squares were more mobile, and separate squares able to provide mutual support. Hicks and his staff led the way with the four field guns, and the cavalry, as before, covered flanks and rear. But the *Jihadiya* were already in action. 'The ring of encircling Dervishes,' wrote Father Ohrwalder:

> was gradually drawing in and enclosing the ill-fated troops. The greatest destruction was done by Abu Anja's men, who may be said to have destroyed the army; hidden behind shrubs and bushes, they fired incessantly at very close range into the midst of the Egyptians. One of Abu Anja's men told me that he alone had fired 150 rounds . . . Dire confusion prevailed everywhere, the troops were suffering terribly from thirst, discipline was gone, and the men could not even lay their guns properly.[46]

The Mahdi, meanwhile, had paraded the rest of his soldiers, led them in prayers, then drawn his sword and pointed it towards the enemy, crying three times '*Allahu akbar!*' Then he shouted to them: 'You will kill this expedition in less than half an hour . . . because the angels and djinns will fight for you . . . And be afraid of neither their numbers nor their guns and arms, because their souls are already caught in our hands.'[47]

And as the *Jihadiya* fell back, tens of thousands of Ansar spearmen, the men of the Black, Green, and Red Banners, filed through the thickets to launch their final massed assault. The leading square, pushing forward to Kashgil, had reached a wooded depression, when suddenly, all around, Ansar warriors sprang from their hiding places and hurled themselves at the Egyptians, some even rising inside the square from shallow holes in the ground roofed with trapdoors. The front face of the square collapsed immediately before the torrent, and the other faces turned inwards and volleyed into the swirling mass, killing enemies and each other. The two flanking squares also delivered an indiscriminate fire into the shambles of the first. But then the thickets on either flank moved and roared and disgorged thousands more screaming Ansar. And all three formations disintegrated into frenzies of shooting, stabbing, and slashing.

The Turco-Egyptian battalions were slaughtered in their squares, most of the dead clustered in one of three discrete heaps, with a further scatter of corpses for about a mile round about, where men had fled and been cut down. It was all over in about a quarter of an hour. Only a few hundred horsemen escaped, and perhaps a similar number were taken prisoner.

Hicks and his staff, seeing all hope gone, had spurred their horses and got clear of the mayhem, but were run down and surrounded by Baggara cavalry. They made a stand in some cultivated ground by a large tree about half a mile from the main battle, and here, for a while, they held their attackers at bay. Hicks' officers and bodyguard fought with the desperation of doomed men. Hicks, it is said, was the last to fall, emptying his revolver, then slashing with his sword, even launching one savage charge, taking down many of his assailants, before he was killed by a spear thrust.

The wreckage of the column was looted of everything of value. The dead were stripped and left for the vultures and hyenas. The 500 or so Ansar killed were buried with honours, before the day was out, as Islamic practice required.[48] The Mahdi lingered near the battlefield a week longer, taking possession of the plunder, especially the war gear, and then returned to El-Obeid, to make a triumphal entry, preceded by thousand upon thousand of his followers brandishing blood-stained spears and chanting 'There is no god but God'. When he appeared in the procession, riding a magnificent white camel, escorted by fanatical adherents, spectators threw themselves down and kissed the ground, and women shouted 'The Mahdi of God'.[49] Muhammad Ahmad, the Dongola boat-builder's son, was now the greatest power in the Sudan.

# CHAPTER NINE

# A CHRISTIAN MYSTIC

When Charles Gordon resigned as Governor General of the Sudan in January 1880, he did not abandon his anti-slavery mission. Two years on, he was in Brussels, taking service with King Leopold of the Belgians, his mission to join Henry Morton Stanley in the Congo, there to further the abolitionist cause by acting to cut off the trade at its Central African source. A deeply religious and moral man, Gordon's other-worldly naïvety continued undiminished to the end. He placed his trust in smooth-talking hypocrites because they were powerful and he needed to believe in them. Just as the Khedive's advocacy of abolition had never been sincere, nor was that of Leopold, who was, in fact, embarking on a career of grotesque colonial exploitation – it would involve chopping off the arms of children as punishment for failure to deliver their rubber quotas – that would become an international scandal. 'No such efficacious means of cutting at the root of the slave trade ever was presented as that which God has, I trust, opened out to us through the kind disinterestedness of His Majesty,' wrote Gordon to Stanley in anticipation of his departure for the Congo.[1]

Since Sudan, Gordon had experienced a number of false starts. A succession of posts – in India, China, Mauritius, and South Africa – had all proved abortive for one reason or another. He had then embarked on a bizarre archaeological pilgrimage to the Holy Land, spending ten months engaged in field reconnaissance to identify biblical locations, largely through reliance on divine inspiration. Results were communicated by letter to various clerical friends at home. His musings included speculation about the Second Coming, which he expected around AD 2000. By coincidence, Gordon had first arrived in Jerusalem on the very day that another millenarian mystic, 1,300 miles away, one with whom his own fate was to become inextricably entwined, had first entered El-Obeid following its capture by his victorious army (17 January 1883).[2]

King Leopold's telegram giving first notice of a possible Congo assignment had reached Gordon at Jaffa in the autumn. But it was not to be. As Gordon sailed for home, the implications of the Hicks disaster were being widely debated, not least in the pages of the London press. And less than 24 hours after posting a letter of resignation to the War Office, Gordon received an unexpected visit from a short, slight, bearded man with piercing eyes and urgent manner: William Thomas Stead, editor of the *Pall Mall Gazette*, pioneer of a new kind of popular, critical, investigative journalism. What, Stead wanted to know, did the greatest living British authority on the Sudan think should be done? Gordon was reluctant to be drawn, but Stead was tenacious, and soon he had the famous general talking. For two hours, Stead listened and made notes. The following morning (9 January), the front page of the *Pall Mall Gazette* blazed with the headline 'Chinese Gordon for the Sudan' above a full report of its editor's scoop interview. The day after, the rest of the press ran the story, and the chattering classes were agog with the idea that Gordon – only Gordon – was the man of the hour, and that he should, as Stead put it, be sent out: 'to assume absolute control of the territory, to treat with the Mahdi, to relieve the garrisons, and to do what he can to save what can be saved from the wreck of the Sudan.'[3]

The mass-circulation press was a new factor in politics. Upper middle-class readers of *The Times* in the 1850s, learning of the military debacle in the Crimea, or the slave trade in Equatoria, may have been an influence on policy. But this was nothing compared with the information revolution of the late-Victorian period. The growth of trade union organisation and the extension of the franchise to lower middle-class and skilled working-class men had helped to create a mass audience for news. Print media expanded to meet the demand. Circulations rose, a plethora of new publications appeared, and the most popular would have print-runs of a million by the 1890s. The new readers were less privileged and therefore less deferential; here was a mass market for journalism that was more edgy, probing, critical. But in the 'new journalism', alongside currents of socially aware radicalism were other currents of flag-waving jingoism. The scramble for empire, the rise of nationalism, the beginnings of a European arms race that would eventually blow the continent apart, these sentiments, too, found increasing expression, especially at the lower end of the market, in what would soon be called 'the yellow press'. Crucially, jingoism seemed a handy antidote to the socialist politics of the emergent labour movement, especially in the context of 'the Long Depression', with its deep pools of discontent, between 1873

**1 Mid-Victorian Enterprise**
Dr David Livingstone – explorer, abolitionist, celebrity-saint – at work on his journal in the
African interior. The Crystal Palace and the Great Exhibition of 1851 showcased Britain's global
industrial leadership.

**2 The East African Slave Trade**
The slave market in Zanzibar. An Arab slave caravan in western Sudan.

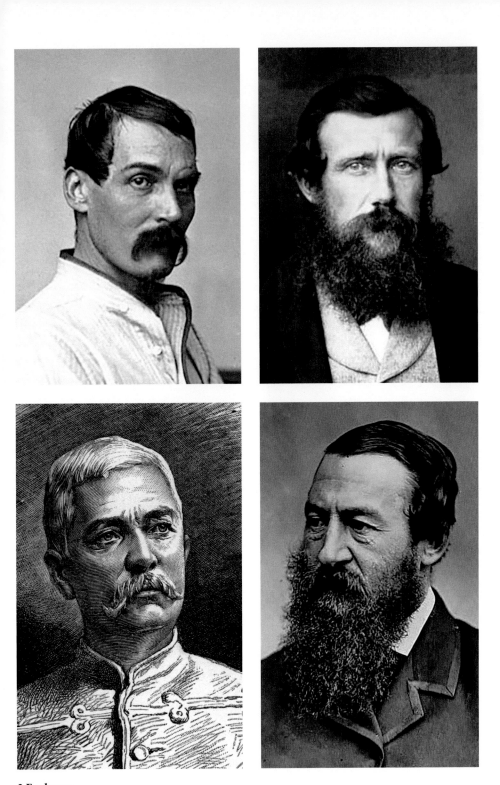

**3 Explorers**
Top: Richard Francis Burton (1821–90); John Hanning Speke (1827–64). Bottom: Henry Morton Stanley (1841–1904); Samuel White Baker (1821–93).

**4 Slavers**
An Arab slave dhow. Cross-section showing the packing of African slaves below deck.

**5 An African King**
Mutesa's capital. Inset: King Mutesa I of Buganda (1837–84).

**6 Finding Livingstone**
Stanley's expedition to find Livingstone crosses the Makata swamp: the rigours of African travel broke the health of many European explorers. The famous meeting between Stanley and Livingstone at Ujiji in November 1871.

**7 The Royal Navy's East Africa Squadron**
HMS *Amazon*, one of a new class of fast armoured steam frigates deployed by the Royal Navy to suppress the slave trade in the Indian Ocean. A Royal Navy pinnace chases down a suspected Arab slave dhow.

**8 The Baker Expedition to Equatoria**
Baker raises the Ottoman flag at Gondokoro on 26 May 1871 and thereby formalises the
Turco-Egyptian annexation of Equatoria. The Battle of Masindi, 8 June 1872: facing a local tribal
insurrection, Baker's micro-army of 120 men was forced to retreat.

**9 Slave Lords**
Top: Barghash bin Said (1837–88), Sultan of Zanzibar; Tippu Tip (1837–1905), Arab-Swahili slave trader. Bottom: Muhammad Ali (1769–1849), ruler of Egypt, conqueror of the Sudan; Al-Zubeir Rahma Mansour (1830–1913), Sudanese slave trader.

**10 Turco-Egyptian Imperialism**
The Khedive Ismail (1830–95). The Khedive Tewfik (1852–92). The *bastinado*: tax-collection in the Sudan was a brutal paramilitary operation.

**11 Abolitionists**
Charles George Gordon (1833–85). Romolo Gessi (1831–81). The emancipation of slaves rescued from a Nile riverboat.

**12 Suez, 1882**
General Sir Garnet Wolseley (1833–1913), commander of the British Army in the Anglo-Egyptian War. Admiral Beauchamp Seymour (1821–95), commander of the British fleet in the Anglo-Egyptian War. The Suez Canal, the British Empire's global choke point.

**13 Industrialised Imperialism**
Admiral Seymour's ironclads bombard the Egyptian forts at Alexandria in July 1882. Royal Navy bluejackets operate a Nordenfelt machine gun from an armoured train.

**14 Armed Counter-Revolution**
Colonel Ahmad Arabia Pasha (1841–1911), leader of the Egyptian Nationalist Revolution of 1882.
'*Vici!!!*' ('I conquered') – John Tenniel's *Punch* cartoon of 23 September 1882 celebrates Wolseley's
victory in jingo style. Wolseley's infantry storm the Egyptian ramparts at Tel el-Kebir on 13
September 1882.

**15 Islamist Insurrection**
Colonel William Hicks (1830–83), commander of the ill-fated Turco-Egyptian expeditionary force
of 1882–3. Muhammad Ahmad, the Madhi (1844–85). Turco-Egyptian soldiers of Colonel Hicks'
army on the march.

**16 A Political Crisis**

Liberal Prime Minister William Ewart Gladstone (1809–98) ponders his options. This cartoon appeared in the *Penny Illustrated* on 11 October 1884; newspaper journalism and public opinion were growing political forces. Khartoum at the time of the 1884–5 siege. The view is looking west, with the Blue Nile in the foreground, the White Nile in the distance. The city fortifications, including the fort at Omdurman on the far side of the river, are clearly shown.

**17 The Gordon Relief Expedition**
Running the Nile cataracts. The logistical strain imposed by distance and the desert were major obstacles to British military intervention in the Sudan. Up against the clock, Wolseley improvised a Camel Corps for a direct dash across the desert ahead of his main force.

**18 British Squares and Modern Firepower**
The Naval Brigade in action against Osman Digna's Hadendowa Mahdists at the Second Battle of El-Teb, 29 February 1884. The Camel Corps in action at Abu Kru, 19 January 1885.

**19 Too Late!**
Brigadier General Charles Wilson's race to
Khartoum on one of Gordon's improvised
gunboats reached the town only after it had
fallen into enemy hands. John Tenniel's *Punch*
cartoon 'Too Late!' on 14 February 1885
expresses the shock to Victorian jingoes.

**20 The Islamist State**
Mahdist emir. The execution of the Batahin.

**21 The Reconquest of the Sudan**
General Horatio Herbert Kitchener (1850–1916), *Sirdar* of the Anglo-Egyptian Army. Kitchener's two-year campaign of reconquest in 1896–8 was an exercise in methodical machine-warfare involving railway building and the massed firepower of steel guns, machine guns, and magazine rifles. E.T. Reed's *Punch* cartoon of 2 December 1893 was entitled 'One of the "Maxims" of Civilisation!'. The British infantry assault at the Battle of the Atbara, 8 April 1898.

**22 Omdurman**
The 12th (Sudanese) Battalion, Anglo-Egyptian Army, await the Mahdist assault at Omdurman on 2 September 1898. Successive Mahdist charges were destroyed by massed firepower.

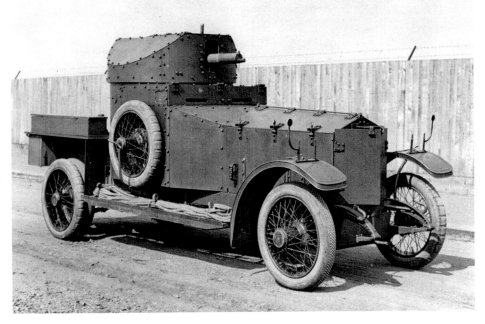

**23 The Anglo-Senussi War (1915–16)**
Senussi warriors marching to war in 1915. Rolls-Royce armoured cars provided mobility,
protection, and firepower during the campaign against the Senussi in 1915 and 1916.

**24 The Anglo-Somali War (1899–1920)**
The Camel Corps of Somaliland in 1913. De Havilland DH9 light bombers helped bring the campaign against the Mullah of Somaliland to a rapid end in 1920.

and 1896. So news became education, entertainment, propaganda, and opiate all at once – with the press not only supplying a ready market, but also, in so doing, shaping public opinion and conjuring political forces.[4]

The creation of celebrities was one aspect of this. The late-Victorian press turned soldiers into 'heroes' of empire. The extraordinary cult that now swelled around the slight, self-effacing person of Charles George Gordon, soon to reach the level of mass hysteria, is perhaps the most overt example – at least until the somewhat similar case of Thomas Edward Lawrence four decades later. The press had in fact both created a problem and proposed a solution. The Liberal government of William Ewart Gladstone had ordered a military takeover of Egypt to protect the Suez Canal and safeguard the profits of London bankers. No remotely comparable interests were at stake in the Sudan, and the government was primarily concerned with its domestic reform programme, not foreign military adventures. But in smashing Arabi and occupying Egypt, the British had inherited an insurgency in the Khedive's southern empire. And the *Pall Mall Gazette* had succeeded in stirring a 'something must be done' jingo storm around this. The *Morning Advertiser* warned that in the event of a massacre of fugitives from Khartoum, 'there would be an outburst of indignation from the civilised world'. The following morning, it spelt out the implication: 'all England has been looking for the employment of General Gordon in the present crisis'. Other Victorian 'heroes' – Samuel Baker and Garnet Wolseley joined their voices to the 'send Gordon' chorus. And, ever alert to popular winds, the Queen let it be known that she was 'very anxious about Egypt'.

Under mounting pressure, Lord Granville, the Foreign Secretary, looked around for a politician's get-out. Well before the press storm broke, Gordon's name had, in fact, cropped up in internal government memos. 'My advice would be,' the Chancellor of the Exchequer had written to the Foreign Secretary, 'to place the whole affair without reserve in Gordon's hands. If the Mahdi is a prophet, Gordon, in the Sudan, is a greater.' Place the whole affair in Gordon's hands: that sounded like a simple solution to a background irritant. Granville decided that Gordon was 'a genius and of splendid character' – albeit marred by 'some eccentricity' – and took soundings. Writing to Sir Evelyn Baring, the new British Consul General in Cairo, he enquired whether Gordon 'might be of use in informing you and us of the situation. It would be popular at home, but there may be countervailing objections'. Popular at home: that was what mattered. The Liberal government wanted a gesture to still the growing clamour for action. Besides, Gordon had proved an effective trouble-shooter in the past; perhaps he could work a miracle now.[5]

Cairo was having its own deliberations. Egypt was now effectively ruled by a British colonial junta of four men. Though lip-service was still paid to the formal independence of the country – and would continue to be until 1914 – this was a convenient political fiction. The Khedive was powerless without the approval of the junta. This comprised, in addition to the Consul General, General Sir Frederick Stephenson, who commanded the British army of occupation, General Sir Evelyn Wood, the '*Sirdar*' of the new Egyptian Army, and General Valentine Baker, the commander of the gendarmerie. Baring, however, was the dominant figure, and would remain so until 1907, when, as Lord Cromer, he finally left Egypt and went into semi-retirement in England. Nicknamed 'Over-Baring', the Consul General was an unashamed Tory imperialist with reactionary opinions about women and 'orientals'. A scion of a top banking family, he had first arrived in Egypt as one of the two foreign 'controller-generals' charged with managing the country's debt. Gordon had noted the obvious conflict of interest and clashed with Baring ('pretentious, grand, patronising') over his own proposal for radical reform to relieve the misery of the *fellahin*. Baring had made it clear that the creditors' interests were paramount. He had proved equally indifferent on the question of slavery. In the business of ruling an empire, men like Gordon were essentially decorative: it was the Baring types who decided.[6]

For this reason – because profit was paramount – the Cairo junta had at first argued for the Sudan to be abandoned. 'They are unanimously of the opinion', went the cable to London on 26 November, 'that the Egyptian government will find it impossible, with the forces at present at its disposal, to hold the Sudan, and that it will eventually be necessary, after withdrawing the garrisons, to fall back from Khartoum on Egypt proper.' Accordingly, Baring at first rejected Granville's suggestion that Gordon be sent out; in particular, he was of the view that, in the context of an Islamic revolt, the appointment of Christians to the Sudan would be counterproductive. But the policy of evacuation was, in the circumstances, bound to be an operation of exceptional difficulty and hazard; so much so, in fact, that the Egyptian minister responsible refused to attempt it. This left Baring with no alternative but to accept the services of a British officer; and there was none better qualified than Charles Gordon.[7]

The decision was now quickly made. Gordon was summoned back from Brussels on the evening of 17 January, and he was at a high-level meeting in the War Office the following afternoon. Wolseley was there, along with Lord Granville, the Foreign Secretary, Lord Hartington, the War Minister, and the only two other government ministers who happened to be in town that day. The meeting was perfunctory: all seemed in agreement as to what should happen. Gordon's instructions – written out in Granville's own hand – were clear. His orders were:

> To proceed to Suakin to report on the military situation in the Sudan and on the measures to be taken for the security of the Egyptian garrisons still holding positions in that country and of the European population at Khartoum. He will consider the best mode of evacuating the interior of the Sudan and of securing the safety and good administration by the Egyptian Government of the ports of the Red Sea coast. He will pay special consideration to what steps should be taken to counteract the possible stimulus to the slave trade which may be given by the revolution which has taken place. Colonel [sic] Gordon will be under the orders of Her Majesty's minister at Cairo and will report through him to H M Government and perform such other duties as may be entrusted to him by the Egyptian Government through Sir Evelyn Baring.[8]

And yet, during this short and apparently conclusive meeting of six men, one whose outcome seemed to have been so succinctly summarised by the Foreign Secretary, a charge of political explosive had been laid whose detonation would shortly rock the country and destabilise the government. To understand why this was so, it is necessary to appreciate three things: first, that different players had different intentions; second, that three separate objectives had become conflated; and that events on the ground would render these unachievable. In any case, the British government was muddled about what it wanted. Prime Minister Gladstone in particular – the most non-interventionist member of his own Cabinet – was misinformed about Granville's instructions and continued to believe that Gordon's mission was merely advisory. Granville and Hartington probably imagined that that was all they had agreed to, but the wording of their instructions rather implied that Gordon was to assume executive power in the Sudan, subject to Baring's authority in Cairo. This, certainly, was how both Gordon and Baring understood matters. The former, who left for Egypt immediately, diverted to Cairo for a conference with the latter, arriving there on 24 January, just six days after leaving Charing Cross. Baring had arranged for Gordon to be appointed

Governor General of the Sudan (by the Khedive), with full plenary powers, (a) to organise the evacuation of the country, and (b) to establish a stable and orderly government. That this was his mission remained Gordon's conviction from the moment he left Cairo for the Sudan on 26 January 1884 to the day of his death in Khartoum precisely one year later.[9]

By the time he reached Khartoum (18 February), Gordon was more convinced than ever that the two executive components of his mission – to evacuate those who wished to leave and to establish a new government authority – were inextricable. More: to do either was almost bound to involve fighting. He had, in fact, already said as much, six weeks before during the *Pall Mall Gazette* interview.

> You have 6,000 men in Khartoum. What are you going to do with them? You have garrisons in Darfur, in Bahr al-Ghazal, and Gondokoro. Are they to be sacrificed? ... How will you move your 6,000 men from Khartoum – to say nothing of other places – and all the Europeans in that city, through the desert to Wadi Halfa? Where are you going to get the camels to take them away? Will the Mahdi supply them? If they are to escape with their lives, the garrison will not be allowed to leave with a coat on their backs. They will be plundered to the skin, and even their lives will not be spared. Whatever you may decide about evacuation, you cannot evacuate, because your army cannot be moved. You must either surrender absolutely to the Mahdi or defend Khartoum at all hazards.[10]

The logic was impeccable. It was the logic of imperial collapse in the face of popular insurgency. There were in total perhaps 24,000 soldiers in 14 separate garrison posts. Many of them had wives and children. There were, in addition, up to 15,000 others – Europeans, native Christians, government employees – who would wish to be evacuated from Khartoum alone. So the minimum number to be moved was perhaps 50,000, and around half these would first have to be brought to Khartoum from various locations across the Sudan – a vast desert country, with primitive communications, now in a state of full-scale war. Ideally, too, government cannon, rifles, and ammunition stores should also be removed. One Egyptian minister had estimated that thousands of camels would be required, and that the operation would take between seven months and a year to complete. Nor was the transport problem the whole of it. Any announcement that Cairo was evacuating its garrisons could be expected to trigger a political stampede in the Mahdi's favour among wavering tribal leaders across the Sudan – unless, that is, a viable alternative government, with its own military resources, could be established. Thus the two substantive parts of Gordon's mission were inseparable.[11]

This explains Gordon's otherwise bizarre plan to establish a government of 'local sultans' in each region under the overall authority of none other than Zubeir Pasha, the former slave lord, who had resided in Cairo under house arrest since 1878. Again, the logic was sound once the 'end of empire' framework was accepted: the Turco-Egyptian colonial regime was finished; the 'local sultans' had ruled before the conquest; and Zubeir was the only Sudanese with a network of connections comparable with that of the Mahdi. Zubeir may have been Gordon's nemesis – embittered against him by the execution of his son – but he was the only other figure of national stature. With alarming consistency, the Governor General argued that, since the slave trade was bound to revive in any case, whoever came to rule the Sudan, it was better to go with Zubeir so that the government garrisons might be saved. (Besides, he told himself, as soon as his immediate mission was accomplished, his plan was to go to the Congo and cut off the trade at source.)

The suggestion, filtered through press and parliament, produced consternation in London. It was inconceivable, of course, that a Liberal government could countenance employing Zubeir as an unofficial colonial viceroy. The scheme came to nothing. But the fact that it was countenanced at all – even securing the support of Baring – was a measure of the contradictions with which Gordon was grappling. Here was a hero of the anti-slavery societies proposing to place Sudan in the hands of a slave lord. (And in fact, even the hope of using Zubeir to save the government garrisons was quite forlorn: unknown to Gordon, his old adversary was already in communication with the Mahdi at El-Obeid.)[12]

The coils began to close at the outset. One prospective 'sultan' – intended as the new ruler of Darfur – having arrived in splendid new uniform with 23 wives and several carriages of baggage, had to be left behind when he began to drink heavily. Another was the Mahdi himself, to whom Gordon addressed a letter offering him the title 'Sultan of Kordofan'; the Mahdi's reply bade the Governor General embrace Islam or prepare to perish. At Berber – a strategically vital river-station 200 miles north of Khartoum – Gordon stopped for two days to confirm the authority of the local governor and establish a council of notables under his presidency; but he fatally undermined the authority of this 'sultan' by confiding the evacuation plan. Something similar happened at Metemmeh, halfway between Berber and

Khartoum, where another petty potentate learned that the government was pulling out. Colonel John Stewart, an officer of the 11th Hussars serving as Gordon's aide-de-camp, had advised against such frankness. Gordon himself later admitted the mistake. Father Ohrwalder thought the Governor General had dealt 'a death-blow to himself and his mission'.

For in bitter truth there were now only two powers in contention: the British Empire and the Mahdi's Islamic *jihad*. The Turco-Egyptian regime's forces were broken, and only British military intervention was now capable of preventing the Mahdi from taking Khartoum. The Sudanese sheikhs not only lacked the power to resist the Mahdi, they had no interest in doing so once it was clear he was going to win, for he posed no threat to the traditional social order. 'How,' asked Hajj Ali Wad Saad, the leading man of Metemmeh, and one held in great respect, 'could I have remained loyal to a government which I knew intended to leave me in the lurch afterwards? I would only have been paving the way for the Mahdi's vengeance.' Though Gordon received a rapturous reception from great crowds of soldiers, government dependents, and local traders when he arrived at the city, this was not for the man alone. As Ohrwalder wisely observed, 'Gordon's name alone could not suppress the revolt, and it was not on account of his name that the Khartoum people rejoiced at his arrival; it was because they looked on Gordon as an English representative, and [assumed] that he was only the precursor of an English expedition to take possession of the Sudan for England.'[13]

Gordon announced a radical programme. Tax arrears were wiped away, and taxes for the coming year halved; the debt records themselves were publicly burned in front of the Governor's Palace, along with the official *kourbashes*. Dozens of chained prisoners were released from jail. The government's abolitionist programme was set aside. 'I know that the hardship which opposition to the slave traffic has caused you is very great,' the Governor General announced. 'Today I desire you to recommence with perfect freedom the traffic in slaves, and I have given orders that public criers shall make this known to all, that they may dispose of their domestics as they may see proper, and no-one in the future shall interfere with the commerce.' The Mahdist army had not yet taken Khartoum, but the slave traders' revolt had already triumphed there. A council of notables was appointed, and measures were taken for the administration of the city and the evacuation of the garrison. All military action against the rebels was suspended, and the gates of Khartoum were left open. This was a peace offensive: an attempt to achieve a negotiated settlement through appeasement.[14]

Gordon's judgement was impaired. He seems to have misread the Mahdi and underestimated the power of his movement; to have exaggerated his own influence over the Sudanese tribes; to have relied too much on his own 'mystic feelings' (his term), while being blind to the 'mystic feelings' animating tens of thousands of Ansar. Father Ohrwalder had a clearer perspective:

> The movement was a religious movement, and was not limited to the Sudan alone; the Mahdi's intention was to subdue the world. He was a prophet, and in his own and the estimation of his followers he was a greater man than the Prophet Muhammad. The world was to come to an end in his time. Had Gordon only known beforehand how boundless was the wild fanaticism, and how completely the Mahdi's followers were intoxicated by it, he would never have accepted the mission.[15]

The stream of telegrams Gordon sent to Cairo, many (though not all) forwarded by Baring to London, bore testimony to a dynamic personality grappling with hopeless contradictions. If Egypt was to be secure, the Mahdi must be 'smashed up'. This could be done if the government sent £100,000 and 200 Indian troops to Wadi Halfa. Later he suggested 3,000 Sudanese 'black troops' could do it. Meanwhile, the evacuation had begun, but completion would be impossible 'until government asserts its authority'. Again, he proposed Indian troops, now to open up the Suakin–Berber route, with some British troops at Wadi Halfa. 'I will do my best to carry out my instructions,' he cabled on 1 March, 'but I feel a conviction I shall be caught in Khartoum.' Again and again, he returned to the question of Zubeir. 'If you do not send Zubeir,' he messaged on 8 March, 'you have no chance of getting the garrisons away.' That same day, he sent a detailed military appraisal to Baring: 'I hear that the Mahdi has raised the tribes, who will try to cut the road to Berber. Tribes will try cut off supplies from Khartoum; will cut telegraph. They will not probably attack directly . . . We have provisions for six months.' Three days later, he wrote to his sister Augusta: 'This may well be the last letter I send you, for the tribes have risen between this and Berber and will try and cut our route. They will not fight us directly, but will starve us out . . .'

The following day, 12 March, the line went dead: a force of up to 5,000 Ansar had swooped on Halfaya, 9 miles downriver from Khartoum, captured the town, and cut the telegraph. The siege of Khartoum had begun.[16]

Communications had never been good in the Sudan. Except for steamboats on the river and a handful of telegraph lines (easily cut), information was transmitted, if at all, at the speed of a camel. Increasingly, though, it was not transmitted at all, for the insurgency was blocking the overland routes. The wheels of decision-making, in any case, tended to move slowly in the late nineteenth century. Gentlemen politicians liked to spend time at their clubs and country seats: ministers were often absent from government offices. The decision to send Gordon had been made at a meeting of the only four ministers who happened to be in London at the time. Besides, major decisions were usually contentious, and where many rancorous men were accorded a voice, as they tended to be in a parliamentary democracy, decisions were liable to be delayed. In short, events were now happening in distant Sudan faster than information could be processed and decisions made in London. In the 14 months between the defeat of Hicks and the fall of Khartoum, the British imperial class was to be consistently behind the curve.

The defeat of Hicks had, in fact, been a decisive event. The capture of El-Obeid in January 1883 had made the Mahdi master of Kordofan. The defeat of Hicks in November 1883 had made him master of the Sudan. When Gordon reached Khartoum four months later, this was obvious, for Darfur, Bahr al-Ghazal, and the Red Sea coast had by then all fallen to local Ansar insurgents.

In the summer of 1882, the Mahdi had appointed a local sheikh of the Rizeigat tribe, Madibbu Ali, to lead the uprising in Darfur. Under his leadership, it had quickly swelled into a conflagration. The Governor, Rudolf Slatin, suffered a major disaster as early as October 1882, when his main field force – 550 regulars, 1,300 *bazingars*, and 6,000 tribal spearmen – was ambushed and virtually annihilated on its way to establish a new government post at Shakka in the Rizeigat country. The Battle of Om Waragat, fought in an area of bog and scrub, bears comparison with the disaster that befell Hicks a year later. Slatin's *bazingars*, armed with old muzzle-loaders, managed only a single volley before being hit by a fanatic charge. The better-armed regulars were unable to prevent the government square collapsing into chaos. The tribal levies on the flanks fled in all directions and were cut down by Rizeigat horsemen. Though Slatin retained control of a contingent of regulars whose concentrated Remington fire eventually drove the attackers back, his command had been reduced to 900 men in just 20 minutes of fighting. These losses were irreplaceable, and the governor was forced to barricade himself behind the walls of Dara. With insufficient men, ammunition running low, and fifth columnists ubiquitous, his position was desperate. Even his deputy, Muhammad Khalid, defected to the Mahdi: he was immediately appointed Emir of Darfur and sent back to take charge of operations against his former colleague. Slatin held out in the hope that relief would come. But news of the destruction of Hicks' column confirmed that the garrison was doomed. The governor surrendered on 23 December 1883. Al-Fasher, the provincial capital, caved in a fortnight later. Well before Gordon's arrival at Khartoum, the whole of Darfur was in Mahdist hands.[17]

In his desperation, Slatin had smuggled letters to Frank Lupton, Governor of Bahr al-Ghazal, appealing for help: there was none to be had, since Lupton was also cut off and faced a rising tide of insurrection. Here was the front line of the East African slave trade, where Arab *jallaba* had their compounds of grass huts and prisoner cages from which armed *bazingar* detachments would raid deep into the surrounding bush in the hunt for black Africans. Here, Gessi's anti-slavery war had ruined many. Here, as much as anywhere, the Mahdi's message found keen listeners. Even so, the struggle see-sawed for a year, until the arrival in late November 1883, following the destruction of Hicks, of Karamallah al-Sheikh Muhammad, the newly appointed Mahdist Emir of Bahr al-Ghazal, at the head of 5,000 men. Like Slatin at Dara, Lupton was compelled to abandon the countryside and hole up at Deim Suleiman, behind a 20-foot wooden stockade, with cannon platforms at the corners and rocket tubes by the gates. But his 1,200 regulars preferred surrender to a Muslim army to a fight to the death under a Christian. Just as Slatin had appealed to him for help, Lupton wrote in desperation to Emin Pasha, the Governor of neighbouring Equatoria. 'The Mahdi's army is now encamped six hours' march from here,' he explained.

> Two dervishes arrived here and want me to hand over the *mudiria* [province] to them. I will fight to the last . . . I will, I hope, from my fort, be able to turn them out again . . . Perhaps this is my last letter to you. My position is desperate, as my own men have gone over to them in numbers . . . I win the day or die, so goodbye . . . If steamers come to you, write to my friends and let them know I died game.

But Lupton did not die game: he was persuaded by anxious subordinates to surrender his post, which he did on 28 April 1884, becoming, like Rudolf Slatin, a prisoner of the Mahdi.[18]

No outside help had reached either Slatin or Lupton because the insurgency had by now swept across the whole of central Sudan. In the east, the tribes had risen under the leadership of Osman Abu-Bakr Digna, the grandson of a Kurdish merchant and slave trader who had settled in the region in the early nineteenth century. The family business – they dealt in cutlery, cotton, gum, ivory, pepper, ostrich feathers, and slaves – had been headquartered at Suakin with branches at Berber, Khartoum, Kassala, and Jedda. Central to its operations had been slave trafficking across the Red Sea between Suakin and Jedda. But Gordon's operations against the caravans in the interior and British naval action against slave dhows at sea during the late 1870s had wrecked the trade. A rich man facing ruin, Osman had spent years arguing for rebellion, denouncing the collaboration between the Khedive and the British. 'Ismail is a Frank!' he was reported saying. 'He is a traitor to the Prophet, and has leagued with infidels to destroy the customs of Islam; and the Christians wish the liberation of our slaves that they may possess them.'

The Suakin slave trader became an early adherent of the Mahdi. He belonged to a Sufi brotherhood, the Majdhubiya, the head of which had been in communication with Muhammad Ahmad even before the latter's *hijra* from Aba Island. Osman had married into the Hadendowa tribe of the Beja people, many of whom were also adherents of the Majdhubiya, and this religious-tribal nexus formed the basis of the Mahdist movement in the region following Osman Digna's appointment as Emir of Eastern Sudan. 'I have sent you Sheikh Osman Digna to help you uphold religion and fight the infidels,' read the Mahdi's open letter to the people of the province.

I have made him a blessed emir over you and over all the nomadic peoples and natives of Suakin province, so that he may lead and guide you, uphold the Faith, and revive the *Sunna* of the Lord of the Prophets and Apostles. Listen to him and obey both his commands and prohibitions! Stand by him. Support and swear allegiance to him. He who swears allegiance to Sheikh Osman swears allegiance to me. He who is martyred while with him is deemed to have been martyred while with me.

The core of the tribal army of thousands that now assembled in the Erkowit Hills west of Suakin were the formidable warriors of the Hadendowa. They were big-boned, bounding men, their frizzy hair glued into crests and plaits (the British would dub them 'fuzzy-wuzzies'), their clothing often limited to cotton trousers, though now with Mahdist-style coloured patches. They carried round leather shields and fought with daggers, boomerangs, short stabbing spears, and long, straight, wide, double-bladed swords; but they would adopt firearms when they could get them. Osman's appeal was not restricted to his fellow tribesmen, however. The Mahdist insurgency was approaching its peak, an intoxicating mix of tax rebellion, slave traders' revolt, religious fanaticism, hatred of the oppressor, and expectations of victory – a mix that percolated not only through the tribes, but also into the garrisons and medinas of the Red Sea ports.[19]

Suakin was pre-eminent. It consisted of an old town built on a coral island in a salt-water lagoon connected by causeway to a newer, bigger, walled suburb on the mainland. The lagoon provided a sheltered habour, but was too shallow for large vessels, so these would anchor in a coastal bay at the far end of the neck of water, three-quarters of a mile long and 500 yards wide, that connected the lagoon with the sea. Though also an administrative centre, Suakin was primarily an emporium, the lives of its 8,000 inhabitants shaped by the caravan routes that extended to Berber on the Nile, 240 miles to the west, to Abu Hamed and Wadi Halfa to the north-west, and to Kassala and Gallabat to the south. Beyond the port lay a sandy plain, dissected by nullahs and spotted with thorn scrub, extending as far as the foot of the Erkowit Hills, about a day's journey away.

Into this zone of broken ground projected a tenuous Turco-Egyptian bridgehead about 50 miles wide anchored on the garrison towns of Sinkat to the west, Tokar to the south, and Trinkitat down the coast from Suakin. But this position was not in the least secure: the area between the government posts was infested with Mahdists. On 16 October 1883, a column of 160 soldiers on their way to reinforce Sinkat was attacked and destroyed; only 25 survived. On 4 November, a column of 550 dispatched to relieve Tokar was routed, losing 160 men. A further attempt to relieve Sinkat on 2 December, this time 700 strong, resulted in an even greater disaster, with only 35 survivors. By now, though, a Turco-Egyptian expeditionary force of 3,500 men was on its way. It was commanded by General Valentine Baker Pasha.[20]

Valentine Baker, the younger brother of Samuel Baker, had been a professional army officer. But he had been dismissed from the service after being convicted and imprisoned for sexually assaulting a young woman in a railway carriage. Taking service with the Ottoman Empire, he had recently, since Arabi's defeat, been appointed commander of the Egyptian gendarmerie. The order to proceed to the Sudan was deeply unpopular with his men. Many officers resigned, many of the rank and file absconded; the morale of those herded onto transports was rock-bottom, their mood insubordinate and mutinous. Their attitude darkened further upon arrival, when the Egyptian policemen encountered the traumatised survivors of previous debacles, heard chilling tales of the numbers and fanaticism of the enemy, and became aware that government support in the region had just collapsed with the news that the British were pulling out. Nonetheless, augmenting his force of gendarmes with a ragbag of detachments, irregulars, and local recruits, supported by four small guns and a couple of machine guns, Baker set out at the head of about 3,000 men intent on driving the enemy away from Tokar.

The task was hopeless. It was not an army, but a rabble. When the clash came, on 4 February 1884, Baker's attempt to advance in three squares folded into a disorderly jumble of men and beasts. A thousand Ansar emerged from scrub and sand hills near the wells of El-Teb and charged the Egyptian gendarmerie on the right side of the government formation. Facing only ragged fire, most of it high, some hitting other Egyptians, the Ansar came on fast and furious and were among their enemies inside a minute, cleaving and spearing through a disintegrating mass. Most of the policemen threw away their arms and attempted to flee. Some simply cast themselves down and waited to be killed. Few tried to defend themselves. The European officers, some of the Turks, a fair few Sudanese stood their ground; but they were islands in a torrent of panic and mayhem. Baker, some other officers, most of the cavalry, a number of the more fortunate fugitives on foot managed to get away; but the bulk of the infantry were cut down, around 2,300 in all.[21]

The First Battle of El-Teb was a disaster on the scale of Shaykan, and Osman Digna might have swept away the foreign lodgement at Suakin but for the cannon of British ships offshore and a party of marines and blue-jackets landed to enforce martial law. Under this umbrella, fragments of the shattered Turco-Egyptian forces gathered, eventually 3,800 men in all. But these were of little military value, being either broken by defeat and desperate to go home, or openly mutinous and in sympathy with the rebels. Beyond the perimeter, the Mahdists held dominion. On 12 February came news that Sinkat – the defenders having been reduced to eating first camels, then cats and dogs, finally roots and leaves – had been captured and the garrison of 450 men annihilated. On 24 February, it was learned that Tokar had also fallen – though in this case, the commandant and the bulk of his soldiers with all their equipment had gone over to Osman Digna. The Tokar commandant had been a supporter of Arabi. Now he told his men that it was better to fight with Muslims against Christians than with Christians against Muslims. They had needed little persuading. So the Mahdist Emir of Eastern Sudan was riding high, his army swelling to 10,000 or more as previously wavering sheikhs committed themselves, his arsenal of captured weaponry now including four Krupp field guns, two Gatling machine guns, up to 5,000 Remington breechloaders, and half a million cartridges, his ranks swelled by a growing cohort of former Turco-Egyptian soldiers trained in the use of modern weapons.[22]

This near-total collapse of Turco-Egyptian power on the Red Sea coast prompted swift and substantial British military action. On 18 February, the very day of Charles George Gordon's arrival at Khartoum, another senior British officer, Major General Gerald Graham, had departed Suez bound for Suakin. And whereas Gordon had been dispatched as lone warrior, Graham was to assume command of a British battle-group of 4,000 men. For the decision to evacuate the Sudan did not, in fact, extend to the Red Sea littoral. The Khedive wanted to retain this sliver of the former Turco-Egyptian Empire in the Sudan, and his British overlords were prepared to underwrite the attempt, partly from a general concern to contain jihadist subversion, partly from a specific concern with the maritime security of the Red Sea. Following the Hicks disaster, Baring had advised evacuation of the rest of the Sudan, but had informed the Egyptian Prime Minister that the British would assist in the defence of both Egypt and the Red Sea ports: Mahdism was to be corralled within the Sudanese wilderness. Initially, however, such assistance had been restricted to the use of British ships to transport troops and guard the ports. The land fighting was to be done by Turco-Egyptian forces raised for the purpose by the Khedive. This policy had been wrecked by Baker's destruction at El-Teb. The British were left with little choice but to send an army or allow the Red Sea to be infested with jihadist pirates.[23]

Nor was that London's only concern. Defeats, like victories, can be contagious; and news of the British Empire's Sudan troubles – coming so soon after Isandlwana, Maiwand, and Majuba Hill – might encourage disturbances elsewhere. As one contemporary British chronicler recorded:

Our government then resolved to send troops to Suakin for a serious contest against Osman Digna, one of our main objects being to counteract the evil effect, on the minds of Muhammadan subjects in India, of

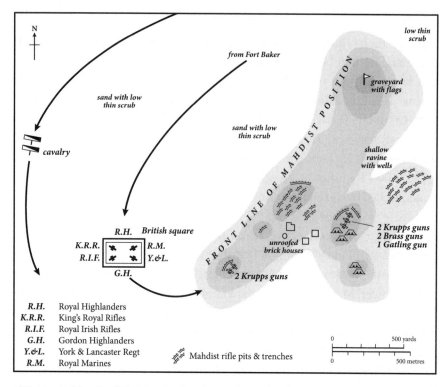

N

*low thin scrub*

*from Fort Baker*

*graveyard with flags*

*sand with low thin scrub*

F R O N T   L I N E   O F   M A H D I S T   P O S I T I O N

*sand with low thin scrub*

*shallow ravine with wells*

cavalry

R.H.   **British square**

K.R.R. ⊞ R.M.
R.I.F.    Y.&L.

G.H.

*unroofed brick houses*

2 Krupps guns
2 Brass guns
1 Gatling gun

2 Krupps guns

**R.H.**     Royal Highlanders
**K.R.R.**   King's Royal Rifles
**R.I.F.**   Royal Irish Rifles
**G.H.**     Gordon Highlanders
**Y.&L.**    York & Lancaster Regt
**R.M.**     Royal Marines

Mahdist rifle pits & trenches

0        500 yards
0        500 metres

6. The Second Battle of El-Teb, 29 February 1884

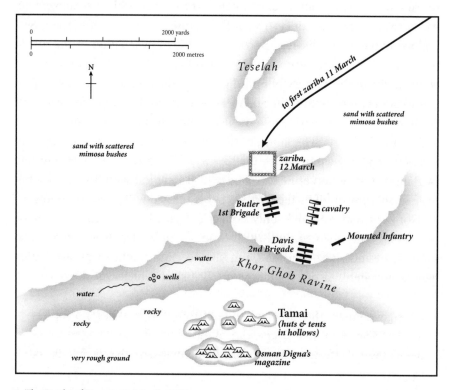

0        2000 yards
0        2000 metres

N

*Teselah*

*to first zariba 11 March*

*sand with scattered mimosa bushes*

*sand with scattered mimosa bushes*

zariba, 12 March

*Butler 1st Brigade*

cavalry

*Mounted Infantry*

*Davis 2nd Brigade*

*Khor Ghob Ravine*

water

wells

water

rocky

rocky

**Tamai**
(*huts & tents in hollows*)

very rough ground

**Osman Digna's magazine**

7. The Battle of Tamai, 13 March 1884

repeated defeats inflicted by the Arabs, not indeed on British forces, but on armies led by British officers. The rumour was arising in the bazaars of the East that the arms of Britain were being beaten from our hands by soldiers fighting under the banner of Islam.[24]

※

General Graham's battle-group arrived even before the news that Tokar had fallen, so his first effort was directed to the relief of the garrison. Even when the truth was out, having already moved his force to Trinkitat, he chose to continue with the original plan of marching on Tokar. British military doctrine in colonial 'small wars' stressed aggressive strategy based on thorough logistics and clear intelligence The aim was to advance as soon as possible, throw the enemy onto the defensive, and, ideally, break the will to resist in a single decisive blow. It was often of secondary importance where the blow fell: the main thing was to bring the enemy's principal forces to battle and destroy them. So Graham's decision to go onto the offensive against the large Mahdist presence around Tokar was an orthodox procedure.[25]

Several days were spent establishing a forward base, Fort Baker, and transporting there a three-day supply of water and rations for the whole army. On the night of 27 February, the army bivouacked at Fort Baker, aware that the Mahdist army lay a few miles distant, at its former position near the wells of El-Teb, where it was entrenched on a low ridge amid hillocks, scrub, and one or two mud-brick buildings.

The night was unsettled: the enemy fired occasional shots, it rained heavily in the early hours, and the soldiers knew they would fight in the morning. The Mahdists had a fearsome reputation, and this would be the first clash with British troops. The *reveille* bugle was a relief: the waiting was over. Breakfast was eaten, the camp cleared, and at 8 o'clock the army began its advance. It was formed into a giant rectangle, two brigades strong, Gordon Highlanders in front, Royal Irish Fusiliers and King's Royal Rifles on the right face, York and Lancasters and Royal Marines on the left, Black Watch at the rear. Gatlings and Gardners were deployed at the front corners, field guns at the rear corners. Mounted scouts moved ahead and on the flanks, with the main mass of the cavalry, 10th and 19th Hussars, coming up behind. All told, there were around 4,000 men, 800 camels, and 350 mules.

Coming abreast of the Mahdist line along the ridge, the British square was peppered with fire from Krupps and Remingtons. It moved wide, passing the enemy front at about 400 yards distance on the right, ready at any moment to scramble its carefully aligned columns into line to face a charge. None came. Osman Digna was too canny a fighter to hurl his men across an open killing-ground. Mahdist tactics were to fight from cover, in loose order, harassing the enemy with fire, launching assaults in sudden, fast, last-minute rushes. But there was a second element to Graham's plan: to manoeuvre right past the Mahdist position, swing around its far flank, and then storm into the rear. As they did so, the British regulars closed into a compact mass, preparing for the close-range charges they would face as they entered the labyrinth of mounds, pits, and thorn bush where the enemy was posted.

From all directions, again and again, groups of Mahdists rose up to hurl themselves at the intruders, only to be mown down by the massed fire of breechloaders and machine guns. 'The Arabs, nearly naked and yelling fearfully,' recalled one sailor:

> came on for the Black Watch, behind whom were most of the bluejackets, with terrible impetuosity, their object being to break the ranks and then do their bloody work in the *mêlée*. Most of them were tall broad-chested fellows, with the fierce glare of wild beasts in their black eyes ... The Gatlings played fearful havoc among them ... Some of the rebels planted themselves firmly at weak points of their defences, and there used their great heavy swords with dreadful effect until shot down or bayoneted by the Highlanders. Again and again, the Arabs rushed on, but only to fall under the hail of bullets, or the stabs and slashes of bayonet or sword. The whole force kept well together, and fought its way right through the rebel position.

It was a one-sided contest: the raw courage of traditional warriors pitted against the mechanised killing of an industrialised empire. The only glitch from Graham's perspective was a premature and costly charge by his cavalry. Brigadier General Stewart had been ordered 'to avoid engaging the enemy until their formation was broken and until they were in full retreat'. Long before this, however, the two regiments of British light cavalry had been led around the square to a position on the right flank. Seeing numbers of the enemy on the plain east of the ridge, they had been formed into three lines and ordered to charge. Cavalry train for years in anticipation of such an opportunity: the temptation to attack can be overwhelming. But the enemy formations were loose, the Sudanese tribesmen agile, and a halt had to be called after a 3-mile gallop, with little achieved. Then it was discovered that the third line – 100 men of the 10th Hussars among the brigade's 740 horsemen – had failed to complete the charge and were being 'cut up' by a large contingent of tribesmen who had appeared out of the scrub. A hundred or so rode bareback and wielded long swords. Behind them came a great mass of spearmen. Lieutenant Colonel Barrow, in command of the second line, wheeled his men around and charged again. The result was a chaotic *mêlée* in which the real threat was posed by spearmen who had gone to ground and were lurking amid the hillocks and bushes, using boomerangs or blades to bring down horses, occasionally stabbing upwards with their short *assegai*-like spears, or rising to cast a spear at the back of a passing trooper; whereas the sabres of the Hussars could not reach men hugging the sand.

Three officers and 20 men were killed and a similar number wounded before the vicious little struggle of the British light cavalry was over. The proportion of fatalities was high: once a man was unhorsed, his prospects were poor. British casualties for the battle overall were 30 killed and 140 wounded. Sudanese casualties may have exceeded 1,000, with most of the wounded shot or bayoneted by the victors, for reports were widespread after the battle of fallen warriors, whether feigning death or oblivious of wounds, rising to strike down infidels who offered succour. The letters, diaries, and memoirs of British participants often recalled the fanatic courage of the enemy. Percy Marling, a veteran who served in the mounted infantry detachment of the King's Rifles at El-Teb, considered the action 'one of the hottest I have seen' and the Hadendowa tribesmen 'the pluckiest fellows I've ever seen'. But no quarter was given: 'We shot or bayoneted all wounded because it wasn't safe to leave them, as they speared or knifed everyone they could reach.'[26]

But Graham's 'shock and awe' did not have the intended effect. Following the battle, he and Admiral Hewett issued a proclamation to the local tribes promising redress of wrongs, describing Osman Digna as a 'notorious scoundrel', and pooh-poohing 'the foolish idea that the Mahdi has come to earth'. They received their reply a week later: a letter signed by 21 sheikhs rejecting the British peace offer and asserting that they stood at the head of 10,000 men. This was no idle threat: it was already clear that large numbers of Mahdists were assembled at Tamai, about 16 miles south-west of Suakin, and that El-Teb had changed little in the strategic configuration on the Red Sea coast. So the day after receipt of the sheikhs' letter, Graham launched a second expedition, this time from Suakin. He again established an advanced post and pushed forward supplies, before marching forth with his main force on 11 March. The following morning, scouts reported a heavy enemy presence ahead. Graham advanced as far as the Tamai Valley, where up to 4,000 enemy were reported, and camped for the night. Again, the British passed a disturbed night, punctuated by shots and alarms, on alert against a sudden rush, aware of the imminence of battle.

The Battle of Tamai on 13 March was almost a disaster. At 8 o'clock in the morning, the British advanced in two squares, Davis's 2nd Brigade on the left, supported by the cavalry, with Buller's 1st Brigade 800 yards to the right rear. The bulk of the enemy was believed to lie concealed in a deep *khor*, a dried-up watercourse, about a mile ahead. As the British approached, some hundreds of skirmishers in rocks and scrub above the depression commenced an inaccurate long-range fire. The advance was very slow and deliberate, with stops to dress ranks; for movement in square is a tricky business. By 9 o'clock, 2nd Brigade was within about 200 yards of the *khor*. A series of minor rushes were beaten back by fire. Then, for whatever reason, Gerald Graham lost his reason and issued a near-fatal order. The Black Watch, who formed the left front and left side of Davis's square, were ordered to charge. When they did so, the York and Lancasters to their right joined the rush forward. But only half of each regiment was involved; the respective halves forming the left and right sides of the square received no orders and remained where they were. The effect was similar to taking the lid off a box: the whole interior of the square was opened up.

The charge slowed at the edge of the *khor*, and the British infantrymen commenced firing as they advanced, scattering the Mahdists to their immediate front. But only 500 redcoats had joined the charge, and many of the several thousand jihadists in and on the far side of *khor* now surged forward on the right, their sudden onrush partly hidden by clouds of black-powder smoke hanging over the battlefield. Everything now happened very fast. With their flank turned by hundreds of enemy warriors, the York and Lancasters tumbled backwards in confusion towards the Royal Marines at the rear of the square. This exposed the flank of the Black Watch, who also recoiled, the whole movement, according to one correspondent, 'resembling the slow swing of a door on its hinges'. Naval machine guns run forward in an attempt to halt the onslaught had to be abandoned. The interior of the square filled with a surging mass of Sudanese warriors fighting with spears and swords against little knots of redcoats standing back-to-back and firing point-blank or thrusting with bayonets. One officer compared the chaos to a rugby scrum. Attempts to improvise a line failed, the Royal Marines were forced to retreat, the broken fragments of the Black Watch and the York and Lancasters conforming; despite every effort of frantic regimental officers, the whole brigade was driven rearwards about 800 yards.

But none of the three regiments broke and ran; that they did not is a testimony to the extraordinary discipline and professionalism of the British armed services – and also perhaps to the excellence of the Martini-Henry, a combined firearm and pike, which soldiers could continue to load and fire between bayonet thrusts even as they fought hand-to-hand. The brigade – its formation shattered, its ranks decimated, its soldiers traumatised – survived as a fighting unit.

Graham and his staff were now on the scene, rallying the men, organising one group of 150 into a mini-square. Highland officers also succeeded in organising one or two smaller clusters. Around these improvised islands of resistance, the rest of the shattered regiments reformed. The process took about 20 minutes. What made it possible – what provided the necessary respite – was the steadiness of Buller's 1st Division. Advancing in echelon at the right rear, Buller's square had clear fields of fire in all directions, and though the Mahdists flowed around it, so that eventually all four sides were engaged simultaneously, no enemy warrior got nearer than about 80 yards without being shot down. Formed shoulder to shoulder, the British infantry fired volley upon volley, each crash of shot cutting down a great swathe, leaving the plain black with dead and dying. As the assault faded away, Buller resumed his advance; and soon, with 2nd Division reassembling, and Stewart's cavalry on the left, the Mahdists found themselves under a converging fire from three directions. At 10.30 a.m., the British commenced a general advance, this time a measured combination of fire and movement, with halts to blast away threatening clumps of flags and spearheads in the scrub punctuating a slow and steady progress across the plain, through the *khor*, and up the slopes beyond. The demoralised Mahdists melted away in front of Graham's little army. From the top of the ridge on the far side of the *khor*, Osman Digna's camp could be seen, and before midday it had been captured and set alight.

Tamai had been a close-run thing for the British. The order to charge a hidden enemy thousands-strong had led to the collapse of a square. The British had lost 91 killed, 110 wounded, 19 missing; 70 of the dead had fallen during the breaking of Davis's square, for any who went down were quickly finished off. The Mahdists may have lost as many as 2,000. Of these, some 600 were counted on the site of the broken square. The disparity in casualties here – 70 British against 600 Mahdists – is testimony to the superiority of breechloader and bayonet over spear and sword in close-quarters fighting.[27]

The Mahdists had suffered up to ten times the casualties of the British at El-Teb and Tamai combined. In other circumstances, this disparity might have been decisive. The Anglo-Zulu War of 1879 had been ended within six months by a single crushing victory at Ulundi. Here were two blows, swiftly delivered and extremely violent, of the kind that British small-wars doctrine expected to break the enemy's will to resist. Graham had hoped at least to secure Suakin and the Red Sea coastal region, perhaps even to collapse the revolt across eastern Sudan as a whole and open the road to Berber. Yet nothing of the sort happened. Osman Digna was still at large. The Mahdist tribal alliance endured. The interior of eastern Sudan remained beyond the reach of British military power. And within a year, the British would again be fighting pitched battles in the immediate vicinity of Suakin. The Anglo-Sudanese War had only just begun.

The mythic archetype of 'the hero' was reconfigured in the age of empire. Charles George Gordon was perhaps the most consummate example of the new class of hero. It was, of course, the persona that mattered, not the person. Gordon in fact was a repressed homosexual who suffered from bipolar disorder and religious mania.[28] Gordon imagined was another matter: a lone, white, Christian warrior – one cast in the form of a medieval Crusader knight, but bearing the modern banner of abolitionism – setting forth to face the dark heathen hordes. Through him, the racism and militarism of late-Victorian jingoism could be sublimated as a civilising mission. Here was a living symbol of 'the White Man's Burden' before the poet could coin the term.[29] And because other European nations also were building empires in Africa and Asia, and because Gordon, a maverick and a mystic, seemed to embody a kind of white evangelical universalism that transcended anything particularly English, he could stand proxy for all colonial land-grabs. 'The achievements and romantic elevation of his character,' wrote a Viennese journalist a few days after his departure from Cairo, 'have made General Gordon's name as familiar here as in England.'[30] So it was across Europe, now and for the next year, as the distant hero battled the forces of barbarism, a quest soon elevated to impending tragedy as his fate hung in the balance. British imperial prestige was, of course, caught in this glare of international spotlights; and this – when the whole of empire was bluff, an impression of power in which few overawed many – was a factor in the political row that now engulfed William Gladstone's Liberal government and almost carried it to oblivion.

The debate really began in the wake of Graham's victory at Tamai. Gordon had argued that a route could be opened between Suakin and Berber that would enable both the evacuation of personnel and the establishment of a new native government. Some senior officers deemed an advance across the desert by Graham's little army of 4,000 men possible but risky. Baring reported this judgement to London in a telegram on 24 March, and offered his opinion that 'an effort should be made to help General Gordon from Suakin'. Queen Victoria added to the political pressure: 'Gordon is in danger', she told Hartington. 'You are bound to try and save him.' But the Cabinet did not agree: the heat was rising, the route was long, the lack of water on the way acute, and the menace of Osman Digna's army – only temporarily cowed as far as anyone could see – remained. On receipt of this news, Baring telegraphed London again; and his missive this time seemed to contain the veiled threat of resignation. For Baring – unlike Gladstone – had no sense that Gordon had exceeded his instructions: it seemed to him that the general was simply attempting to implement the dual policy of evacuation and stabilisation that had been agreed. This being so, Baring felt honour-bound to stand by Gordon. 'No-one can regret more than I do', he wrote, 'the necessity of sending British or Indian troops to the Sudan, but, having sent Gordon to Khartoum, it appears to me that it is our bounden duty, both as a matter of humanity and policy, not to abandon him.' The word 'abandon' dropped in London, in the words of Lord Granville, like a 'heavy cannon-ball'.

It would soon become a barrage. Already the Queen was repeating it: 'If not only for humanity's sake, for the honour of the government and the nation, he must not be abandoned.' Gladstone was compelled to move a short political distance – the minimum he could get away with – to placate the jingoes and steady the government. The Queen was assured that her ministers were seeking intelligence about the true situation from General Gordon himself, and that 'there will be every disposition to support him to the full extent which national interests will permit'. The first of a series of disingenuous do-nothing interventions by Gladstone, this mealy-mouthed formulation sufficed for now.[31]

The government respite was short-lived. A bane of the Liberals that summer of 1884 was to be a young Irish journalist called Frank Power. One of the new breed of adventurer-correspondents now to be found wherever colonial small wars were fought, he had avoided the Hicks disaster – in which his companion Edmund O'Donovan of the *Daily News* had perished – but had stayed on in Khartoum afterwards, despite the growing danger, scenting good copy. Taken on by *The Times* – and helped by Gordon, keen to get the message out – he managed, intermittently, to file a series of alarming dispatches.[32] On 1 April, *The Times* carried a report in which he wrote, 'We are daily expecting the British troops. We cannot bring ourselves to believe that we are to be abandoned by the government.' That word again; and this time, in the public domain. But Baring's and the Queen's prior use of it were not, and this allowed Gladstone a parliamentary triumph over the opposition in which he castigated them for charging the government with a policy of 'abandonment' on the basis of a newspaper report. 'But what is Mr Power in relation to us? . . . he is the correspondent of *The Times* . . . And yet the Right Honourable Gentlemen takes an opinion of Mr Power, transmitted to *The Times*, as virtually equivalent to an official declaration of policy conveying to the mature conviction of General Gordon. Really, sir, it is a farce to treat it in such a spirit.' Knowing what he knew, this was consummate deceit; but it quelled the opposition for another couple of weeks.[33]

On 17 April, however, *The Times* published another Power dispatch, far more despondent: 'Khartoum is at present the centre of an enormous rebel camp . . . The situation is now very critical . . . Because I am confident that General Gordon is abandoned by the government, and that without Zubeir Pasha he can never beat the rebels, I fear that he will be driven to retreat to Central Africa.' This brought forth a display of semantics brazen even by Gladstone's standards. Gordon was not surrounded, he told the House, but 'hemmed in'. This turned out to mean that 'there are bodies of troops in the neighbourhood forming more or less a chain around it'. But, he continued, 'I draw a distinction between that and the town being surrounded, which would bear technically a very different meaning.' Despite laughter on the opposition benches, and the dismay of many of his friends, Gladstone was again able to move on.[34]

In fact, having sailed through the spring storm, the government was able to proceed with little regard for the Sudan for the best part of three months, a political passage made possible by the disruption of communications between Cairo and Khartoum. This suited Gladstone well. The government could maintain the fiction that it was acting appropriately by consulting the man on the spot. He, of course, was unable to respond, since he was receiving government telegrams, if at all, only after inordinate delay. His own messages back were almost as intermittent. A momentary difficulty for the government arose with the publication of an official 'Blue Book' on 1 May which contained all the telegrams between Gordon and the government. Though these were a context-less jumble hard for the uninitiated to decipher, one phrase stood out, used in the last of Gordon's telegrams to get through, where he branded the government with the words 'indelible disgrace'. This caused a media flurry, a renewed opposition attack, and yet another display of Gladstonian rhetoric. He lashed the Tories as warmongers, demanded to know whether they would send an army to Khartoum, and denounced any such policy as 'a war of conquest against a people struggling to be free'.

This, of course, was rank hypocrisy: what had not applied to Arabi, a liberal Egyptian revolutionary, now applied to the Mahdi, a reactionary mystic leading a slave traders' revolt. Nor was it enough on this occasion to still the storm, and Hartington, fearing a government defeat, his conscience in any case troubled, was compelled to make a significant concession. Gordon's position was unenviable, he admitted. He may have 'departed in some respects from his original purpose'. But, on the other hand, he may simply have overestimated his chances of success, and found that 'the execution of his original intentions . . . was perfectly impossible'. As for an expedition, following full enquiries, if it seemed necessary and practical, 'then I believe that this country will be prepared to grudge no sacrifice to save the life and honour of General Gordon'.[35]

This calmed matters through the early summer. The dialogue of the deaf between London and Khartoum continued. No news was taken as reason for no action. But as parliament's summer recess approached, Hartington's mind was brought to focus on a matter that troubled it more and more. He, as War Minister, was the politician most responsible for Gordon. He did not believe that the general had exceeded his instructions. He considered him a blameless public servant put in danger by order of his government. And Hartington had fought off a censure motion in May by implying, quite clearly, that a rescue mission would be mounted if necessary and practical. On 29 July, therefore, he circulated a memorandum to his fellow ministers putting 'the relief of General Gordon' once more 'under the consideration of the Cabinet'. Two days later, sensing resistance, he followed up with a personal letter to the Prime Minister, setting out his case and concluding, 'It is a question of personal honour and good faith, and I don't see how I can yield upon it.' This was an unmistakable threat of resignation, and Hartington's departure, above all on this so sensitive question, would have blown up the political alliance on which the administration was founded. To save his government, on 5 August, William Gladstone himself proposed a government motion for the grant of £300,000 'to undertake operations for the relief of General Gordon, should they become necessary, and to make certain preparations in respect thereof'. It was passed overwhelmingly. The caveats were void. The military planning immediately went into top gear, £750,000 had been spent before a month was out, and General Sir Garnet Wolseley arrived in Cairo to take command of the expeditionary force on 9 September. The redcoats were coming.[36]

The attention of the whole world was now focusing on Khartoum. The Scramble for Africa, that fatal collision between European imperialism and the people of the continent that was fast gathering momentum, found its epicentre here in the summer of 1884. The exponential growth of industry, the ruthless struggle for markets, the plundering of natural resources, the conscription of native labour, the debt-peonage to foreign bankers, the laying waste of the world and its people by rampaging capital accumulation, all this, in a sense, was now converging in an epoch-defining military confrontation around a distant desert town. On one side stood a maverick British general, the wreckage of a failed Turco-Egyptian colonial project, and a British expeditionary force belatedly on its way to rescue what it could. Against it was a traditionalist revolt of Arab tribesmen, an eruption of rage from the social depths, canalised by religious mysticism, powered by bitterness at lives ruined by taxation, official corruption, military occupation, and abolitionism; a revolt that was both a nationalist revolution against foreign domination and a religious counter-revolution to restore the status quo.

Babikr Bedri, serving in the trenches south of Khartoum, was perhaps typical of the Mahdi's core supporters. He had been born to poor but loving parents in a village by the River Atbara in 1861, but the family had relocated to Rufa'a on the Blue Nile, about 80 miles south-east of Khartoum, when he was four. Here, on the edge of the Jazira district, he attended a religious school – a mix of rote learning, savage beatings, and domestic chores – and by the time he was 19 was able to recite the whole of the Qur'an from memory. He then entered a theological college at Madani, 40 miles upriver, and it was here that he became an adherent of the Mahdi. By the time he returned to his home village – enjoying a brief premarital fling with a local woman called Zahra – the insurrection in the Jazira had begun. When the local sheikh of the Halawin joined the revolt, Babikr Bedri followed his lead and became actively involved in the fighting. 'Then I put on the *jibba* and devoted myself both outwardly and inwardly to the Mahdist cause,' he later recalled, 'as did my mother also, though my father and my teachers merely made a show of doing so. And I exposed myself in the attacks on the government steamers without precautions, longing for martyrdom.' Around this time, accompanied by his mother and another relative, he made the pilgrimage to the Mahdi, 'full of single-hearted devotion and eager desire'. His father was called up to serve at the siege of Khartoum while he was away, and he left instructions that Babikr was to remain at home to tend the family farm when he returned from his pilgrimage. But the young man was not to be restrained – 'passion for the holy war had mastered my mind' – and he followed the army and joined the siege. 'I was in the most advanced of the positions surrounding Khartoum, so that at night we could see the glow of the enemy's cigarettes and hear their conversation; nor could we leave our trenches in the daylight to get water, but only at night.'[37]

The Mahdist movement was first and foremost a movement of religious youth. A generational conflict divided families, pitting volatile young men against more cautious fathers, uncles, and teachers. This conflict extended to the higher reaches of the social hierarchy, where younger men among tribal sheikhs and religious *ulema* were more likely to commit to the Mahdi than older men. Even when the movement became hegemonic, the youth remained the vanguard. It was young men like Babikr Bedri who were most willing to hurl themselves against breechloaders, machine guns, and steel cannon. This was what gave the movement its inner strength, for in all conflict, especially in war, it is the psycho-social magnetism of the militant minority that carries forward the mass. Most men are cautious, inclined to keep their heads down and hang back; they provide social and moral weight on the battlefield, but rarely become actual killers – unless and until the enemy breaks and runs.[38]

The Mahdist *jihad* created a large cadre of exceptional fighters. Babikr Bedri described a classic of Ansar battle-craft during the struggle around the village of Buri outside Khartoum – a sector of the line that was dubbed, with the grim black humour common to trench-fighters, *Dar al-Akhira*, the 'Last Home' before paradise. In response to a Turco-Egyptian sortie:

Abdullah al-Nur jumped up, and we went out with him to an open place
in which were a few small bushes, where he harangued us, saying,
'Companions of the Mahdi, do you not see the *houris* of Paradise as they
glide there gracefully, waving to you with their white kerchiefs?' He was
boiling and foaming as though possessed, and we attacked the enemy
until they fell back before us to the fortifications. There was an officer
with them who tried to rally them, kicking them and shouting at them,
and Abdullah al-Nur rushed at him and stabbed him in the stomach with
his spear . . . And we fell upon them and forced them to a final retreat
within their fortifications.[39]

Babikr Bedri and his comrades from the Jazira had been among the
forward elements of the Mahdist forces now mustering from all directions
at Khartoum. Just four days after his triumph over Hicks at Shaykan, the
Mahdi had sent a petulant letter to his father-in-law, Muhammad al-Tayib
Ibn al-Basir, a leading commander in the Jazira, repeating his injunction to
invest the city:

> As I ordered you to carry on the *jihad* by besieging Khartoum, you may
> not depart from this command . . . On the arrival of this letter, rouse up
> all the Muslims who are with you, join together, rise up and besiege
> Khartoum. Block the roads in all directions. Embarrass the Turks in the
> city, those infidels, and all who are united with them. Let them see your
> courage and valour before Allah, until they listen to Allah's commands,
> or are destroyed as those before them tasted the punishment for their
> deeds. Their firepower will not avail them as Allah's command has gone
> forth. Be zealous in the righteous fight, and there is no doubt that we
> shall be victorious over them by Allah.[40]

Khartoum was to be destroyed. Not only was it the centre of the Turco-
Egyptian colonial administration; it was also a modern, secularist, cosmopolitan capital, filled with venal officers, bureaucrats, and foreign merchants.
Not only was it built on the profits of colonial oppression, but, viewed
through Muhammad Ahmad's religious lens, it seemed a den of vice and
irreligion. One of many: for Khartoum was but a stepping-stone on the road
of a global *jihad* intended to sweep the world, carrying the Ansar – like their
forebears, the followers of the Prophet, in the seventh century AD – to Cairo,
Mecca, Jerusalem, Beirut, Damascus, Baghdad, and Constantinople.[41]

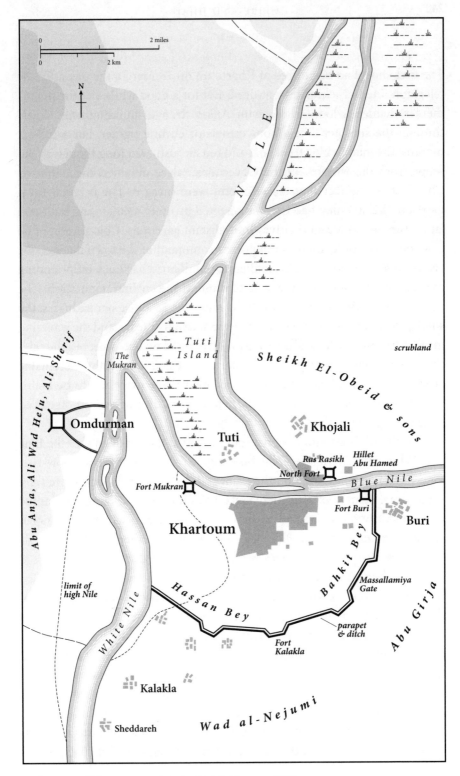

8. The Siege of Khartoum, 12 March 1884–26 January 1885

The first shots had been fired at Khartoum on 13 March, the day after the telegraph line to the north went dead. But for a good while yet, the investment remained a loose affair, with Ansar strength building only slowly through the summer, like a boa-constrictor curling tighter. For a full six months, the man in blue frockcoat and red tarbush, watching though a telescope from the window of the Governor's Palace, retained the initiative. This despite the fact that his resources were meagre. The original town garrison of 2,000 men had been augmented by up to 4,000 more, but these latter were demoralised fugitives from distant garrisons. Colonel Henry de Coëtlogon, the officer left in temporary command of the town defences by Hicks, considered a third of his soldiers to be militarily useless. Compounding the security problem was the state of mind of the civilian population. The usual three parties were present: the clandestine Mahdist sympathisers, the solid government loyalists (whether by conviction or fear), and the wavering mass of trimmers whose allegiance would depend on outcome; but the relative proportions were, for the most part, concealed behind the inscrutable faces of colonial subjects. Suffice to say, internal security had to be maintained, even though the length of the defences, hastily improvised, stretched the garrison far too thin.[42]

The city of Khartoum lies on a spur of land at the confluence of the Blue and White Niles. Most of the buildings in 1884 were small, low-rise, mud-brick dwellings, even on the main east–west street, though there were some larger houses of rich merchants and officials. The more substantial government buildings included the Governor's Palace, which faced north and looked out across the Blue Nile, a hospital, an arsenal, and a barracks. There were also several mosques and churches. Some discerned a measure of romance about the place. Journalist Frank Power thought the white-sailed boats on the Nile at early morning, with a village, a fringe of palms, a field of *durra*, and the red desert beyond, made a lovely picture. The town markets also added some colour; they included workshops for the manufacture of mats, cotton goods, and filigree silverware. But Colonel Stewart considered the place wretched. A wide, flat, barren plain of sand and stone extended in all directions. Summer temperatures were scorching, and this was also the time of high water, when much of the plain was inundated and marshy. The town was full of rotting refuse and stank so badly that some European residents carried camphor to their noses when they ventured out. The population fluctuated around the 50,000 mark. More than half of these were black slaves. The owners were Syrians, Turks, Copts, Albanians, and Jews. 'Of the floating population,' opined Stewart, 'the Copts are mostly employed in government service or trade. The Turks, Albanians, etc are generally irregular soldiers and loafers. The European element is represented by about a hundred individuals, mostly Greeks. There are also some Italians, French, Austrians, and Germans.'[43]

The defence problem was acute: though the Blue and White Niles protected the city on three sides, the south-eastern side was wide open, the curving landward wall of the city running for a full 5 miles between the two rivers. The wall, reinforced by several projecting forts along its line, was a formidable defence-work, made more so by the digging of a ditch in front of it, spiked with spearheads, and the sowing of crow's feet and a 500-yard-wide belt of broken glass beyond. A further refinement was the planting of improvised mines – biscuit boxes filled with powder, nails, and bullets buried a couple of feet underground and attached to electric trigger wires. This much had been done by Coëtlogon. Gordon did more. He was in his element, being a master of improvisation and a man of restless energy. A new fort was built at Buri at the eastern limit of the line. Outworks at Omdurman on the west bank of the White Nile, on Tuti Island north of the city, and around the village of Khojali on the north bank of the Blue Nile were strengthened with mines and wire entanglements. Dummy figures were set up as targets along the river. Outlying posts were connected by telegraph to a central command-and-control station. Civilian volunteers were enrolled as militia and given arms. A contingent of black troops was raised from among the slaves of masters who had joined the Mahdi. Commanded by a black officer, and fighting to maintain their new-found freedom, they were, in Power's opinion, 'the only troops we can depend on'. Much of this military work was left to Colonel Stewart, while Gordon himself set about turning the city into a self-sufficient miniature state, with its own paper currency, price controls, anti-hoarding raids, and a workshop manufacturing uniforms; he even issued a campaign medal inscribed 'The Siege of Khartoum 1884', cast in silver for senior officers, tin for junior officers and other ranks.[44]

Obstacles and firepower act as multipliers in defence, but no works are stronger than the garrison available to man them, and Gordon's little army was quite inadequate for the task. The defence of Khartoum faced four critical problems. First, the full circuit – land wall, river line, and outworks – was about 15 miles in extent: barely one soldier for every five yards. Second, most of the soldiers were demoralised, and a good number, along with many civilians, in sympathy with the enemy; the known Mahdist practice of welcoming fellow Muslims who deserted acted as a potent corrosive. Third, existing stores of food in the town were sufficient for several months, but then they would run out, and enemy infestation of the surrounding countryside would eventually make foraging impossible. Fourth, the rivers were the main defence, but the waters would begin to fall at the end of summer, creating new avenues of approach where no substantial defences existed, notably at the western end of the land wall. Time, in short, favoured the Mahdi, for Gordon's position could only worsen as his own improved. In an effort to redress the balance, Gordon went onto the offensive.

All Nilotic civilisations had used boats to police their domains. A modern industrialised version – the steam-powered gunboat – was already symbolic of European imperialism across much of Africa and Asia. River boats had been employed to good effect by both Baker and Gordon in Equatoria, and Gordon had formed a small flotilla at Khartoum while serving as governor general. These 'penny steamers' were now transformed into a formidable force of five armoured gunboats and used to project military power along the rivers to disrupt Mahdist operations. All five vessels were small side-wheel steamers, varying between 110 and 160 feet in length, 10 and 14 feet in width, with a pair of paddle-boxes amidships and a tall, thin funnel astern of them. They were relatively underpowered, becoming more so due to lack of parts and poor maintenance, with theoretical speeds of 10 knots in some cases down to 5. The high fuel-consumption of their antiquated boilers necessitated frequent stops to cut wood. Originally civil vessels, Gordon had them converted into gunboats with the addition of baulks of timber, sheets of metal plate, and home-made sandbags. The little ships sprouted palisades along the sides, sheds over the paddle-boxes, miniature bastions fore and aft, and keep-like towers around funnel and bridge-house, coming to resemble little floating forts. These defences were bullet-proof, though not resistant to shot or shell. They might have a brass 9-pdr fore and aft, a couple of Gardners amidships, and a hundred or so riflemen acting as marines.[45]

'The ships' companies were an interesting example of river piracy,' wrote Commander Charles Beresford RN, who inherited command of one of these gunboats in January 1885:

The steamers had been cruising up and down the Nile since October, a period of four months, during which the crews lived on the country, raiding and fighting. Everything was filthy and neglected except the engines. The fore-hold was crammed with ammunition, *durra* grain, wool, fuel, and miscellaneous loot. The main-hold was inhabited by women, babies, stowaways, wounded men, goats, amid a confusion of ammunition, sacks of grain, wood fuel, bedding, and loot. The after-hold held the possessions, including loot, of the commandant. Below the forward turret, slave-girls ceased not from cooking *durra*-cakes. Rats swarmed everywhere; the whole ship exhaled a most appalling stench; and the ship's company shouted and screamed all day long.

Beresford described the ship's serving personnel in equally vivid colours:

First there was the commandant, who was theoretically in chief command of the ship, and who commanded the soldiers on shore. Then there was the officer commanding the regular soldiers, Sudanese. He was black, and so were his men, who were freed slaves. The officer commanding the artillery was an Egyptian. The Bashi-Bazouk contingent was composed of Shaigiya [tribesmen], of black slaves, and of half-castes. Their officers were Turks, Kurds, and Circassians. The captain of the ship was a Dongolese [from northern Sudan], and his sailors were blacks. Under the captain were numerous petty officers, such as the chief of the sailors, the chief of the carpenters, and so forth. The chief engineer and his staff were Egyptians. The *reis* (pilot) and his assistants were Dongolese.[46]

The gunboat flotilla – much of which eventually escaped downriver to join the relief expedition – was Gordon's elite strike-force. At first, it was employed on abortive peace missions, the steamers arriving at riverside villages flying white flags, the government officers going ashore intent on winning 'hearts and minds'. Not for long: the shooting started soon enough. 'River pirates' they then became. The gunboats were constantly active, cruising in different directions, on reconnaissance missions, to forage for supplies, to rescue beleaguered garrisons, to bombard Mahdist positions, to land raiding parties. Gordon's steamer campaign reached its climax towards the end of the summer. His ultimate intention was to open up the entire river from north to south, providing Khartoum with a wind-pipe, cleaving Mahdist territory into two halves. The first phase of this effort focused on the Blue Nile and an attempt to clear the route as far south as Sennar. This was, in fact, the culmination of a three-year struggle for control of the Jazira.[47]

The Jazira was an extensive, fertile, relatively well-watered region that straddled the Blue Nile between Khartoum and Sennar, a distance of about 180 miles. Sennar itself, just beyond the Jazira, was important in its own right, being the centre of a grain-growing region and a source of supply for Khartoum. The Mahdi had begun his mission – on Aba Island in the White Nile – near the western edge of the Jazira, and his adherents in the region were numerous. But proximity to the centre of government power at Khartoum, and the ease with which government forces could enter the Jazira by moving up the rivers, had encouraged many tribal leaders to remain loyal or neutral. In consequence, between August 1881, when the Mahdist insurgency began, and August 1884, when the Jazira was finally cleared of government forces, a fierce seesaw struggle had raged across the region, with half a dozen major campaigns before Gordon's final steamer offensive.[48]

A leading commander, Muhammad Osman Abu Girja – described by Wingate as a 'redoubtable ex-Nile boatman' – had arrived to take command of the Mahdist forces operating against Khartoum in April.[49] It was his slowly strengthening investment of the city that had brought Babikr Bedri and his family to the siege lines; and it was this threat to the security and provisioning of the city that prompted Gordon and his officers to launch a counter-offensive by steamer. They were encouraged by the ease with which initial attacks by Abu Girja's Ansar were repulsed: 'we fought them on land and from the steamers on the river,' reported one Bashi-Bazouk officer, 'until we killed most of them and routed them'. On 27 July, the government launched a combined land and river assault on the eastern end of the Mahdist line south of the city, a three-day operation in which four steamers providing covering fire for an advance by 800 regulars and Shaigiya tribesmen. Under a deluge of cannon, rocket, and rifle fire, a Mahdist fort was destroyed, hundreds of Ansar killed, a large quantity of arms and food captured, and Abu Girja was driven several miles upriver to a second position at Gereif. The steamers, supported by armoured barges adapted into floating gun-platforms, followed them, bombarding the fort at Gereif for eight hours before retiring.[50]

This victory was followed a month later by another thrust in the same direction. Muhammad Ali Hussein, Gordon's most able officer, led the expedition. At first, it was rewarded with startling success. Abu Girja was driven from his second position at Gereif, and government forces then steamed up the Blue Nile all the way to important market town of Abu Haraz, not far short of Sennar. Here, Muhammad Ali secured another victory, driving Abu Girja away from the river and seizing arms, ammunition, and supplies. 'We are going to hold out here forever and are pretty well matched with the Mahdi,' wrote Gordon gleefully. 'He has cavalry and we have steamers ... We have provisions for five months and hope to get in more.' Two days later, a similar operation was mounted at Halfaya, 10 miles north of Khartoum, cutting a swathe through the Mahdist encirclement of Khartoum. 'We have (thank God) succeeded in taking Arab camp and killing Arab commander-in-chief (RIP),' Gordon telegraphed. 'This victory clears our vicinity on three parts of a circle ...' The intention now was to push still further north, to recapture Berber and open up the whole river line from Dongola to Sennar. Gordon was buoyant, his sense of mission restored. 'There is one bond of union between us and our troops,' he wrote. 'They know if the town is taken they will be sold as slaves . . .'[51]

Only a few days later, that fate suddenly loomed larger. Disaster struck on 5 September. Seeking to consolidate the government advantage, Muhammad Ali had been authorised to mount a fresh attack up the Blue Nile, on the village of El-Eilafun about 25 miles south of Khartoum. A primary objective was to capture or kill El-Obeid, a local sheikh renowned for his piety who had great influence over the Jazira tribes. Muhammad Ali landed, captured the village, and seized a large supply of provisions; but El-Obeid escaped inland. Gordon had warned against leaving the river, where the gunboats provided protection and a line of retreat. The further government forces moved inland, the more the advantage shifted to the Ansar. Muhammad Ali nonetheless decided to pursue the quarry, heading for the village of Umm Dibban, about 20 miles away, where the rebel sheikh was reported to have taken refuge. The country was thickly wooded. The guides were enemy sympathisers. The result was a miniature Shaykan. Ambushed and assailed on all sides, a thousand of Gordon's elite black troops perished with their commander.[52]

This was a shattering blow. It transformed the balance of forces at a stroke. The combination of steamers, a contingent of highly motivated ex-slaves, a first-class native officer, and a resolute garrison commander had allowed the government to punch well above its weight for several months. Now, just as the Nile began its annual fall, the receding waters opening the approaches to the city, the Mahdist concentration in the siege lines coming to a peak, the Governor General's right arm had been severed. Gordon – who had received little news from Cairo in the months past – wrote what proved to be a last despairing letter to Baring. 'How many times have we written asking for reinforcements, calling your serious attention to the Sudan? No answer at all has come to us as to what has been decided in the matter, and the hearts of men have become weary at this delay.' He dispatched the letter with Colonel Stewart, now sent north by steamer, not to retake Berber, simply to rush the enemy batteries in an effort to get through bearing messages.[53] Was there a rescue mission? Were the British coming? When might they arrive? Would they be in time? The Governor General wanted to know. Otherwise, all he could do now was hunker down, eke out his supplies, and hope for the best, as the enemy vice closed around the city of Khartoum.

# CHAPTER TEN

# A MODERN CRUSADER

Garnet Wolseley had been lobbying for a Gordon relief expedition from the outset, in large part because he had no doubt who should command it. Following Tel el-Kebir, his star was at its zenith, and he was anyway a Liberal favourite, due to his support for army reform and a long record of success in the field. A modern machine soldier – once asked why he never suffered a reverse, he replied, 'The reason is that I never fight unless I know that I am certain to win' – he was felt to be a safe pair of hands. He was duly appointed, in preference to the senior men on the spot; a decision made more certain by the fact that Wolseley was the leading advocate of the Nile route, whereas both General Stephenson, commander of the British army of occupation, and General Wood, commander of the new Egyptian Army, favoured overland routes.[1]

The 'battle of the routes' had begun long before any expedition had been authorised; indeed, the disagreement among senior officers, both army and navy, had provided Gladstone with a handy additional pretext for his persistent procrastination. Several routes were considered, but only two were ever serious contenders: the Suakin to Berber route across the eastern desert; and an ascent up the Nile from Cairo. Everyone agreed that both main options involved major logistical and military problems. Stephenson summarised these in relation to the Suakin–Berber option as: 'a) opposition from hostile tribes, b) oppressive heat, and c) want of water'. The combination was potentially fatal, since enemy resistance, even if not decisive, might be sufficient to delay movement until the water ran out. The distance between the O-Bak wells, the last on the road – where in any case the supply was 'small and bad' – and Berber was a full 58 miles. A Victorian field force might expect to march 12 miles a day. But in the presence of the enemy, if square formation was necessary, progress might slow to a crawl. Established Mahdist tactics were to commence action

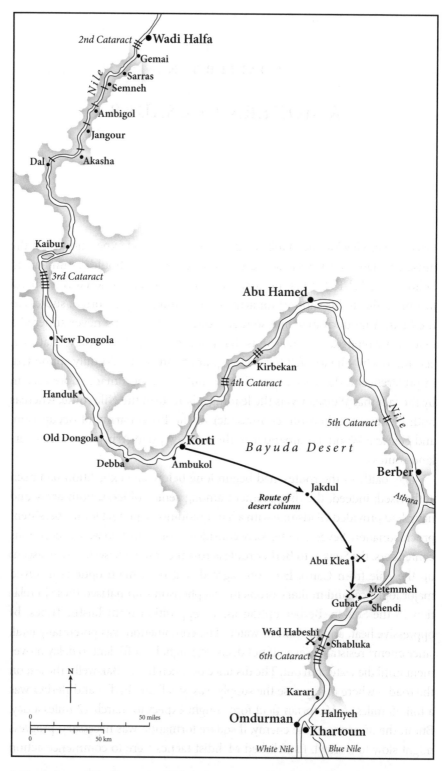

9. The Sudanese Nile, illustrating Wolesley's 1884–5 and Kitchener's 1896–8 campaigns

with long-range harassing fire, the skirmishing sometimes continuing for days, before launching a fanatic charge against a degraded force. The implications were obvious. It was questionable, anyway, whether the wells on the route could supply more than relatively small detachments of a few hundred or so: too small to be safe, for, as Wolseley explained, 'Our recent experience has shown us the warlike character of the tribes living about [the route]; their hostility would render the march of small detachments along it extremely dangerous'. The only solution would be to build a desert railway, and though preparations for this were made, the fall of Berber in May 1884 finally put paid to plans to relieve Khartoum from this direction.[2]

Wolseley may have been right about the Suakin–Berber route; but he was wrong about the Nile route. Like so many others, he underestimated the power of the jihadist insurgency and its potential, in alliance with the forbidding geography of the Sudan, to wreck any British relief expedition, from whatever direction. The principal argument in favour of the Suakin–Berber route had been the overall distance: a mere 245 miles from the Red Sea to the Nile. The distance from Cairo to Berber was six times greater. The movement of men, beasts, and supplies along the route involved a complex coordination of rail, boat, and camel transport, none of it adequate to the task in hand, all of it subject to shortages, bottlenecks, and breakdowns. Troops shipped from Britain were landed at Alexandria after 10–15 days at sea. They were then taken by train to Cairo (120 miles), and from there by train to Assiut (another 230 miles). Stores accumulated here because of limited carrying capacity on the next leg of the journey. This was by river vessels – Thomas Cook tourist steamers and a variety of tugs, barges, and native craft – as far as Aswan (320 miles). A delay of ten days arose here when Cook ran out of coal and an argument about contractual obligations ensued. At this point, the southward journey encountered the first of six 'cataracts'. These constituted a logistical problem of the highest order.

All six cataracts – each of them an extent of rock and rushing water several miles long – presented grave impediments to river passage, especially during a falling Nile, when the traditional numbering of the cataracts became misleading, with the rapids almost continuous in many places. At each cataract, it was necessary to disembark men, equipment, and stores, bypass the obstacle, and resume the river journey on the far side. At the First Cataract (Aswan-Shellal), this involved travelling 7 miles on a narrow-gauge railway. A second flotilla of boats – steamers and native craft – then provided transport on the next leg down to Wadi Halfa (210 miles). Here lay the

Second or Great Cataract, again with railway bypass, this one 33 miles long, down to Sarras, where the journey continued either by boat or camel depending on availability. The long stretch from Sarras, on the Egyptian-Sudanese border, to Korti, destined to become the advanced based of the expedition – a total of 330 miles – included the Third Cataract (at Hannek) and two minor cataracts, some 22 miles of white water in all. The line of communications from Alexandria to Korti was therefore 1,250 miles in length, divided into nine stages, 390 miles traversed by train, 530 by steamer, 330 by camel or boat.[3]

'The Nile expedition was a campaign less against man than against nature and against time,' explained Colonel Colvile in the *Official History*. 'Had British soldiers and Egyptian camels been able to subsist on sand and occasional water, or had the desert produced beef and biscuit, the army might, in spite of its late start, have reached Khartoum in November. But as things were, the rate of progress of the army was dependent on the rate of progress of its supplies. As the difficulty of feeding each man increased with his distance from Alexandria, it was Lord Wolseley's endeavour to keep his army as near the base as possible, until such a time as the state of his supplies would enable him to launch it from the fighting base ... the troops had therefore to be halted at such positions on the river as would allow them to arrive at the fighting base as soon as the supplies were ready for them, and at the same time to be the fewest number of miles from the source of supply.'[4]

The essence of the logistical problem was the need to supply a force of 11,000 British soldiers, 7,000 Egyptian soldiers, 8,000 camels, and many thousands of native workers along a 1,250-mile line of communications, and then to project two spearheads, one across the desert, the other upriver, all the way to Khartoum, a further 250 miles. Such was the length of the line of communications, and the labour required to work it, that the bulk of the supplies – mainly food, fodder, and fuel – were simply consumed *en route*. A baggage camel, for example, would eat the equivalent of its own load in just 30 days or 390 miles of journey. The time taken to accumulate stores at the advanced base also increased consumption, since men and beasts waiting in camp still had to be fed. And the length and complexity of the line had another consequence: losses to poor packing, mishandling, theft, and accident were high. Half the hospital supplies were stolen, a third of the biscuits arrived uneatable, and half the tea and a quarter of the sugar transported by whaler were spoiled by damp. 'The supply question,' Colvile explained, 'divided itself into two distinct phases: a) the supply of the troops locally up to the moment of leaving the fighting base; and b) their supply from that moment.' Wolseley – ever attentive to logistical problems – had instructed his commissariat officers to ring-fence 'the 100 days' rations per man' that was to supply the spearheads when they moved on Khartoum. General Redvers Buller, who had reached Cairo ahead of Wolseley, found the calculations alarming: 'What we want is to have supplies for 10,000 men for 100 days at Dongola. Of course, we also have to supply the 10,000 men from other stores on their way up to Dongola . . . Now one day's supply for 10,000 men weighs about 17 tons, so 120 days will mean 2,040 tons.' In total, around 40,000 tons of general stores and 30,000 tons of grain had to be moved to supply the Gordon Relief Expedition.[5]

Nothing was straightforward. At the outset, the railways were quite inadequate. Track was in poor condition. Some of the bridges were unsafe. There were not enough sidings. There were too few carriages. Engines were old and broken down. Wheels were worn and crank pins off-centre. Sand clogged all working parts, and heat affected pumps and injectors. There was a lack of spare parts. The coal was of bad quality. There were hardly any native staff. Sterling work was done by the Royal Engineers to improvise a functioning military rail service out of the decay – the 1,000 tons of supplies moved by rail in October was doubled the following month – but, even without breakdowns, with the system running at capacity, the railway links on the line of communications remained bottlenecks.[6]

A different set of problems arose on the river. Large civil steamers could not negotiate the cataracts at all. Small military steamers could do so only with great effort and risk. Native river craft – *kyassas* and *nuggars*: wooden cargo boats with lateen sails – were not available in sufficient quantity, nor, with a falling Nile, could they manage the rapids south of Wadi Halfa. The gap was filled by 800 'whalers'. These, based on the design of the traditional Canadian boats Wolseley had used in his 600-mile ascent of the Red River in 1870, were purpose-built for the expedition at 47 separate boatyards in Britain. About 32ft long, 7ft broad, and 2ft 6in at the sides, they were sleek, fast, manoeuvrable, and of shallow draft. The whaler fleet was the baby of Colonel William Butler, an eccentric Irishman whom Wolseley had first encountered on the Red River – an intrepid scout travelling in the opposite direction in a birch-bark canoe in company with five Native Americans. Musing over the cataracts problem at the War Office, Wolseley had issued a peremptory summons – 'I want to see you here tomorrow' – and Butler had been appointed to get the boats built and crews for them recruited. An army man with river expertise, he had rejected navy advice to the effect that the cataracts constituted insuperable barriers on the prospective line of communications. 'I have not seen the Nile above Cairo and its neighbourhood,' he wrote, '. . . but I have had considerable and varied experience in ascending rapid and dangerous rivers. Water is water, and rock is rock, whether they lie in America or in Africa, and the conditions which they can assume towards each other are much the same the world over.' Some 380 Canadian *voyageurs* (river boatmen) and 270 West African 'Kroomen' (ex-slaves recruited into Royal Naval service) were engaged as expert crew. The whalers proved their worth: they were capable of ascending the rapids with minimal losses, were light enough to be portered around anything impassable, and, unlike camels, their crews consumed only a tiny fraction of what they could carry.[7]

Not that Butler's operation was trouble-free: it was simply that he had the right kit for a tough job. A number of the whalers were damaged in transit. Many arrived with the wrong gear: each boat had 26 separate items (masts, sails, oars, rowlocks, rudder, yoke, tiller, and more), each set fitted only vessels made by one of the 47 boatyards, and boats and gear had got mixed up on their way to Wadi Halfa. Still, the whalers passed the test of the rapids. In the treacherous 200-mile stretch of water between the Second and Third Cataracts, which involved seven major and numerous minor obstacles, and where the configuration of cliffs, rocks, and white water changed daily as the river fell, native *kyassas* and *nuggars* were wrecked, but Butler's whalers were manhandled through. He wrote of one personal exploit:

> Before us lay a troubled mass of water growing rapidly stiffer, until at the head of the rapid a large rock stood full in the centre of the stream. Round this rock, the current broke furiously, and between the two severed rushes lay the usual interval of seething and whirring but comparatively quiet water. The art of forcing up a rapid consists in running up this lane of easier water, clinging to it as long as possible, and leaving it only at the very edge of the rock. Then, with all the strength of oar and paddle, the effort is made to lift the boat over and through the neck of the rush. It is at this point that the art of steering tells.

During the campaign, only a handful of boats were damaged, and only six men drowned: trifling losses for the logistical gain. As Evelyn Wood, the General of Communications, opined: 'The striking success of the expedition was the whalers. At high or low Nile, with and without wind, in good and bad weather, up or down stream, the whalers proved the most certain transport for men, stores of all kinds, and eventually all the sick and wounded were brought down in them.'[8]

Camel transport constituted another nest of problems. As well as baggage animals on the line of communications to supplement train and boat, the plan was to create a camel corps for a dash across the desert, for which a large supply of both riding and baggage-camels was needed. An original order for 1,200 camels had to be increased to 4,000, but procuring these proved hard; the purchase price rose, but the quality fell. Eventually, 1,700 riding camels and 1,200 baggage-camels were acquired, but at first there were saddles for only 150 of the former and 500 of the latter. All sorts of inappropriate saddles were used as substitutes, animals were overloaded, and care was neglected; in consequence, the camels developed sores, became sick, and eventually broke down. Fodder was also in short supply. To reduce the logistical load, only limited quantities had been transported upriver, in the expectation that *durra* and chopped grass could be sourced locally. This expectation was disappointed, and lack of fodder became an additional constraint on the deployment of transport. A perennial shortage of good camel-drivers compounded matters. 'It only requires working daily convoys,' explained Lieutenant Colonel Furse, Director of Transport, 'to see the material difference it makes having good and bad drivers. The time taken in saddling and turning out, the great length of time occupied in loading, the number of loads that require to be readjusted just after starting off, all add to the time the animal is kept at work and deprived of his rest . . .'[9]

Given the multiple difficulties, the achievement was remarkable. The Nile expedition was a triumph of Victorian enterprise and improvisation in the face of great obstacles. By Christmas 1884, barely three months after setting out, Wolseley had most of his strike-force assembled at his advanced base. 'Korti,' recalled Commander Charles Beresford RN,

> was a city of tents arrayed amid groves of fronded palm overhanging the broad river; beyond, the illimitable coloured spaces of the desert, barred with plains of tawny grass set with mimosa, and green fields of *durra*, and merging into the far rose-hued hills. All day long, the strong sun smote upon its yellow avenues, and bugles called, and the north wind, steady and cool, blew the boats up the river, and the men, ragged and cheery and tanned saddle-colour, came marching in and were absorbed into the

great armed camp. Thence were to spring two long arms of fighting men, one to encircle the river, the other to reach across the desert, strike at Khartoum, and save Gordon.[10]

The camp was a pleasant refuge after the rigours of the journey south, with local villagers hired to provide essential services, the troops at ease. Great bonfires were lit and double rations issued for the seasonal celebrations. The band of the Royal Sussex played to regular evening assemblies of officers and men. Christmas-night entertainment on a huge open-air stage erected by Royal Engineers included comic, sentimental, and patriotic songs, along with dances, burlesques, and pantomimes.

Beyond the campfires, around which thousands of young men eager for war were talking and singing and laughing, stretched hundreds of miles of dark desert, at the end of which lay the beleaguered city and the lonely warrior they had come to rescue. And from him came news, somehow smuggled north. A letter dated 4 November which read: 'At Metemmeh waiting your orders are five steamers with nine guns. We can hold out 40 days with ease; after that, it will be difficult. The Mahdi is here about eight miles away. All north side along the White Nile is free of Arabs; they are on south and south-west and east of town some way off. They are quiet. I should take the road from Ambukol to Metemmeh, where my steamers wait for you.' Then a verbal message, issued in Khartoum on 14 December, delivered to Korti on the 30th: 'The enemy cannot take us except by starving us out. Our troops suffer from want of provisions: the food we have is little – some grain and biscuit. We want you to come quickly. Do not scatter your troops. The enemy is numerous. Bring plenty of troops if you can.'

The need for relief was clearly urgent. It was on its way. At 3 o'clock on the afternoon of the very day that Gordon's verbal message arrived at Korti, Brigadier General Sir Herbert Stewart, commander of the Camel Corps, set out across the Bayuda Desert, bound for the Jakdul Wells.[11]

⬛

The destruction of Muhammad Ali's expeditionary force on 5 September had crippled Gordon's strike capacity and compelled him to abandon his grand scheme to open up the whole river from Dongola to Sennar. Instead, all he could do now was sit tight, eke out his rations, endeavour to maintain morale, and somehow communicate the urgency of the situation to Cairo and London. Thus, on the night of 9/10 September, Colonel John Stewart, accompanied by *Times* correspondent Frank Power, French Consul Henri Herbin, and a group of Greek and Syrian merchants, set sail in the steamer *Abbas*, bound for Dongola and Egypt. Stewart had been reluctant to go, but Gordon had insisted that his duty was to carry messages north. The *Abbas* had been provided with underwater buffers to protect against submerged rocks, and two sailing boats were taken in tow in case of mishap. Two large steamers, *Mansura* and *Safiya*, were to escort the *Abbas* past two danger points, the narrow Shabluka Gorge (the Sixth Cataract) and the heavily garrisoned town of Berber, and then to continue for two days further to ensure safe passage before turning back to Khartoum.

Though the flotilla took fire from the banks at various points, all went well up to and past Berber. Then Stewart, in defiance of Gordon's orders, perhaps afflicted with concern and guilt, ordered the two escort steamers to head back immediately. Too soon. The Mahdists, who had earlier captured two steamers, now sent one of them, the *El-Fasher*, downriver after the *Abbas*. Stewart, unaware that he was pursued, had cut the two sailing boats adrift, in order to gain speed in the descent of the Fifth Cataract; these, with their Greek and Syrian passengers, were promptly captured by the *El-Fasher*. The *Abbas*, however, sailed on – the Mahdists having decided not to risk the rapids – passing Abu Hamed on the great bend of the river, arriving at the Fourth Cataract, almost 500 miles downriver of Khartoum. Then, on 18 September, disaster struck. The *Abbas* hit a rock, became wedged, and could not be got off. Stewart took refuge on an island to await the arrival of the sailing boats he assumed were still following. After two days, he sent men ashore to seek help from the local sheikh, offering presents and rewards in return for the use of camels and safe passage. The reception was positive: Stewart, Power, and Herbin were invited to the sheikh's house to discuss arrangements. As soon as they were seated, they were surrounded by armed men and hacked to death.

This was a blow no less severe than Muhammad Ali's defeat – though it was to be a month before Gordon heard rumours of it, and another month before he received confirmation. He had not only lost his second-in-command – 'a brave, just, upright gentlemen' – along with one of his precious steamers; his journal, correspondence, and cypher book had all fallen into the hands of his enemies. The Mahdi later informed Gordon of this huge intelligence coup in a gloating letter. 'We never miss any of your news,' he wrote, 'nor what is in your innermost thoughts and about the strength and

support – not of God – on which you rely. We have now understood it all.'
After providing details on Gordon's orders, plans, garrison, armaments,
supplies, and deployments – all gleaned from the cache of captured
documents – he again appealed to his enemy to surrender and become a
Muslim, or 'face war from Allah and his Messenger'.[12]

But Gordon knew that a relief expedition was on its way. Operating for
much of the time undercover in northern Sudan was an exceptionally tall,
moustachioed, 34-year-old intelligence officer with piercing blue eyes who
was reputed to speak Arabic so well that he could adopt dialect and pass
himself off as a local. Despite being a loner, a repressed homosexual, and a
man who disdained the company of fellow officers, Major Horatio Herbert
Kitchener was destined for an illustrious career. Right now, however, his
mission was a mix of intelligence gathering, liaison with local sheikhs,
raising irregular forces among friendly tribes, and, not least, communications with Gordon, now only possible by getting trusted natives to smuggle
messages in and out of Khartoum.[13] On 20 September, three Arabs had
arrived from Dongola with a message from Kitchener for Stewart. 'Can I do
anything for you or General Gordon?' Kitchener had written at Debba,
south of Dongola, on 22 August. 'I should be awfully glad if you would let
me know. The relief expedition is evidently coming up this way, but whether
they will go by Berber or attempt the direct road from here, I do not know.'
The relief expedition! It was coming. The following day, Gordon had the
news announced on notices, with pictures of British and Sudanese soldiers,
which were pasted throughout the town, and ordered the firing of a 100-gun
salute 'to let the Arabs know of the advanced expeditionary force'.[14]

Other forces were also in motion. The summer of 1884 had afforded the
beleaguered city of Khartoum something of a respite. Many of the Mahdi's
warriors were still engaged elsewhere. The fighting had only recently ended
in the Bahr al-Ghazal, a seesaw struggle continued in the Jazira, and a
murderous little war still raged against Nuba tribesmen in the mountains
of southern Kordofan. The high Nile, meanwhile, protected the city against
direct assault, while Gordon's aggressive use of his elite strike-force of steamers
and black riflemen had broken through the siege lines. Only on 8 August did
the Mahdi set out from his main base at Rahad (about 50 miles from
El-Obeid). His leisurely progress towards Khartoum was part pilgrimage,

part propaganda, part military muster. This was to be the greatest gathering of Mahdist power so far. A hundred streams of recruits flowed into the main procession as it moved towards Khartoum. Some came on camels, horses, and mules, but most on foot, tens of thousands of Ansar fighters, tens of thousands more who were families and slaves. They fed off the land, or at pop-up markets along the way, or from what they could hunt; but they also herded thousands of cattle as a mobile food-store. The Mahdi rode his magnificent camel in their midst, and carried a portable *minbar* on a baggage camel, a robust wooden pulpit from which he would preach to great assemblies of his followers when they camped, his strong voice reaching across the stillness of the desert to carry the 1,300-year-old message of Muhammad to a new generation of holy warriors. When the great host reached Omdurman on the west bank of the White Nile opposite Khartoum, on 23 October, it may have become 200,000 strong, of whom perhaps 60,000 were fighting men. Others continued to arrive through November, and with the men already in the lines south and north-east of the city, and Mahdist army may have totalled 100,000 in all.[15]

Sheikh El-Obeid and his sons commanded the forces at Khojali on the northern bank of the Blue Nile, Abu Girja and Wad al-Nejumi the forces holding the lines south of the city between the two rivers. Most of these men were drawn from the Jazira and the Nile tribes. Now an army from the west, from Darfur and Kordofan, commanded by the Khalifa Abdullahi and Hamdan Abu Anja, sealed the investment, establishing a vast camp in the near desert and a ring of trenches close around the government fort at Omdurman. When these looped around the eastern side of the fort, the Ansar digging in as the Nile fell, the garrison's communications with Khartoum were severed and the defenders began to starve. The fire from fort and steamers was heavy, but the trenches were deep-cut, and the Ansar could not be dislodged; and the return fire, from captured Krupps, Nordenfeldts, and Remingtons, was equally heavy – heavy enough to defeat an attack by Gordon's two remaining steamers, sinking one, damaging another.

The fort commandant, Brigadier General Farajallah Raghib, was one of Gordon's most senior and trusted officers. But even the strongest allegiances are brittle in a collapsing state. Farajallah had known and respected Muhammad Ahmad before his manifestation as the Mahdi. And Mahdist strategy was to win by diplomacy, inducement, and example wherever it could be done. 'Do not think,' the Mahdi wrote to Farajallah, that if you surrender, we will come for your property or possessions. On the contrary, you will be promoted and stand among the ranks of our beloved companions. I believe my warnings have already reached you . . . you should know that whoever disbelieves in me will be tormented in this world and the next . . . You yourself have witnessed my victories when I was still weak, with few men. Now I have the weapons of Rashid Bey, Al-Shallali, Hicks, and garrisons of Darfur and Bahr al-Ghazal.

On 15 January, Farajallah and his 240 men surrendered. The commandant set aside the uniform and tarbush of an Ottoman officer for the patched *jibba* and turban of a Mahdist emir. Not only was Gordon's west-bank bridgehead extinguished, allowing the enemy vice to tighten around city, but Farajallah's defection encouraged other men to review their allegiance.[16]

Some had been in active communication with the Mahdi all along. Others were lying low, concerned not to compromise themselves given a likely change of masters. A good number were active sympathisers, working, openly or clandestinely, in the Mahdi's interest – for the same mix of motives as animated so many other Sudanese living under the lash of Turco-Egyptian colonial rule. But the army – and government service more generally – was a special case, since it had been the core support of the Arabi revolution, and many of the officers and soldiers defeated at Tel el-Kebir had afterwards been shipped to Sudan. The Turco-Egyptian apparatus was not only rotten with demoralisation and corruption: it was permeated with revolutionary ideals. Arabi may have been a liberal nationalist, where the Mahdi preached Islamic fundamentalism, but the latter was still a fellow Muslim fighting an anti-colonial war against British imperial domination. Ahmad Awwam al-Husseini was a case in point. He had worked as a clerk in Arabi's Ministry of War, and then been exiled to Khartoum following the defeat of the revolution. In July 1884, he published a pamphlet, *Awwam's Advice to the Educated and Common People*, in which he railed against 'the Turco-Egyptian government that has turned this country to ruin and sacrificed souls by kindling the flames of war and thundering her rifle-shots among her subjects, the true believers'. He denounced the Ottoman Sultan and the Egyptian Khedive for 'an awful crime and an indelible sin' in handing Sudan over to the British. He described the leader of the Sudanese *ulema* (the clerics) as a 'hypocrite' and 'blind man' for his alliance with Gordon and opposition to the Mahdiya, which he considered a struggle for the cause of Islam against a government that had betrayed the *umma* (the Muslim community). Oddly, despite his subversive activities, Awwam continued to be employed as a translator for many months by both Colonel Stewart and General Gordon. But after someone attempted to set fire to the town's ammunition supply on 29 September, he was arrested and, with support from a delegation of Khartoum dignitaries, hanged.[17]

By New Year, however, the fifth column was not Gordon's primary problem: it was food. The town was now in a state of famine, with civilians dying of hunger every day, and the soldiers, though their needs were prioritised, enfeebled and lethargic. The supply of grain and biscuit ran out, and the few remaining cattle were slaughtered. Early in January, Gordon made a public announcement that any townspeople who wished to leave the town and join the Mahdi were free to do so. Many did (and were well received). Crops were reaped on Tuti Island under enemy gunfire. A requisition squad searched the town for hidden stores. Gum was collected. The pith of palm trunks was mixed with a little *durra* to create a species of bread. By the second week of January, donkeys, mules, dogs, and rats were being eaten. Prices skyrocketed as Gordon's paper money lost all value. The trickle of desertions became a stream. Those who remained were wracked with hunger, dysentery, and despair. Their leader scanned the northern horizon with his telescope every day, many times a day, always hoping to see the smoke of steamers.[18]

Garnet Wolseley's proposal to create a camel corps to form a desert column was only the latest in a long series of disagreements between 'our only general' and the Duke of Cambridge, the head of the British Army. Though the two men were in harness – Wolseley, as Adjutant General, was Cambridge's No. 2 at Horse Guards – it was a most unhappy arrangement, for Wolseley was a field commander and the standard-bearer of reform, while the Duke was an ageing, gout-ridden, desk-bound conservative who owed his position to royal rank (he was Queen Victoria's cousin). The proposed camel corps was yet another affront to military tradition. Wolseley wanted to create a mobile *force de frappe* composed of picked men from the Guards and the Cavalry – an elite of the elite. The Duke objected that this would damage the integrity of fine regiments. But he was unable to come up with an alternative, so Wolseley got his way. 'These Camel Corps,' he insisted, 'will really be worth any brigade of troops I could collect here. In fact, they will be, in reality, the very finest troops in the world.'[19] This may well have been true. The corps was formed of four regiments, each of 400 men: the Heavy Camel Regiment was recruited from the Life Guards, the Blues, the Dragoon Guards, the Dragoons, and the Lancers; the Light Camel Regiment from the Hussars; the Guards' Camel Regiment from the Coldstream, Grenadier, and Scots Guards, plus a detachment of Royal Marines; while the Mounted Infantry Camel Regiment was formed of 25-man contingents from a number of regiments of the line. Their distinctive uniform comprised a white pith helmet with blue sun goggles and green fly net, light-grey summer tunic, light-brown corduroy breeches, blue puttees, and boots. They carried rifle, sword-bayonet, a bandolier holding 50 rounds, plus pouch, haversack, and water bottle.[20] Today, we would call them 'special forces' – except that time was lacking to turn them into a wholly effective military force before they were deployed.

Learning to ride was the first problem. 'We had a mounted parade,' recalled Private Marling of the Mounted Infantry, 'at first at a walk, and did fours, right and left and wheeling, and only about six men fell off. Then Curly Hutton sounded the trot, and in two minutes the air was thick with Tommies flying about at every angle. Twenty-three camels got loose and went off with their tails in the air, towards the setting sun, and we never got back five of them. Curly Hutton came off on his head.'[21] Learning to ride a camel was, though, a minor problem compared with learning to maintain one. Camels are big, smelly, intractable beasts, liable to bite, often infested with tics, and endowed with a number of revolting habits: in consequence, few men warm to their camels. Yet, despite their phenomenal powers of endurance in desert environments – they can manage up to 100 miles without water – they require much skilled care to remain healthy. This, in Wolseley's new Camel Corps, was in short supply. Nor were there enough animals – far from it – so those available were not only inexpertly laden (often using inappropriate saddles), but were overloaded, underfed, worked too long, and denied the rest they needed. So they developed sores, became exhausted, and gradually broke down.[22] Logistical collapse – the failure of its camel transport – would eventually bring the Desert Column to defeat.

Some officers saw this coming. Brigadier General Sir Charles Wilson, the expedition intelligence officer, was one of them. Wolseley's plan was to send the Desert Column on a fast dash across the Bayuda Desert from Korti to Metemmeh, while a slower River Column took the long way round, infantry in boats, cavalry and camels following the bank. Ideally, the two arms of the expeditionary force would unite for an advance in force on Khartoum. To buy time, the Camel Corps was to send a small advance contingent from Metemmeh to Khartoum on Gordon's steamers. Twenty-nine red uniforms were supplied so that they could arrive at the town dressed as 'redcoats'. The hope was that this modest display of British imperial power would have disproportionate moral effect. But the plan contained other options. As Wolseley cabled Baring, 'I shall be able to communicate with Gordon by steamer, learn exact position, and, if he is *in extremis* before infantry arrive by river, to push forward by camel corps to help him at all hazards.'[23]

The Desert Column was commanded by General Sir Herbert Stewart, a Wolseley loyalist, supported by Wilson as second-in-command and Charles Beresford RN in command of the Naval Brigade. Speed was of the essence, but the camel shortage imposed delay from the outset. Instead of a direct 150-mile dash from Korti to Metemmeh, it was necessary to convoy to the Jakdul Wells, just beyond the midway point, establish an advance post there, then return with the camels for a second convoy. A deleterious effect on the camel train was immediate, made worse, in Wilson's view, by the decision to march mainly at night.

> I contend that . . . when the camels are loaded in the dark, the loads are badly put on, and that sore backs are started before the loads can be properly adjusted by daylight; that owing to the constant long halts, necessary to keep the column together in the dark, the loads remain on the camels' backs for an excessively long time, 15 or 16 hours out of the 24; that the camels start on empty stomachs, contrary to the habit of the beast; that much harm is done to the camels by marching, in close order, in the dark over rough ground; that the camels get neither proper rest nor food . . . There is ample water, abundant vegetation, and an almost limitless supply of *savas* grass, the best of feeding for camels; and here ours are failing before we have commenced, simply because we will not give them time to feed, and when in camp tie them down so tightly they cannot move.

So problematic were the camels that Wilson wondered at the whole concept of a Camel Corps. 'It would be heresy to say the camelry is a mistake; but if Tommy Atkins cannot march in such a climate as this, we had better give up fighting.'[24]

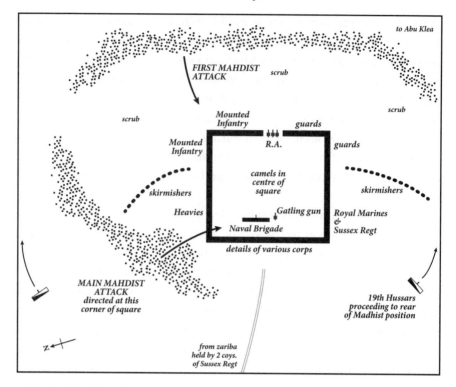

10. The Battle of Abu Klea, 17 January 1885

It took two weeks to complete the concentration at the Jakdul Wells, a small plain enclosed by a punchbowl of rock containing two large pools that now became the Desert Column's forward depot, with a small fort and 150-strong garrison. When the column moved out for the advance to Metemmeh, it comprised 1,800 combatants and 1,100 transport camels. They included the Heavy, the Guards, and the Mounted Infantry Camel Regiments, 250 men of the Royal Sussex, also on camels, two troops of the 19th Hussars, Beresford's Naval Brigade with a Gardner machine gun, three Royal Artillery 7-pdr mountain guns, plus Royal Engineers and a Field Hospital.[25] On the second day out, the Hussars, scouting ahead, brought news that the enemy was deployed in force in a range of low hills straddling the track to the wells of Abu Klea.

The column's delay in reaching thus far had allowed time for this challenge to be mounted. The Mahdi, alerted to its approach, had ordered the Emir of Berber to mobilise. A formidable force of Ababda, Bisharin, Danagla, and Ja'aliyin tribesmen, reinforced by *Jihadiya* riflemen and Kordofani spearmen from the Mahdi's army, perhaps 10,000 Ansar in all, under the command of Abd al-Majid Muhammad, was now blocking the road, intent on denying Stewart's column of thirsty men and beasts access to the wells.[26] A long line of banners could be seen flapping in the breeze, war-drums were pounding, and little puffs of smoke in the distance revealed the presence of enemy riflemen. Stewart decided it was too late in the day to mount an attack, so halted and formed a *zariba* of thorn bush, biscuit box, and camel saddle to camp for the night. But the British were already in rolling ground, and numbers of enemy riflemen crept forward, occupying high ground above the *zariba*, from which they maintained a harassing fire through the evening and into the darkness. At sunrise the following morning, the fire grew hotter. Breakfast was served amid whizzing bullets.[27]

Stewart and Wilson had expected a dawn attack: the entire column had been roused and stood to arms. But none came; whereas the enemy fire was taking a steady toll, as it was bound to do, for Mahdist marksmanship was better than anticipated – 'we did not realise that we had such good shots in front of us' (Wilson) – and a *zariba* of 1,800 men and 2,900 camels was a dense target. Attempts to suppress the fire using cavalry and skirmishers were insufficient. In any case, the column had to move to water or die of thirst. So at 9 o'clock, three hours after sunrise, orders were issued to form square preparatory to an advance.[28]

The sick, the stores, and most of the camels were left in the *zariba*, guarded by a detachment of the Royal Sussex. Colonel Barrow's Hussars were sent out on the left to keep enemy riflemen on the hills in check, while detachments of Mounted Infantry and Scots Guards were deployed as skirmishers on the flanks. The main formation was a 1,200-man square, with Mounted Infantry left front, Guards right front, Heavies and Naval Brigade left rear, Royal Sussex right rear. The three 7-pdr guns were placed in the centre of the front face. The Gardner was with the Naval Brigade at the left-rear corner. About 150 baggage-camels – for water, ammunition, and *cacolets* (for the wounded) – filled the centre. Its progress was very slow, since the ground was formed of rocky hillocks and deep ruts, a route chosen because it was clear of covered areas where the enemy might mass for a rush. The camels in particular slipped and stumbled and fell behind, causing the rear of the square to bulge, necessitating frequent halts to dress formation. Firing was constant. The Mahdist marksmen took a steady toll. British cavalry, skirmishers, and mountain guns fired back to cover the advance of the square. Perhaps, had the Mahdists refused to close and continued the battle as a firefight, Stewart's command might have been destroyed, for the square was slow and dense. But when the skirmishers were within 200 yards of the line of flags marking the main enemy position, and the square, 300 yards further back, was halted again to dress ranks, thousands of Ansar warriors rose from the wadi and surged forward.[29]

They were, thought Wilson, 'a beautiful and striking sight'. They came on in three giant wedges, each headed by a mounted emir or sheikh with a banner and his personal retinue, followed by row upon row of tribal spearmen charging on foot.

> I remember experiencing a feeling of pity mixed with admiration for them, as I thought they would all be shot down in a few minutes. I could not have believed beforehand that men in close formation would have been able to advance for 200 to 400 yards over bare ground in the face of Martini-Henrys. As they advanced, the feeling was changed to wonder that the tremendous fire we were keeping up had so little effect. When they got within 80 yards, the fire of the Guards and Mounted Infantry began to take good effect, and a huge pile of dead rose in front of them. Then, to my astonishment, the enemy took ground to their right as if on parade, so as to envelop the rear of the square.

Hitting an impenetrable wall of fire to their front, the Ansar torrent seems to have surged around the British left. Skirmishers racing ahead of them, seeking the security of the square, blocked the field of fire, allowing the Ansar following on their heels to close with their enemies. As they did so, they found the left-rear angle of the square unformed, with soldiers still struggling to haul camels inside.[30]

Now were discovered other problems with the Camel Corps. Recruited from the most prestigious regiments, the Camel Corps had a disproportionate number of young aristocratic officers who had never been in battle. Many regarded war as a lark. Winston Churchill, who served as an officer in the Sudan (and elsewhere) in the late 1890s, later wrote of the typical attitude at the time: 'Nobody expected to be killed. Here and there in every regiment or battalion, half a dozen, a score, at the worst 30 or 40, would pay the forfeit; but to the great mass of those who took part in the little wars of Britain in those vanished light-hearted days, this was only a sporting element in a splendid game.'[31]

Another problem was that fighting a square was an infantryman's job, but the two officers at the endangered spot were a sailor, Commander

Beresford of the Naval Brigade, and a cavalryman, Colonel Burnaby of the Heavies. 'It does not pay to pick a cavalryman to do infantry work,' would be General Buller's wry comment on Abu Klea when he heard reports of it. Mobility was in the DNA of both cavalry and naval officers, whereas the rigid discipline of the firing line was less familiar. Beresford ran his Gardner gun out of the square on the left, while Burnaby wheeled two companies of his Heavies in such a way as to widen the gap.[32] 'They were tearing down upon us with a roar like the roar of the sea,' recalled Beresford:

> an immense surging wave of white-slashed black forms brandishing bright spears and long flashing swords; and all were chanting, as they leaped and ran, the war-song of their faith ... and the terrible rain of bullets poured into them by the Mounted Infantry and Guards stayed them not. They wore the loose white robe of the Mahdi's uniform, looped over the left shoulder, and the straw skull-cap. These things we saw in a flash, as the formidable wave swept steadily nearer.
>
> I laid the Gardner gun myself to make sure. As I fired, I saw the enemy mown down in rows, dropping like ninepins; but as the men killed were in rear of the front rank, after firing about 40 rounds (eight turns of the lever), I lowered the elevation. I was putting in most effective work on the leading ranks and had fired about 30 rounds when the gun jammed.[33]

The Gardner, the mechanical machine gun favoured by the Royal Navy, had five barrels side-by-side firing .45-inch calibre rounds held in clips and fed vertically by lever. Thus each turn of the lever fired five rounds, and the rate of fire could be as high as 120 rounds a minute. Mounted on a wheeled carriage, it was nonetheless heavy and cumbersome, and efficient operation was the work of several men, much like a light artillery piece. But the biggest problem was the machine's proneness to jamming.[34] Beresford and his chief boatswain's mate attempted to unscrew the feed-plate to clear the obstruction, but the enemy were upon them. All the bluejackets around the gun perished, except Beresford, who found himself 'carried bodily backwards by the tremendous impact of the rush'. Colonel Burnaby was cut down 30 yards outside the square (and would die where he lay in a brother officer's arms immediately after the battle), and those of his Heavy Camels who did not fall with him were thrust back against men of the Royal Sussex who had been attempting to close the gap.[35]

The crush as the front ranks of Ansar struck the collapsing side of the square and the rear ranks concertinaed into them was such that many men could not use their weapons. Beresford found himself facing an Arab holding a spear over his head that was jammed against his back by the pressure behind, while he himself was incapable of drawing either sword or pistol. Some of the attackers broke clean through. Wilson watched in astonishment as 'a fine old sheikh on horseback' planted his banner in the centre of the square before being shot down. 'I had noticed him in the advance, with his banner in one hand and a book of prayers in the other, and never saw anything finer. The old man never swerved to the right or left, and never ceased chanting his prayers, until he had planted his banner in our square.'[36]

Stewart's column might have been destroyed. Hundreds of men of fanatic courage had penetrated the British formation. Four factors combined to prevent this. First was the exceptional quality of British regulars, who were, in terms of training, discipline, and morale, second to none; the fact that the men of the Desert Column did not panic at this supreme moment of crisis was crucial. Second was the superiority of the breechloader-and-bayonet weapon system over that of spear and sword in close-quarters fighting. Third was the presence of a mass of camels in the interior of the square that created a solid barrier against the Arab eruption and prevented the surge from carrying away the opposite sides of the broken formation. Fourth was the fact that the right front of the square had been on slightly raised ground when the formation halted, and this now provided a ready firing platform when the rear ranks turned to face the *mêlée* behind them. As Colvile later explained in the *Official History*, 'The camels, which up to this time had been a source of weakness to the square, now became a source of strength. The spearmen by weight of numbers forced back the rear face of the square onto the camels; these formed a living traverse that broke the rush and gave time for the right face and front face to take advantage of finding themselves on higher ground, and to fire over the heads of those engaged in a hand-to-hand struggle, on to the mass of the enemy behind.'[37]

A storm of lead shot fired at point-blank range crashed into the rear ranks of the dense mass of Ansar spearmen packed inside the square. The effect was immediate. The Martini-Henry volleys, crashing out every few seconds, brought down dozens at a time. The rest wavered, turned, and retreated – not in panic, but sullenly, many still defiant. 'Their desperate courage was marvellous,' recalled Beresford:

I saw a boy of some 12 years of age, who had been shot through the stomach, walk slowly up through a storm of bullets and thrust his spear at one of our men. I saw several Arabs writhe out from a pile of dead and wounded, and charge some 80 yards under fire towards us, and one of them ran right up to the bayonets and flung himself upon them and was killed. I saw an Arab, who was wounded in legs, sit up and hurl his spear at a passing soldier. As the soldier stopped to load his rifle, the Arab tried to reach another spear, and failing, caught up stones and cast them at his foe; and then, when the soldier presented his rifle and took a deliberate aim, the Arab sat perfectly still looking down the barrel, till the bullet killed him.[38]

Loud cheering broke out across the square, and for a time the victors were wild with excitement, officers struggling to reform ranks lest a second assault be mounted. But there was none: the Mahdist energy was spent. The battle had lasted barely 10 minutes, but in that time at least 1,100 Sudanese had been shot down, while the British had lost 9 officers and 65 men killed, 9 officers and 85 men wounded, many of them severely – almost 10 per cent of the Desert Column's strength. Both sides were damaged. Though the Mahdist army had not been broken, Abu Klea had served a bloody lesson in modern firepower, and only the bravest of the Ansar would join any future charges of spearmen. On the other hand, the British were in no condition to follow up their victory. Instead, having collected themselves, they counted their dead, picked up the wounded, gathered up abandoned kit, and staggered towards the wells, 3 miles off, with raging thirst, 'their tongues so swollen as to cause intense pain, their lips black, their mouths covered with white mucus' (Beresford). The wells turned out to be pits of sand filled with muddy water that looked like white tea; but Beresford found it 'cool, sweet, and delicious'. The force then bivouacked for the night in bitter cold. Many could not sleep. Beresford joked with a brother officer that it would be hard to die without knowing who had won the Derby.[39]

Stewart now made a most difficult decision. At a council of war, some officers had argued that the column would not be able to withstand another attack and should retreat to the Jakdul Wells. The implications were dire: rations consumed, camels worn down, men demoralised, the enemy emboldened, and the relief of Gordon ever more remote. Stewart therefore decided to establish a small fort at Abu Klea to protect the stores and the wounded, guarded by 100 Royal Sussex, and to march with the rest of the column on Metemmeh – a forced march of about 25 miles through the night of 18/19 January with the intention of reaching the river by dawn. The cautious Wilson tried to change his mind, and even the gung-ho Beresford had grave doubts: 'It was a desperate venture, for the men had had no sleep for two nights, had fought a battle in between, had suffered agonies of thirst and the exhaustion of hunger.'[40]

The column set out at 4 o'clock on the afternoon of 18 January. A good pace was established at first, but the march slowed during the night, as native drivers nodded off, camels wandered in search of grazing, loads fell off, and tired men lost their way in the darkness. Control broke down, because, with the enemy close, orders had to be given in whispers and passed along the line, and, in a straggling column of shadows, messages failed in transmission. What had been a good pathway, 'showing up white in the darkness' (Wilson), ceased to be so as the column entered the Shebakat bush country, a region of tall savas grass and acacia thicket. 'The column got into terrible disorder here. The mounted portion got through fairly enough, but the baggage-camels got jammed and entangled in the bush: many were left behind, others were extricated with difficulty. The confusion was endless, and the noise of men swearing and 'grousing' camels could have been heard miles away. The passage through the bush would have been troublesome enough in daylight for a convoy as large as ours; at night, with no moon, it was exceedingly difficult. Halts were frequent, and for a long time we made little progress . . .' The column averaged barely a mile an hour during 14 hours of marching.[41]

Dawn revealed that the column had wandered off course and was still 5 miles from Metemmeh. After a brief halt to reorganise, Stewart pressed on, determined to reach the river without having to fight a battle. But at 7.30, topping a gravel ridge that offered a clear view over the Nile, with Metemmeh on the west bank and Shendi on the east, large numbers of Ansar could be seen streaming into position to contest the advance. The enemy's war-drums were beating, and the Hussars, scouting ahead, had already come under fire. Stewart ordered a *zariba* constructed so that his exhausted men could break-fast, aware that he was now going to have to fight to reach the river.[42]

The situation was perilous in the extreme. Though there were about 250 yards of open ground around the *zariba*, and though a small knoll to the south-west had been occupied to prevent its use by the enemy, the more distant ground was covered in thin scrub as far as the eye could see: ideal cover for Mahdist riflemen. A dangerous firefight continued all morning, with a steady stream of casualties, one of whom was Stewart himself, hit in the groin, a wound that would eventually prove fatal. Command was assumed by Charles Wilson.

The position was untenable. The enemy refused to attack: they seemed set upon slow attrition. The men were exhausted, their improvised shelter of saddles and boxes was inadequate, the baggage-camels were taking numerous hits, and the water situation would soon turn critical. The decision – to advance and attempt to reach the river – was unavoidable. Wilson divided his force, leaving Colonel Barrow with half the Heavies, the Naval Brigade, the Hussars, the 7-pdrs, and the Gardner to defend a strengthened *zariba*, while forming the remaining 900 men into a square, moving off at 3 o'clock. This time, there were no skirmishers to obstruct the field of fire, but the square halted periodically to deliver volley-fire into the bush to suppress snipers, supported by machine gun and artillery fire from Barrow's *zariba*.[43]

The men in the *zariba* watched as the square disappeared from view over the gravel ridge. Then they heard 'the steady roll of volley firing' (Beresford) that indicated that the square was under attack. Then, after five minutes, silence. It was a while before they knew what had happened.[44]

As at Abu Klea, the Mahdist musketry had died away, and a great surge of spearmen had raced towards the British formation. The numbers who charged at the Battle of Abu Kru seem to have been fewer – Wilson estimated only 800, as against 1500 at Abu Klea – and now there was no disorder in the British ranks, no gaps, only solid lines of riflemen with clear fields of fire. And there was superb fire-discipline – so much so that when the first fire had little effect and the bugle sounded 'cease firing', the men answered the call and the momentary rest steadied them, and when the enemy reached to within 300 yards and the bugle sounded 'commence firing', the effect was devastating. 'All the leaders with their fluttering banners went down,' recalled Wilson, 'and no-one got within 50 yards of the square. It only lasted a few minutes: the whole of the front ranks were swept away; and then we saw a backward movement, followed by the rapid disappearance of the Arabs in front of and all around us.' Between 250 and 300 Ansar were shot down in the attack. Not a single man was wounded in the square during the charge.

Abu Kru was a tactical triumph of machine power over raw courage. But the strategic situation of the Desert Column was more critical than ever. Before the charge of spearmen, the Mahdist riflemen had accounted for 23 killed and 98 wounded.[45] This meant the column had now lost 15 per cent of its effectives. The wounded, moreover, were a major impediment, since they had to be tended, guarded, and transported. The rest of the men were utterly spent: in the previous four days, they had fought two battles, endured an exhausting 14-hour night march, suffered agonies of thirst, and not had any proper sleep. The camels were quite broken down, having been over-worked, underfed, and underwatered for the best part of a week. 'Can it be wondered at that the poor beasts were hardly able to crawl down to the river with their loads,' Wilson wrote:

> and that they were practically useless without some rest and food. The result almost justified the *mot*, that we thought we had found in the camel an animal that required neither food, nor drink, nor rest: we certainly acted as if the camel were a piece of machinery. The sore backs from careless loading in the dark, and from tumbling about during night-marches, were sickening to look at.

The horses were equally done in, rendering the Hussars 'almost useless as cavalry' by the time they reached the river.

Despite this, Wilson considered himself duty-bound to continue offensive action. A sapper and cartographer, not a fighting general, he consulted with the wounded Stewart and with brother officers. The former was too much the Wolseley loyalist to question the orders issued in Korti, while the latter were woefully short on combat experience. Standard doctrine in small wars 'against savages and semi-civilised races by disciplined soldiers' was to remain active and aggressive. The stress was on 'boldness', 'vigour', 'resolute action', 'the maintenance of the initiative', 'the importance of following up successes'. As Colonel Callwell later wrote in what became the official British Army manual of colonial warfare, 'It cannot be insisted upon too strongly that in a small war the only possible attitude to assume is, speaking strategi-cally, the offensive.' Wilson's conclusion was that 'the political effect of not taking Metemmeh would be so bad that its capture ought to be attempted'.[46]

Much that happened over the next two weeks would have had a comic-opera character had the situation not been so perilous. Wilson established a camp at the village of Abu Kru (called Gubat by the British). The immediate priority was to reunite the two parts of the Desert Column – the men left in the *zariba* had no water, the men who had advanced to the river had no food – so 600 men marched back to the *zariba* to bring the rest down. Beresford and Barrow had failed to prevent wholesale looting of the stores; a lack of grip by inexperienced officers had led to a breakdown of discipline and control. The following day (21 January), having consulted with the wounded Stewart, for whom Wolseley's instructions to 'attack and occupy' Metemmeh were paramount, Wilson launched 750 men against the formidable mud-walled town. They manoeuvred round it for several hours, exchanged brisk fire with the defenders, then gave up and marched back to their camp, destroying three small villages on the way. The 7-pdrs had made no impression on the walls. The numerous enemy had shown no sign of giving up. The task had been hopeless with the force available. Mahdist morale had not collapsed as British counter-insurgency doctrine expected.[47]

During the battle, Gordon's four steamers had arrived at Metemmeh. The cargo included Gordon's journal, written up to 14 December, with this final plea: 'NOW MARK THIS, if the expeditionary force, and I ask for no more than 200 men, does not come in ten days, *the town may fall*; and I have done my best for the honour of our country. Goodbye.' But there was other news: enemy forces were reported approaching Abu Kru from both north and south. This compelled further delay. The column was reorganised into a more secure defensive position, with two camps, one by the river to guard access to water, the other to hold the high ground overlooking it. These forts were to be held by 900 men, but they would have only 400 camels and 100 horses, and since they were also encumbered with wounded, they would be effectively immobilised. Meanwhile, a column of 300 men and 1,000 camels was to return to Jakdul to resupply and also carry dispatches for Korti. Contributing further delay was Wilson's decision to make a steamer reconnaissance downriver to evaluate the enemy threat reported from that direction. Not until the morning of the 23rd did two steamers, the *Bordein* and the *Telahawiya*, depart for Khartoum. Beresford, who, as ranking naval officer, should have commanded 'the river dash', was incapacitated by a boil on his bottom, so Wilson himself led the expedition, taking two officers and 20 men of the Royal Sussex, about 250 Sudanese troops, and a *nuggar* (under tow) filled with *durra* for the starving garrison.[48]

The little flotilla's chances of success were not high. The distance was the best part of 100 miles against the current, and the steamers were heavily laden, low in the water, and slow; frequent stops, moreover, were necessary for 'wooding'. The steamers were 'the size of "penny" steamers on the Thames, which a single well-directed shell would send to the bottom, with crews and soldiers absolutely without discipline'. Mahdist batteries lay in wait at various points along the banks, and the Shabluka Gorge, the Sixth

Cataract, was not only a major obstacle in itself, but a potentially perilous ambush-position. In the event, the sinister-looking ramparts of mud-and-sand were silent as the flotilla passed by – ominously so, it turned out, for the Mahdist garrisons were busy elsewhere. Only on the sixth day out, approaching Khartoum, did the steamers come under fire, and soon they were running a gauntlet of field guns and rifle fire. Abreast of Tuti Island, the fire reached a crescendo, the rolling of musketry continuous, a loud rushing of shells incoming from emplacements at Omdurman and Khartoum. 'We kept on to the junction of the two Niles,' Wilson recorded in his journal, 'when it became plain to everyone that Khartoum had fallen into the Mahdi's hands; for not only were there hundreds of dervishes ranged under their banners, standing on the sandspit close to the town ready to resist our landing, but no flag was flying in Khartoum and not a shot was fired in our assistance.'

Wilson gave the order to turn and run at full speed downriver, back through the tunnel of fire. 'The sight at this moment was very grand: the masses of the enemy with their long fluttering banners near Khartoum; the long rows of riflemen in the shelter-trenches at Omdurman; the numerous groups of men on Tuti; the bursting shells, and the water torn up by hundreds of bullets and occasional heavier shot . . . it seemed almost impossible that we should escape.' They did, but only to be shipwrecked in the rapids and deserted by many of the Sudanese. Beresford, his boil lanced, was forced to mount a hair-raising rescue mission. Wilson's little party – bedraggled, exhausted, traumatised – finally returned to the British camp at Abu Kru on 5 February, carrying the dismal news that the Gordon Relief Expedition had failed.[49]

Chastened by the bloodbath at El-Obeid, when he had ordered a massed assault, the Mahdi had chosen to invest Khartoum in close siege and attempt to starve it out. Hearing of the approach of the Desert Column, he had dispatched reinforcements northwards to assist Abd al-Majid Muhammad in attempting its destruction. Learning of the setbacks at Abu Klea and Abu Kru, he knew that relief was coming to the beleaguered city, and he assumed it would be soon. In this, he was mistaken: the Desert Column was now too crippled to attempt an advance on its own, and the River Column was still two months away; the 2 steamers and 250 men actually on their way could hardly prevail against his 100,000 holy warriors. But Muhammad Ahmad, believing time was short, resolved to storm the city. His intelligence was excellent, for the place was full of sympathisers and spies; in any case, Gordon had let go a large contingent of civilian refugees, who carried lurid stories of conditions inside Khartoum to Mahdist interrogators. Supplies were exhausted. Famine stalked the streets. Soldiers collapsed at their posts. The defence had reached its limits. This was known. And the Nile had been falling for five months, the receding floodwater exposing a wide mudflat beyond the western edge of the main defences.

Late on 25 January, the Mahdi crossed to the east bank of the Nile to address his soldiers before a dawn attack the following day. Mounted on his camel, he warned them of the deep ditch and the field of iron spikes they must cross. 'Do you wish with all your hearts to fight for God?' he then asked. 'Yes!' they answered. 'Swear allegiance to me unto death!' he called. 'We swear allegiance to you unto death,' they answered. Then he told them they should spare Gordon and all others who offered no resistance. Finally, the multitude swore the accustomed oath of Mahdist warriors before battle: 'We swear by God and His Prophet, and we swear by you, that we will not worship any but God, that we will not steal, that we will not commit adultery, that we will not disobey your lawful commands, that we will not flee from the Holy War. We swear to renounce this world and chose the next.' The Mahdi then pointed his drawn sword towards the city and cried aloud, '*Allahu akbar!*' The banners were unfurled and the Ansar columns marched towards the city.[50]

Despite the racket, perhaps because of their exhaustion, most of the garrison seems to have been asleep when the attack came in the half-light of morning on 26 January. The Ansar crept forward on their bellies and then, on signal, rose to hurl themselves towards the enemy in two massive columns, one on the south-east formed of Jazira and Blue Nile men under Abu Girja, one on the south-west of Baggara, Dighaim, and Kinana from Kordofan under Wad al-Nejumi. Cannon from the Mahdist trenches and lines of *Jihadiya* riflemen posted between the columns gave covering fire. Men coiled in agony as they trod on caltrops, or they were blown away by biscuit-box mines; but these were few among the thousands surging forward, banners snapping above them, spearheads and swords flashing in the rising sun, the ancient Islamic war-cry *Allahu akbar!* sounding above the crash of guns.[51]

Babikr Bedri was in Wad al-Nejumi's column. 'The route of my party was from the south-west, where the White Nile had first risen to flood the ditch and then ebbed again, leaving it filled with earth and silt. I was among the foremost, and did not realise that I had passed the ditch until I found myself close to a machine-gun that was firing on us.' Some, in fact, sank to their waists in the mud and could not get out, but others simply clambered over them; and in many places, the way, though muddy, was passable. Obstacles, in any case, are designed to slow movement so that attackers can be destroyed by fire; undefended, they are always surmountable. And undefended they now were, for acts of resistance by a garrison brought to breaking point by hunger and despair were few. The machine-gunners facing Bedri and his group simply fled into a tent and let it down on top of themselves; and there, writhing in its folds, were hacked to death. Some units fought hard, sustained by a resolute officer, but most fell apart, either at the first onset, or once it was known the enemy had breached the walls. At the Kalakla Gate, the colonel of the 5th Battalion stripped off his uniform and fled into the desert. At the Massallamiya Gate, the general in command of all five forts did the same, leaving the gate open behind him. Through it poured Wad al-Nejumi's Baggara, who then swung north-east, following the wall on the inside to Buri Fort, where regulars of the 2nd Battalion supported by Bashi-Bazouks put up the fiercest resistance, dying almost to the last man.[52]

Tens of thousands of Ansar were soon inside the city. A long pent-up flood of rage now flowed through its streets. The Mahdi's injunctions to his followers to grant quarter and abstain from looting were lost in the moment. Men were shot, speared, stabbed, beheaded, thrown down wells. Women were raped. Houses were ransacked for loot, owners tortured to reveal hiding places. Some officers, fearing the worst, shot their wives and children and then turned their guns on themselves. For the most part, only slaves were spared; for they, of course, were chattels, soon to become the property of new masters.[53]

No-one is sure of Gordon's precise fate. Different stories emerged from the mayhem. It seems certain that he was killed at his palace, but whether he was shot before he had been recognised or was speared as he confronted the mob, his body then tumbling down the steps, we do not know. But for sure his head was cut off, wrapped in a cloth, and carried to the Mahdi's camp, where Slatin saw it. 'His blue eyes were half-opened; the mouth was perfectly natural; the hair of his head and his short whiskers were almost quite white.' The Mahdi was displeased: he had wanted Gordon a prisoner – perhaps in the naïve belief he might be converted, probably out of some mix of curiosity and respect, maybe as a bargaining chip. Nonetheless, he allowed the head of his fallen foe to hang on a tree in Omdurman, to take the curses of the faithful. It seems unlikely, in any event, that Gordon would have allowed himself to have been taken alive. A lonely man tormented by repressed homosexuality, now approaching late middle-age, suffering bouts of deep depression, possessed by a brooding, mystical, evangelical faith, there was a smell of death about him long before the end. In his last year, he wrote often of the possibility, even likelihood, that he would die in Khartoum. 'This may be the last letter you will receive from me,' he had written to his sister Augusta, always his closest confidante, on 14 December, 'for we are on our last legs . . . I am quite happy, thank God, and . . . have *tried* to do my duty.' Charles George Gordon did not expect to survive the fall of the city: he had already decided that his mission on earth was over; that he was being summoned to his Maker.[54]

Wolseley had been living on his nerves. He had rated Stewart's mission 'a great leap in the dark', and then found himself, for the first time in his life, 'chained to the rear', reliant for news on occasional out-of-date messages brought in by steamer or camel. He maintained his gravitas, but he began smoking heavily, and he wrote privately to his wife Louise that 'my very heart is being consumed with anxiety about Stewart's column'. When he heard that it had reached the river, he telegraphed an optimistic report to London, but was concerned to learn that Stewart was wounded and Wilson – 'no soldier' – had assumed command. So Major General Redvers Buller was dispatched to take over. The hammer-blow fell early on 4 February. 'Oh my dear child, I am in despair,' Louise was told. 'News just in that Khartoum was taken by treachery on 26 January. My steamers reached Khartoum on the 28th, just in time to see it occupied by the enemy . . . Poor Gordon! For his sake, I sincerely hope he is dead . . .' Soon after came confirmation that he was. Wolseley was consumed with regret and recrimination. Gordon had been a personal friend. Things could have been done better. A career of unbroken success was now sullied by signal failure. 'My mind keeps thinking how near a brilliant success I was, and how narrowly I missed achieving it.'[55]

It was necessary to apportion blame. Two men were accused: William Ewart Gladstone and Charles Wilson. 'If anything can kill Gladstone,' Wolseley wrote on 5 February in his acerbic campaign journal,

> this news ought to, for he cannot, self-illusionist though he be, disguise from himself the fact that he is directly responsible for the fall of Khartoum

and all the bloodshed it entails; that it was owing to his influence, active measures for the relief of Gordon were not undertaken in time. Whilst Gordon was starving, this arrogant minister who poses as a great statesman, but without any just claim to be considered one, was discussing to himself whether Gordon was 'hemmed in' or 'surrounded' ... Never were the destinies of any great nation committed to a more incompetent pilot. And yet a pack of fools and theoretical vestrymen contrive to worship him with an almost idolatrous reverence.[56]

In an entry on 11 March, equal venom was directed at the hapless Wilson, the engineer and mapmaker on whom responsibility for the command of a doomed mission had accidentally fallen. He was responsible for 'all those delays'; he had 'lost any nerve he ever possessed'; he must 'never again be employed on active service'. 'Great God, it is too dreadful to dwell upon the hairbreadth by which we failed to save Gordon and Khartoum. I still think if Stewart had not been wounded, we should have saved Khartoum. Is is then to be wondered at that I hate the sight of Sir C Wilson? ... He is one of those nervous, weak, unlucky creatures that I hate having near me on active service ...'[57]

In truth, of course, great events have multiple causes: no one man was to blame for the failure of the Gordon Relief Expedition. But Garnet Joseph Wolseley carried a larger share than most, for it was he who had lobbied so hard for Gordon to be sent to Khartoum in the first place, and then for an expedition to be dispatched to relieve him; an expedition which he had always intended should be commanded by himself. In doing so, he underestimated the enemy, minimised the difficulties, and, once in the field, launched highly risky operations without adequate logistical support. The vainglory of a colonial militarist lies at the heart of the story. Wolseley's scapegoating of Wilson was shabby and dishonourable behaviour. It did not save his reputation: he would never hold field command again. 'The sun of my luck set when Stewart was wounded' was how he later described the end of his career as a fighting general.[58]

In the short run, though, the government, not the soldiers, took the blame. 'Too late,' cried Queen Victoria when she heard the news. 'These news from Khartoum are frightful,' she telegraphed Gladstone, Granville, and Hartington, 'and to think that all this might have been prevented and many precious lives saved by earlier action is too frightful.' The Prime Minister's private secretary described it as 'the blackest day since the horrible

Phoenix Park murders'. The newspapers were selling as soon as they hit the streets, with people standing on the pavements to read them. The West End clubs were full at noon with members eager to talk. Egyptian stocks were down. The yellow press transformed Gladstone's honorific initials G.O.M. ('Grand Old Man') into M.O.G. ('Murderer of Gordon'). Conservative Associations all over the country recorded their 'deep regret and bitter humiliation'. Gordon prints, photos, busts, and plates sold out. The Liberal government found itself in the eye of a perfect jingo storm.[59]

Wolseley had cabled for instructions, 'the object of my mission to this country being no longer possible'. He was taken aback by Hartington's reply two days later: 'In addition to the primary object of saving Gordon's life, if it be still possible, we desire to check the Mahdi's advance in the provinces of the Sudan which he has not yet conquered by any means in our power. It is even possible that a subsequent advance and recapture of Khartoum may be necessary'. To facilitate this, in addition to leaving Wolseley 'entirely unchecked' (the Queen's words) to pursue matters as he saw fit, the government was prepared to send out another expeditionary force, this to Suakin, to operate against Osman Digna, build a railway to Berber, and hook up with Wolseley's force on the Nile. This was an extraordinary volte-face by a supposedly non-interventionist government. 'We cannot flatter ourselves,' Wolseley wrote to the Duke of Cambridge a month later, 'that we are here to fight for an oppressed people, to help a population struggling to be free, or to put down slavery. None of the spurious and claptrap pretexts under which we so often invade uncivilised countries will serve here: we are now to crush the Mahdi, who, unless crushed, will crush Egypt, and in doing so bring down the whole Turkish Empire about the Sultan's head.' That some spectre of Islamic *jihad* spreading its shadow across the region panicked London into uncharacteristically abrupt escalation seems likely. But the Liberal government had a more immediate political purpose. The jingoes wanted revenge, a bloodbath, a killing field of 'niggers'. The government scraped a majority on a censure motion at Westminster – but only by letting loose the dogs of war in Africa.[60]

Dawn on 10 February revealed the enemy still in position on the rocky hills at Kirbekan, apparently intent on blocking the road to Abu Hamed. The River Column, the slower arm of Wolseley's giant pincer, had been edging

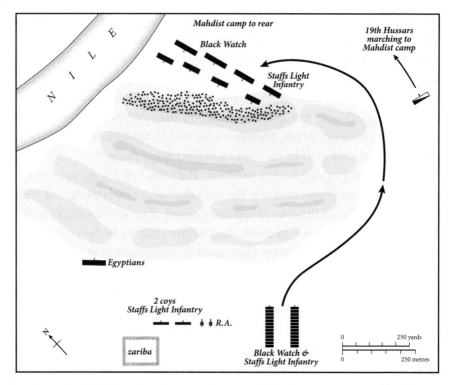

11. The Battle of Kirbekan, 10 February 1885

forward for more than a month, moving north-east along the upper arm of the giant Nile bend. Enemy interference had been minimal, but there were never enough camels, most of the *voyageurs* had departed for home at the termination of their contracts, native allies had proved tardy in the matter of supplies and auxiliaries, and the hazards of the Fourth Cataract – 'tumbled masses of black rock' (Colvile) – had caused considerable delay. Beyond the cataract, the ground was broken and threatening.

> Instead of the rolling plains, so favourable to long-range fire, and so fatal to an enemy whose strength lies in the impetuous charge of his spearmen, are here found cramped and tortuous passages, down which a company could scarcely march in line. The rocky ground is almost impassable for cavalry. On every side extend rugged ridges, behind any one of which thousands of Arabs might be concealed, ready to spring out on a column, with a minimum of exposure to themselves in the open.[61]

General William Earle, in command, received a halt order from Wolseley once it was known that Khartoum had fallen, pending instructions from London. Two days later, the commander-in-chief – now 'entirely unchecked' and urged to 'crush the Mahdi' – wired that the advance was to resume. Wolseley's objective was Berber. Buller, now in command of the Desert Column, was to cooperate with Earle in the attempt to recapture the town. It was hoped that this operation could be coordinated with that of the Suakin expeditionary force, whose ultimate objective was also Berber. Here was a grand strategic plan involving three separate British forces converging across several hundred miles of desert to establish a new forward base for the reconquest of the Sudan: a heady conception.[62]

The Mahdists, emboldened by the capture of Khartoum, were deter-mined to fight on each of these three fronts. Having fallen back before the advance of the River Column until now, up to 2,000 local tribesmen had installed themselves in a strong defensive position astride the road to Abu Hamed. In a chain of hillocks strewn with boulders running down to the river, they had constructed rough stone breastworks. Behind these hillocks ran the road, and on the far side, about 600 yards from the hillocks and parallel with them, was a great ridge of serrated rock, perhaps 300 feet high and 600 yards long; this, too, was heavily occupied, the spears and banners of the defenders visible along the summit. A frontal attack on the hillocks was liable to be costly and hazardous, whereas a flank attack would have been met by enfilade from the ridge. Earle therefore decided upon a wide envelopment on the east to encompass both hillocks and ridge; the aim was to storm the entire enemy position from the rear and cut off the enemy's escape-route.

It was a miniature battle. Colvile reports that most of the Mahdists had slunk away before the collision, leaving only a few hundred to face the British attack. Earle's total force comprised fewer than 1,200 combatants, and some of these were left in a *zariba* to guard boats and baggage. The British suffered minimal casualties on their approach, and the hills were quickly taken by men of the Black Watch and South Staffordshires. 'In open attack formation,' recalled one young captain, a certain Ian Hamilton, 'our men went for them; destroyed their grand counter-charge of spearmen by fire and then stormed the heights from the rear! No-one escaped.' Despite the speed and ease of the victory, however, the brief flare-up of fighting in the rocks had been savage enough, the Arab dead anywhere between 200 and 700, the British losses 10 killed and 47 wounded. Among the British

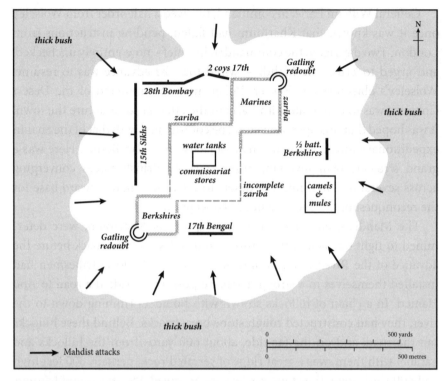

12. The Battle of Tofrek (or McNeill's *zariba*), 22 March 1885

fatalities, moreover, was the commanding general and both regimental colonels. All three were buried by a solitary palm tree on the riverbank. Colonel Henry Brackenbury – the complete army bureaucrat, in Hamilton's judgement – assumed command. The River Column then resumed its advance towards Abu Hamed, taking punitive action along the way against the property of those deemed complicit in the death of Colonel Stewart and his party five months before.[63]

The Suakin Expedition of March 1885 was a political war, fought to deflect criticism from the Liberal government back home. Having withdrawn from the theatre in March 1884, the British suddenly stormed back into it, General Graham again in command, now at the head of 11,000 troops, plus Lucas and Aird railway contractors to lay a line from Suakin to Berber. This was an operation fully comparable in scale with that of Wolseley on the Nile; at a stroke, it doubled the number of British troops operating in the Sudan. Graham's mission, as before, was to secure the Red Sea coast, crush Osman Digna, and open the cross-desert route to Berber. His method, too, was similar. He first lunged towards Hasheen, about 10 miles west of Suakin, where his 10,000 men fought a somewhat chaotic battle on 20 March against about 3,000 Mahdists operating in an area of hill and scrub. The enemy proved resilient and daring, giving ground in the face of direct attack, but continuing to swarm and occasionally launch counterstrikes. With no clear outcome, Graham had to content himself with building a fort and then withdrawing. He claimed his objective had been to guard his right flank for a prospective advance on Tamai, establish an observation post in the hills, and assist in overawing the local tribes. But five days later the fort was dismantled and the place abandoned.[64]

The main operation – a lunge south-west towards Tamai, Osman Digna's reputed headquarters and stronghold – went ahead nonetheless. As before, it was necessary to establish an intermediate position, an advanced depot, where water, stores, and ammunition could be accumulated. This mission was entrusted to Major General John McNeill, who set out from Suakin on 22 March at the head of the Berkshire Regiment, the Royal Marine Light Infantry, 15th Sikhs, 17th Bengal Native Infantry, 28th Bombay Native Infantry, four Gardners managed by bluejackets and marines, and a squadron of 5th Lancers. The combined force numbered 3,300 men, but they were encumbered by a disproportionately large baggage-train, including up to 1,200 camels. Progress, through ever thickening bush, was painfully slow, the men wilting under a burning sun, and the Lancers reported enemy hovering. So, at 10.30, 6 miles out from Suakin, the decision was taken to halt and form *zariba*.

With Lancers providing an outer line of pickets, infantry an inner line, the work of fortification was begun, some men cutting bush and dragging it into position, while others stood to arms; those not so employed were served rations or lay down to rest. Because of the great bulk of the baggage, the plan was to form three interconnected square *zaribas* arranged diagonally, a large central one for the water and commissariat stores, two smaller ones at opposite corners to act as fighting positions, the Marines to the north-east, the Berkshires to the south-west, each with a two-gun Gardner redoubt at the furthest corner. This layout was designed to ensure that any rush of spearmen towards the central square would be met by converging fire from two sides. But the *zariba* was unfinished when, at 2.30 in the afternoon, the Lancers

galloped in on every side with the enemy following close behind. The attack
had come very suddenly.

Moving with the alacrity of irregulars, their approach covered by thick
bush, the Mahdists surged into the open ground around the *zariba* in one
vast mass, perhaps 2,000 strong. The Marines holding the north-eastern
square and a half battalion of Berkshires holding the south-western square
stood their ground, as did another half battalion of Berkshires caught in the
open to the east of the *zariba*, who immediately formed a small square of
their own. Two lines of Indian infantry, the 15th Sikhs facing west, the 28th
Bombay Infantry facing north, also remained solid, delivering heavy volleys
with their Snider rifles that crushed the attack to their immediate front. Not
so the 17th Bengal Infantry, facing south, who, disordered by retiring cavalry
and spooked by the speed of the enemy charge behind, managed one scattered volley, then fled for cover to the unfinished *zariba*. The rout triggered
a stampede of animals and native drivers which compounded the chaos.
What seems to have just saved the south-western square from disintegration
was the decision of regimental officers to turn the rear line of Berkshires
holding the western face to deliver close-range volleys into the mass of
Arabs pouring through the gap in the defences behind. Eventually all who
entered the south-western *zariba* were shot down: 112 bodies were later
counted within it.

But the crisis was not over. The sheets of fire issuing from the Anglo-
Indian line in and around the *zariba* had the effect of hustling many of the
attackers towards the undefended south-eastern sector. Here stood the great
mass of baggage-camels, assembled for the return journey to Suakin. In a
frenzy of howling and hacking, the attackers started another stampede. The
panic-stricken animals fled in all directions, but mainly northwards, towards
the *zariba* held by the Marines and the square in the open ground beyond
held by the half battalion of Berkshires. Such was the animals' terror that
they trampled down the thorn-bush fences and went right through the
Marines' position. 'Suddenly, from the bush,' recalled one officer:

> all along the face of the *zariba* fronting Tamai burst out a clamour of
> savage cries, and the next instant the whole assemblage of transport
> animals plunged forward. There was multitude of roaring camels, appar-
> ently heaped one upon another, with strings of kicking and screaming
> mules, entangled in one moving mass. Crowds of camp-followers were
> carried along by the huge animal wave, crying, shouting, and fighting.

All these surged up on the *zariba*, any resistance being utterly hopeless. This mass of brutes and terrified natives swept all before it, and a scene of indescribable confusion ensued.

Again, the superlative discipline of British regulars was decisive. When the surge of animals had passed through, the Marines rallied immediately and resumed firing, both rifles and Gardners. Few Mahdists seem to have penetrated the square during the camel surge – only 12 bodies were counted afterwards – and the swirling mass around the position was now shot away. The half-square of Berkshires also stood firm, firing disciplined volleys through the crisis of battle, accounting for about 200 of the enemy in all during the 20 minutes the whole affair lasted.

Suddenly it was over. The battlefield was littered with dead and wounded, 250 British, perhaps 1,000 Sudanese, no less than 900 camels.[65] McNeill's advanced force had been crippled. Nor had the morale of the enemy been broken, for the relief convoys organised by General Graham over succeeding days were constantly harassed by riflemen sniping from the bush and occasionally charged by spearmen. The British response, once logistical arrangements were complete, was to launch a massive column – according to official returns, 8,175 officers and men, 1,773 native workers, 1,361 horses, 1,639 camels, and 930 mules – in the direction of Osman Digna's base at Tamai. It was inevitable that Osman Digna – wily old guerrilla that he was – would simply fall back, contenting himself with long-range harassing fire and little more, leaving Graham's mailed fist punching air. Then it turned out that the wells at Tamai were more or less dry, leaving the British with no option but retreat. In any case, whereas Osman Digna knew exactly what the British were up to – for the bush was riddled with Mahdists – Graham had no idea where his enemy was. The British lost only one man killed, six wounded, and seven stricken by heat in the entire operation. All they had to show for their effort was the destruction of one miserable village. The Red Sea front was again in stalemate.[66]

General Buller arrived at Abu Kru to take command of the Desert Column on 11 February. His instructions were to take Metemmeh and then cooperate with General Earle's River Column in the capture of Berber. Buller was a somewhat enigmatic figure. Despite red-faced bad temper, he was popular with the troops and inspired confidence. Though a *bon vivant* fond of food and drink, he was a trusted fighting general of the Wolseley Ring. A firm hand who could be relied upon to impose order amid chaos, he would nonetheless crash to disaster in the opening campaigns of the Boer War in 1899. But that was in the future. Right now, he made a brisk assessment, decided that his commander-in-chief's plan was hopeless, and made arrangements for an immediate pullback to the Jakdul Wells. The problem was plain enough: the camel transport was close to collapse. There had been too few animals to start with, many had already died, and the remainder were exhausted and emaciated. This was immediately confirmed on the first leg of the retreat, when 100 more camels collapsed and had to be left in the desert. The transport crisis meant that it was now impossible to move all 1,700 men in a single convoy, so part of the force was sent on to Jakdul with most of the 800 camels, while the rest camped at Abu Klea – despite the fact that the water supply was meagre, the fodder minimal, the enemy still hovering, apparently undaunted by a fierce little firefight on 17 February when they had been driven off with some loss.

It was six days before the camels returned for the second convoy, and then it was a three-day march to the wells. By now, uniforms were in tatters and boots falling to bits, rotted by water and eaten by ants, so that many men marched barefoot or wearing cut-up rifle buckets tied to their soles. The Mahdists let them go: it is anyone's guess what would have happened had they attacked. The second leg of the journey, from Jakdul to Korti, was staggered over several days. Most men continued on foot; there was no choice, for the Heavy Camel Regiment was down to 32 camels, the Mounted Infantry to 95, the Guards to 200. Wolseley had accepted Buller's decision when first reported, and any doubts would have been dispelled when he saw the condition of the Desert Column as the men staggered into Korti over several days in early March: it was obvious, he admitted, that 'the troops in the desert had . . . become practically incapable of undertaking any enterprise involving mobility'. But the implications were grim: 'Every retrograde step is regarded by uncivilised races as a sign of weakness and fear . . .'[67]

On the giant chessboard of the Sudan, the British had three separate pieces in play – the Desert Column, the River Column, and the Suakin Expedition. Each, in its immediate vicinity, was tactically dominant. Even in the direst of circumstances, when close terrain, or poor intelligence, or simple accident had placed one of these pieces in danger, the discipline and firepower of British regulars had always prevailed. But tactical dominance – victory in battle – does not win wars. Strategic dominance is decisive. What mattered, finally, in the Sudan campaigns of 1884–5 was the relationship between force, space, and logistics. The British dominated the immediate combat zone, but nothing else; the Mahdists controlled the rest. The British squares lumbered about, like some species of slow-moving animal, while Mahdist riflemen and spearmen swarmed around them, receding when they advanced, infiltrating forward if they retreated. And in this asymmetrical war between square and swarm, regular and irregular, firing line and skirmish cloud, the British blundered about blind, never really sure where the enemy was, when he would show up, whether he would attack; whereas the Mahdists always had a thousand eyes watching. Because, moreover, they depended for supply on flotillas of boats or great trains of camels humping water barrels, biscuit boxes, and ammo cases, the British were often barely able to move at all. The vastness of the Sudan, the barrenness of the desert, the crushing heat, and the invisibility of an exceptionally dangerous enemy combined to reduce them, for much of the time, to virtual immobility.

The enemy and the country had both been underestimated. First, Gordon had been unable to carry out an evacuation and ended up surrounded at Khartoum. Then, Wolseley had been unable to reach him in time and Gordon had perished in the sack of the city. Now, Wolseley's revised plan for a three-pronged drive on Berber in preparation to 'crush the Mahdi' had collapsed. He halted operations and informed the government that he was reorganising the army and going into summer quarters. Not until cooler weather in the autumn would it become possible to resume the offensive. This was too much. The war was set to drag into a second year, tying down more than 20,000 British soldiers, almost 15 per cent of the army, and in order, at great cost and risk, to secure control over what *Daily Mail* correspondent George Steevens would later call 'a quarter of a continent of sheer squalor'. As Gladstone put it to his colleagues – moral rectitude again ascendant over political expediency – was there 'any obligation of honour or any inducement of policy . . . that should lead us, in the present state of the demands on the Empire, to waste a large portion of our Army in fighting against nature, and, I fear, also fighting against liberty (such liberty as the case admits) in the Sudan?' Was there, his memorandum asked, 'the moral basis of the prolonged military operations'?

The blow fell on 13 April 1885. Wolseley, now in Cairo – to which he had relocated as a more convenient headquarters for the direction of the two forces, one on the Middle Nile, one on the Red Sea, over which he now held supreme command – received a telegram from War Minister Hartington: 'In the condition of imperial affairs, it is probable that the expedition to Khartoum may have to be abandoned, the troops brought back as soon as possible to Egypt.' A few days later, the decision was confirmed.[68] The jingoes and militarists were back in their box. The war was over. The Sudanese had defeated the British Empire.

# Part IV
# The Spectre of *Jihad*

# CHAPTER ELEVEN

# AN ISLAMIC CALIPHATE

Omdurman was a place of ceremonies. The great mosque, the religious court, the marketplace, and the parade ground had become theatres of spectacle. Sometimes special preparations were made. On one occasion in late 1889, three wooden scaffolds were erected in the marketplace. The regime's power was to be displayed in an elaborate ritual of public execution. The victims were to be the Batahin.

They were one of the wilder tribes of the Jazira, notorious as highway robbers and rebels against authority. Their offence now was reluctance to answer a call to arms. The days of jihadist enthusiasm were long gone. There was growing resistance to conscription to fight the regime's endless wars. The Batahin had been selected to be made an example. Government soldiers had been dispatched to make summary arrests, and 69 men had been apprehended, put in chains, brought to Omdurman, and incarcerated in the *Saier*, the grim state prison. Their trial had been perfunctory. The presiding *qadis* of the religious court enjoyed independence only in minor cases; in all important matters, they deferred to the theocratic dictator, the Khalifa Abdullahi, the successor of the Mahdi. The court's judgment had, unsurprisingly, been unanimous: the Batahin were guilty of disobedience. 'And what is the punishment for disobedience?' the Khalifa had demanded to know. 'Death,' came the judges' reply.

After midday prayers, the *ombeya*, the great war-horn, sounded across the city and the *nogaras*, the giant kettledrums of the army corps, were beaten, summoning the people to the spectacle. The Khalifa rode to the parade ground with his entourage, dismounted, and seated himself on a small *angareb*. Thousands of warriors and residents assembled to watch. The prisoners were brought out, hands tied behind their backs, their women and children running after them, crying, screaming. The Khalifa whispered instructions. The women were constrained as the men were marched away to the marketplace. There they were divided into three groups. One group of 18 was hanged from the scaffolds, their bodies twitching at the end of camel-hair ropes until the last breath. A second group of 24 were forced to kneel and were then decapitated by swordsmen. The remaining 27 were mutilated, the right hand and left foot of each severed, the victims left writhing until they bled to death. Shouts of exultation greeted the agonies of the condemned. The Khalifa summoned one of the *qadis*, who happened to be of the Batahin, and told him, 'You may now take what remains of your tribe home with you.'[1]

Muhammad Ahmad had devoted his life to an elusive chimera: what might be called a 'Community of Purity'. The inhabitants of one of the poorest places on earth were enjoined to eschew worldly things, set aside petty quarrels, and devote themselves to prayer, self-discipline, and the ascetic life. At Omdurman – the new capital of an Islamic state created by holy war – daily prayers and weekly attendance at mosque were mandatory. A vast covered space, a roof of mats supported on forked sticks, was laid out, and here, each Friday, the Mahdi led the prayers of tens of thousands.

But this was only the beginning. From the Mahdi's secretariat poured forth a stream of proclamations, injunctions, and appeals to the men who formed the infrastructure of the new state. Other messages were sent to foreign potentates and peoples, announcing the success of the Mahdiya and demanding recognition of Muhammad Ahmad's spiritual leadership. For this was only the beginning of an intended international *jihad*. The immediate target was Egypt, and the Khedive Tewfik and the Egyptian *ulema* and *umma* were the recipients of many letters. 'I do not desire power, prestige, or material possessions,' wrote the upstart ruler of Sudan to the Khedive. 'If you accept my guidance and revert to Allah sincerely, I will offer you the safe conduct of God, his Prophet, and his Mahdi. We will be on hand for the sake of religion, to expel the enemies of Allah from the land of the Muslims, and eradicate them to the last man if they do not surrender or revert to God.'[2]

Within months of the fall of Khartoum, the Mahdi was dead. On 16 June 1885, he was struck with fever. Its precise nature is unknown, but disease stalked the huge, growing, insanitary encampment that Omdurman had become, and it could have been any one of several things. It matters not:

whatever it was, it killed him in a week, throwing his entourage into crisis, sowing dismay and doubt among the rank and file. How could the Mahdi die? How could the chosen of God, the successor to the Prophet, the man whose divine mission was to destroy the Turks, restore the faith, and lead the prayers in the great mosques of Cairo, Damascus, Baghdad, Constantinople, and Mecca, how could this man be dead?

The Khalifa Abdullahi did his best to sustain the myth of the Mahdi. For long Muhammad Ahmad's second lieutenant and presumed successor, he had received a final deathbed endorsement, leaving the assembled Mahdist notables with little choice but to accept him as their new leader. He moved immediately to secure his power. 'You are the friends of the Mahdi,' he told the crowds, 'and I am his Khalifa. Swear that you will be faithful to me.' The passing of the Mahdi changed nothing, he told them. The war would continue. The Prophet Muhammad had also passed away before his mission was complete: the great Islamic conquests that followed had been the work of his successors. So it would be now.[3]

But matters were not so simple. The Mahdi had created a tribal confederation and led a tribal insurrection that had made him master of a million square miles of territory. The Sudan had been a construct of 60 years of Turco-Egyptian colonialism. The Mahdist revolt had turned that construct into an independent African country. Now must come the transition from 'Call' to 'State' – from holy war under charismatic leader to political regime with formal governmental infrastructure. No sound basis for this transition existed. It was not simply that Abdullahi was not the messiah figure that Muhammad Ahmad had been. Nor that the faith of many had been shaken, their public observances often now a cover for private doubts. The problem was more basic, and the premature death of the leader merely made the contradictions more stark. The ideology of Mahdism was based on a religious myth: not simply that Muhammad Ahmad was the Messenger of God, but also the more generic notion of a human world whose dominant feature was holy war between believer and infidel. This had been false in the seventh century, when the first Islamic Caliphate was created. It was hardly applicable to an age of railways, steamboats, and telegraphs. The Mahdist leadership might make show of Islamic piety and have recourse to Qur'anic quotations; but, confronted with Sudanese realities during the 14 years the Mahdist state endured, it was not medieval religious doctrine that determined their actions. What emerged was a dictatorship of special type – a centralised military autocracy with theocratic trappings – and one which empowered reactionary tribal elites – warlords, sheikhs, slave traders, patriarchs.

The Khalifa himself was a powerfully built man in his 40s, now somewhat stout, and already white-haired. He wore traditional dress, but of the finest cotton, and was invariably attended by 15 small boy-slaves. His occasional charm was a mask. He harboured the suspicions and fears of the tyrant. Though his tastes in food were simple and his piety punctilious – he would lead the prayers at the Great Mosque in Omdurman five times a day – he nonetheless lived the life of a voluptuary. 'Shortly after he had established himself as supreme ruler,' noted Father Ohrwalder, 'he thought to surround himself with all the pomp and splendour of a Sudanese sultan, of which the most important item is a very extensive harem.' He always had four legal wives (though he would periodically divorce one and introduce another), and his harem eventually contained some 400 women, mainly slave-concubines, drawn from all quarters of his domain. Managed by a cohort of madams and eunuchs, the harem formed a walled compound of large detached houses and courtyards; funds for food, cosmetics, jewellery, and rich clothes were always ample.[4]

Other members of the Mahdist elite also built houses and harems in Omdurman. Khartoum was deliberately destroyed, the population forced to move at short notice, most of the buildings demolished and cannibalised for the materials to construct a new desert metropolis on the west bank of the White Nile. The city eventually sprawled for 6 miles, and as well as the houses of the Mahdist notables, the mud-and-straw huts of the common people, and the shops and stalls of the souks, there were new public buildings – the domed mausoleum of the Mahdi erected over his tomb, a place of veneration and pilgrimage; the Great Mosque, that forest of sticks and mats, and, communicating with it, the enclosure of the Khalifa, with its reception rooms, private apartments, harem, stables, storerooms, and slave quarters; the *Beit al-Amana*, the state arsenal, its walls lined with captured cannon, rifles, and ammunition; the military workshops, where gunpowder and munitions were manufactured; the *Beit al-Maal*, the state treasury, a huge enclosure divided into courtyards filled with goods from all parts of the Sudan; the fearsome *Saier*, where 'complete silence prevails, broken only by the clanking of chains, the hoarse orders of the hard-hearted warders, or the cries of some poor wretch who is being mercilessly flogged' (Slatin); and the post office, where the camels of the cross-desert service were stalled, the central hub of the Khalifa's communications system.[5]

Most important were the barracks. As the Sudanese historian Ismat Hasan Zulfo put it, 'The Mahdist revolution . . . was born by the sword, lived by the sword, and perished by the sword.'[6] It was not simply that military insurgency had created the Mahdist state: it was that the very existence of the state, its ability to contain the contradictions that threatened to tear it apart, came to depend upon military power, permanent war, and a 'state of tension'. This, in the nature of things, was inevitable. The regime existed to wage *jihad*. It offered nothing material; no economic development or social reform; on the contrary, it regressed to medieval forms of exploitation and oppression. Its promise was for some sort of redemption through *jihad*. The Mahdist mission was to restore the true faith by force of arms. The waging of holy war necessitated taxation, conscription, and requisitioning. This strengthened the central state, which, on the one hand, dressed its surplus appropriation in a mantle of Islamic piety, and on the other, used the military force thereby accumulated to crush dissent. Permanent holy war was the very essence of Mahdism throughout its existence as a political force. Leadership was therefore based on apostolic succession. The Khalifa was the successor to the Mahdi, and he had been the successor to the Prophet; *ipso facto*, the Khalifa was the duly appointed servant of Allah on earth, and to defy him was to defy God.

The army was formed of two main components: the permanent garrisons; and the 'volunteers'. All able-bodied men were considered to be holy warriors, liable for military service, who could be called up to fight, usually as spearmen, when required. Far more important were the permanent garrisons, the largest of which, accounting for half the army, was stationed at the capital. Here was the Khalifa's strategic reserve, from which contingents might be dispatched on foreign expeditions or on internal security operations. The Omdurman garrison included (in 1895): the Khalifa's private guard (2,000 men); the *Mulazimiya*, a mix of tribal sheikhs' sons and black slave-soldiers, many recruited from the old *Jihadiya*, all armed with rifles (15,000 men); and the soldiers of the Black and Green standards, mainly spearmen (45,000 foot and 3,500 horse). The other half of the standing army was distributed across the six provinces (*imalas*) into which the country was divided for administrative purposes, each headed by an *amil* (provincial governor), supported by an emir (army commander) and a *qadi* (Islamic judge), each with its own miniature *beit al-maal* (treasury) and a bureaucracy of minor officials and clerks. The entire army, in 1895, numbered 34,000 riflemen, 64,000 spearmen, 7,000 cavalry, and 75 cannon.[7]

If the *Mulazimiya* were the Khalifa's Praetorian Guard, the Baggara, and especially his own tribe, the Ta'aisha, were his Cossacks. For thousands of years, every Nilotic state had based itself on the labour of the *fellahin*. The villagers who cultivated *durra*, beans, and dates, reared sheep and goats, and operated little cranes and water wheels along the banks of the river, because they were settled, because their means of livelihood could not be spirited away into the desert, were preyed upon by tax collectors. Partly for this reason, the river tribes had rallied to the Mahdi out of hatred for the Turks; his movement had been an alliance of riverine peasants and desert nomads. But the Sudanese *fellahin* soon discovered that, as so often before, they had merely exchanged one master for another. In the end, the difference between the Khedive's soldiers and the Khalifa's seemed slight, especially set against the hard toil and modest rewards of peasant labour; the bitterness against those who took without having worked was much the same. The old game of cat-and-mouse between tax collector and peasant farmer – the class war between state and village – resumed. Evidence of cultivation was erased and harvests were carried to distant granaries to evade the tithe. People disappeared when government officials drew up poll-tax registers. Animals were moved to another village when it was known the soldiers were coming. So the government used the army to collect the taxes: 20 or 30 *Jihadiya* or Baggara, armed with guns and *kourbashes*, would come to the village when payment was due – just like the Turks.[8]

The Baggara – the cattle-herding, slave-raiding nomads of Kordofan – had always been remote from government control. And these were Abdullahi's people. So as relations soured with the riverine tribes, he came to rely on them more. They predominated in the army, alongside the *Mulazimiya* and the *Jihadiya*, and large numbers were moved into Omdurman, where local residents were displaced to make room for them, they were supplied direct from the *Beit al-Maal*, and their bullying and plundering went unchecked. Babikr Bedri – the young religious enthusiast who had fought at Khartoum – bore testimony to their oppression, both on campaign, when they would plunder fellow soldiers, and on tax-collecting missions in the villages, when 'the bearded ones' (as they were known) would take by force whatever they pleased. Father Ohrwalder at Omdurman had a grandstand view of the Baggara takeover:

> The revenue of the *Beit al-Maal* is expended almost entirely on the Baggara. All the fertile islands in the neighbourhood, and the

best-cultivated portions of the Nile banks as far as Berber, have been made over to them, whilst the original owners of the soil have been turned out without a piastre's compensation. They are, therefore, owners of all the best lands, and serve as a foreign garrison in occupation of a conquered country. Woe to the native who happens to have a Baggara as neighbour! His cattle are robbed, and he must share the product of the fields with his overbearing master. Wherever they go, the Baggaras take their horses with them, which must be fed and cared for at the expense of the local inhabitants. Complaints against Baggaras are not taken the slightest notice of . . .'[9]

The regime's dependence on *Mulazimiya* and Baggara increased as religious passion waned. Because so much of Sudan's limited wealth was turned into a state monopoly – symbolised by the great granaries and slave compounds of the *Beit al-Maal* – elite factions competed for political power, triggering a succession of conspiracies, uprisings, purges, show trials, and grotesque rituals of public execution. Tyrannies follow a common trajectory: fear and suspicion make them repressive; that makes them more unpopular; they then become yet more paranoid. Many leading men were purged: one, the state treasurer, was hanged for saying the country was being over-taxed; another, the supreme judge appointed by the Mahdi himself, was starved to death in prison. Many lesser men also perished or were incarcerated in the *Saier*, where prisoners were loaded with chains, packed into airless rooms so overcrowded it was impossible to lie down, and left slowly to starve unless they had relatives able to supply them with food – if they did not die first from one of the diseases that festered in the animal squalor of the place.

People whispered of the horrors of the *Saier*. They could see those of the head-pit. 'There in a dirty pit near the market-place,' recalled Father Ohrwalder, 'lay the decaying heads of all his [the Khalifa's] principal enemies . . . all huddled up together in a heap . . . Gradually the skin and hair dropped off, leaving only the bare white skulls, deep eye-holes, and grinning teeth, and yet these were the skulls of crowned heads, prophets, and patriarchs gathered together in a narrow pit . . .'[10]

Some threats to the rule of the Khalifa were real enough. The jostling of rival factions at the top of the Mahdist state was one. The greatest danger was posed by the *Ashraf* (the Arabic plural of *sherif*, meaning a descendant of the Prophet, or, in this case, a kinsman of the Mahdi). The Mahdi had drawn upon his extended family and personal network to staff his move-ment. Many therefore held senior positions in the state inherited by the Khalifa, forming a powerful faction rooted in the riverine tribes to which they belonged – in opposition to the Khalifa, his brother Yacoub, the Ta'aisha tribe, and the Baggara of Kordofan. Some were dispatched on distant campaigns and perished; some were dismissed and either driven into exile or executed; but this merely brought the simmering conflict to boiling point. On 23 November 1891, the *Ashraf* assembled their supporters, mainly men of the Danagla and Ja'aliyin tribes, in the vicinity of the Mahdi's tomb, intent on a display of force as they presented their demands – effectively for the ending of the supremacy of Yacoub and the Baggara. But they were surrounded by loyalist forces and hopelessly outgunned – 100 Remingtons against 1,000. After a brief exchange of fire and a handful of casualties, the confrontation was ended by negotiation and seeming compromise. But Abdullahi had no intention of keeping his word. With the immediate crisis over, he ordered the arrest of seven *Ashraf* notables, including two uncles of the Mahdi, who were promptly condemned, sent into exile, and summarily executed *en route.*[11]

The *Ashraf* had drawn upon the discontent of the *Aulad al-Balad* – the soldiers recruited from the riverine tribes, resentful of the licence given the Baggara. But the desert sheikhs had no more reason to favour rule from Omdurman than village leaders on the Nile. The government could do nothing for them. They preferred to be left alone to raise cattle and traffic gum, ivory, and slaves down the camel tracks. Governments were prone to making unwelcome demands. The Sudan had been strapped together by the Turco-Egyptian Army in the 1820s. It had been united during the Mahdiya by its hatred of that army. Now that it was gone, the Sudan had no particular reason for staying together, and a fair few good ones for not doing so. If the villages waged a low-intensity class war against the Khalifa's tax collectors, there was always a limit to their resistance, for they could not escape, being anchored by their bean plots and palm groves. The desert was another matter. Here, in places, something approximating full-on military occupa-tion was needed to keep the country's centrifugal tendencies in check.

The camel-owning Kababish of northern Kordofan, who had a strong commercial interest in the trade with Egypt, had resisted Mahdist authority from the outset. Their power was broken in a savage military campaign during 1887; Ohrwalder reported mass executions at El-Obeid, a large haul of captured camels, and the public display on the Omdurman gallows of the defeated rebel leader's severed head. More intractable was the resistance of Darfur. Far distant from Omdurman and with a long history as an independent sultanate stretching back to the seventeenth century, this westernmost province of the Sudan was the focus of large-scale military operations involving almost 20,000 men for two years. First, Yusuf Ibrahim attempted to restore the sultanate, but was defeated, forced to flee, and eventually hunted down and killed; his head joined the rest at Omdurman. Then a new Mahdi arose among the Fur, one Abu Jummaiza, and the war in Darfur was renewed, the rebels winning a succession of victories and eventually bottling up the main Mahdist army in Al-Fasher. Only the sudden death of Abu Jummaiza from smallpox, an event which shook the morale of the rebels and caused many to disperse, allowed the Mahdists to return to the offensive, crush the revolt in a major battle outside the town in February 1889, and dispatch a fresh consignment of heads to Omdurman.[12]

A different kind of war raged further south. The conflicts in northern Kordofan and Darfur were struggles between rival Arab potentates. In parts of southern Kordofan, across much of Bahr al-Ghazal, and sometimes extending into Equatoria, the conflict was effectively a class war between black tribesmen and Arab slave traders. For the Mahdi had attracted to his banner hundreds of former slave traders, driven into the shadows by government anti-slavery drives, and these now resumed activity. Like so much else in the new Sudan, the slave trade was a government monopoly, so the traders became contractors, organising large-scale raids in the south, then trafficking their captives north to a government station, where the men were usually taken into the army, the women and children sold in state-controlled markets inside the *beit al-maals*. Sudan under the Khalifa was a profoundly patriarchal society, the condition of all women oppressive; but that of hundreds of thousands of slave women, torn from their families and homes, was surely the worst, a combination of hard labour, serial rape, and savage beatings. Not all were black women from the south. The Khalifa's endless wars – both internal and on the frontiers – were a far more lucrative source of slaves than raids. Women were booty, another form of male property, like camels, cattle, and grain, to be used by their captors as labourers, domestics, and concubines.

But there was resistance. In 1885, some 300 black soldiers, former Turco-Egyptian regulars who had been captured and enrolled into the Mahdist army, mutinied against their maltreatment at El-Obeid. They fought a fierce gun battle with the Arabs in the town, then marched off, their numbers swelled to around a thousand by escaped slaves. They took refuge in mountain country at Golfan, and when attacked by a strong government force, said to number more than 10,000, they routed them with volley-fire from the cover of rocks. Only later did they succumb to another large-scale expedition.

For a while, the Shilluk were spared, for they did military service under the Mahdists; but when they resisted an attempt to plunder grain and cattle in 1891, they were targeted for punitive action. They fought back with great courage, spears against Remingtons, but their resistance was smashed, the men slaughtered, the women and children shipped as slaves to Omdurman.

The Khalifa made no attempt to subjugate Equatoria: he treated it as a hunting-ground, dispatching large raiding parties to seize ivory and slaves. But the black tribes fought back, sometimes with encouragement and assistance from Emin Pasha, Gordon's old governor, who was still at large; on one occasion in 1891, a Mahdist emir returned to Omdurman to report that a *zariba* had been overrun with everyone killed and a government steamer captured.

Most serious of all, by the 1890s, was the deteriorating situation in the Bahr al-Ghazal, the traditional slave hunting-ground where Arab north met African south in fatal collision. Gordon and Gessi had triggered a slave war here in the late 1870s, tipping the balance against the *jallaba* and their *bazingars*, allowing black tribal warriors to exact bitter vengeance at a thousand little skirmishes in the bush. Now other forces had come into play. One day in late 1894, Rudolf Slatin was summoned before the Khalifa to translate several captured documents. They were written in French. The Belgians of the Congo Free State, it turned out, had entered into alliance with local rulers in the Bahr al-Ghazal. Slatin had no doubt of the implications:

> These various black tribes have no love for the Arab slave-hunters, and would aid any power which would guarantee their protection. The recruitment of 4,000 or 5,000 local levies possessing fighting qualities of a high order would, for such a power, be a matter of no difficulty; and in the space of four or five years, an army from 15,000 to 20,000 men might be raised, by which not only Darfur and Kordofan, but indeed the whole Sudan, could be conquered.[13]

The Mahdist state was weakened by factional struggle, the secessionism of desert sheikhs, the bitterness of the over-taxed, and mass resistance to the slave trade. Mahdism had morphed from an anti-colonial Islamist insurrection in 1885 to a military dictatorship based on coercion and terror in 1895. Devoid of any trace of political idealism, incapable of imagining, let alone enacting, any kind of social reform, the regime offered nothing to the great mass of Sudanese except taxes, conscription, and poverty. If the loyalty of the dominant court faction was to be secured by state largesse, and if the power of a traditional ruling class of sheikhs and slave traders upheld, no general improvement was possible. What filled the vacuum – between promise and practice – was the ideology of holy war. Unable to escape the surreal logic of the myth without destroying its own *raison d'être*, compelled by this fact to wage holy war *à l'outrance* ('to the limit'), the regime propelled itself to its doom, attempting to build a military empire on an impoverished economic base of *durra*, cattle, and slaves. The contradiction worked on the morale of the Sudanese like an acid.

Mahdist armies surged following the fall of Khartoum in January 1885. Kassala was captured by Osman Digna in July, Sennar by Wad al-Nejumi in August, both towns key strategic assets in the south-east, close to the Abyssinian border. But Egypt was the main priority. Sudan was on the periphery of the Islamic world, whereas Egypt, like Syria and Iraq, formed part of its inner core. Either the Mahdists took Egypt, or their global *jihad* would stall and wither in the desert. Perhaps it could be taken on the run? Perhaps the Egyptian *fellahin* would explode into revolt as the Sudanese had done, inspired by the example of victorious holy war in the south? The British certainly thought it possible. 'The struggle with the Mahdi, or rather with Mahdism,' Wolseley had warned his government, 'must come sooner or later. Eventually you will have to fight him to hold your position in Egypt. No frontier force can keep Mahdism out of Egypt, and the Mahdi, sooner or later, must be smashed, or he will smash you.' So Mahdist forces were soon in motion, occupying Dongola behind the departing British in July 1885, then advancing to the border, a force of northern Sudanese around 8,000 strong under Muhammad al-Kheir and Abd al-Majid. Troops were rushed to meet them, and the police deployed on the streets of Cairo and elsewhere, especially in the frontier districts, to deal with any jihadist outbreaks. On 30 December, Generals Stephenson and Grenfell launched their combined Anglo-Egyptian force, 5,000 men in all, against Mahdist defensive positions in and around the village of Ginnis. In a succession of well-executed manoeuvres and firefights, the Mahdists were driven away with heavy loss, estimated at 800, compared with just 40 among the attackers.[14] It would take more than local forces to crack open the Egyptian frontier and perhaps trigger an Egyptian *jihad*.

The death of the Mahdi in June, the defeat at Ginnis in December, and the fact that the country had been ravaged by famine and smallpox that year seems to have broken the spell. Father Ohrwalder thought 'the glow and fervour of religious enthusiasm was gone'. But the Khalifa, the ruler of a state founded on the ideology of holy war and now in command of an army of 100,000 rifles and spears, could not stand still. The *jihad* was a process of perpetual motion. So ultimatums were sent from Omdurman to Muslim rulers in Egypt and Arabia demanding submission to the Khalifa of the Mahdi, followed by personal letters to Queen Victoria, the Ottoman Sultan Abdul Hamid II, the Egyptian Khedive Tewfik, and the Abyssinian Emperor John IV.[15] This was the diplomatic arm of a military offensive. Since the *jihad* was fuelled by taxes, requisitions, and the slave trade, it engendered mass resistance, so for much of the time the Mahdist army was engaged in internal wars. But whenever possible, forces were directed against external enemies – often with little regard for rational strategic purpose, but simply because the opponent could be 'othered' as an enemy of Islam. This was above all true of the massive, brutal, pointless war of aggression waged against the Abyssinians from 1885 to 1889.

Emperor John had sent a peace proposal to Omdurman, arguing that Christians and Muslims should not fight over religion, and that Abyssinians and Sudanese had common enemies in the Europeans. The Khalifa had replied that John should become a Muslim and that if he did not, he would be treated as an enemy of God and the Prophet, and the Khalifa would destroy him. A full-scale invasion of Abyssinia followed in 1888. This turned into an apocalyptic campaign of massacre, destruction, and enslavement, prompting a massive Abyssinian counter-attack that culminated in a ferocious battle at the frontier town of Gallabat on 12 March 1889 between perhaps 120,000 Abyssinians and 80,000 Mahdists.

It might have been a crushing defeat, but for the accident of the Abyssinian Emperor's death in battle, causing his army to withdraw rather than renew their attack. The Mahdist army returned to Omdurman triumphant. The Emperor's head was displayed on the gallows, and the Khalifa claimed a great victory. But in fact the war had ended with nothing changed, despite vast expense in blood and treasure. It had been fought to a stalemate, because the Sudanese-Abyssinian frontier was as 'natural' a frontier as it was possible to conceive. Abyssinia (today's Ethiopia) was a vast upland plateau, cut by numerous ravines and watercourses, green and fertile and productive, home to an ancient and largely self-contained civilisation of Christian tribal warriors. Around 50 per cent of John's men were armed with breechloaders, 20 per cent with muzzle-loaders, the rest with spears, swords, and shields; of these, up to 40 per cent were mounted. Given the geography, the social cohesion, and the military organisation of Abyssinia, there was never any possibility of the Mahdist state conquering the country; indeed, a decade later, the Abyssinians would inflict the greatest defeat by native forces on a European army of the entire Scramble for Africa, destroying an Italian invasion force of 20,000 men at the Battle of Adowa. At most, the Khalifa's war was a series of gigantic armed raids. But the booty taken did not begin to compensate for the terrible attrition. The Sudanese-Abyssinian War of 1885–9 bears testimony to the madness of the Islamist regime.[16]

It was equally evident on the Egyptian front. Despite the distraction of the Abyssinian campaign, the Khalifa had launched Wad al-Nejumi on a fresh invasion of Egypt. 'Wad al-Nejumi, you are a thing of scorn,' the Khalifa had berated the veteran Mahdist commander on a visit to Omdurman. 'Those who were your companions have all achieved martyrdom. And you, how long will you remain in terror of death?' Nejumi was not trusted and was being deliberately undermined and set up for failure. The command in the north was divided and rancorous. The army was too small – a mere 5,000 (with 8,000 camp-followers) – for an invasion of Britain's increasingly well-defended Egyptian colony. The logistics were virtually non-existent, the expectation being that the army would live off local supplies – that is, plunder the peasantry. In the event, access to the Nile banks was problematic, with Anglo-Egyptian troops shadowing the Mahdist advance and gunboats cruising up and down the river, both intent on denying the invader access to food and water. On 2 July 1889, at the village of Argin, Nejumi launched a frontal attack in an effort to reach the river, but was repulsed by the fire of a 2,000-strong Anglo-Egyptian flying column supported by several steamers. The Mahdists lost 900 killed. Their morale was shattered. Babikr Bedri, still serving under his old commander, was there: 'We returned defeated and dispirited to the camp, where we spent the night, and in the morning there was not a single one of us that had any desire for the holy war.'[17]

Some senior commanders urged retreat, but the decision was to push on, against the odds, no doubt in fear of the Khalifa's retribution. They managed another 25 miles or so. Then they came to a temporary halt, the little army diminishing by the day, soon down to around 3,000 warriors and 4,000 camp-followers. The animals wasted away or were slaughtered for food. The people suffered agonies of thirst and hunger. Many were reduced to eating roots, stalks, and seed pods. Bedri did not taste bread for 27 days and was left weak in body. He saw Nejumi overcome by dizziness taking the evening prayers. A foraging expedition near the river was the occasion of profound personal tragedy. A shell exploded near a hut in which he, his brother, and his brother's daughter had taken refuge. A fragment entered the hut, took off the top of the little girl's head, killing her instantly, and lodged in his brother's hip, inflicting a wound that was soon infected, killing him also a day or two later.[18]

The British knew the condition of the Mahdist army and appealed to Nejumi to surrender. General Sir Francis Grenfell, the *Sirdar* of the Anglo-Egyptian Army, wrote as follows: 'The Khalifa Abdullahi dismissed you, and appointed his cousin Yunus in your place; and has now sent you here without ammunition or supplies, so that he may be rid of you and your army, for he fears your strength. I advise you to surrender, and you will find here every-thing that you want . . .' Grenfell then listed the good things in his gift. But the veteran commander – who had destroyed Hicks at Shaykan and Gordon at Khartoum – would not betray his allegiance. He would fight one more time. He instructed his secretary: 'Write to the general and tell him that I have sworn to the Mahdi and his Khalifa to wage the holy war, and that I will fight on; and that if we kill him and his men, we shall get everything he has mentioned in his letter, but that if he kills us, he will get nothing but a war-worn *jibba* and a discarded spear.'[19]

Bedri was spared the final collision: he was captured shortly before it took place. But he was shown the corpse of Wad al-Nejumi when it was brought in from the battlefield: 'All that appeared of his wounds was a ragged gash in his leg, for he was wearing his *jibba*. There was dust in his fine beard as though he had just returned from reviewing his army, and there was no sign about him of the ugliness of death. May Allah have ample mercy upon him.'[20]

Seventy-five miles from the border, just south of the village of Toski, Nejumi's further advance had been blocked by Grenfell's cavalry and camel corps on 2 August 1889. A British infantry brigade was on its way, but Grenfell decided to attack immediately with the two brigades, one Egyptian, the other Sudanese, on hand. The Mahdists were in the hills a few miles from the river, only about 3,000 strong, at the end of their resources. He had 4,000 men of the new Anglo-Egyptian Army – well armed, highly trained, eager for war – with which to crush them. The Egyptian and Sudanese infantry advanced on the hills, delivering concentrated fire that shattered the Ansar formations, then stormed each position at bayonet point. Nejumi, badly wounded early in the day, refused to flee. He was still trying to rally the last of his followers at the end of the battle when he was killed. Toski was a dismally one-sided affair: for the loss of 25 killed and 140 wounded, Grenfell had annihilated the Mahdist invasion force, killing 1,200 and taking 4,000 prisoners (warriors and camp-followers).[21] The Khalifa's second invasion of Egypt was over. The villages of Upper Egypt had not stirred: the Mahdists had been left to march and fight and die alone – unsuccoured, unsupported, seemingly unwanted.

Lack of enthusiasm for the holy war also affected operations on the Red Sea. Between 1883 and 1885, Osman Digna had organised the local Hadendowa in a powerful anti-colonial insurgency that had kept the British bottled up in the port of Suakin, their two successive attempts to break out defeated by a combination of logistical challenges and guerrilla resistance. But the Khalifa's permanent war was another matter – especially given the cost of facing British firepower – and Osman Digna's support drained away. The veteran Mahdist commander met recalcitrance with terror: two leaders of the Amarar tribe were executed. Baggara and others, 4,000 of them, were dispatched from Omdurman as reinforcements: the oppressive presence of these outsiders deepened resentment. The mosaic of local tribal allegiances – pro-British, neutral, wavering, pro-Mahdist – was shifting. Though Osman pushed forward again, occupying Handub, a mere 15 miles north of Suakin, and tightening the siege around Suakin in the autumn of 1887, he was no more capable than before of taking the port. A year later, the Suakin garrison having been increased to 5,000 men, 750 of them British, he was counter-attacked and his lines broken. Soon after, in January 1889, he was ordered to abandon Handub and fall back on Tokar, 55 miles south of Suakin. Aware that local loyalties were changing – and that increasing numbers of tribesmen wanted an end to the disruption and hardship of the war – the more hard-line British officers pressed for decisive action against Osman Digna. London gave the go-ahead early in 1891. Colonel Holled-Smith led a small Anglo-Egyptian force of 2,000 men in an attack on Tokar on 19 February 1891. It was the same story as at Toski: drilled and disciplined precision, Egyptian and Sudanese battalions advancing to the assault,

crushing fanatic charges with fire, storming enemy positions with the
bayonet. Around 700 Mahdists were shot down for the loss of just 58 Anglo-
Egyptians.[22]

The old ferocity of the Ansar diehards was still there, but the numbers
were now too few. Osman's total force was down to around 4,000, and he
committed only 2,000 to the battle – concerned, perhaps, to retain an intact
nucleus around which fresh forces might be gathered. So few could not
prevail against ordered Martini-Henry volleys. A measure of the shifting
balance – evident at both Toski and Tokar – was that the new Anglo-
Egyptian Army eschewed the lumbering squares of earlier campaigns to
attack in line, confident that two ranks of trained men armed with breechloaders could smash anything ahead of them and, if necessary, change front
fast enough to secure a threatened flank.

The Abyssinian war had ended in mutual prostration. The second
Egyptian invasion had been annihilated. The insurgency in eastern Sudan
had been driven off the coast. The Khalifa's much-vaunted global *jihad* had
vanished in the sand. The vast expenditure of blood and treasure, the
draining of Sudan of its young manpower and all-too-meagre resources,
had been for nothing, mere waste, a chasing of rainbows. And this was also
the time of the Great Famine. The harvest was poor in 1888 and the grain
price increased five-fold. Partly it was because the rains failed, but also it
was because the war had drained the land of cultivators. Needless to say, the
men of the politico-military complex – the Mahdist leadership, the loyal
sheikhs and imams, the merchants, the *Mulazimiya*, the Baggara – did not
go short. But everyone else did. Refugees from hunger poured into
Omdurman from the countryside, and the city, already a place of heaving
squalor, filled with scenes of appalling suffering. The starving collapsed in
the street and dead bodies lay everywhere unburied. The Nile was contam-
inated by corpses. The hyenas broke into houses and carried off the dying.
Camels, cattle, mules, and donkeys disappeared; even the bones were ground
into powder to make a sort of bread. Market traders wielded clubs against
the poor, and fights erupted over filthy scraps. A few, utterly deranged, ate
their own children. 'Perhaps the most horrible scenes occurred at the places
where animals were slaughtered,' wrote Father Ohrwalder:

> Hundreds of starving men and women would be seen standing around
> with cups or gourds in their hands, ready to catch the blood before it fell,
> and then, as the animal would be writhing on the ground in its death-

agony, they would fall upon it to catch the blood as it flowed out of its wound, whilst a crowd would be struggling on the ground for the few drops which had escaped and become mixed up with the dust and sand. These struggles generally ended in fights, in which the receptacles were broken, and the people besmeared with their contents, which added to the grim ghastliness of this dreadful sight.[23]

The national crisis of 1889–91 – military defeat, acute social distress, collapsing faith in the regime and its mission – occasioned the internal coup which broke the power of the *Ashraf* and established the supremacy of the Baggara. From late 1891 until the end, the Khalifa, his brother Yacoub, and the Ta'aisha tribe had tight control over the Mahdist state, their grip enforced by their well-fed, heavily armed standing army of *Mulazimiya* and Baggara at Omdurman. This was sufficient, for the time being, for the purposes of internal security. But on the frontiers, the balance of power was shifting. Arab sheikhs eager to break free of Omdurman, and African chieftains determined to resist the slave traders, were discovering powerful allies – the French, the Belgians, the Italians, and the British. For the Scramble for Africa was now at fever-pitch, the European powers in a heady race for empire from Cairo to the Cape, from Senegal to the Horn.

The British, in addition, had a score to settle. The Khalifa's son warned his father of the danger in the north: 'You know well enough that the English have an axe to grind with you: they want to avenge the death of Hicks, of Gordon, and of all the Englishmen who were killed in the Sudan. The Egyptians too want to avenge the death of their Turko-Egyptian armies and the loss of the lands they once ruled. Now they are coming to avenge themselves and reconquer the country.'[24]

# CHAPTER TWELVE

# OMDURMAN

The new Prime Minister was a great Tory gentleman who bore the burdens of high office lightly. Born to rule, Robert Arthur Talbot Gascoyne-Cecil, 3rd Marquess of Salisbury, was a direct descendant of William Cecil, Elizabeth I's chief minister, whom she had ennobled as Lord Burghley. His preference was to retire to the family's country seat, Hatfield House in Hertfordshire, where he conducted scientific experiments in his private laboratory and took tricycle rides round the grounds. He carried out the business of government mainly by letter. So occasional were his visits to Westminster that it was said that he sometimes failed to recognise members of his own Cabinet. He took the view that it was not the business of gentlemen who happened to chose politics as a pastime to upset the status quo by legislation. 'We must work at less speed and at a lower temperature than our opponents,' he explained to one over-enthusiastic colleague, in obvious reference to the reforming zeal of Gladstonian Liberals. 'Our bills must be tentative and cautious, not sweeping and dramatic.' In this regard, Lord Salisbury's three administrations (1885–6, 1886–92, and 1895–1902) were models of Tory success, taking no action of noticeable effect in relation to any of the major domestic questions of the day.[1]

Two such questions were of especial importance. There was 'the social question', which, since the banking collapse of 1873 and the onset of the Long Depression, had become acute. 'Each succeeding winter brings up afresh the great question, what to do with the unemployed,' wrote Frederick Engels in 1886; 'but while the number of the unemployed keeps swelling from year to year, there is nobody to answer that question; and we can almost calculate the moment when the unemployed, losing patience, will take their own fate into their own hands.' He was right: the explosion came just a year later. What gave it exceptional force was its fusion with that other great unsettled issue: Irish Home Rule. The agitation of Irish nationalist politicians like Charles Stewart Parnell at Westminster, combined with a bitter land war between Catholic peasants and Protestant gentry in the Irish countryside, had been the backdrop to Gladstone's failed attempt to steer Home Rule through parliament between 1880 and 1886.[2]

On 13 November 1887, the Social Democratic Federation and the Irish National League called a joint demonstration to protest against the plight of the unemployed and the use of coercion in Ireland. Tens of thousands of working-class Londoners, many of them Irish migrant workers, answered the call. The police, with soldiers in reserve, attacked the demonstration and it turned into a riot: 75 were injured, 400 arrested. More demonstrations followed, with further violent clashes, and at least two protestors were killed by the police. Then the East End erupted, with strikes of, first, women match-makers, then gas-workers, and finally dockers, 60,000 of them, who shut down the Port of London for a month in August/September 1889, crippling the trade of the British Empire, to win a stunning victory that launched a wave of 'New Unionism' among the unskilled. Over the following year, the number of trade unionists in Britain more than doubled from 860,000 to almost 2 million.[3] The British working class was providing its own answer to 'the social question'.

But theirs was not the only one. Across Europe, conservatives alarmed by the rise of labour were discovering antidotes in nationalism, racism, and jingoism. Intellectuals, politicians, industrialists, and empire-builders embraced the idea that the masses – the dark, threatening masses stirring in the social depths – could perhaps be distracted by a new kind of 'bread and circuses': the glory of empire. French philologist, philosopher, and historian Ernest Renan was explicit: it was 'the only way to counter socialism', and 'a nation that does not colonise is condemned to end up with socialism, to experience a war between rich and poor'. Cecil Rhodes, the diamond magnate and colonial pioneer who did more than anyone to establish British imperial rule in Southern Africa, found himself thinking along precisely these lines after witnessing a rowdy meeting of the unemployed in East London. 'On my way home,' he later recalled, 'I pondered over the scene, and I became more than ever convinced of the importance of imperialism ... The Empire, as I have always said, is a bread and butter question. If you want to avoid civil war, you must become imperialists.'[4]

The jingoism of the 'new imperialism' found expression in newspapers, magazines, and comics like the *Boy's Own Paper*; in children's books, campaign histories by veterans and war correspondents, and popular novels by writers like Rider Haggard and G.A. Henty; in the music of Elgar, the poetry of Kipling, and in countless theatre, opera, and music-hall productions; and in an endless stream of empire-themed badges, flags, souvenirs, pictures, and advertisements. Above all, there were great state pageants, like the 1897 Diamond Jubilee of Queen Victoria, which were transformed into popular celebrations of imperialism. The *Daily Mail*'s star reporter, George Steevens – who would soon be on the Nile with General Kitchener's army – watched the London parade, in which soldiers marched of 'every colour, every continent, every race, every speech – all in arms for the British Empire and the British Queen . . . A living gazetteer of the British Empire . . . How small you must feel in the face of the stupendous whole, and yet how great to be a unit in it.'[5]

Here was 'Tory democracy' incarnate on the streets of London: a vast crowd of ordinary men and women waving flags, cheering the British Army and Empire, bewitched by the symbols and celebrities of nationalism. Here was the political base for the 20-year ascendancy of the Tory Party between 1886 and 1906. Here was the rationale for Benjamin Disraeli's transformation of the Tories into a conservative party with a popular message for a new age of mass politics. 'He made the Conservatives a great force in democratic politics,' wrote Winston Churchill. 'Tory democracy – working men by hundreds of thousands who voted Conservative – became the dominant factor.' It was the surging popular jingoism stoked by the Tories that finally wrecked Gladstone's Liberal Party. It may have broken on the rocks of Home Rule, but it was swirled to destruction by the deep waters of the new imperialism. The instinct for reform and improvement was trumped by that for conquest. 'England without an empire!' exclaimed Joseph Chamberlain, Salisbury's Colonial Secretary. 'Can you conceive it? England in that case would not be the England we love.' Observing the Diamond Jubilee, Fabian socialist Beatrice Webb noted dismally in her diary, 'Imperialism in the air. All classes drunk with sightseeing and hysterical loyalty.'[6]

Dividing the working class to prevent a socialist majority was one effect of the new imperialism. But hard material interests were also at stake. The Long Depression – when growth rates were often half what they had been between 1848 and 1873 – meant idle capital and idle hands. The industrial bourgeoisie responded to the crisis in various ways. Big firms gobbled up small firms and then created cartels to manage competition among them and protect prices and profits. National governments abandoned free trade and imposed import tariffs on foreign goods to prevent home firms being undercut. Capital responded to sluggish domestic demand by flowing overseas in pursuit of cheap raw materials, captive colonial markets, and new investment opportunities. The state began investing heavily in infrastructure – especially railways – and in armaments: a double-edged boon, since many firms grew rich on state contracts, while growing military power made the state a more effective defender of business interests. And with larger units of capital involved in ever bigger investments, the banks played an increasing role as lenders of finance. Concentration of capital; protectionism; colonialism; militarism; financialisation: these processes gave rise to a new kind of capitalism involving a tight nexus between state, banks, and industrials.

This was an ever more dangerous world – a world on the road to 1914. 'When competition has finally reached its highest stage', explained the Russian revolutionary Nikolai Bukharin in 1915:

> when it has become competition between state-capitalist trusts, then the use of state power, and the possibilities connected with it, begin to play a very large part . . . The more strained the situation in the world sphere of struggle – and our epoch is characterised by the greatest intensity of competition between 'national' groups of finance-capital – the oftener an appeal is made to the mailed fist of state power.[7]

This was for the future: the rising temperature between the great powers would eventually cause an explosion inside Europe. But in the 40 years before the First World War, Africa and Asia acted as shock-absorbers, soaking up the surplus capital of a stagnant European economy, providing the mass markets that for a while prevented a European war. Until 1876, most of Africa had been an unknown 'dark continent' as far as Europeans were concerned. Their influence had been largely limited to trading stations on or near the coast. Most of the rest of Africa had remained a patchwork of polities at many different stages of development. This political geography was completely transformed in the generation after 1876 by British, French, Portuguese, Spanish, German, Belgian, and Italian imperialism. Africa supplied gold, diamonds, copper, tin, rubber, cotton, palm oil, coffee, cocoa, tea, and much else to the growing cities and industries of Europe. The continent's inhabitants, including increasing numbers of white settlers, provided markets for European manufactures. Colonial infrastructure projects, such as railway construction, made European bankers, industrialists, and bondholders rich.

Because of this, and also because geopolitical tension was rising, the carve-up of Africa was competitive and contested. The great powers seized colonies even when they had no particular value simply to pre-empt their rivals. They used them as barriers to block one another's expansion and as platforms for the projection of military power into one another's 'spheres of influence'. They also wanted them as bargaining chips in imperial horse-trading. The French, who eventually controlled virtually the whole of the Maghreb (Morocco, Algeria, and Tunisia) and West Africa, dreamed of an empire extending across the continent from the Atlantic to the Indian Ocean. The British, by contrast, talked of an empire extending north–south 'from Cairo to the Cape', linking existing possessions in Egypt, East Africa, and South Africa. Other players added further complication: the Portuguese already controlled Mozambique; the Germans grabbed Tanzania; the Belgians were colonising the Congo; the Italians occupied chunks of Eritrea and Somaliland and had designs on Abyssinia.[8]

The Sudan – from which the British had 'scuttled' in 1885 – had come to matter a great deal by 1895. The British and the French, at loggerheads for centuries and now the two principal imperial powers involved in the Scramble for Africa, were in conflict over the Nile Basin. The British had already usurped the French in Egypt – evicting Napoleon's army in 1801, buying a controlling share in the Suez Canal in 1875, taking over the country as a whole in 1882. From the French point of view, as well as completing a band of blue from the Atlantic to the Indian Ocean, control of the Nile Basin might offer some leverage in relation to the Nile Valley as a whole. Yet it was mainly British explorers and soldiers – Livingstone, Burton, Speke, Grant, Baker – who had mapped the Lakes, and it was British officers – Hicks, Gordon, Stewart, Graham – who had done the fighting in the Sudan. Though no vital British interest was immediately threatened, all imperial statesmen became anxious when rivals were on the move. Though the Salisbury government was eager to avoid open clashes with other powers – 'British policy is to drift lazily downstream, occasionally putting out a boat-hook to avoid a collision' was how the Prime Minister explained the policy – it was willing to give far greater licence to the men on the spot than the Liberals had ever done. The ideal was private imperialism that cost London nothing. Work was entrusted to local affiliates: the Royal Niger Company, the British East Africa Company, the British South Africa Company – or, in the case of Sudan, the British-controlled puppet regime in Cairo.[9]

Also useful were good relations with secondary powers in a position to interpose between British territory and the pushy French. So in 1894, in return for recognition of British pre-eminence in the Nile Basin, London granted King Leopold II leave to extend his Central African empire over much of the Bahr al-Ghazal. Millions died in the Belgian Congo, possibly as many as half the population, due to war, starvation, and disease between 1885 and 1908, as the entire territory was transformed into a vast forced-labour camp, where native workers who failed to meet rubber and ivory quotas had their hands cut off. What mattered to the British, however, was Leopold's value as a buffer to French expansionism. Coming from the opposite direction – the coast of the Horn – were the Italians, whom the British considered a potential counterweight to both the French and the Mahdists. Italy, though, was a relatively underdeveloped European power, whose corrupt ruling class was prone to overreach itself; Bismarck's comment was that 'Italy has a large appetite and rotten teeth'. So it proved: an Italian army of 20,000 suffered catastrophic defeat at the hands of the Abyssinians at Adowa on 1 March 1896. The danger then was that the entire Italian position on the Horn might collapse, unhinging the British foothold on the Red Sea coast, perhaps in the context of a regional realignment around a French–Abyssinian–Mahdist axis. Kassala, held by the Italians since 1893, was at immediate risk, but Suakin might be the next domino to fall. Its retention had enabled the British to guard the Red Sea maritime route, block arms supplies to the Mahdist state, and reduce jihadist influence in Arabia; or so some Sudan hands argued. But there was a wider consideration, made explicit in a cable from Salisbury to Lord Cromer (as Sir Evelyn Baring, the Egyptian Viceroy, had now become) in March 1896. After wishing that 'our friends, the Italians, had less capacity for being beaten', the Prime Minister opined that 'it would not have been safe either from an African or European point of view to sit quite still while they were being crushed'. Native victories over European armies set a bad example.[10]

Adowa put wind in the sails of Britain's prophets of empire. Alfred Milner, the former Financial Secretary in Egypt, published his *England in Egypt* in 1893, with its clarion call to take up what Kipling would, before the decade was out, dub the 'White Man's Burden'. 'The book was more than a book,' proclaimed Churchill. 'The words rang like a trumpet-call which rallies the soldiers after the parapets are stormed, and summons them to complete victory.' Another enthusiastic advocate for a forward policy was Reginald Wingate of the Egyptian Intelligence Department. Three books, his own *Mahdism and the Egyptian Sudan* (1891), based on captured documents, and Father Ohrwalder's *Ten Years' Captivity in the Mahdi's Camp*

(1893) and Rudolf Slatin's *Fire and Sword in the Sudan* (1895), both of them edited volumes of memoirs, functioned as effective black propaganda. The implication was obvious: Egypt was flourishing under British administration, while the Sudan languished under a regime medieval in its barbarism. Had the time not come to exact vengeance from the murderers of Gordon?[11]

Even so, there was the cost. But to this, too, the Sudan hands had an answer. The Egyptian finances were now in good order and getting better. Milner was able to report (in the fifth edition of his *England in Egypt*) that by 1893 the revenues were showing a surplus over expenditure of £720,000, the reserves stood at £3,554,000, and annual payments on state debt had fallen from 66 per cent of income to 45 per cent; this, moreover, had been achieved despite substantial reductions in taxes on the peasantry.[12] The bondholders were being paid, yet Egypt was self-sufficient and stable: an ideal colonial set up. The most visible expression of this success was undoubtedly the new Anglo-Egyptian Army.

Formed of 18 battalions of infantry, 10 squadrons of cavalry, a camel corps of 8 companies, and 1 horse and 4 field batteries, it numbered about 20,000 men. Of the infantry battalions, 12 were conscripted Egyptian *fellahin*. The burden fell relatively lightly in a country of 10 million, and recruiters were usually able to pick only fit and willing men. Pay was adequate, and service was for six years with the colours and nine in the reserves or the police. The other six infantry battalions were formed of black Sudanese. These were largely volunteers who enlisted for life – men choosing to become professional soldiers, a good many of them former slaves. 'Many of the black soldiers,' reported George Steevens, 'have fought against us in the past, with the same energy and enjoyment as they now exhibit in our service. After each victory, the more desirable of the prisoners and deserters are enlisted, to their great content, in one black battalion or another.' The black battalions turned out to be the army's elite. Most senior regimental officers were British – three or four per battalion – but many junior officers were Egyptian or Sudanese. Each battalion of 760 men was armed with the single-shot Martini-Henry breechloader. The cavalry squadrons (all Egyptian) and the camel corps companies (half and half), each 100 strong, were also equipped with Martinis. The artillery was a mix of 18-pdr, 12-pdr, and 9-pdr quick-firers; and there were also some of the new 650-rounds-a-minute Maxim machine guns. On campaign, the uniform was usually khaki-covered tarbush with neck-flap, brown woollen jersey, sand-coloured trousers, and dark-blue puttees.[13]

Initially deployed in the defence of Suakin and the Egyptian frontier – and found to be an effective fighting force – this new army was poised, in 1896, to attempt a reconquest of the Sudan. Whether it would be so used still hung in the balance. Reginald Wingate was one of those urging that it should be. If Milner was able to report growing Egyptian strength, Wingate, at the centre of the intelligence web for a decade, was able to report a corresponding weakening of the Mahdist regime: the balance of forces was shifting in Britain's favour. Another of the men on the spot eager for action was one Horatio Herbert Kitchener.

Like Charles Gordon before him and T.E. Lawrence later, Kitchener had found purpose in life serving in the East. Such was his addiction – to his profession and his chosen theatre of action – that between 1878 and 1914, he did not spend a single winter at home. Born into a minor landowning family in Ireland in 1850, he had opted for a military career and pursued it with relentless determination. Tall, lean, handsome, with piercing blue eyes, he was also detached and aloof, having about him 'a strange atmosphere of loneliness'. This, almost certainly, was connected with repressed homosexuality. Any open expression at the time would have meant professional and social extinction. One of Kitchener's senior officers, Hector Macdonald, would in fact be driven to suicide by exposure as a homosexual in 1903. The only safe option was total celibacy and the sublimation of sexuality in obsessive work. But this made him uptight, a poor mixer, and too focused on his own advancement. Though he did form some very strong male friendships, they were few and intimate, and he was unpopular with most fellow officers. His rapid rise made him an object of envy and resentment. His lack of empathy did not help, and was a serious flaw in a military leader, indeed any kind of leader. Even humanity in the abstract was a matter of indifference: Kitchener was an ambitious social climber devoid of idealism, vision, or wider purpose. But this peculiar disposition made of him a certain kind of instrument: a technocrat, a machine soldier, an organiser of industrialised warfare, an embodiment of the systematic violence of empire.

Cromer knew him to be the man for the task in hand. 'He is cool and sensible, knows his subject thoroughly, and is not at all inclined to be rash,' he assured Salisbury. Much later, when the struggle for the Sudan was over, Cromer expanded on this 'man of the moment' theme. 'When once the

British and Egyptian troops were brought face to face with the enemy, there could . . . be little doubt of the result.' The problem had been to reach this point. 'The speedy and successful issue of the campaign depended, in fact, almost entirely upon the methods adopted for overcoming the very exceptional difficulties connected with supply and transport of the troops.' What had been needed was not so much a great captain as an efficient manager. 'The main quality required to meet those difficulties was a good head for business . . . Lord Kitchener of Khartoum won his well-deserved peerage because he was an excellent man of business; he looked very carefully after every important detail, and enforced economy.'[14]

Kitchener, now in his late 40s, was one of the most experienced of the old Sudan hands. He had spent several years in the mid-1870s working on a military survey of Palestine and become fluent in Arabic. He had been present at the bombardment of Alexandria in 1882, and had then served as second-in-command of an Egyptian cavalry regiment following the British invasion. His combination of linguistic skill, preference for independent action, and single-minded focus on professional advancement qualified him well for his role as Wolseley's intelligence officer in the campaign of 1884–5; Kitchener much preferred to don Arab robes and go undercover in native villages than frequent the officers' mess. He then served against the Mahdists in the eastern Sudan during the late 1880s, before taking over as *Sirdar* – commander of the Anglo-Egyptian Army – in 1892. Unsurprisingly, Kitchener had firm views on what should be done in the Sudan, and they were of course the hawkish views of an ambitious senior officer eager for war. While serving at Suakin, he had told Samuel Baker that the issue came down to a choice between 'anarchy – a return to savagedom and great danger to Egypt . . . or the development of an enormous trade in central Africa, under a good government'. Here was the heart of the matter: whether Sudan was to be run by a medieval elite of Arab slave traders or a modern elite of British policemen and coolie capitalists.[15]

There is little evidence that many Sudanese wanted to be 'liberated' by the British. Many of them, despite the oppressive character of the Khalifa's regime, proved willing enough to fight, often with great courage, to defeat the invasion. There is equally little evidence that many Egyptians wished to play the role of 'liberators'. On the contrary, when they got the chance, as events had shown in 1882, and would show again in 1919 and 1956, they demonstrated a much more active interest in liberating themselves from British colonial domination. Yet the British had no intention of paying for the 'liberation' of the Sudan: Kitchener's campaign was authorised only on the basis that it would not involve British troops or cost British taxpayers. In the event, mission creep and the jingo press combined to ensure a substantial British contribution in 1898; but that was not foreseen when Salisbury gave the go-ahead for the first stage of what eventually turned into the reconquest of the Sudan. Meanwhile, the gap between ambition and resources was made good by conscription and the lash.

The campaign which culminated in the Battle of Omdurman on 2 September 1898 was the operation of a modern industrial machine against an essentially medieval opponent: one of the most unequal campaigns in military history. Kitchener would finally bring to bear the massed firepower of 22,000 men equipped with modern artillery, machine guns, and breech-loaders. The combination of greater numbers and improved weaponry would give him something like 25 times the firepower of Stewart's square at Abu Klea. This is what turned Omdurman into a one-sided massacre. His real problem – which had also been Wolseley's – was getting such firepower to the battlefield. In the vastness of the Sudanese desert, logistics were all. Had a railway existed beyond the Egyptian border in Gordon's day, he might have been rescued. As it was, Wolseley's dependence on river steamers impeded by cataracts, and camel caravans supplied from meagre desert wells, had resulted in fatal delay and lack of punch. In Kitchener's campaign, railway power was to be decisive. But its construction was a major engineering project requiring tens of thousands of workers to labour long hours in crushing desert heat. Government parsimony meant that everything was done on the cheap. Kitchener's railway was built by the forced labour of conscripts and chain-gangs, subject to frequent floggings and occasional hangings. 'There was no trouble about labour,' explained *Daily Mail* correspondent G.W. Steevens. 'The railway battalions supply that. The railway battalions are raised by conscription, only instead of fighting with Martini and bayonet, the conscripts fight with shovel and pick. I have heard it called the *corvée* in another form; so, if you like, it is. But it is no more *corvée* than the work of sappers in any European army.' Except, of course, that the Egyptian conscript was the forced labourer of a colonial power.[16]

The first phase of the operation, between June and September 1896, was the advance to Dongola, in Sudan's northern province. At dawn on 7 June, Kitchener's army stormed the trenches of the Mahdist advanced post at

Firket, achieving complete surprise, killing the enemy commander and 800 of his men, taking more than 1,000 prisoners. As Kitchener noted in his dispatch to Cromer the following day, the battle had shown the quality of the Egyptian troops – about which there had previously been doubt – but also the continuing resilience of the Mahdist warriors. 'The Dervishes made a more stubborn resistance than I expected. Numbers had to be killed as they would not surrender, though in a hopeless condition . . . The Dervishes were like rats in a trap, and most that escaped did so by swimming the river, naked and without arms.'[17] The next three months were spent awaiting the arrival of new steamers, pushing forward the railway, and dealing with various calamities – an outbreak of cholera, which killed 280 soldiers and 640 labourers, a series of violent storms in which tents, telegraph lines, and railway embankments were swept away, and an accidental explosion that crippled the *Zafir*, the first of Kitchener's new river gunboats.

Meanwhile, the Mahdist Governor of Dongola, Wad Bishara, proved a wily opponent, refusing to commit his forces to destruction in the face of the invaders' vastly superior firepower. When Kitchener was finally ready for a second thrust, he hoped to repeat the success of Firket and catch the Mahdist army at Kerma in a dawn attack on 19 September. Instead, Wad Bishara slipped away in the night, crossing from the east to the west bank of the Nile to take up a fresh position at Hafir, leaving his opponent punching air. When the Anglo-Egyptians reorganised to attack the new position, the Mahdist emir again wriggled away before his army could suffer serious damage, falling back on Dongola. Even here, he declined to fight, allowing Kitchener to march into the town unopposed on 23 September. The *Sirdar* immediately dispatched an advanced force to seize Merowe, another 150 miles upriver, with orders to halt there and await further instructions. The northern province had been overrun, though less by battle than by engineering: the railway had enabled Kitchener to bring to bear such force that the enemy had declined to fight. It would soon extend all the way from Wadi Halfa to Kerma, 200 miles inside Sudan. But there, in May 1897, this particular line would come to rest.[18] For Kitchener was working on another, far more ambitious railway plan – one that would be hastened to fruition by alarming news from Wingate's intelligence department.

The plan was to run a line direct from Wadi Halfa to Abu Hamed, cutting off the entire Nile bend by taking it across the Nubian Desert – more than 230 miles of almost waterless waste, but barely a third the distance involved following the river. To pay for this, Cromer now abandoned the policy of

economy and urged Salisbury to come up with £500,000 of British government money. This *volte-face* was the Consul General's response to Wingate's
report that a French mission was in Addis Ababa seeking the Emperor of
Abyssinia's consent to a French sphere of influence in the Nile Basin. Here
was the French–Abyssinian–Mahdist axis beginning to take practical shape.
Lord Salisbury may have prepared tricycle rides around his English park,
but, willy-nilly, he now found himself bounced into a race up the Nile to
plant the flag in Equatoria.

He could hardly have held out had he wished to. Kitchener, on a flying
visit to London, flush from the capture of Dongola, had the backing of Queen
Victoria, the Duke of Cambridge, and the whole jingo faction; on the eve of
the Diamond Jubilee, here, it seemed, was the great imperial warrior everyone
had been waiting for. Kitchener was able to telegraph the good news
to Cromer before starting on his return journey to Cairo: 'Government
have approved of scheme proposed, and authorise expenditure on railways
and gunboats. The approximate estimate I submitted to the Chancellor of
Exchequer was – railway, £240,000; construction, £30,000; gunboats, £75,000;
armament, stores, etc, £55,000; transport, £100,000. Total, £500,000.'[19]

Railways were at the heart of turn-of-the-century imperialism. The
biggest infrastructure projects of their age, they returned gargantuan profits
for the consortia of banks, industrial suppliers, and construction firms
involved. They were also vital strategic assets. Their capacity to move armies
and deliver victories had been demonstrated in both the American Civil
War and in Bismarck's wars against Austria and France. They had become
major arteries of military power in a global struggle for empire. As European
industrialism's most visible and impressive exports, they were also symbols
of a dawning modernity, of machine-powered progress – monuments of
steel and steam gifted by a 'superior civilisation' to the 'backward races';
emblems, therefore, of the white man's right to rule.

Cecil Rhodes, dreaming of a British line from Cairo to the Cape, loaned
a number of 70- and 80-ton locomotives for the Sudan Military Railway
(SMR), and Kitchener insisted on a 3-foot 6-inch gauge, to match that of
Britain's South African colonies. Steevens considered the SMR to be 'a
civilised weapon' and 'the deadliest weapon that Britain has ever used
against Mahdism'. He contrasted 'the extempore, amateur scrambles of
Wolseley's campaign and the machine-like precision of Kitchener's'. It was
the essence of victory: 'The Battle of the Atbara was won in the workshops
of Wadi Halfa,' he affirmed.[20]

The second phase of Kitchener's campaign – achieved in two jumps, the first to Abu Hamed, the second to Berber – was accomplished as easily as the first. A flying column of 2,700 men and 1,300 camels under Major General Archibald Hunter marched 130 miles from Merowe to Abu Hamed in eight days, pounced on the enemy at 2 o'clock on the morning of 7 August, and won a crushing victory with the loss of only 27 killed as against ten times that many Mahdists. The effect was to panic the enemy into abandoning Berber, a further 120 miles upriver, which Kitchener then captured on the run, before it could be reoccupied, taking possession on 10 September. This was a huge strategic leap at virtually no cost. It was now possible not only to complete the cross-desert railway to Abu Hamed, but to continue it southwards; it would eventually run all the way to Fort Atbara, a short distance beyond Berber, at the confluence of the Atbara and the Nile, affording Kitchener a railhead a mere 200 miles north of Omdurman. Possession of Berber also allowed the road to Suakin, the shortest route between the Nile and the Red Sea, to be reopened.[21]

That the railway was a mortal threat was well understood by the Mahdist high command. The loss of Berber was a major setback – the result, it seems, of the local commander's fright when he did not receive immediate reinforcement by the Emir Mahmoud, the young, capable, but brutal commander of a large Mahdist army dispatched northwards by the Khalifa to block the Anglo-Egyptian advance. Mahmoud's army – it would eventually number around 18,000 warriors – was a far more serious threat than anything Kitchener had faced until now. In relation to it, he was, for the time being, perilously overextended, for it would take many months for the railway construction gangs to catch up with the military vanguard.

Lieutenant Edouard 'Percy' Girouard, a Canadian railway engineer, was a minor genius in the matter of industrial organisation. He created a moveable 'railhead' – a canvas town of 2,500 workers – who were organised on 'Fordist' principles of strict division of labour, and were supplied with all their needs, both industrial materials and human supplies, by two trains each day. The railway would eventually extend almost 600 miles, and Girouard succeeded in pushing it forward at the extraordinary rate of one and a half miles a day; but even at this pace, it was not destined to reach Fort Atbara until 3 July 1898. Winston Churchill, a young subaltern serving with the 21st Lancers who also doubled as correspondent for the *Morning Post*, was among the most intelligent of the many participants who left accounts of the campaign. Like Steevens, he was unequivocal about the central (if unglamorous) significance of the railway: 'The eye is fixed on the fighting brigades as they move amid the smoke; on the swarming figures of the enemy; on the general, serene and determined, mounted in the middle of his staff. The long trailing line of communications is unnoticed . . . Victory is the beautiful, bright-coloured flower. Transport is the stem without which it could never have blossomed.' Once the railway was complete, he felt, the matter was settled: 'though the battle was not yet fought, the victory was won . . . It remained only to pluck the fruit in the most convenient hour, with the least trouble and at the smallest cost.'[22]

This was not the only reason for the long delay – it lasted the best part of a year – before Kitchener was on the move again. The Khalifa's army was around 100,000 strong. A third of these were riflemen. Many – especially the *Mulazimiya* and the Baggara, the regime's Praetorians and Cossacks – were highly motivated. To be certain of victory – and anything less than certainty was not to be contemplated – the *Sirdar* needed a strong contingent of British regulars. For a good while, neither Cromer nor Salisbury were moved to provide them – reducing Kitchener to a state of anxiety bordering on hysteria and mental breakdown. For the façade – of poise and authority – was precisely that: the body-armour of a highly neurotic personality. In the face of difficulty, Kitchener could succumb to crippling indecision; and when ambition hit a barrier, he became irritable and petulant. Cromer worried about him. 'He complains of the strain,' he cabled Salisbury, 'and, generally, leaves on my mind the impression that, for the moment, his nerve has gone.' Kitchener seems to have been brought to a pitch of nervous tension by anxiety that he might suddenly be denied the culminating glory of a decisive victory over Mahdism: 'I hope there will be no question about finishing the whole thing at Omdurman next year,' he wrote to one of his intimates. 'You have no idea what continual anxiety, worry, and strain I have through it all. I do not think I can stand much more, and I feel so completely done up that I can hardly go on and wish some leave, or I shall break down. I have had none for three years now.'[23]

What mattered to Cromer and Salisbury was not so much the Mahdists as the French. Aware that their rivals were intent on 'setting up a French principality at Fashoda [in Equatoria]', they saw Kitchener's army at Berber as one piece among many on the larger chessboard of Africa. Sitting where it was, it was capable of putting into check any untoward French move. That consideration seems to have been the reason for a sudden change in British policy when Wingate reported that the Khalifa was about to march on Berber at the head of his main force. The British imperial elite could not allow their Berber rook to be taken by the Mahdist queen – as much as anything, for fear that it would allow a French pawn to occupy Fashoda. Accordingly, on 23 December 1897, the British Cabinet agreed to send whatever British reinforcements the *Sirdar* required to meet the military emergency. By the end of January, Kitchener had his Anglo-Egyptian Army concentrated in an entrenched camp at Berber, and the first of the new British contingents had arrived, a brigade under the command of Major General Gatacre comprising the 1st Battalions of Warwicks, Lincolns, Camerons, and Seaforths. The fire-power of this single British brigade was equal to that of three Egyptian and Sudanese brigades combined, because the British infantry had been re-equipped since the campaigns of the 1880s with the Lee-Metford magazine rifle.[24]

Wingate's intelligence had been misleading. The Mahdist high command was in fact divided and unable to decide. Only the army of Emir Mahmoud was on the move – a force of perhaps 18,000 Mahdists as against 13,000 Anglo-Egyptians – while the Khalifa remained at Omdurman. Kitchener's prediction – that 'the fight for the Sudan would appear likely to take place at Berber' – turned out to be wrong. The immediate struggle was with only a fraction of the main Mahdist army, and Mahmoud was too sensible a commander to hurl his warriors across open ground against trenches defended with breechloaders, machine guns, and modern artillery, backed by the fire of a flotilla of river gunboats. Instead, he took up a strong defensive position a short distance east of the river, by the dried-up bed of the Atbara, forming a wide circular *zariba* inside a shallow crater-like depression, giving protection from long-range artillery fire, but with high ground in the centre, such that tiered trenches afforded the defenders three banks of fire. Kitchener marched out to confront Mahmoud, but was then confounded by the enemy position. He knew that he faced 'a force of Dervishes of better fighting qualities and far greater numerical strength than we have ever met before'. That force was now in front, yet hardly anything of the enemy could be seen save a few fluttering flags. The crater was largely silent. Kitchener was overcome with an attack of the dithers. How many men might go down to rifle fire on the approach? What terrible damage might those waiting fanatics do at close-quarters inside the *zariba*? Might two years' toil unravel in 20 minutes of chaos? He even cabled Cromer for advice: should he attack or not? Nothing happened for several days.[25]

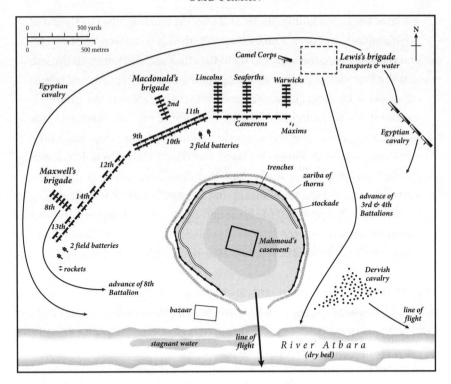

13. The Battle of the Atbara, 8 April 1898

Then senior colleagues persuaded him to take the risk. On 7 April 1898, the Anglo-Egyptian Army marched out to attack Mahmoud's *zariba*, and on the following day, a little after 8.00 a.m., the *Sirdar* ordered a massed infantry assault supported by artillery and machine guns. The cavalry swept around on the left to block any escape across the Atbara bed, Gatacre's British regulars stormed forward in heavy columns on the left, while Macdonald's and Maxwell's Sudanese attacked in a long double line to their right, with Egyptians in reserve. As the attackers reached the lip of the crater, 300 yards from the *zariba*, they paused to unleash crashing volleys at the defences, in the same instant that fire exploded along the enemy lines. Then they moved forward again, taking casualties as they went, and soon they were at the *zariba*, attempting to tear their way in. 'Now the inside suddenly sprang to life,' reported Steevens. 'Out of the earth came dusty, black, half-naked shapes, running, running and turning to shoot, but running away.' The interior was a warren of hillocks and scrub, trenches and stockades, a labyrinth of danger. But Remington and spear could not stand against Lee-Metford and bayonet.

For now began the killing. Bullet and bayonet and butt, the whirlwind of
Highlanders swept over. And by this time, the Lincolns were on the right,
and the Maxims, galloped right up to the stockade, and withered the left,
and the Warwicks . . . were volleying off the blacks as your beard comes
off under a keen razor. Farther and farther they cleared the ground –
cleared it of everything like a living man, for it was left carpeted thick
enough with dead. Here was a trench: bayonet that man. Here was a little
straw *tukl*: warily around to the door, and then a volley. Now in column
through this opening in the bushes; then into line, and drop those few
desperately firing shadows among dry stems beyond. For the running
blacks – poor heroes – still fired, though every second they fired less and
ran more. And on, on the British stumbled and slew, till suddenly there
was unbroken blue overhead and a clear drop underfoot. The river![26]

The attackers had gone straight through the *zariba* in a single sweeping
storm of fire and steel, taking 650 casualties themselves, but slaying 2,500 of
the enemy, scooping up several hundred prisoners, including Mahmoud
himself, and putting the rest to flight.

A victory for modernity, for sure; but not for civilisation. The Mahdist
wounded were routinely shot or bayoneted; very few wounded men were
taken prisoner. The captured enemy commander was paraded through the
streets of Berber on 14 April, shackles riveted to his ankles, a halter round
his neck, his hands bound behind his back. He was driven forward under
the whips of his guards as the crowd shouted abuse and pelted him with
refuse – a scene which must have reminded some of Kitchener's classically
educated British officers as something akin to a Roman triumph.[27]

A pause in the fighting followed as the heat rose to its summer zenith, with
temperatures as high as 55°C. A second British brigade arrived, and
Kitchener concentrated his army at a new forward base, Wadi Hamed, just
60 miles north of Omdurman. A curious paralysis seems to have overcome
the Mahdist command. No initiatives were taken, no attempts made to
disrupt the steady build-up of destructive power of men and machines just
a few days' march away. The guerrilla war whose unleashing might have
bogged the invaders down in months of frustrating attrition and escalating
cost appears never to have been contemplated. Perhaps the regime, hollowed

out by larceny, corruption, and brutality, could now survive only as a centralised military force. Perhaps the Khalifa had accumulated too many Sudanese enemies to operate as a freedom fighter in the bush. So when the orders went out to the Mahdist emirs, it was to mobilise all able-bodied men and bring them to Omdurman – not, as they might have done, to attack the enemy's long, thin, easily broken line of communications. But many did not come. Some disaffected tribes ignored the summons altogether, and many individuals either dodged the draft or slipped away later. Morale was damaged by an upsurge in official plundering, of both farmers and traders, in that final summer, but also by growing awareness of the obvious imbalance of military force, especially when news arrived of the destruction of Mahmoud's army on the Atbara. The veteran soldier Babikr Bedri was caught up in the dragnet, but all enthusiasm for holy war was gone. His father's prognosis was grim: 'I'm always thinking about the Khalifa's army and the government army. I believe they'll meet at Karari [immediately north of Omdurman: the Sudanese name for the battle], and after a bit I see the Khalifa and his army going pitter-patter, pitter-patter to Omdurman, running away from the government army. I can see no victory for them at all.' The markets shared the prevailing pessimism: the price of *durra* rocketed in the Omdurman *souks*.[28]

The Anglo-Egyptian advance began on 24 August – 22,000 men, a third British, two-thirds Egyptian and Sudanese, organised in six infantry brigades, with a regiment of British cavalry, a regiment of Egyptian cavalry, and a total of 44 field guns and 20 Maxim machine guns. On the river supporting them was a flotilla of ten gunboats mounting a further 36 cannon and 24 machine guns.[29]

For two weeks, contact with the enemy was minimal. Mounted patrols were seen occasionally, but no large bodies, and such small parties as were encountered soon fell back and disappeared. The Khalifa surely knew he was doomed; or was his religious conviction so profound as to imagine some miracle possible? Either way, he did not lack courage, and he was, anyway, caught in the coils of the myth – the myth of the holy war – on which his theocratic dictatorship was based. To surrender or to flee was tantamount to a denial of the Mahdi, if not of God himself. Still, he might have decided to fight in the streets of Omdurman, preventing Kitchener from deploying his firepower to maximum effect, involving the invaders in a more dangerous struggle in the close terrain of a mud city several miles across. But he did not. On 1 September, Anglo-Egyptian cavalry patrols

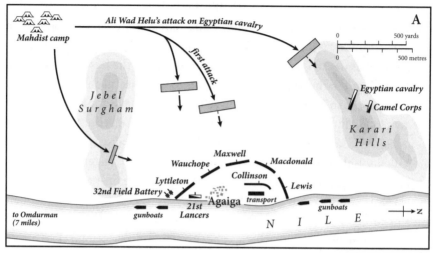

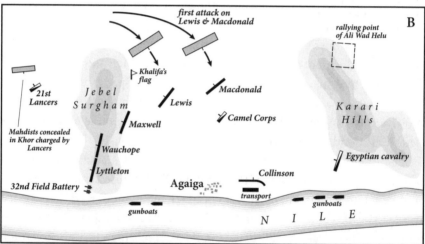

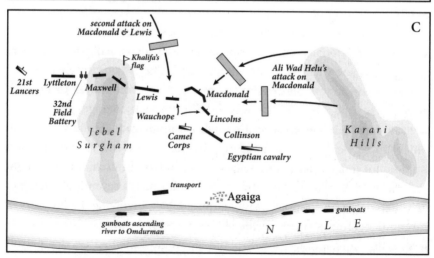

14. The Battle of Omdurman, 2 September 1898

scouting southwards towards Omdurman from a newly established main camp on the western bank of the river saw them: the main field army of the Mahdist Empire, tens of thousands of them, heading north from the city, to confront the infidel at the Karari Hills.[30]

Journalist George Steevens was present:

> In front of the city stretched a long white line – banners, it might be; more likely tents; most likely both. In front of that was a longer, thicker, black line – no doubt a *zariba* or trench. Then they did not mean to fight after all. Only as we sat and ate a biscuit and looked – the entrenchment moved. The solid wall moved forward, and it was a wall of men. Whew! What an army! Five huge brigades of it – a three-mile front, and parts of it eight or ten men deep. It was beginning to move directly on our hill, and – tum, tum, tum – we heard the boom of a war-drum . . . The five corps never broke or shifted, the rigid front never bent; their discipline must be perfect. And they covered the ground. Three miles melted before them . . .

The scouts raced back to report what they had seen. How many? Perhaps 50,000. How acting? Advancing rapidly, in fine order, with great confidence.[31]

The Anglo-Egyptian Army spent the night under arms. They were deployed in a line forming an obtuse angle with both flanks resting on the river, the mass of the Karari Hills away to the right, the Jebel Surgham to the left, a wide expanse of flat desert in front. The British, under Gatacre, were on the left: Lyttleton's 2nd Brigade (Rifles, Lancashire Fusiliers, Northumberland Fusiliers, Grenadier Guards) and Wauchope's 1st (Warwicks, Seaforths, Camerons, and Lincolns). Three brigades of Egyptians and Sudanese then manned the centre and the right, Maxwell commanding the 2nd, Macdonald the 1st, Lewis the 3rd, while Collinson's 4th Egyptian formed the main reserve, posted behind the line near the village of Agaiga.

The expectation was that the Khalifa would mount a night attack in an effort to minimise the effect of the Anglo-Egyptian Army's massive superiority in firepower. This, like the prospect of a street battle, was a worry for Kitchener; his ideal, of course, was pitched battle on open ground in the full light of day. In the event, there was no night attack. Nor, when the sun came up on 2 September, were there any enemy to be seen. Surely, then, the Khalifa had decided to fall back and fight a defensive battle at Omdurman, after all? Surely he would not be so crazy as to rush the Anglo-Egyptian line in broad daylight?

But at 6.00 a.m., a trooper of the 21st Lancers galloped down Jebel Surgham, across the plain, and through the waiting line: they were coming.

Steevens recalled the electric atmosphere as the enemy first appeared far away on the slopes of Jebel Surgham and through the heat haze on the plain: 'a flicker of white flags began to extend and fill the front . . . The noise of something began to creep in upon us; it cleared and divided into the tap of drums and the faraway surf of raucous voices . . . They were coming on.'[32] Winston Churchill was awestruck:

> The emblems of the more famous emirs were easily distinguishable. On the extreme left, the chiefs and soldiers of the Bright Green flag gathered under Ali Wad Helu; between this and the centre, the large Dark Green flag of Osman Sheikh al-Din rose above a dense mass of spearmen, preceded by long lines of warriors armed presumably with rifles; over the centre, commanded by Yakoub, the sacred Black Banner of the Khalifa floated high and remarkable; while on the right, a great square of Dervishes was arrayed under an extraordinary number of white flags, among which the red ensign of the Sherif was almost hidden. All the pride and might of the Dervish Empire were massed on this last great day of its existence.[33]

The conduct of the Mahdist army on 2 September 1898 was characterised by, on the one hand, the astonishing courage of the rank and file, and, on the other, the shocking stupidity of the leadership. Not only did the Khalifa launch his men on a series of suicidal frontal charges, but he failed dismally to coordinate attacks to ensure maximum pressure on the British line. The battle was a shambles. Despite this, the Anglo-Egyptian force would find itself wrong-footed and, at one point, in danger of losing an entire brigade, perhaps more, owing to the unexpected determination, resilience, and ferocity of their opponents.

There was little time to observe the spectacle. The Mahdists were already in motion, and they did not pause, advancing towards the enemy with all their customary speed. The British guns opened at long range at 6.30 a.m., and from that moment the roar of battle rose steadily as ever more guns joined in along the line, together with the gunboats, anchored on the river's edge on either flank. The British on the left stood in double rank behind a *zariba*, the Egyptians and Sudanese lay side-by-side in a shelter trench. Soon, the shriek of shrapnel, Maxims, and breechloaders was deafening. 'No white troops,' reported Steevens:

would have faced that torrent of death for five minutes, but the Baggara and the blacks came on. The torrent swept into them and hurled them down in whole companies. You saw a rigid line gather itself up and rush on evenly; then before a shrapnel shell or a Maxim, the line suddenly quivered and stopped. The line was yet unbroken, but it was quite still. But other lines gathered up again, again, and yet again; they went down, and yet others rushed on. Sometimes they came near enough to see single figures quite plainly. One old man with a white flag started with five comrades; all dropped, but he alone came bounding forward to within 200 yards of the 14th Sudanese. Then he folded his arms across his face, and his limbs loosened, and he dropped sprawling to earth beside his flag.[34]

What Steevens noticed is that when the Mahdists were stopped, usually hundreds of yards short of the Anglo-Egyptian line, they were not so much driven back as destroyed outright. Entire bodies of the attackers simply ceased to exist. The courage was breathtaking. Then, gradually, the fire died down, and by 8.00 had ceased entirely. 'The last shell had burst over the last visible group of Dervishes; now there was nothing but the unbending, grimly expectant line before Agaiga and the still carpet of white in front.'[35]

It appeared to be over, and at about 8.30, after half an hour of expectant waiting, the bugles sounded the advance, and the Anglo-Egyptian line moved forward in an echelon of brigades, Lyttleton's 2nd British leading on the left beside the river, Macdonald's 1st Egyptian forming the right rear on the other flank out in the desert. The Anglo-Egyptians found themselves advancing across a carpet of dead and dying, among whom were many still-dangerous enemies, men only lightly wounded or lying low, awaiting a chance to rush forward with spear or sword, or try a close-range shot with a Remington.

Then, around 9.40, a heavy crackle of fire was heard in the rear. Soon, it was a crashing roar as the battle burst back into full vigour. Two massive blocs of Mahdist warriors, perhaps 30,000 men in all, were in motion against the exposed right rear of the British line. What was happening? The main attack on the *zariba* seems to have been mounted by only one large corps of the Mahdist army, the 10,000 men of Osman Azrak's White Banner. Their attack had collapsed, hardly anyone getting closer than 300 yards of the enemy line, leaving 2,000 casualties behind, Osman Azrak himself among the dead. Now, though, the men of the Black Banner (under the Khalifa), the

Dark Green Banner (Osman Sheikh al-Din), and the Bright Green Banner (Ali Wad Helu) were hurling themselves against Lewis's and Macdonald's brigades.

If the first phase of the battle had been a methodical execution from a prepared position, the second phase was a sudden crisis that took the British wholly unawares. What followed seems to have been exceptionally close-run. Had the Dervish attacks been better coordinated, such that both main blocs, the Black Banner approaching from the south-west, the Green Banners from the north-west, struck the exposed Anglo-Egyptian brigades at the same moment, the latter might have been enveloped and overwhelmed. Had that happened, the whole outcome of the battle might then have been in the balance. For the Anglo-Egyptian formation was neither a square nor a line, but an echelon of brigades between which wide gaps had opened as it wheeled southwards to cross the Jebel Surgham, with Lyttleton's British brigade as pivot, Macdonald's on the outer flank; in fact, the gap between Macdonald's brigade and Lewis's, next on the left, had stretched to a perilous 800 yards.

As it was, the Black Banner came on first, at about 9.40, and Macdonald deployed his brigade with four battalions in line, but with the right-hand one bent back, so that half these men faced forward and half at right angles, to guard against the end of the line being flanked by the Green Banner. Macdonald was therefore able to meet the onslaught of the Khalifa's corps with the fire of around 3,000 men, supported, to some degree, by that of Lewis's men to his left rear. What followed was a stunning display of fanatic courage by 200 Baggara horsemen. One eyewitness later described it as follows:

The Baggara cavalry on this occasion showed remarkable and reckless daring. They evidently intended to break through our lines and divert our fire, so as to give the Dervish infantry an opening. To carry this out was hopeless, for it meant riding to certain death – but they galloped forward in loose open order, their ranks presenting one long ridge of flashing swords. Every soldier in the Sirdar's army watched breathlessly this daring feat. Nearer and nearer they came, until the foremost horseman emerged almost within 200 yards of Macdonald's lines. A continuous stream of bullets from our lines was emptying the saddles, but on they came until not a single horseman was left. One Baggara succeeded in getting within 30 yards of the lines before he fell.

The whole Dervish cavalry had been annihilated. There is no instance in history of a more superb devotion to a cause, or a greater contempt for death.

This, however, was but a prelude to a display of almost equally reck-less courage on the part of the Dervish infantry in their last despairing effort. The latter, although they had seen the fate of the cavalry, swept like a great white-crested wave towards our ranks, without the slightest pause or hesitation. Hundreds planted their banners defiantly in the ground, and gathered round them to drop lifeless at the foot, as the price of their devotion. The carnage was fearful, as the dauntless fanatics hurled themselves to inevitable death. Most noticeable of all was the Emir Yacoub, who bore forward the great Black Banner of the Khalifa (his brother) surrounded by his relatives and devoted followers. Although decimated by the hail of bullets before and around them, they surged forward, until only a mere handful of men remained around the flag; and these, never faltering, rushed onwards until they dropped dead.[36]

Steevens described the resolute firing that destroyed them.

The *fellahin* [Egyptian infantry] stood like a wall, and aimed steadily at the word; the chargers swerved towards Macdonald. The blacks [Sudanese infantry], as cool as any Scotsman, stood and aimed likewise; the last Baggara fell at the muzzles of the rifles. Our fire went on, steady, remorseless. The Remington bullets piped more and more rarely over-head, and the black heads thinned out in front. A second time the attack guttered and flickered out. It was just past ten.[37]

But it was still not over. Before the Khalifa's attack had entirely collapsed, Osman Sheikh al-Din's and Ali Wad Helu's Green Banner men surged forward from the direction of the Karari Hills to the north, the tremendous speed of the Mahdist formations again taking the plodding Anglo-Egyptian battalions by surprise. It was five minutes past ten. Macdonald's brigade, which had just managed to shoot away an entire corps of perhaps 15,000 men, immediately faced a second onslaught by a similar number, coming against both its right front and right flank. And now, in an extraordinary display of cool-headed command on Macdonald's part and superb drill and discipline on that of his soldiers, this second attack was met and defeated. Measuring distribution of force with the precision of a structural engineer, he shifted his battalions one by one from their west-facing position on the left to a north-facing position on the right. Cyril Falls describes it with the admiration of one professional soldier for another:

> The Khalifa's men came on in enormous strength with their usual courage, but the combination of artillery fire and volleys from the infantry mowed them down. Just before the remnant dispersed, Osman's force swept forward in even greater strength. Macdonald had already ordered his left battalion to move across and deploy on the right part of the right battalion, which he had already moved to face the new front, and it actually reached its position before the troops on the left had finished dealing with the southern attackers. Next he transferred another battalion to the new alignment, while the half battalion in the centre wheeled on it with the batteries and machine-guns conforming. And finally the last battalion, having completed the rout of its assailants, extended the new line to the left.[38]

The last charge was pressed with the gritty resolution of the first. As before so many times, as the Dervish formations came on, they had to be annihilated by fire if the attack was to be repulsed. 'It was their largest, best, and bravest army that ever fought against us for Mahdism,' says Steevens, who had watched it all:

> and it died worthily of the huge empire that Mahdism had won and kept so long. Their riflemen, mangled by every kind of death and torment that man can devise, clung around the black flag and the green, emptying their poor, rotten, home-made cartridges dauntlessly. Their spearmen charged death at every minute hopelessly. Their horsemen led each attack, riding into the bullets till nothing was left but three horses trotting up to our line . . . Not one rush, or two, or ten – but rush on rush, company on company, never stopping, though all their view that was not unshaken enemy was the bodies of the men who had rushed before them. A dusky line got up and stormed forward: it bent, broke up, fell apart, and disappeared. Before the smoke had cleared, another line was bending and storming forward in the same track.[39]

Nor was it all hopeless self-sacrifice. The top leadership was rotten, but there was cunning and craft in the Mahdist army. This was the explanation of the battle's most famous incident, the charge of the 21st Lancers, when the regiment thought it was attacking 300 enemy isolated on the southern fringe of the battlefield, only to find a deep ravine packed with 3,000 spearmen suddenly yawn open in its path. Too late to rein the horses in, the 400 troopers had no choice but to plunge through the mass and try to hack their way to the other side. 'The pace was fast and distance short,' recalled Churchill, an eager participant:

> Yet, before it was half covered, the whole aspect of the affair changed. A deep crease in the ground – a dry watercourse, a *khor* – appeared where all had seemed smooth, level plain; and from there sprang, with the suddenness of a pantomime effect and a high-pitched yell, a dense white mass of men nearly as long as our front and about 12 deep. A score of horsemen and a dozen bright flags rose as if by magic from the earth. Eager warriors sprang forward to anticipate the shock. The rest stood firm to meet it.

In the two minutes of chaotic, close-quarters collision that followed, the 21st Lancers lost 5 officers, 65 men, and 119 horses.[40]

By mid-morning, it was finally over. In the short space of four hours, the Anglo-Egyptian Army had killed 11,000, wounded 16,000, and taken 4,000 prisoners: the enemy's casualties amounted to half their own army's strength and exceeded the entire strength of Kitchener's. The fact that the Mahdists moved with exceptional speed – such that flight would have been relatively easy for most – underlines the extraordinary bravery implicit in these losses. Some men, though, did indeed slink away. One such was Mahdist veteran Babikr Bedri, whose faith in the regime had finally collapsed during the abortive invasion of Egypt ordered by the Khalifa in 1889. He and his comrades, serving with the Black Banner, watched as the broken bodies of the first attack, that of the White Banner, were carried past on stretchers. Four men were carrying or supporting each wounded man. 'Look here,' Bedri said to his companions, 'if one of us gets wounded, I shall get "wounded" too, with his blood; and the rest of you can carry us away, since that seems to be allowed.' As the attack of the Black Banner wilted in the storm of fire, as the brave were killed and the timid cowered or shammed death, Bedri's group went to ground at a little hillock of sand and bushes, keeping their heads down in the hail of bullets. 'I rubbed my face into the sand trying to bury my head in it, thoughtless of suffocation, so distracted was I by fear of death, which in dangers no less acute than this I had sought so eagerly.' Then the man to his right was wounded, and Bedri ripped off his turban, smeared it with blood, and wrapped it round his arm. 'Now two of us are wounded,' he declared; and the whole group, as planned, sought escape from the killing field.[41]

Despite the upsets – the two onslaughts on Macdonald's exposed brigade and the precipitous charge of the 21st Lancers – the victory was overwhelming. In Steevens' words, 'It was not a battle, but an execution.' The Anglo-Egyptian casualties were slight: around 200 British and 300 Egyptians and Sudanese. Many of the soldiers were sickened by it. One NCO thought the battle 'like murder'; another 'more like a butcher's killing-house than anything else'. As the victors advanced across the battlefield, seemingly wounded men would occasionally rise from the ground to shoot or stab. This was taken as sufficient justification for the routine bayoneting of the wounded; but something uglier was at work. 'It is certain,' wrote Ernest Bennett of *The Westminster Gazette*:

> that in many cases wounded Dervishes, unarmed and helpless, were butchered from sheer wantonness and lust of bloodshed. The whole formed a hideous picture, not easy to forget. Some of the wounded turned wearily over, and paid no attention to our advance. For many of them, indeed, the bitterness of death was already past. They lay in the scorching heat, with shattered bodies and shattered hopes, awaiting the final thrust of the merciless bayonet. Many of them were doubtless good as well as brave men. They had trusted in Allah that he would deliver them, but their prayer had been in vain.

Some soldiers boasted of their genocidal prowess. One reported killing 'about 25', each time proclaiming 'another one for Gordon'. The young Winston Churchill wrote home that the victory had been 'disgraced by the inhuman slaughter of the wounded'. He cited the particular case of Colonel John Maxwell, commander of 2nd Brigade, who made no attempt to control his men, and later, put in charge of the occupation of Omdurman, privately admitted to having 'quietly made away with a bunch of emirs'. Not that there was any succour for those left alive. Kitchener's economies had pared his medical services to Crimean inadequacy, leaving his force ill-equipped to deal with its own wounded, let alone the enemy's. But few cared. A jingo mood of vindictive vengeance was symbolised by the commander-in-chief's decision to dig up the Mahdi's body, blow up his tomb, and retain his skull as a souvenir.[42]

Not all the killing was gratuitous brutality. Many Sudanese soldiers had real scores to settle. Bedri bore witness to one example. He saw a black soldier leading a slave woman by the hand through the streets of Omdurman. Then he saw a man he recognised, Ibrahim Tamim, a merchant from Aswan, running after them and grabbing the woman's hand to take her back. The soldier loaded his rifle and shot him. Then the soldier and the woman walked on, laughing. Bedri had been only 200 yards away, and when he enquired about the incident afterwards, he learned that she had been Ibrahim Tamim's concubine, and the soldier was her brother. The slaves were taking their vengeance.[43]

⬛

The war was not quite over. While Kitchener raced up the Nile to confront Major Marchand, whose expeditionary force of 4 white officers and 500 Sengalese troops had established themselves at Fashoda and staked a French claim to Equatoria, other commanders led flying columns into the hinterland to suppress hold-out garrisons and run down renegade bands. The most important of these was that of Colonel Reginald Wingate, the veteran intelligence chief, who now headed up a flying column of 3,700 mainly Sudanese soldiers whose job was to kill or capture the fugitive Khalifa. He had fled into eastern Kordofan, where he remained at large for more than a year following the battle. But he was finally cornered, his escape-routes blocked, at a place called Umm Diwaykarat in November 1899. He had with him some of the Old Guard of Mahdism, the bravest and most loyal, many of them Ta'aishi Baggara, such as his two surviving brothers, but also some of the *Ashraf*, including the Mahdi's son.

Wingate's men made a march through the bush by moonlight, taking position on high ground around the Khalifa's camp, preparatory to a dawn attack. They were pre-empted. For the last time, the horns and drums of the Mahdist *jihad* were heard; for the last time, the Ansar launched a screaming charge; and for the last time, they were scythed by artillery, machine guns, and breechloaders. The cease-fire was sounded at 6.25 a.m.

Half an hour later, Wingate's little army marched on the Mahdist camp. Though they took many prisoners, the Khalifa was not among them. Before the firing had ended, knowing the day was lost, that the end had come, he and his closest companions had unrolled their sheepskins, knelt in prayer, and waited for the enemy's bullets to take them. And there the Sudanese soldiers and their British officers found them, behind a double line of the riflemen of the bodyguard, lying in death with their faces turned towards Mecca, the Khalifa and the emirs of Mahdism.[44]

# CHAPTER THIRTEEN

# A 'MAD MULLAH'

Some time before the Khalifa of the Mahdi perished in a hail of bullets in remote eastern Kordofan, Muhammad Abdullah Hassan decided that he, too, had a divine mission to rid his country of Christians and restore the true faith of Islam. His country was even poorer, if that were possible, than the Sudan. At least the Sudanese were blessed with the Nile, their little agricultural villages strung along its banks like beads on a blue thread. Most of Somaliland comprised semi-arid wasteland, parched for much of the year, punctuated only by occasional blobs of green and clusters of mud houses around oases and wells, with wide expanses of rock and thorn scrub between. Much of the landscape was hilly, even mountainous, and rivers ran in the rainy season, but the plains and plateaux were scorched by sun and hot winds for much of the year, with temperatures soaring above 40ºC. Farming of any kind was barely possible, and most of Somaliland's 1 million or so people were nomadic stockmen, their poverty absolute, save for the sheep, goats, cattle, donkeys, and camels they herded between patches of water and grazing. The search for these provided Somali life with its eternal rhythms and tensions. A Somali clan was often on the move, travelling light, with few belongings. Its huts comprised circles of sticks bent together at the top, yurt like, over which were thrown fibre mats. These could be dismantled and stowed on camel-back in a trice, the inverted stick-shelters then having the appearance of giant storks' nests. In the dry season, water and grazing in one place were soon exhausted, so Somali life was an endless rotation. And when the rains failed and the pools and wells ran dry, then the struggle for existence became a war. So the Somalis were a race of fighters.

The harshness of Somali life made its people frugal, resilient, and tough. The myriad miniature wars arising from the country's scarcities made every man a warrior, equipped with small, round, animal-hide shield, stabbing

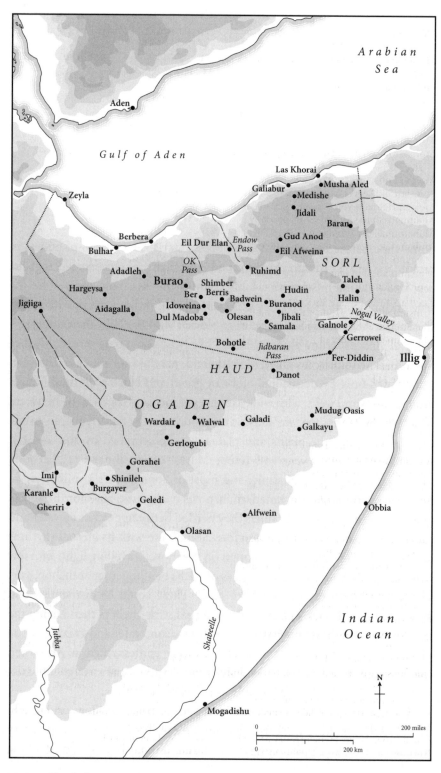

15. Somaliland, illustrating the Anglo-Somali War of 1899–1920

spear, and sword or knife. The better-off men rode to war on camels or ponies, but most were footmen, though capable of tremendous speed. Masters of desert survival and tactics, they fought as skirmishers, but close in, favouring ambush and the sudden rush in thick bush. In the face of injury, illness, and pain, they were exceptionally stoical. Wounds were plastered with camel dung and left to fester and heal. Most older men carried marks of battle on their bodies. The explorers Richard Burton and John Hanning Speke travelled in Somaliland in the mid-1850s – seeking an alternative route to the sources of the Nile. Speke noted 'scarcely a man of them who does not show some scars of wounds . . . some apparently so deep that it is marvellous how they ever recovered from them'.

Burton and Speke were not the first Europeans to visit the region. The British seizure of Aden on the Arabian coast in 1839, and its subsequent development as an important port and garrison, had drawn the gaze of the outside world to the line of shimmering white sand on the opposite shore. Burton and Speke, dispatched by the East India Company, were only the latest in a succession of officers sent out to explore the region and put out diplomatic feelers. One of the poorest places on earth, devoid of natural resources, it would have been of no conceivable value to anyone except the Somalis were it not for its location, on the Horn of Africa, where the Red Sea met the Indian Ocean on what would soon become, with the opening of the Suez Canal, one of the world's busiest maritime routes. Even before then, Somaliland was playing a role in the building of global empire, having become, among other things, a handy meat larder for Aden. So some Europeans established little posts on the coast, and when some of them did this, others, in fear of missing out, soon followed: Somaliland had ended up partitioned into 'spheres of influence', a French enclave in the north, a much larger Italian one in the south, and a British chunk in the middle. The European presence was not, by any standards, very oppressive. No attempt was made to control or tax the natives: given the poverty, the nomadic way of life, and the virtually non-existent communications, the cost of any such attempt would have far outweighed the proceeds. The Somali tribes were left pretty much to themselves. More onerous than the European presence was encroachment on Somali land and rustling of Somali stock by Abyssinian tribesmen along the western border; though even this was a less pressing matter for most than disputes among the Somali tribes themselves.[1]

Nonetheless, Muhammad Abdullah Hassan thought the Europeans should leave. Had they confined themselves to their respective coastal enclaves, all might have been well. But they did not: they imported their imperial rivalries into the Horn of Africa. As in the affairs of the Sudan, the Abyssinian victory over the Italians at Adowa in 1896 seems to have been a tipping-point. At issue was a shift in the regional balance of power in favour of France. A particular concern was the plan to construct a railway line from Djibouti on the coast of French Somaliland, to Addis Ababa in Abyssinia, and perhaps eventually all the way to the Upper Nile. To scotch the emerging French–Abyssinian axis, the British dispatched a high-level diplomatic mission to the court of Emperor Menelik, one bearing a great wealth of gifts, with a view to settling the border line and establishing friendly relations.

To secure agreement, the British handed over 13,500 square miles of Somali territory, including valuable wells and grazing, to the Abyssinians. The interests of Somali camel-nomads were neither here nor there.[2] But to those inclined to view geopolitics through a religious lens, it could hardly pass unnoticed that this was an arrangement between two outside Christian powers, Abyssinia and Britain, to the disadvantage of native Somalis, who happened to be Muslim. Certainly that is how Muhammad Abdullah Hassan viewed matters. He perceived a hostile encirclement of British, French, Italian, and Abyssinian Christians in the Horn of Africa, representing a growing existential threat to the Islamic integrity of Somaliland. And just as the Mahdi had once been inspired by an Islamist network that extended across Africa westwards to the Atlantic and northwards to the Mediterranean, so now Muhammad, in the easternmost reaches of Africa, was inspired by the example of the Sudan.

The year of his awakening had been 1884. Eighteen years old, a tall, slim, sinewy youth with dark skin and African-Arab features, he had undertaken the Hajj pilgrimage to Mecca. This had been an ecstatic 'born-again' experience for the impressionable young man from the Somali bush – made more so by his meeting with Muhammad Ibn Salih al-Rashidi, founder of the fundamentalist Salihiya brotherhood, with its strict adherence to *shariya*. Muhammad Abdullah Hassan headed homewards with a new-found sense of piety and purpose. Along the way, his dhow put in at the port of Suakin on the East Coast of Sudan; and here he heard extraordinary news. A religious leader had risen among the people, and he had led them, under the banner of Islam, to a succession of great victories over the corrupt colonial authorities that had ruled the land. Sudan had been liberated and restored to the true faith. Surely, thought the young Muhammad, what had been done in Sudan might also be done in Somaliland. By whom was as yet unclear: there is no evidence that Muhammad yet imagined that he might be Somaliland's leader-in-waiting. He was young and unlearned; his spiritual apprenticeship had barely begun; it would, in fact, continue for the next ten years. By the end of this time, however, he had become well known among his own people, the Dolbahanta, for his piety and wisdom. He had made the pilgrimage to Mecca six times more, and had graduated as a senior *wadad* (as the Somalis called their mullahs) and become the leader of the Somali branch of the Salihiya sect.[3]

Though well travelled – in his youth he had served on Arab dhows and an Italian steamer – he was by origin a poor Somali of the nomadic tribes of the interior, and by education an adherent of an exceptionally austere brand of Islam. The cosmopolitan society of Berbera appalled him. He considered the sight of Somali children in the streets wearing Christian crucifixes to be offensive (they were homeless orphans taken in by a French Catholic mission), and he resented the willingness of established Muslim brotherhoods to tolerate such anathemas. Returning from his final pilgrimage in 1895, he moved back to his home, Kirrit in the Dolbahanta tribal territory of his mother's family, and there launched his mission to redeem Islam and reclaim Somalia. Men learned in the Qur'an, so long as they are of good character and sound judgement, often become leaders in traditional Islamic societies. So it was with Muhammad Abdullah Hassan. By the middle of 1899, his ascendancy among the Dolbahanta was unrivalled, and he moved with his followers to Burao in the Ain Valley, a place of great strategic importance, for it was the oasis which, in the dry season, was the main water source not only for the Dolbahanta but also for the Habr Toljaala and the Habr Yunis; and these latter were the tribes over which Muhammad now sought to extend his sway.

It was at Burao in August 1899 that Muhammad announced his mission: to lead a holy war to cleanse Somalia of infidels and backsliders. This was a claim to supreme theocratic authority and pan-tribal leadership, such that to oppose him henceforward would amount to apostasy. He was no longer simply *a* mullah; he was *the* Mullah, the spiritual leader sent by Allah to restore Islam to Somalia. The British Consul General in Berbera immediately proclaimed him a rebel and outlaw, and warned everyone against giving him assistance. But this counted for little. At this moment, the British presence in Somaliland consisted of 10 officials, 130 Indian *sepoys*, and the occupation of 3 coastal towns (Berbera, Bulhar, and Zeyla). The Mullah, by contrast, commanded 5,000 Dervish warriors, 1,500 of them mounted, 200 armed with modern rifles, making him the most formidable military power in Somaliland. Pro-British tribes were raided, camel caravans looted, and a large-scale Abyssinian incursion knocked back, the long-suffering Ogaden tribesmen who rallied to the Mullah's banner fighting with such ferocity that they recovered all their plundered stock and left their enemies in fear of them.[4]

Within a year of Omdurman, and before the last embers of the Mahdist insurgency had been extinguished, the British were facing another *jihad* in North-East Africa. Not only was it inspired by the example of Sudan, but a good number of former Mahdists eventually found their way to the Mullah's army.[5] The Somali uprising, therefore, has its place among the unintended consequences of the destruction of the Egyptian nationalist movement in 1882. And, ironically, it presented the British with a far more intractable military problem than Colonel Arabi's large, modern, well-equipped army had done. For the latter had offered itself for destruction by a superior force on a conventional battlefield; and it had indeed been destroyed in the space of an hour. Even the military problem of the Sudan had eventually been resolved by an expensive logistical fix – the construction of a railway line – to deliver the necessary firepower to the battlefield, given that the highly centralised Mahdist state could manage nothing more subtle than massed frontal assault by dense columns of spearmen. The war in Somaliland, which was destined to last, on and off, for two decades, was to prove altogether more difficult – despite the fact that the social and military structure of the country was far less advanced than that of either Egypt or even Sudan.

The two Nile states were based on the tribute and manpower of agricultural villages. Even the desert tribes were involved in long-distance trade as well as nomadic pastoralism. This created the socio-economic foundation for relatively strong centralised governments in Cairo and Khartoum/Omdurman respectively. In Somalia, on the other hand, there was very little agriculture, not much trade, and no tradition of political organisation above tribal level. In practice, therefore, the Mullah's insurgency never amounted to much more than large-scale rural banditry. Tribesmen who joined him and became Dervishes enjoyed religious sanction when they raided the stock and carried off the women of other tribesmen who had either sided with the infidel or simply attempted to remain neutral. The fact that the Mullah attracted followers from different tribes, that he achieved a rudimentary centralisation, that he was able to import firearms, that he commanded shock formations of religious fanatics, that his sadistic authoritarianism inspired terror, gave him a distinct advantage. This meant, in practice, that Somali tribal leaders had to choose a protector: the Mullah or the British. They were caught on the horns of this dilemma. Their priority was to maintain access to their watering places and grazing lands, and to ensure the security of their stock from hostile raids. But achieving this depended upon accurate assessment of the relative strengths of the two warring parties; and to miscalculate was to expose their tribe to the ravages of vengeful enemies.

Even less than in the Sudan was this a national liberation struggle. In the Sudan, the Mahdi's followers had had the bitter experience of Turco-Egyptian colonial rule. The fact that they vested their hopes in the false promise of Islamism does not alter the anti-imperialist inspiration of their revolt. The primary targets of Mahdist insurrection between 1881 and 1885 were Turco-Egyptian garrisons. In Somalia, no comparable grievance underpinned the Mullah's insurgency. The primary targets were other Somali tribes; the prizes fought over were flocks and herds, the measure of victory the captured stock. Islamism became the excuse for a 20-year campaign of robbery with violence in which scrubland poor preyed upon scrubland poor. It could never have been otherwise in a society as basic and impoverished as early 20th-century Somalia.

But the primeval character of this remote struggle over water, grazing, and stock in a semi-arid waste gave rise to a military problem of epic proportions for the colonial authorities. The Somali Dervishes proved to be hardy, fleet-footed, and fanatically brave warriors. Their knowledge of the landscape and their superb informal intelligence network afforded them strategic dominance in the interior; the steady accumulation of imported arms made them increasingly dangerous opponents on the battlefield; and their leader proved to be a master of manoeuvre, ambush, and evasion, as well as a man of exceptional willpower and endurance in the face of every setback.

The Somali Tribal Levy, raised in the early months of 1901, had performed well. Trained and led by Captain Eric Swayne, an experienced Indian Army officer, assisted by 20 other British officers and 50 Punjabi drill instructors, they comprised 1,500 men in total, 500 mounted, 1,000 on foot, the bulk of them armed with surplus Martini-Henry rifles. In their first expedition, they had carried the war to the enemy, penetrating far into the Somali bush, sometimes marching 30 miles a day, enduring great hardship, but always persisting. A large detachment had fought a major action at the wells of Samala on 2 June, where 500 men had defeated 5,000 Dervishes, killing some 600 of them as they hurled themselves at the government *zariba*. Hotly pursued by Swayne's flying column, the retreating Dervish host had then fallen apart and been driven into the desert, where hundreds more are thought to have died of thirst. A three-month campaign, in which the Levy covered some 1,170 miles and inflicted an estimated loss on the enemy of 2,000 in killed, wounded, and missing, thus culminated in a manhunt which appeared to have broken the power of the Mullah; all at a cost of just 46 casualties.

But matters were not so simple. The Levy returned to base, and the Dervishes percolated back through the bush. The Mullah had been damaged, but certainly not broken. His retreat had easily outpaced Swayne's pursuit, and he now demonstrated an extraordinary capacity for recovery, his movement, with its core following of well-armed religious fanatics, easily able to regenerate by recruiting another cohort of young tribesmen with a prospectus of action, a modern rifle, and spoils of war in the form of stock and women. The Dolbahanta tribal elders had warned of this. Persuaded to break with the Mullah, they now found themselves exposed to his vengeance as the government withdrew from the bush. 'What use are our spears to us?' they asked. 'We might as well throw them away and take to sticks! If you go back now, we will surely be punished for leaving the Mullah, and making our peace with the government. We shall have to do everything he tells us, and under his orders even attack government tribes again.'[6] Here was the whole long story of the war. The government held the ground on which its soldiers stood. The Mullah was a brooding menace, if not an actual presence, in all the rest. And because his movement was not a formal state, anchored in space, but a mobile insurgency, sustained by his will, cemented together by religion, powered by plunder, it was able to flow away into the wastes in the face of superior force, then flow back again as that force retreated, often enough having exhausted itself in weeks and months of flailing air in its efforts to strike at an ever-elusive enemy.

Less than a year after the Battle of Samala, news reached Berbera that the Mullah was stronger than ever. He was again dominant over the Dolbahanta, and his force was reported 15,000 strong, almost all on ponies, one in ten rifle-armed. Mounting a succession of *razzias* (raids), he was carrying off so much of the livestock of pro-government tribes that the entire fabric of the colonial regime's mesh of alliances was in danger of unravelling.[7] The risk was that the whole interior might be consumed in a jihadist insurgency – as in the Sudan – making the small colonial enclaves on the coast untenable.

So Colonel Swayne (his local rank) again mobilised the Somali Tribal Levy, now reinforced by 450 Yaos of the 3rd King's African Rifles, and set off from the government post of Burao in May 1902 intent on bringing the Mullah to decisive battle. Collecting local contingents of tribal irregulars along the way, the government columns made huge captures of stock and finally goaded the Mullah into making a stand. On 3 October, Swayne's scouts reported large enemy forces nearby. Pushing forward to contact, the government column entered a zone of thick bush in the vicinity of Erigo where visibility was barely 5 yards. They were deep inside the Haud, a water-less expanse 100 miles wide, and were therefore accompanied by a huge train of camels, 2,000 carrying water tanks, another 2,000 supplying milk and meat. Early on 6 October, in bush as dense and dangerous as ever, scouts reported the enemy 2 miles away, advancing rapidly, coming on in great force.

A halt was called, and a three-sided square formed around the transport, with a looser defence by three companies at the rear. After a brief pause, the column edged forward again. Then, within two minutes, the firing began. Hundreds of Dervishes were yelling Islamic war-cries and firing rifles from the thickets at ranges of 20 yards or so. Thudding into such a dense mass, the Dervish fire immediately caused men and camels to drop. In the initial chaos and terror, the newest Somali levies posted on the left panicked and fell back, spooking others into joining them, disrupting the whole square. In the debacle, a machine gun was lost (and would not be recovered until 1920). Swayne now took personal command of a half company on the front face that had stood its ground, leading a short charge which drove the enemy off. This gave confidence to another company on the front face to advance, while the broken units rallied and returned to the line. But it was too late to save the transport. 'The transport camels had all stampeded ... owing to the noise caused by the firing in such dense bush,' reported Colonel Swayne, 'and some thousand camels with water tins and ammunition boxes jammed against each other, rushed away into the jungle, scattering their loads everywhere.'

The enemy were driven off by the aggression of the Somali and Yao soldiers – advancing and firing into the bush ahead, supported by case-shot from two 7-pdrs – and it was then possible to recover most of the camels. But serious damage had been inflicted on Swayne's force. Casualties – among officers, soldiers, and camel-drivers – were 101 killed and 86 wounded. The morale of the Somalis had been shaken by the battle and their losses. They were left in awe of the Mullah and the courage of his followers. And they had been taunted by their enemies during the fighting for serving under Christian officers against men with whom they shared blood and faith. Swayne was told by his officers that 'they could not rely on the men'. This, compounded by lack of maps, water, and reliable intelligence of the enemy's whereabouts and intentions, made retreat the only safe option. 'Should a sudden panic occur again,' Swayne wrote, 'I don't think I could save the force or even the transport left behind us.'[8]

For sure, the Mullah's cause had again suffered tremendous damage. His total casualties were estimated at 1,400, and government forces and their tribal allies had recovered 25,000 camels, 250,000 sheep, 1,500 cattle, and 200 ponies. His forces had been defeated in pitched battle, and he had been driven from British Somaliland and forced to take refuge in Italian territory. The scale of the achievement – measured against the expenditure of force and the casualties taken – was considerable. But Swayne had proved even less able during the second expedition than the first to translate immediate tactical success into lasting strategic gain. Whereas his offensive power had been augmented by Samala in 1901, it had been crippled by Erigo in 1902. The Mullah was still at large, his core following intact, and he was soon rebuilding his strength at the Mudug oasis, far to the south, beyond the reach of British power.[9] Stronger action was going to be necessary to extinguish the Somali jihad, and Swayne's local levies could not be relied upon to take it – they were too few, they had panicked on the battlefield, and their loyalty was now suspect. Imperial troops were going to be needed.

That local forces had been left to manage the war against the Mullah alone up until this point was a direct consequence of the Anglo-Boer War. Between October 1899 and May 1902, the British Empire had been involved in an exceptionally protracted and hard-fought war against the Afrikaner farmers of South Africa – a war that eventually saw the deployment of almost half a million imperial troops against barely a twentieth of that number of Boer guerrillas. The end of the war, however, meant that veteran combat soldiers with first-class modern weaponry and valuable counter-insurgency experience were available in numbers for redeployment from the Cape to the Horn.

An ambitious new plan was conceived to employ three flying columns, advancing from different directions, so as to block escape-routes and trap the Mullah in a pocket where he could be killed or captured. One column, comprising 1st King's African Rifles (Sikhs), 2nd King's African Rifles (Yaos), and three companies of 1st Bombay Grenadiers, 1,750 men in all, would advance from the north-west on the Berbera-Bohotle line. A second, comprising British, Boer, and Punjabi Mounted Infantry, Bikaner Camel Corps, 2nd Sikhs, 6th King's African Rifles (Somalis), and two mountain guns, 2,300 men, would advance from Obbia on the south-east coast, permission having been obtained from the Italian authorities to operate in their territory. A third prong would be formed by 5,000 Abyssinians, who were to march from the interior down the Webi Shibeli valley.

Colonel Swayne was sceptical about the deployment of regulars, even in such modest numbers, because of the supply problem. A railway was considered too expensive. Some new roads were laid down, wells were improved, a telegraph line was erected, forward depots were established along the prospective line of march. But the enemy was elusive, and it would be necessary to follow him into the semi-arid bush. This meant there was no alternative to camel transport. And while Somalia was full of camels, they were the prized property of the tribes whose support it was necessary to cultivate, and the great majority of them in any case were milch camels, kept to supply the staple food of the nomads, not burden camels. The British were therefore compelled to import large numbers of beasts to support their operations; and of these, there were never enough.[10]

The Mullah was in effective control of a territory about 200 miles across, extending from the Nogal Valley in the north to the Mudug oasis in the south. His strength was estimated at 2,500 mounted riflemen, 5,000 other horsemen, and 16,000 spearmen.[11] These figures are likely to have been exaggerated, perhaps grossly so, and to represent only a snapshot in time, for the Mullah's forces, like most irregular forces, were in constant flux. Moreover, the Mullah had major logistical problems of his own. His loosely structured bands of Dervishes were fast-moving and expert at desert survival; they were capable of dissolving into the bush, quickly outpacing pursuit, and re-congealing in another place. But their slow-moving stock was a highly visible and vulnerable asset; and so was that of the tribes allied to the Mullah. It was necessary not only to protect the animals from capture, but also to maintain access to water and grazing. Nonetheless, in addition to the mobility and prowess of his warriors in the bush, the Mullah was possessed of three other signal advantages: excellent intelligence about the movements of the enemy; the fact that he occupied a central position in relation to separate, converging enemy columns; and his own instinctive feel, perhaps amounting to minor genius, in the practice of guerrilla warfare.

By the end of March 1903, the Obbia column had captured Galkayu, south of the Mudug oasis, and established itself at Galadi, on the Abyssinian border. But the Mullah had retreated westwards, into the forbidding Ogaden region, the Abyssinians, who should have prevented this, proving unreliable British allies. Orders from London had enjoined caution in such circumstances: 'If the Mullah should be driven from the Mudug, or should retire therefrom without contesting your seizure of that district, you should endeavour, if the conditions of the country and of your force permit, to pursue him with mounted troops; but this pursuit should not be pushed to any greater distance than four or five days' march to the south or westward.'

On the other hand, the men on the ground were expected to exercise their judgement; and British small-wars doctrine encouraged aggressive action. So Lieutenant Colonel Cobbe set out from Galadi at the head of a column of about 500 men, heading west towards Wardair, where the Mullah had last been reported. But he lost his way and, finding himself in thick bush with water running out, decided to retreat and establish a temporary *zariba* at Gumburu Hill. Cobbe was, in fact, in trouble: enemy activity was increasing, and his water shortage was acute. He was forced to send out reconnaissance columns to gather intelligence and search for pools. When one of these, a company of 2nd King's African Rifles (KAR) under Captain Olivey, dispatched a message on the morning of 17 April reporting that it was being advanced upon by a considerable force of Dervish horse and foot, Cobbe sent out a second column to rescue it. This comprised another company of 2nd KAR along with 50 men of the 2nd Sikhs and two Maxims under Colonel Plunkett. Just as Plunkett was setting off, another message arrived from Olivey, this one reporting that he was now within a mile and a half of the main camp. All appeared well as Plunkett's force left the *zariba* to meet the returnees. In fact, nothing more would ever be heard from either Captain Olivey or Colonel Plunkett.

Cobbe learned of the destruction of the two detachments around midday, when Somali scouts dispatched to investigate sounds of firing in the distance returned with the news. Exactly what had happened had to be pieced together later. Plunkett seems to have exceeded his orders and, having linked up with Olivey, formed the 230 Sikhs, Yaos, and Somalis of the combined force into a square and advanced a further 6 miles. In an open spot amid otherwise thick bush, he encountered a Dervish force of 4,000 horse and 10,000 foot commanded by the Mullah in person. While the Dervish cavalry, firing from the saddle as they came, hurled themselves against three sides of the square, the Dervish infantry assailed the rear. Despite the shattering fire of Maxims and Martinis – it would leave perhaps 2,000 enemy dead and wounded around the square – the Dervishes came on again and again with fanatic courage. Eventually, with ammunition running out, Plunkett gave the order to break up the square, charge with the bayonet, and attempt to force a way back to Cobbe's *zariba*. This, of course, was a hopeless prospect. The Battle of Gumburu turned out to be a small-scale battle of annihilation. Nine British officers and 187 native soldiers were killed; a further 29 men were wounded; only 6 emerged unscathed.[12]

While Cobbe's battered force retired on Galadi, another drama played out about 100 miles to the north, where a 600-strong detachment of the Berbera column under Major Gough had set out for Danot, about 50 miles south-east of Bohotle. Responding to reports of a strong enemy presence, Gough then pushed on to Daratoleh, a further 25 miles to the south-east. This advanced column comprised 10 British officers, 45 Bikaner Camel Corps, 50 Somali Camel Corps, 55 Somali Mounted Infantry, 30 camel-mounted 2nd KAR, 12 pony-mounted Sikhs, and a Maxim gun. Gough advanced in open square. 'Definite formation was almost impossible,' reported the Reuters correspondent:

the bush lying in large clumps, dense and widespread, 10 to 12 feet in height, 80 to 120 feet in thickness. The tracks, mere lines of footprints, bordering the different bunches of bush, swept and swerved between them, making any regular line of front impossible, any pattern of the parade-ground kind of square impracticable ... In the waste places of the earth, where the unexpected happens, and men fight with their lives in the slides of their rifles, notions that are comfortably orthodox drop away, and men, falling foul of the precedents of Aldershot, hang together with an instinctive common sense.

On 22 April, less than a week after Gumburu, in a region of dense bush 2 miles short of Daratoleh, Gough's little column was attacked by a force estimated at 300 riflemen and 500 spearmen. The fighting started at 10.30 and lasted for seven hours. The first half of the battle was a sustained firefight at ranges of between 50 and 20 yards. 'The Maxim under Sergeant Gibb,' Gough later reported, 'was moved from place to place as occasion arose, and the enemy always giving way when it opened fire.' But ammunition began to run low, whereas the Dervishes seemed to be reinforced and pressing harder on all sides. Gough was forced to order a succession of bayonet charges into the bush – a desperate expedient, since it was bound to unhinge his defensive formation and expose both individual units and the camel transport to enemy rushes. But it worked, allowing him to organise a fighting retreat back towards Danot. This was exasperatingly slow, as he was now encumbered with many wounded, and the enemy continued to press their attacks until dusk; it seems certain that the force, with 25 per cent of its effectives down, would have been annihilated like Plunkett's had the enemy been present in greater numbers and fought with more determination.[13]

The Abyssinian Army advancing from the west also clashed with sizeable Dervish forces, first at Burhilli on 4 April, then Jeyd on 31 May, on each occasion claiming a thousand or so enemy casualties. But shortage of water and grain slowed Abyssinian progress, preventing a junction with the British columns, and eventually compelling retreat. Here was the whole story of the campaign. Somalia's desolation and distances, and the consequent logistical constraints on the mobility of large forces, had prevented the three separate columns from converging to form a net around the Mullah. The Dervishes had easily outpaced pursuit when they needed to, only closing with the enemy when they chose. Though usually driven off with great loss when they engaged – owing to the extreme disparity in firepower – they nonetheless succeeded in inflicting sufficient damage on Cobbe's and Gough's columns to defeat the campaign. This was confirmed when, as soon as the British had fallen back on their main base at Bohotle, the Mullah crossed back from Abyssinian into British territory and reoccupied the Nogal Valley. He made the strategic impasse plain in a letter sent to the British authorities at Berbera:

> We have fought for a year. I wish to rule my country and protect my own religion ... We have both suffered considerably in battle with one another. You have heard that the Dervishes have run away. They have not done so. I have moved my camp, but I have not run away ... When I get news of good grazing, I go to that place ... I have with me camels and goats and sheep in plenty ... I will take many rifles from you, but you won't get any rifles or ammunition from me ... I have no forts, no houses,

no country. I have no cultivated fields, no gold or silver for you to take. I have no artificers . . . If the country was cultivated or contained houses or property, it would be worth your while to fight. The country is all jungle, and that is no use to you . . . The sun is very hot. All you can get from me is war, nothing else . . . If you wish war, I am happy; if you wish peace, I am also content. But if you wish peace, go away from my country to your own . . . Send me a letter saying whether you want war or peace.[14]

The British chose war. This was mission creep. Spooked by the spectre of *jihad*, ever cognisant that empire depended ultimately on bluff, a façade of power, what imperial statesmen liked to call 'prestige', they were now too far steeped in Somali blood to draw back. But the new commander appointed to lead a fourth expedition, Major General Sir Charles Egerton, another Indian Army career professional, was under no illusions about the challenge:

Strategically, the Mullah has all the advantages. Separated from our nearest outpost by about 150 miles of country, he could calmly await the advance of our troops and either fight or decline to fight as seemed best; for there was no containing force to keep him where he was, while the whole of Somaliland to the south, from the Nogal to the Equator, was open to him. Our force, on the other hand, was in the worst strategic position possible.

The issues, as ever, were long distances, poor communications, and the logistical nightmare of supplying any sizeable regular force on active operations in Somalia's desolate wastes.[15]

The new British plan was, in effect, to swing a sledgehammer across these wastes. Egerton would command an 8,000-man field force, one-third of them Indians, the rest locally recruited auxiliaries and irregulars. This would require an immense number of camels, at least 10,000 beasts, to supply milk, carry loads, and mount the tribal contingents, including the *illalos*, the irregular scouts who were to play an essential role in tracking and locating the enemy. A large corps of sappers and coolies was also essential, to build roads, bore wells, and establish depots along the line of communications. The plan was to use feints and false intelligence combined with lines of posts and flying columns to hustle the Mullah northwards – rather than allowing him to escape south and east again – and to corner him in a pocket where he could be brought to decisive battle.[16]

The plan almost succeeded. The pick of the Mullah's forces, estimated between 6,000 and 8,000 strong, were found concentrated at a watering-place located in a wide, bush-covered depression at Jidbali in the northeastern Nogal. Exceptionally dry weather had compelled the Mullah to attempt to hold ground: his vast herds needed access to the water and grazing nearby. This was Egerton's opportunity, and, on 10 January 1904, he concentrated a strike-force of 2,500 men, comprising a mounted brigade of British Mounted Infantry, Indian Mounted Infantry, Bikaner Camel Corps, and Tribal Horse, an infantry brigade of Hampshires, Punjabis, and Sikhs, a section of mountain guns, and six Maxims. Leaving all baggage in his camp under strong guard, he advanced in double echelon, with artillery and machine guns in the centre, cavalry on the flanks. When contact was made, Egerton ordered Lieutenant Colonel Kenna's mounted brigade to make a wide turning movement to the north to threaten the enemy's right flank and line of retreat, while the infantry echelon continued forward. At about 800 yards from the enemy *zariba*, the British and Indian infantry halted, knelt or lay down, and opened fire, supported by the mountain guns and Maxims. The Dervishes, in the main *zariba* and the bush on either side, returned a ragged fire, and then mounted a series of attacks, coming forward in skirmish order, in a succession of rushes from cover to cover, halting and firing at intervals. Few got closer than 400 yards, such was the fearsome fire from Egerton's echelon. Having tried to break through on the left front, they then mounted two determined attacks on the right front and flank, but these too were smashed by fire. Then, at 10.00 a.m., after just half an hour of fighting, the whole mass broke and fled, pursued by a hot fire of infantry, until this was masked by the mounted troops, who now turned the action into a one-sided manhunt, which continued for 16 miles, until horses were spent and ammunition exhausted.

Around 700 Dervishes were killed in the battle, and a greater number may have been slain in the pursuit. British losses were 27 killed and 37 wounded.[17] The Mullah, his forces shrinking through mass desertion, fled westwards, seeking refuge in Italian territory. Here he found breathing space while the British again sought Italian permission to operate in their territory. Then the fight was renewed, from the sea, when three British cruisers, the *Fox*, the *Hyacinth*, and the *Mohawk*, landed a party of bluejackets equipped with Maxims in the early hours of 21 April to storm the Dervish fortifications at Illig, supported by naval gunfire. The action was a minor masterpiece of amphibious operations – in which, of course, the British excelled – and the Mullah was again on the run. But logistics had prevented Egerton from cooperating with the naval operation, so the Mullah was able to disappear into the interior of Italian Somaliland, last news of his whereabouts reaching the British command in late April – after which, the desert fell silent.[18]

The fourth expedition had ended very differently from the third. The British had lost only 34 killed and 64 wounded, and had inflicted over 2,000 casualties on the enemy and captured 304 prisoners, 473 rifles, 223 ponies, 24,376 camels, and 36,415 other livestock.[19] The Somali *jihad* seemed a broken force. The Mullah had been soundly beaten in battle and had lost most of his following and livestock. The perception was that he had ceased to be a major military problem and become, at most, a minor political one. Consequently, when the Italian Consul at Aden, Giovanni Pestalozza, negotiated a peace settlement with the Mullah, granting him refuge and security in Italian Somaliland, the Illig Agreement was welcomed by the British as well as the Italians.[20] It seemed to promise much for no cost: an end to the long war with the Dervishes. Many assumed that, with his cause so damaged, his prestige so dented, the Mullah would now fade into obscurity. They were wrong.

Muhammad Abdullah Hassan's belief that he had a divine mission to purge Somalia of Christians, their presence being in his eyes an offence to Islam, and to punish all Muslims who had aided and abetted them, was an absolute, the guiding principle of his life. Religious bigotry, surpassing willpower, and uncommon cunning in politics and war were his dominant characteristics. His core following comprised an alliance of religious enthusiasts and tribal bandits. To sustain, and augment, this following, he could not stand still. His personality was magnetic, but it generated expectations that had to be fulfilled if the spell was not to be broken and the movement dissolve. The vision of *jihad* and the promise of loot had to be turned into action. And this combination allowed the Mullah to bounce back after every defeat – not only to retain the allegiance of his core, but to regenerate his movement around this nucleus, recruiting fresh cohorts of young Somali warriors attracted by the mix of religion, plunder, and adventure. Islamism was the magic ingredient. It elevated Mullahism into a pan-tribal movement capable of reaching out to all Somalis, and it sanctified and fanaticised its adherents, turning tribal raiders into holy warriors. Thus, each time the Dervishes surged, they quickly achieved military supremacy in the Somali bush, becoming a mortal danger to tribal leaders who withheld allegiance.

Within a year of the Illig Agreement, the Dervishes were again raiding far and wide. The British were in a quandary. They remained determined to hold the coast – because of Aden and the sea route to India – but they could not decide whether to withdraw completely from the interior or to maintain some sort of administration. The dilemma was encapsulated in two contrary recommendations, one from Winston Churchill, then serving as Under Secretary of State for the Colonies, who penned a 'Minute on the Somaliland Protectorate' following a brief stopover at Berbera in October 1907, the other from Reginald Wingate, now Governor General and *Sirdar* of the Sudan, who delivered two reports to the Colonial Office in June 1909, following a fact-finding visit to Somaliland the previous month. Churchill argued for withdrawal on the grounds of cost. Somalia was a wilderness of stone and scrub, utterly impoverished and worthless, peopled by rifle-armed zealots. The cost of further military expeditions followed by permanent annexation of the interior would, in any circumstances, be wholly dispro-portionate to any possible material gain. Wingate, an Omdurman veteran, an imperialist hawk, and a man obsessed by the danger of jihadist conta-gion, took the opposite view. Only if the Mullah was vanquished could the interior be abandoned, for otherwise the coast would never be secure, and complete withdrawal from Somaliland was out of the question – it would damage British prestige, leave Aden exposed, and allow the Mullah unchal-lenged control of the country. Conclusion: full-scale war, in alliance with the Italians and the Abyssinians, to crush the Mullah once and for all.[21]

In October 1909, the British Cabinet made its decision: withdrawal to the coast. This was, in effect, a victory for the second phase, beginning in 1905, of the Mullah's long war against the British Empire. The British hoped that by arming loyal tribes in the interior they might create an effective buffer between the Dervishes and the coast. What actually happened was that the influx of guns fuelled a flare-up of ferocious tribal feuding. Such was the tempest of raid and counter-raid, with loss of stock and consequent famine, that on one estimate as many as a third of the male population of Somalia may have perished. Into the maelstrom advanced the Mullah, the superiority of his forces generating shock waves that drove inland tribes north and east and triggered further rounds of violence as refugee communities fought over water and grazing in overpopulated land. Horace Byatt, the new Commissioner of British Somaliland, summed up the situation in a memorandum dated 30 April 1912:

> Anarchy is steadily spreading over the country, with a prospect under the present system of becoming permanent ... The present situation is profoundly unsatisfactory, and the future holds out a prospect of development for the worse rather than the better. In view of this prospect, it is desirable, and even necessary, to reconsider the question of the attitude to be adopted henceforward towards the affairs of Somaliland. The policy of non-intervention and inactivity has been given full operation for two years, and has disappointed hopes and expectations. Tribal organisation – the first line of defence – has finally and completely given way, and there has been a steady and serious diminution of the authority and prestige of the government among the tribes who are its nearest neighbours.[22]

Berbera, in short, was in danger.

The main British response to the security crisis was the creation of a 150-man Camel Corps. It was commanded by a young political officer called Richard Corfield, who had served previously in Somaliland, Nigeria, and South Africa (where he had been one of Baden Powell's scouts). The corps took time to assemble: riding camels and saddles had to be imported from India, local men recruited and trained. It was organised in 2 companies, each of 4 sections of 18 men, and supplied with a Maxim gun team. Though well armed, it was conceived as a coastal 'constabulary' for the defence of Berbera, its zone of operations limited to a 50-mile radius (later extended to 100 miles), not as a military force designed for long-range 'hunt and pursuit' operations. British policy remained unchanged in its fundamental objection to any attempt to contest control of the interior. In practice, however, this proved unworkable.

The Camel Corps was, in fact, a superb instrument of counter-insurgency warfare. Instead of the heavy infantry columns of the third and fourth expeditions, there was now a fast flying column able to carry the war to the enemy and deliver potentially destructive fire. Corfield was an effective commander – eager, enterprising, able to bond with his men and achieve real *esprit de corps*. The Mullah, on the other hand, seemed to be losing some of his agility. Perhaps because he had been given time to consolidate his grip over a large swathe of the interior, perhaps because he had been influenced to do so by the Sultan of Yemen, who favoured the strategy, but perhaps also because he had grown old, fat, and diseased in body, he had taken to building forts. These were highly visible targets and fixed assets to be defended: the Mullah was sacrificing much of his traditional mobility and elusiveness.[23] The greatest of the forts – there were eventually about 40 of them – was Taleh in the eastern Nogal, which became, in effect, the Mullah's fortified capital. It consisted of a circular walled enclosure surmounted by 13 mini forts, all of massive stone construction, 12–14 foot thick at the base, 6 foot thick at the top, and 40 foot in height. The interior contained wells, granaries, and space for hundreds of head of stock. Three covering forts of even greater height and strength lay 200 yards beyond the main circuit.[24] Taleh was to be the Mullah's powerbase from 1913 to 1920.

In this reconfigured war, Corfield was increasingly confident that his rapier-like column of camel police could penetrate deep and strike hard with relative impunity. He was building alliances with friendly tribes, and they were eager for the British to extend the mantle of protection. Here, again, was the old dilemma asserting itself. To secure the coast meant stabilising the interior; this depended on friendly relations with local tribes; this in turn depended upon British protection against Dervish retaliation. The British were being pulled back, willy-nilly, into the interior in order to secure the coast. Logic was on Corfield's side, when he, supported by friendly tribal elders, agitated to be given a looser rein: to be permitted to push his Camel Corps beyond the 100-mile limit into the Mullah's heartland. The Berbera authorities remained cautious. A reconnaissance was agreed, but Captain Summers, commander of the Somaliland Indian Contingent, was detailed to accompany Corfield as a restraining influence: the over-enthusiastic colonial policeman was to be kept in check by a military professional.[25]

The Camel Corps moved out of Burao on 8 August 1913, 110 mounted men armed with Martini-Henry carbines, each carrying 210 rounds, supported by a Maxim gun with 4,000 rounds, and 150 camp-followers bringing water, rations, and 10,000 reserve rounds. They were soon joined by 300 Dolbahanta tribesmen eager to regain looted stock. Contact was made with the enemy on the first day, and all military precautions against surprise night attack were taken when the column formed its first camp. The following morning, the column moved off early, but scouts immediately reported approaching enemy. The order to dismount and form a line of action was given in the vicinity of the ominously named Dul Madoba ('Black Hill'). Corfield was still in thick bush and wanted to advance his line to an area of open ground about 200 yards ahead. He was not given the time. The line halted in the bush, the Maxim in the centre, the Dolbahanta on the extreme left, the camels 30 yards to the rear. Corfield and Summers held a hasty conference. The latter advised a square. The former wanted to deploy his full firepower. Before more could be said, the enemy was spotted approaching through the bush 100 yards away, firing as they came. It was 6.50 a.m. The Camel Corps was now committed to action in a loose skirmish line, without flank or rear protection, in thick bush, against an enemy force of perhaps 2,000 riflemen. The Dolbahanta bolted as soon as the battle opened and were seen no more. The 100 cameliers (10 had earlier returned to Burao with broken-down animals) were then on their own.

The Dervishes came on in a series of waves, each one approaching, firing, then melting away under the steady hail of shot from the police line. The first wave was beaten back entirely, but the second enveloped the right flank and caused a precipitous retreat to the rear; though some men were rallied, 24 broke and ran, almost 25 per cent of the force. Meanwhile, the Maxim gun packed up. It had fired only three belts before being damaged by enemy bullets. Corfield, in the thick of the fight, tried to get the feed-block out to get it working again. He was suddenly hit in the head by a bullet and instantly killed. Summers now took his place in trying to fix the Maxim, but soon discovered the damage was irreparable; at which point, he was wounded for the first time.

The second wave of Dervish attack now receded, and the Camel Corps survivors adjusted into an irregular square, using the dead bodies of camels and ponies to improvise a *zariba*. Wave after wave was launched against the little band of cameliers, the firing often point-blank, the opponents sometimes grappling hand-to-hand, individual Dervishes occasionally breaking into the *zariba*. But each time – inexplicably, miraculously – the attackers seemed to shrink back into the bush just as they were on the verge of overwhelming the position. It went on like this for five hours. Summers was wounded twice more, and Mr Dunn, Corfield's No. 2, was left in effective command. Then, around midday, physically and mentally exhausted, their ammunition spent, around 400 of their number stricken around the *zariba*, the Dervishes drifted away and left the Camel Corps in possession of the field.

Of the 110 camelry who had set out from Burao the day before, in addition to 10 who had fallen out on the road and the 24 who had fled, 35 had been killed and 17 seriously wounded. Just 24 men remained able to fight, and even some of these were wounded. These survivors now staggered on for 6 miles to find water at Idoweina. The pools in the sandy river bed when they got there were shallow and fouled with animal droppings; but they drank the slime to stay alive. They were met by a rescue party early in the afternoon of the following day and escorted back to Burao. Corfield's Camel Corps was a broken reed.[26]

It had been the smallest of battles in the remotest of places: 100 Somali policemen in what the *Pall Mall Gazette* called 'this waste corner of the earth'. But another of the new class of war correspondents was on hand to paint Dul Madoba in jingo colours – Alan Ostler of the *Daily Express*. The British public was told of the heroism of this tiny force and its daring young commander; of the damage to imperial prestige (apparently, in Aden, Somalis were spitting at British officers); of the menacing advance of Dervish power in the Horn of Africa. Official assessments were hardly less alarmist. The Camel Corps had been destroyed, the 'friendlies' among the Somali tribes were cowed, the Mullah was in effective control of virtually the whole of the country outside Berbera. Refugees huddled on the coast – a makeshift relief camp accommodated 2,000 at Berbera – and the fear was that the entire structure of tribal allegiances on which British security depended was set to shatter. To underline the shift in the balance of power, on the night of 12/13 March 1914, 40 pony-mounted Dervishes entered Berbera itself, shot up the native town, then disappeared back into the bush: the Mullah's men had penetrated to the very centre of British power in Somaliland, causing 'great consternation and confusion in Berbera'.[27]

By this time, anyway, a reversal of policy had been agreed: the British would return to the interior in force. Corfield's Camel Corps was recon-structed in a larger and more military form. The Somaliland Camel Corps would henceforward comprise 18 British officers and 500 Somali rank and file, two companies on camels, a third on ponies. The Somaliland Indian Contingent – 400 picked men from the Indian Army – would also take part in active operations, supported by a new temporary garrison of 400 additional Indian soldiers. The Somali service immediately attracted a rush of good offi-cers: here was a chance of active operations in an empire otherwise almost wholly at peace. Appointed to command was an excellent officer, Lieutenant

Colonel Tom Ashley Cubitt. What makes a great leader, one of his subordinates, Captain Wiart, asked himself: 'so often argued and probed since time immemorial . . . to me it rests simply in the quality of the man. He has it or he hasn't. Tom Cubitt had it, and the troops felt it and responded immediately.'

A new forward policy was adopted. The aim was to drive the Mullah eastwards, freeing up the traditional watering and grazing places of friendly tribes in the west. This meant, first and foremost, an assault on the Dervish forts at Shimber Berris, 150 miles from Berbera, at the head of the Ain Valley. Three forts had been constructed at the top of an escarpment in a range of steep-sided rocky hills. The walls, of mud and plaster, were 10 foot thick at the base and 25 foot high. Each fort was capable of holding 50–70 men, and was well provided with access galleries and firing ports. The surrounding bush had been cleared to provide good fields of fire. The ravine below was honeycombed with caves, which provided additional cover and firing positions.[28]

The first attack was launched on 19 November 1914 by 14 officers and 520 men. The first fort was rushed by a party of Indian *sepoys*. But the second resisted strongly, the walls impenetrable, the defenders beating back their Somali assailants with fire, killing one British captain and severely wounding another. Though the Dervishes had been taken by surprise – they had known nothing of the column which had left Burao two days before until they found themselves under attack – it had not been possible to take the position 'on the rush'. The walls were strong, the defenders determined. Cubitt broke off the action.

Four days later, the attack was renewed, now with the use of an old 7-pdr mountain gun, which had been rushed from Burao. This made all the difference: though little actual damage was done, the defenders seem to have been unnerved by the shock-and-awe effect of even light shell-fire on stonework, and they fled away eastwards, leaving Cubitt's Somalis in possession of all three forts. But with no explosives available, it was impossible to destroy the forts, and the Camel Corps lacked the strength to install permanent garrisons. The column returned to base; and a fortnight later, the Mullah sent out a new garrison to reoccupy Shimber Berris. The struggle for the position was turning into a decisive test.

The following February, now supplied with explosives from Aden and India, Cubitt marched out again, 15 officers, 570 rank and file, six machine guns, and two 7-pdrs, plus explosive charges and hand-grenades. Cubitt's report was a succinct summation:

The two flanking forts were captured after two hours' fighting, but the enemy developed a heavy fire from the caves, from the middle fort, and from the vicinity of the fort. The guns were brought forward and with machine-guns engaged the middle fort and the caves at close range. The enemy's fire slackened, and Dervishes were observed to be evacuating the fort and retiring southwards up the ravine. I dispatched a company against this fort, but, although unable to gain an entrance, the company remained around the fort and enabled the pioneers to place a charge of guncotton against the door, under a hot fire from the occupants inside. The fort and its defenders were blown up, hand-grenades were thrown into the caves known to be still occupied, and the two flanking forts were also blown up.[29]

Despite the unexpected determination of the Dervish resistance, the battle at Shimber Berris on 4 February 1915 had ended in complete victory at minimal cost. Altogether, since November, British casualties amounted to just 9 killed and 40 wounded. For this modest loss, the colonial authorities had secured the western part of Somaliland, pushing the Dervishes far from Berbera and easing the pressure on friendly tribes nearby.

But the forces to follow up this victory were not available. On 4 August 1914, Britain had declared war on Imperial Germany. On 31 October, the Ottoman Empire had entered the war as Germany's ally, placing the entire British position in the Middle East in imminent peril. The skirmishes of the Somali war vanished into obscurity. No-one cared any more. No troops were available. No interest or capacity existed for a further forward move.

Not the least reason for this was that the spectre of *jihad* – exorcised from the Sudan in 1898, restricted to the stone and scrub of the Somali outback ever since – was suddenly transformed into a global demon. The First World War may have been the first fully modern war, the first war of global empires hyper-charged by machine power and industrialised carnage. But, across much of North Africa, the Middle East, and Central Asia, it echoed with the ancient call to Islamic *jihad*.

# CHAPTER FOURTEEN

# THE KAISER'S WAR

'The Syrian army is as fanatical as the hordes of the Mahdi. The Senussi have a hand in the game. The Persian Muslims are threatening trouble. There is a dry wind blowing through the East, and the parched grasses wait the spark. And the wind is blowing towards the Indian border.' The words were fiction, but they reflected the anxieties of British imperial statesmen in the middle of the First World War. John Buchan has them spoken by the Foreign Office mandarin 'Sir Walter' to his hero 'Richard Hannay' in the 1916 novel *Greenmantle*. Buchan was in a position to know, having been appointed Foreign Office director of information.[1] Of the 270 million Muslims in the world in 1916, 100 million were ruled by the British Empire, mainly in India, Egypt, and the Sudan. A further 20 million were ruled by the French, mainly in North and West Africa, and another 20 million by Russia, mainly in Central Asia. By contrast, Imperial Germany, against whom these three Entente powers were ranged, had almost no Muslim subjects at all. As archaeologist, Arabist, and self-appointed expert on Middle Eastern affairs Max von Oppenheim had explained to German Chancellor Bernhard von Bülow in 1908, in the event of:

a great European war, especially if Turkey participates in it against England, one may certainly expect an overall revolt of the Muslims in the British colonies . . . In such a war, those colonies would be, along with Turkey, the most dangerous enemy of an England strong on the seas. British soldiers would be unable to invade inner Turkey, and, in addition, England would need a large part of its navy and almost its entire army in order to keep its colonies.[2]

In pursuit of this global *jihad*, German statesmen, army officers, and a small cohort of orientalists, adventurers, and spies set to work to suborn the rulers of the Ottoman Empire and secure a political alliance. Of the mere 30 million Muslims ruled by other Muslims, more than half were subjects of the Ottoman Sultan, whose sway extended east–west from Macedonia to the borders of Persia, north–south from the Caucasus to the Yemen. Here lived around 12 million Turkish Muslims and a further 6 million or so Arab Muslims. The Ottoman Sultan, moreover, had recently made what might be described as an 'Islamic turn'. Traditionally, the sultans laid claim to the title of 'caliph' – a specifically Islamic concept that combined political and religious authority in succession to the Prophet. Of late, Sultan Abdul Hamid II had chosen to lay greater stress on his caliphate. He had, for example, built a railway from Damascus to Medina – the Hijaz Railway – ostensibly at least to facilitate the passage of Hajj pilgrims to the Holy Land. An act of piety, it was paid for partly by government borrowing (from foreign banks), partly from public donations collected (with more or less coercion) across the Ottoman Empire.

The Islamic turn was a reaction to the long-term crisis of what the Russian Tsar had dubbed 'the sick man of Europe'. A ramshackle, polyglot construction of the sixteenth century, the Ottoman state upheld the power of traditional elites and thereby hard-wired conservatism, lethargy, and stagnation into its social order. As Europe industrialised during the nineteenth century, the Ottoman Empire languished in medieval backwardness. In 1914, despite its vast extent and half a century of railway building, it still had less than 3,250 miles of track – compared with 40,000 miles in Germany, a country with barely one-fifth the land mass. As for industry, coal production was just 0.3 per cent of that of Britain, iron and steel production was insignificant, and there was no chemical production of any kind.[3] This economic weakness, combined with the empire's vast geographical extent and its ethnic and religious diversity, meant that it was disintegrating. Most of the Balkans had been lost, the Greeks, Serbs, and Bulgars establishing independent states. The whole of North Africa was gone, the Ottoman grip first loosened by local strongmen, then broken by the European powers, the French in Morocco, Algeria, and Tunisia, the Italians in Libya, the British in Egypt. The speed of collapse had accelerated since 1911, with first the Italo-Turkish War, then the Balkan Wars. This military crisis had radicalised the Young Turk regime, which had come to power in Constantinople in 1908, transforming it into a nationalist dictatorship in search of a powerful ally in a war of *revanche*.

Like the Arabi movement in Egypt in 1882, the Young Turk movement was dominated by middle-ranking army officers and other professional men who wished to reform an antiquated social order, build modern infrastructure, and create the basis for national independence and prosperity. But the intractable contradictions of Ottomanism – the weakness of the popular movement, the conservatism of traditional elites, the insurgencies of national minorities, the continuing predations of the imperial powers – conspired to drive them towards an increasingly authoritarian form of rule. By the outbreak of the First World War, the Ottoman Empire was dominated by a triumvirate of three CUP (Committee of Union and Progress) leaders – Enver, Talaat, and Djemal. All three, but Enver especially, saw war as an opportunity for regeneration and recovery. They were hazy and conflicted about its precise form. Was Ottomanism to be the basis of the empire's reconstruction as a great power? If so, what was Ottomanism in an age of nation-states? Or was pan-Turkism the big idea, the aim being to recast the Empire in nationally homogeneous form? In which case, a war of conquest in Central Asia must be the implication, to liberate the Turks living under Tsarist rule and unite them with their brothers and sisters in Anatolia. Or was Islamism the key? Should Constantinople rally the Muslim majority of the Ottoman people, both Turks and Arabs, and appeal to the Muslim masses living under European colonial rule to rise in holy war against their oppressors? Whatever it was to be, a backward empire, deeply in debt, with poor communications, without a modern arms industry, could not contemplate entering the First World War without a powerful ally.

Though the leadership of the Ottoman Empire dithered between the Entente and the Central Powers – and did not in fact enter the war until three months after it started – all logic favoured a German alliance. Britain, France, and Russia had all seized Ottoman territory in the past, while France had further ambitions in Syria, and Russia in the Caucasus, the Balkans, and the Straits. Russia in particular was a historic enemy, against whom the Ottomans had fought a long series of wars, stretching back to the sixteenth century; and the Tsars made no secret of their continuing ambition to take Constantinople itself and gain control of the shipping lane through the Straits from the Black Sea to the Mediterranean. No such conflict of interest stood in the way of an alliance between Ottoman Turkey and Imperial Germany. The ground, moreover, had been well prepared. The Kaiser had made official visits, donned the Turkish fez, and allowed it to be believed that 'Hajji Wilhelm' had converted to Islam. German engineers had built the 'Berlin-to-Baghdad' railway. German firms had re-equipped the Ottoman Army with Krupp guns and Mauser rifles, and German officers had reorganised and retrained it on modern lines. This special relationship was now underpinned by a promise of generous wartime subsidy. Two trainloads of gold were dispatched as advanced payments in October 1914. The aim was not only to harness 18 million Turks and Arabs to the German war-machine; it was also to attempt to unleash the revolutionary potential of the 140 million Muslims living under British, French, and Russian rule. Constantinople was to be the launchpad of a global *jihad*.

'Turkey herself is not really the important matter,' explained the huge, domineering, cigar-chomping Prussian aristocrat Baron Hans Frieherr von Wangenheim, the German Ambassador in Constantinople, to his American counterpart, Henry Morganthau. 'Her army is a small one, and we do not expect it to do very much. For the most part, it will act on the defensive. But the big thing is the Muslim world. If we can stir the Muhammadans up against the English and the Russians, we can force them to make peace.'[4] Other Germans shared this perspective: they deprecated the military potential of the Ottomans, but viewed them as a potential catalyst of holy war beyond their borders. 'Turkey is militarily a nonentity,' thought Helmuth von Moltke, the Chief of the German General Staff. 'If Turkey was described before as a sick man, it must now be described as a dying man . . .'[5] What mattered was not the Ottoman peasant-conscript's questionable fighting capacity, but his exemplary jihadism. 'Our consuls in Turkey and India, our agents, etc, must rouse the whole Muslim world into wild rebellion against this hateful, mendacious, unprincipled nation of shopkeepers [the British],' proclaimed Kaiser Wilhelm. 'If we are going to shed our blood, then England must at least lose India.'[6]

This was the danger perceived by the British. Viewing the Turks through an orientalist lens, they considered the Ottoman Army to be a second-rate force. 'I should say it was [a] militia only moderately trained, and composed as a rule of tough but slow-witted peasants as liable to panic before the unexpected as most uneducated men,' wrote one British staff officer in November 1914. Another thought the Turks 'an enemy who has never shown himself as good a fighter as the white man'. General Sir Ian Hamilton, slated for the Gallipoli command, exuded the orientalist confidence of his class: 'Let me bring my lads face-to-face with the Turks in the open field, we must beat them every time, because British volunteer soldiers are superior individuals to Anatolians, Syrians, or Arabs . . .'[7]

Racism would prove a poor guide in such matters. The British would crash to defeat again and again – not only on the bloody hills of Gallipoli peninsula in 1915, but at Kut in Mesopotamia in spring 1916, and at Gaza in Palestine in the opening months of 1917. The Turkish soldier – often outnumbered three or four to one, usually underfed, often short of ammunition, sometimes dressed in little more than rags – was to fight against the odds through four years of modern industrialised warfare before he was finally broken. This his enemies would learn the hard way. And this would make the danger they had perceived from the outset – of global *jihad* – so much the greater.

'O Muslims, who are obedient servants of God!' intoned the Sheikh al-Islam in Constantinople on 14 November 1914. 'Of those who go to the *jihad* for the sake of happiness and salvation of the believers in God's victory, the lot of those who remain alive is felicity, while the rank of those who depart to the next world is martyrdom. In accordance with God's beautiful promise, those who sacrifice their lives to give life to the truth will have honour in this world, and their latter end is paradise.'[8] Here was the official launch of the German grand plan to trigger anti-colonial revolt in the British, French, and Russian Empires.

The British, in no doubt of the implications of the German–Ottoman alliance, had already taken pre-emptive action. Egypt was the immediate worry. Four classes of 'sedition-mongers' were identified by *The Times*: 'the Khedive and his supporters, the extremist nationalists, German agents, and Turkish agitators'. Though the 'extremist party' was considered 'numerically small' – a statement that appears to have been based on no evidence at all – the real worry was the potential mobilising power of *jihad*. 'Religion was the side on which this town population was most easily approached by intriguers, and it is noteworthy that the connexion between Egypt and Turkey was popular among them, and among some of the *fellahin* for religious reasons.'[9] A particular concern was the Anglo-Egyptian Army. Though this artefact of British colonial rule had given good service during Kitchener's reconquest of the Sudan, its loyalty could hardly be taken for granted in a world war that pitted the British Empire against Egypt's supposed Ottoman suzerain. A troubling complication was that the Khedive Abbas Hilmi II, the figurehead ruler of Egypt, was, in fact, displaying marked sympathy with Constantinople.

The 'Veiled Protectorate' had become untenable. The army commander in Egypt, Lieutenant General Sir John Maxwell, a veteran of Omdurman, therefore imposed martial law on the country on 2 November – just two days after the Ottoman declaration of war – explaining that he had been directed 'to assume military control of Egypt in order to secure its protection.' Five days later, a second proclamation informed the Egyptian people that they were at war with the Ottoman Empire; apparently: 'Great Britain was fighting both to protect the rights and liberties of Egypt . . . and to secure to her the continuance of the peace and prosperity which she has enjoyed during the 30 years of British occupation.' The somewhat anomalous situation thereby created – where the Egyptian people were at war with their ostensible sovereign, the Ottoman Sultan, and his local representative, the Egyptian Khedive – was not resolved until 18 December. It was then announced that the Ottoman Sultan's suzerainty had been terminated, Abbas Hilmi had abdicated, and his uncle, Hussein Kamel, was the new Khedive. The coup was marked by an official inauguration ceremony on 20 December. In the laconic words of Lord Cromer, the departing Khedive had 'preferred to throw in his lot with the enemies of Great Britain, being probably under the impression that he was joining the side which would be ultimately victorious in the war now being waged. In adopting this course, he committed political suicide.'[10] To quell any local doubts about the appropriateness of these proceedings, a garrison of 100,000 imperial soldiers was soon in occupation of Egypt.

Equally peremptory action was taken in Khartoum, by Sir Reginald Wingate, another Omdurman veteran, who now combined the roles of Governor General of Sudan and *Sirdar* of the Anglo-Egyptian Army. Wingate summoned the Sudanese sheikhs and *ulema* to a meeting on 8 November and instructed the Grand Mufti to read a proclamation in Arabic. After reciting the many benefits of British rule in Sudan, this went on to explain that war with the Ottoman Empire had been forced on Britain by 'this syndicate of Jews, financiers, and low-born intriguers, like broken gamblers staking their last coin, and in deference to the urgent demands of Germany and our enemies, who have gone to war with the one power who, by her actions and the sentiments of her people, has ever been a true and sympathetic friend to the Muslims and to Islam'. If some of the assembled dignitaries, who included the eldest son of the Mahdi, found this last claim somewhat surprising in the light of Sudan's recent history, they gave no intimation: the British war effort was given formal approval.[11] With most of the 20,000-strong Anglo-Egyptian Army stationed in Sudan, it could hardly have been otherwise.

The Government of India had also been taking pre-emptive action that busy first November of the war. It had landed two brigades of troops at the head of the Persian Gulf, mainly to secure the oilfield at Ahwaz, the oil port at Abadan, and the 100-mile pipeline connecting the two. For oil was already a matter of acute geopolitical importance. Britain's new class of 'super-dreadnought' battleships depended upon oil – which burned more fiercely and gave off more heat than coal – to enable them to combine speed with heavier armour and batteries of 15-inch guns. The Royal Navy would have been crippled without Persian oil. But there was another consideration – the potential resonance of the Ottoman call to *jihad* in Mesopotamia, and the fear that it might become 'a dry wind blowing through the East' setting alight 'the parched grasses' of India's 55 million Muslims. The danger proved all too real. The Anglo-Indian landing at Basra triggered a surge in local Ottoman support. The Arabs may have had little love for the Turks, but most had even less for the British. Large contingents of tribal irregulars would fight alongside the Ottoman Army in Mesopotamia, their service inspired in part by jihadist enthusiasm. 'It is well known,' wrote Iraq's most senior Shia cleric to a leading sheikh on the Persian Gulf:

> that one of the most important duties towards the domain of Islam is the defence, at all costs, of the Muslims' seaports against attack by the infidels, and since yours is one of the most important of those ports, hence it is your duty to protect that port to the utmost that you are able. Likewise, you have a duty to lead the local tribes in that region, and it is required of you to inform them that it is forbidden for any Muslim to assist the infidels, and that their support must be for the Muslim war-effort. We trust in your zeal and sense of honour to make every effort to repel the infidels. And if God so wills it, may he support you in vanquishing his enemies.[12]

Would the East catch fire? Many British administrators feared so. 'Whence comes that wind?' asks John Buchan's 'Sir Walter'. 'There is a *jihad* preparing ... Supposing there is some Ark of the Covenant which will madden the remotest Muslim peasant with dreams of Paradise?'[13]

The war in the Middle East opened with an ambitious double offensive.[14] The main thrust of the Ottomans, against the Russians in the Caucasus, crashed to disaster at Sarikamish, where an ill-equipped army of 100,000 was destroyed by the winter cold of the 'Turkish Siberia' in January 1915.

The dream of a pan-Turkish insurgency across Central Asia thus perished in the snows of Sarikamish. A secondary thrust, by 13,000 men, across the Sinai Desert to the Suez Canal in February 1915, was shot away by the regiments of Indian *sepoys* entrenched to defend it. Another dream faded: that the Egyptian *fellahin* would answer the call of their Muslim brothers and rise against their British colonial masters.

But no rapid counterstrokes were possible. The Russian Army was almost as deficient in materiel as the Ottoman, and the mountainous terrain and ferocious climate of the Caucasus, this ancient battleground of Slavic Christian and Turkish Muslim, played to the advantage of the defender. The British found themselves facing equally daunting logistical challenges on three widely separate fronts: on the tiny battlefields of Gallipoli, where patches of ground sometimes no larger than tennis-courts became the slaughter-pens of massed Turkish machine guns; in the Sinai Desert, where it took two years of engineering work to build a railway, wire road, and water pipe to enable an army of sufficient size to be deployed for an assault on Palestine; and in the sand and scorching heat of Mesopotamia, where the serial mismanagement of the Anglo-Indian officer caste reached Crimean proportions, and it was not until March 1917 that a British army finally made it to Baghdad. In every case, the Turkish peasant-conscript defending a trench proved himself to be as formidable a fighter as any to be encountered on any of the many battlefields of the First World War.

This was not the least reason for the urgency with which the British pursued an alliance with Hussein, Emir of Mecca, the ambitious Hashemite ruler of the Islamic Holy Land. The Arab Revolt – the war which would transform the Oxford archaeologist and wartime officer T.E. Lawrence into a celebrity – began in the Hijaz region of western Arabia in June 1916 and erupted across Syria between June 1917 and October 1918. Prior to the outbreak, General Maxwell had stressed the political and military importance of an agreement with Hussein: 'As all the great camel-raising tribes are pan-Arab,' he explained in a cable to London, 'a satisfactory settlement of the Arab question would go far to make a serious invasion of Egypt impossible . . . I feel certain that time is of the greatest importance, and that unless we make a definite and agreeable proposal to the Sherif [Hussein] at once, we may have a united Islam against us.' Maxwell relied heavily on the intelligence assessments of the Cairo spy chief, Gilbert Clayton, who was firmly of the view that an Arab alliance was essential. Failure in this regard would:

throw the Young Arab party definitely into the arms of the enemy. Their machinery will at once be employed against us throughout the Arab countries, and various Arab chiefs, who are almost to a man members of, or connected with, the Young Arab party, will undoubtedly be won over. Moreover, the religious element will come into play, and the *jihad*, so far a failure, may become a very grim reality, the effects of which would certainly be far-reaching, and at the present crisis might well be disastrous.

The alliance between the British Empire and the Hashemite rulers of the Hijaz was an attempt to avoid this 'very grim reality' by trumping the Ottoman call to *jihad*. It was characterised by exceptional duplicity, for it was based on false promises, the British and the French having a secret agreement to carve out the Arabs and divide up the Middle East between themselves at the end of the war. But that was in the future. For the present, the Hashemites proved to be allies of unexpected (and, to some degree, unwelcome) prowess; by the end of the war, the 25,000 or so Bedouin guerrillas of the Arab Revolt had more Ottoman troops tied down east of the Jordan than there were Ottoman troops confronting General Allenby's 350,000 men in Palestine.

The third and final phase of the war, the slow collapse of the Ottoman Army in the face of the British Empire's massive preponderance of force, began with the fall of Baghdad (March 1917), continued with the fall of Gaza (November 1917) and then Jerusalem (December 1917), and culminated in the collapse of the Ottoman Fourth, Seventh, and Eighth Armies in Palestine and Syria during the Megiddo Offensive (September/October 1918). The war in the Middle East was ended by the Armistice of Mudros on 30 October. By this time, the danger of *jihad* had been almost entirely dispelled. In the last phase of the war, the power and success of British forces discouraged any attempt at rebellion. Nor was this all: a new wind was blowing. It was represented by 'the Young Arab party' referred to by Clayton in his intelligence assessment in late 1915. This party was active in the cities of the Middle East – in Baghdad, Damascus, and Beirut – and the Hashemite leaders of the Arab Revolt were in contact with this nationalist underground. It was active, too, among Arab officers serving in the Ottoman Army, a fair number of whom deserted and became officers in an embryonic Hashemite regular army. This fresh current of secular nationalism would predominate in the post-war Middle East. The days of the First Modern *Jihad* were drawing to a close. Nonetheless, as long as the war lasted, and certainly until late 1917, the British imperial establishment remained on high alert against the danger that the Turco-German grand plan to trigger an Islamist uprising inside the British Empire might succeed.

⬚

The ambition was boundless. It reached across Persia to Afghanistan and India. Because of its strategic location, wedged between Russian Central Asia, British India, and Ottoman Mesopotamia, Persia had been effectively partitioned into three spheres of influence. The Anglo-Russian Treaty of 1907 had created a Russian-dominated zone in the north and a British-dominated one in the south-east, with a buffer zone under Persian control in between. The agreement had helped terminate 'the Great Game', which had pitted the Russians and the British against each other in a struggle for control over the approaches to India for much of the nineteenth century; part and parcel of the diplomatic realignment that created the Triple Entente in the years leading up to the First World War. Enver hoped to drive an Ottoman wedge into Persia and use it to unhinge the Tsarist grip on the Turkish peoples east of the Caspian Sea and that of the British Raj on the Muslim peoples of north-west India. The plan was to suborn King Habibullah of Afghanistan's long-standing neutrality and turn his country into a launchpad for Islamist subversion. Perhaps a German-backed Ottoman/ Afghan army might descend through the Hindu Kush, stir the turbulent Pathan hill-tribesmen on the North-West Frontier into revolt, and erupt into the valley of the Indus, where it might hope to rouse its teeming millions against their colonial masters.

The predominantly Muslim Punjab was the centre of a new, more radical nationalism born of a split in the Congress Party in 1907. Young militants were carrying out terrorist attacks – 'propaganda of the deed' – culminating in the attempted assassination of the British Viceroy, Lord Hardinge, in 1912, when a home-made bomb was hurled at the howdah of his elephant. German agents were soon at work in this fertile ground, where local revolutionaries saw Britain's war as India's opportunity. Hardinge was ever on edge and kept his police hard at work ferreting out conspiracies, both real and imagined, including one to launch a full-scale revolt in late 1915, when he claimed 'ample evidence that German assistance, financial and otherwise, has been given to agitators'.[15]

The decision to send a diplomatic mission from Germany to Persia and Afghanistan was made as early as August 1914. A 'Berlin Committee' of Indian revolutionaries gave encouragement, and a second mission soon followed. The adventurer-diplomat and Farsi-speaker Wilhelm Wassmuss – later dubbed 'the German Lawrence' – established himself in Persia and succeeded in organising some of the Persian tribes into a low-level insurgency against the British. Werner Otto von Hentig and Oskar Niedermayer, both German Army officers, pressed on to Afghanistan. Leaving Persia in two separate parties, the better to avoid detection and interception, they trekked across the ferocious Iranian desert, lost half their men, and almost died of thirst. They then crossed the Afghan border and journeyed on under escort to Kabul, arriving there three months after setting out, only to be kept waiting several weeks more before finally being admitted to the royal presence on 20 October.

Habibullah declined to accord the German emissaries diplomatic status, and responded to the gifts they brought with studied indifference; they were left feeling like travelling salesmen. Things were no better during the serious horse-trading that followed at a succession of meetings. Hentig and Niedermayer urged Habibullah to break his treaty with the British and allow Ottoman troops passage through Afghanistan. Given that he shared borders with both Russia and Britain – whereas the Germans and Ottomans were far away – and given, too, that he was a recipient of British subsidies, this was asking much. The King – a wily opportunist – made full use of the fact that he was being courted by two parties to raise his price. Hardinge was fully informed by his spy network of the proceedings at Kabul, and was induced to raise the level of British subsidy to ensure continuing Afghan allegiance. Meanwhile, the German emissaries continued to be strung along, gaining the impression that a German–Afghan treaty was imminent. A document was drawn up which committed the Germans to supplying 100,000 modern breechloaders, 300 artillery pieces, and £10 million in cash, and also to providing direct military support were Afghanistan to join the war as a belligerent. Plans were drawn up for the remodelling of the 70,000-strong Afghan Army, and contact was made with the more radical mullahs on the North-West Frontier. The Viceroy – the newly appointed Lord Chelmsford – organised a display of British airpower, with bombing and strafing, for the benefit of the tribal leaders who controlled the mountain roads to India.

In the event, the Viceroy's aerial spectacle was superfluous. Habibullah had informed himself of developments in the distant European and Middle

Eastern theatres of war, and had taken careful measure of the likely balance of forces in his own, concluding that the proposed German–Ottoman–Afghan axis would be suicidal. He summoned a *jirga* – a traditional Afghan assembly of tribal elders – and announced that Afghanistan would remain neutral. In May 1916, the German emissaries departed empty-handed. Niedermayer retraced his steps across Persia, suffering great hardship on the way. Hentig chose the eastern route, through China and the United States. Habibullah was rewarded for his loyalty with fresh shipments of Anglo-Indian gold.[16]

Greater success attended Ottoman efforts at the opposite end of their continent-spanning battle line: in the Western Desert. Just as British commanders were coming to terms with defeat on Gallipoli, in November 1915, a jihadist tribal insurrection exploded out of Libya across the Egyptian border.

It had been brewing a long time. A full nine months earlier, a small boat loaded with arms and ammunition, operated by a Beirut gun-runner, and carrying two enterprising Ottoman officers, Nuri Pasha, half-brother of Enver, and Jafar Pasha al-Askari, an Iraqi Arab, had come ashore at Dafnah on the Libyan coast. Two days later, the officers had met with Sayid Ahmad al-Senussi, the current leader of a politico-religious Islamist movement founded in the middle of the nineteenth century that had spread its influence across much of the Sahara, establishing *zawiyas* or 'lodges' in most of the major oases of the Western Desert. The movement was embedded in a Berber social order of nomadic tribesmen and oasis villagers, a society of 'desert and sown', in which the nomads traded animal products and long-distance exotica for the foodstuffs and artefacts produced by the villagers. The resident *ikhwan* or 'brothers' of the Senussi order were organised as both religious community and military force, living in the mud villages of the oases, where there were mosques, *madrasas*, barracks, and armouries amid houses, courtyards, gardens, and narrow lanes.

The Berber wore their religion loosely, and the Senussi dominant among them were tolerant and easy-going; they were not *shariya* fanatics like the Sudanese Mahdists. But they were certainly fighters. Filling the vast desert spaces between Italian-dominated coastal Libya, French-dominated Central Africa, and British-dominated Egypt and Sudan, they sometimes waged war against European colonialism. Though they had declined to make common cause with the Mahdists – despite much urging – they had fought the French and especially the Italians in the recent past. When the Italians invaded Libya in 1911 and quickly defeated regular Ottoman forces on the coast, the Senussi had mounted sustained guerrilla resistance in the interior; in fact, it would be 20 years before the Italians succeeded in suppressing the Senussi and beginning the colonisation of Cyrenaica. This ugly little war – of punitive columns, aerial bombing, and a trail of atrocities – was ongoing when the First World War broke out. The Senussi leader was therefore reluctant to start another war against the British. This remained his stance despite the lobbying of the two Ottoman officers, and the blandishments of the German Kaiser, who sent a message in Arabic, carried in an embossed casket. 'Praises to the most High God,' it began:

Emperor William, son of Charlemagne, Allah's Envoy, Islam's Protector, to the illustrious Chief of Senussi. We pray God to lead our armies to victory. Our will is that thy valorous warriors shall expel the infidels from territory that belongs to true believers and their commander. To this end, we send thee arms, money, and tried chiefs. Our common enemies, whom Allah annihilate to the last man, shall fly before thee. So be it. William.

Needless to say, Sir John Maxwell and his officers were hard at work to counter these efforts and maintain peace on the western frontier. So too was the Senussi court astrologer, who, according to Jafar, was 'forever fiddling with an astrolabe' and making 'divinations and auguries', all of which 'pointed to the same conclusion: that all our operations would end in complete failure'. Thus did a medieval mystic delay the plans of modern warlords. But Sayid Ahmad's control over the Berber tribes was loose; he was not the autocratic ruler of a centralised state as the Khalifa had been. And the inward flow of guns and gold was destabilising the desert, making it easier for Nuri and Jafar to engineer cross-border raids that might bounce the Senussi into war. A chaotic flare-up in November 1915 – involving German submarines, renegade Senussi regulars led by the Ottoman officers, and a pro-Senussi tribe living on the Egyptian side of the frontier – culminated in British abandonment of their exposed frontier camp at Sollum and a pullback towards Mersa Matruh. Willy-nilly, a war had started, and the Senussi leader's prestige was now at stake. Would he stand by loyal tribesmen who had been attacked by infidels or not? Besides,

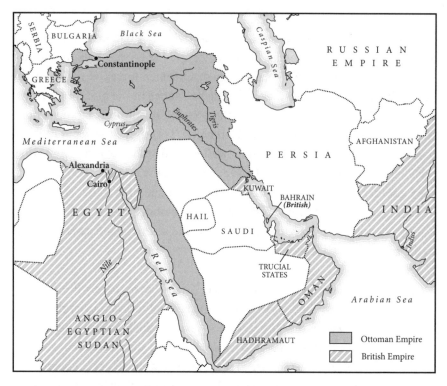

16. The Ottoman Empire and the Middle East at the time of the First World War

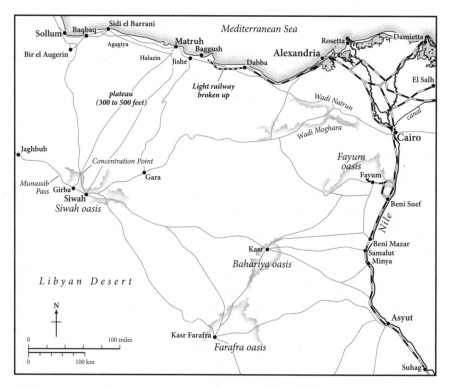

17. The Western Desert, illustrating the Anglo-Senussi War of 1915–16

Nuri and Jafar told him, Italy had joined the Entente, which meant 'there was no way of getting rid of them and saving his country unless he salvaged what he could from the situation by joining the Ottoman side wholeheartedly'. Now was the time, they argued, to make common cause with the Muslim masses living under infidel rule; 'much better to take advantage of such circumstances and not let the opportunity slip by'.[17]

So war it was.

It was Christmas Day 1915. The Western Frontier Force moved out in two columns. The right column, mainly infantry, a mix of Londoners, New Zealanders, and Sikhs, backed by some guns, was to advance south-west from Mersa Matruh, the British forward base. It would head down the Khedivial Motor Road, to engage a large Senussi force established in the Jebel Medwa hills. The left column, mainly mounted, British Yeomanry and some Australian Light Horse, was to make a wide turning movement through the desert to come in behind the enemy position. The estimate of enemy strength was 5,000, though in truth it was only 900 regulars, four mountain guns, and two machine guns, with an indeterminate number of Bedouin tribal irregulars hovering. The Senussi regulars, the *Muhafiziya*, were trained soldiers who wore khaki uniform and Arab headdress. Jafar, despite excessive weight, was an efficient and energetic officer who had done much to turn the seven 350-strong battalions of *Muhafiziya* into effective soldiers. They were equipped with modern magazine-rifles, either Italian captures or German imports. The tribesmen – usually bearing single-shot breechloaders – were another matter. 'These would take part with us in an action,' Jafar later explained, 'if they saw we were going to be successful, but, if the contrary, would retire to their camps and lie low.'[18]

Jafar had pushed his force forward to Jebel Medwa following the British decision to concentrate at Mersa Matruh. Sollum, more than 250 miles west of Alexandria, had been too exposed when fighting flared on the frontier. Mersa Matruh, roughly 150 miles west, had therefore been chosen as the assembly-point for the Western Desert Force. It was served by a single-gauge railway as far as Dabaa, and then by a good road, the Khedivial Motor Road, beyond there. Jafar's advance was wholly in keeping with the German–Ottoman grand plan. 'We lived in hope that some of the Egyptian tribes would join our forces, stage internal revolts in Egyptian cities, and so allow some of our bands to infiltrate into Egypt and start guerrilla operations, thus distracting and tying down enemy troops as much as possible.' The Ottoman–Senussi strategy was to advance on a broad front, with the aim of penetrating deeply into Egyptian (and Sudanese) territory with small forces at different points – thereby stretching the defence, and increasing the chances of triggering local uprisings. The war, in fact, was to have this peculiar character: that it would be fought in three widely dispersed sectors – on Egypt's Mediterranean coast, in the oases of the Western Desert, and in the semi-arid wastes of distant Darfur – creating a front extending some 1,250 miles. 'The idea,' explained Jafar, 'was to engage as many British troops as possible along a front extending all the way from the Mediterranean to the south of Darfur. Obviously, this front was hardly in the same class as the Hindenburg Line – it consisted of isolated units scattered over a vast expanse of howling wilderness and empty desert. Communications between these units were very poor, so each one operated on its own initiative, trying to carry out guerrilla operations and bring the tribes inside Egyptian territory over to our cause.'

Things were edgy in Egypt. The Sollum debacle had been bad enough: the news had caused 'serious unrest' in Alexandria. As *The Times* explained: 'Should the Senussites have gained any striking advantage, hostile outbreaks in Egypt itself, where agitation was rife, would have been very probable. Even in Alexandria, the Senussi had many adherents, and his prestige was increased by the measures which General Maxwell now ordered, the withdrawal of the Egyptian garrisons from Sollum, Sidi el-Barrini, and other outposts.' As the *Official History* intoned, 'It was important that the Senussi should be defeated, but equally important to move carefully and risk no initial reverse.'[19]

Much was at stake, then, when Major General Alexander Wallace ordered the Desert Force into action on 25 December. They had previously fought a successful minor action on 11–13 December, using guns, armoured cars, and mounted infantry to drive a small enemy advanced force out of nearby Wadi Senab. But now a full-scale battle was in prospect, the intention being to destroy the enemy force if possible, or at least drive it away. The attackers achieved partial surprise – the Senussi outposts were unaware of their approach before dawn – but not enough to avoid a frontal firefight of opposing infantry in the Jebel Medwa. Numbers, and more powerful artillery, including naval gunfire offshore, eventually prevailed, and Jafar's *Muhafiziya* broke and ran at around 10 o'clock. Had the cavalry of the left column got into their rear, the Senussi might have been destroyed; but they had moved more slowly than anticipated, and communications now broke down, allowing the bulk of the enemy to escape down the Wadi Majid. The British had suffered 64 casualties, the Senussi many more, perhaps 300.[20]

Jafar withdrew inland, taking up a new position about 20 miles south-west of Mersa Matruh, at place called Bir Tunis (in his account) or Halazin (in the British *Official History*). Torrential rain stalled further operations for a while. December to March is the rainy season on the coast, liable to transform the landscape into a sea of mud and immobilise all military forces; so it was for ten days after Wadi Majid. Then, air reconnaissance having spotted the enemy camp on 19 January, a column of infantry, cavalry, artillery, and armoured cars was dispatched to pinch out the Senussi force. The Ottoman–Senussi command again handled their units with skill. The battle took the form of a tiny desert Cannae defeated by firepower. While the Senussi centre fell back on prepared positions, drawing advancing Sikhs, South Africans, and New Zealanders down upon them, their comrades on both right and left developed wide flank attacks that threatened to sweep into the enemy rear. The British formation came to resemble a giant horseshoe. But they broke through in the centre, and held on the flanks, thereby registering another victory, though a more costly one than Wadi Majid, taking more than 300 casualties. And again they were unable to mount a destructive pursuit: the horses were exhausted, the armoured cars bogged down, and water had run out.[21]

Having cleared the enemy from vicinity of Mersa Matruh, the Western Desert Force was now readied for an aggressive thrust along the coast back to Sollum. Wallace, disabled by an old wound, tendered his resignation, and Maxwell appointed Major General William Peyton to command the second stage of the campaign. This was not the only change. The British, in the maelstrom of the First World War, were evolving new ways of fighting colonial 'small wars'. To some degree, this reflected tactical developments in conventional warfare: the dominance of firepower and a 'storm of steel' on the battlefield that made it impossible for dense infantry lines to carry enemy positions in frontal assault. There had been a shift to loose skirmish lines employing 'fire and movement' tactics to get forward, and this would soon be followed by a further shift, where formal lines dissolved entirely, to be replaced by 'blobs' or 'worms' formed of small, self-contained, all-arms platoons or sections using their initiative and adapting to the exigencies of the battlefield. Still, in the 'close terrain' of trench-war battlefields, despite the growing role of artillery, armour, and airpower, infantry remained dominant. But in the 'open terrain' of expansive colonial theatres – above all, in the desert – mobility was at a premium, since the enhanced firepower of modern armies was of no avail if the enemy could not be located, reached, and brought to battle. The lunge at Sollum involved a marked change of gear. 'Two thousand camels had now been allotted to the Western Frontier Force,' explained the *Official History*,

> which thus for the first time became completely mobile, able to advance a considerable distance from Matruh and remain in the desert for a long period. The force itself was changing in composition. It had been joined by the headquarters and the remaining troops of the 2nd Mounted Brigade. The Royal Navy Armoured Car Division, the heavy cars of which had been found unsuitable for desert warfare in the wet season . . . had been replaced by the Cavalry Corps Motor Machine-Gun Battery, with 17 light armoured cars and 21 motor-bicycles.

The resulting combination of mobility and firepower – supported by aerial reconnaissance – was to be decisive.[22]

The two Ottoman officers, Jafar and Nuri, made their stand at Agagiya, about 65 miles short of Sollum, on 26 February. They had taken position in some sand hills a few miles inland – safe from naval gunfire – and their 1,600 men, supported by three cannon and five machine guns, were entrenched behind wire, ranged in depth, facing north. While the 3rd South African infantry mounted a fixing attack against the enemy front, with 1st South African infantry in support, the Dorset Yeomanry, under covering fire from two armoured cars, moved to flank the enemy on the right. A Senussi attack on the opposite flank was beaten off, but the attack in the centre bogged down in the dunes – they were 4 miles long and 3 wide – the South Africans taking three hours to battle their way through to the southern edge. It was then 3.15 in the afternoon. The enemy were already retreating into the desert, a mile-long trail of Bedouin and baggage-camels, the *Muhafiziya* with machine guns forming flank and rear guards.

Colonel Souter, at the head of three squadrons of Dorset Yeomanry, examined the ground, decided it was suitable for cavalry action, and ordered his men to attack in two lines. 'Several machine-guns opened fire, well handled at first, but as the Yeomanry approached, the shooting became wilder and finally ceased. Fifty yards from the rearguard, Souter gave the order to charge, and, cheering loudly, the Dorsets dashed at the enemy.

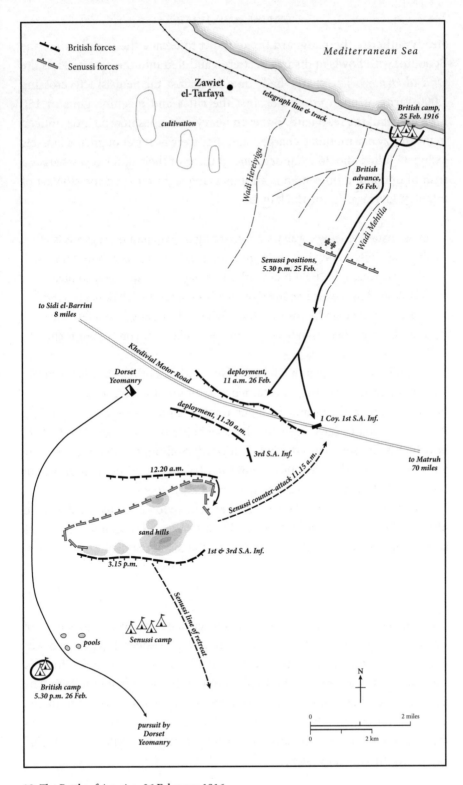

Steady hitherto, the rearguard broke ranks to escape the sword, while the Bedouin, with howls of dismay, scattered and fled into the desert.' Thus the *Official History*. The charge had come in against the Senussi left, crossing 1,000 yards of open ground against the rifles and machine guns of 150 *Muhafiziya* of the rearguard. But even heavy casualties may be little noticed in the frenzy of a mounted charge – and they were heavy enough, the Dorsets losing 32 killed and 26 wounded, one in three of their number – whereas a rush of oncoming horsemen is an unnerving sight for even the stoutest of infantry. Jafar was in the thick of it:

> In an instant, enemy cavalry were charging down upon us, regardless of life and limb. Soon they were in among us with their swords drawn, while we fought back with our rifles in savage close-quarters combat. I was slashed by a sword on my right arm and my pistol fell to the ground, and glancing behind I saw the officer who had wounded me a few paces away, having fallen from his horse, hit by a bullet from one of our men.[23]

Though Nuri escaped the debacle, Jafar and two other Ottoman officers were among those captured. Sustained pursuit into the desert prevented the fugitives from rallying and brought total Senussi losses to around 500. Agagiya proved to have been the decisive battle on the coast. The British, now highly mobile, pushed forward towards Sollum, the Bedouin melting away before the advance. Only a handful of Turks stood by their guns, but they inflicted no casualties as the British took the town.[24]

But the war was far from over. Another Senussi force, led by Sayid Ahmad himself, had occupied four Western Desert oases, and another force was mobilising, that of the Sultan of Darfur, in the distant Sudan.

The Bahariya, Farafra, Dakhla, and Kharga oases form a semi-circle of watering places on the desert caravan routes of western Egypt. Each was home to some thousands of people, who lived in mud houses and cultivated bean plots and date palms, and each lay 100 miles or so from the Nile. The Senussi forces that infiltrated into the oases during February 1916 numbered hundreds rather than thousands. The real danger was that they might act as the catalyst of a tribal-jihadist insurgency along the Nile. 'The Arabs,' explained the *Official History*, were, in fact, in a strong position. They might not be formidable in fighting qualities, were probably far less so than the battalions under Jafar on the coast, but they were desert bred, and with a small amount of camel transport could cover great distances. As a consequence, they were within striking distance of the Nile Valley at several points on a wide front, but were for the time being out of reach of British forces, which were not mobile or inured to the conditions of desert warfare. There was the additional danger in that Upper Egypt, threatened from Kharga, contained a large and highly excitable population, with a considerable proportion of Copts [Egyptian Christians], against whom the flame of religious fanaticism was easily fanned.

Maxwell took the threat seriously – regular air-reconnaissance flights kept the oases under observation – but it took time to improvise an appropriate military force. This took the form of a new Imperial Camel Corps. Built up company by company and formed of picked men, it was to reach brigade strength by the end of 1916. Many were recruited from the Australian Light Horse, but there were also British Yeomanry and Australian, New Zealand, and British Territorial infantry. The Camel Corps became the backbone of the defence of western Egypt, supplemented by patrols of light Ford cars and light Rolls-Royce armoured cars. Further mobility was provided by an existing narrow-gauge railway, which ran for about 80 miles from the Nile at Qara to the Kharga oasis. Maxwell's first moves, while his mobile forces were forming, were to dispatch strong garrisons to various locations along the Nile, including the Fayum district, which received a full mounted brigade, and to dispatch a 1,600-strong battle-group down the light railway to the Kharga oasis. He also ordered further railway construction and the establishment of blockhouses along major routeways. These measures created a strategic framework both for the operation of the camels and cars in the clearing of the oases and for longer term security in the Western Desert. In the event, resistance was minimal; without a spine of professional officers and regular soldiers, the Senussi tribesmen simply escaped across the desert in the face of superior firepower. They re-congealed at the Siwah oasis, an exceptionally remote location, 300 miles west of the Nile, 200 miles from the Mediterranean coast – the place where Alexander the Great, almost two and half millennia before, had imagined himself to be a god. Here, Sayid Ahmad, the latter-day prophet of another god, was destined to make his final stand.

Defeat had undermined his prestige, and Sayid Idris, a rival for the Senussi leadership, had taken the opportunity to open peace negotiations with the British and the Italians. Though not concluded for many months, the effect was to leave the rebel leader politically isolated and militarily vulnerable. Fearing he would escape deeper into the Sahara, Lieutenant General Archibald Murray – who had taken over from Maxwell in Egypt – ordered a rapid-reaction operation by a wholly motorised force of light cars and armoured cars. The operation was a triumph of mobility – the task force crossing 200 miles of waterless desert to reach the enemy in a matter of days in late January–early February 1917 – but it lacked the strength to manoeuvre so as to cut off the enemy retreat. The Senussi suffered about 250 casualties, but Sayid Ahmad and the bulk of his following disappeared into the desert. This, however, proved the end of the struggle for control of the western oases. The further diminution of Sayid Ahmad's standing, combined with the demonstration of British reach, induced his rival to come to an agreement in April 1917: in return for recognition of his leadership of the Senussi brotherhood, Sayid Idris agreed to hand over all Ottoman officers and all British and Italian prisoners-of-war, and to accept the effective demilitarisation of the Western Desert.[25]

'To my mind there is little or no doubt that Ali Dinar is acting on instructions and advice from the Senussi and his Turco-German advisors,' wrote the Governor General of Sudan, Sir Reginald Wingate, to General Maxwell in February 1916. Wingate was building up military forces in western Sudan, preparatory to a pre-emptive strike, and requested reinforcements. 'It might be necessary to deal him a blow,' he continued, 'before our enemies' propaganda and intentions have sufficient time to materialise; the main point, however, is to prevent trouble spreading into Kordofan and our own tribes becoming restive and unsettled owing to apparent inaction or pusillanimity on our part.' He figured some airpower would be handy. 'If it were possible to send up a flight of aeroplanes, it would be immensely useful in discovering the whereabouts of enemy concentrations in these huge desert tracts west of Nahud.'[26]

The Governor General's aim was to terminate the rule of Ali Dinar, the Sultan of Darfur, a former (lukewarm) Mahdist who had made his escape to the west around the time of the Battle of Omdurman. Overcoming various rivals for control of his homeland, he had re-established Darfur as an independent sultanate, beyond the reach of Anglo-Egyptian power. It was a conservative regime of sheikhs, imams, and slave traders, but highly centralised under the autocratic rule of the Sultan, with strong elements of Mahdist practice in its administrative, religious, and military arrangements.[27] Aware of his vulnerability, Ali Dinar had welcomed the outbreak of war between the British and Ottoman empires, endorsing the Ottoman call to *jihad* and establishing relations with the Senussi. 'We have been moved by religious zeal and fervent faith to rise by the power and might of Allah for the protection of the religion of Allah against the enemies of Allah, the infidels and opponents of *shariya*, who are our neighbours in the Sudan,' he wrote to Sayid Ahmad in January 1916. 'We shall shortly proclaim the *jihad* for the sake of Allah, and you shall hear how the enemies of Allah will suffer hardship at our hands.' He responded to Wingate's military build-up with defiance: 'You Christians are infidels and dogs,' he wrote to the Governor General on 7 February. 'Your destination is hell, to which you will ultimately go. You have chosen to die.'[28]

In reality, the Sultanate of Darfur was doomed. The British evacuation of Gallipoli had flooded Egypt with troops, and large numbers were deployed in the spring of 1916 along the whole Western Desert front to deal with the threat of the Ottoman/Senussi *jihad*. At the same time, the British were pushing eastwards into Sinai, building a railway, a wire-mesh road, and a water pipe, so as to drive Ottoman forces eastwards from the Suez Canal and Egypt. With so much recent experience of jihadism, they were taking no chances.

The force assembled at Nahud – the Darfur Field Force – numbered 2,000 men. Commanded by Lieutenant Colonel Kelly, it comprised five companies of camel corps, two of mounted infantry, eight of Sudanese infantry, three of Egyptian infantry. There were 6 mountain guns and 12 Maxims. Transport was provided by 1,200 baggage-camels. Kelly's advance into Darfur began in mid-March. For two months, the campaign was a matter of steady advance and tentative clashes. The Sultan's army was estimated to comprise about 3,000 rifle-armed infantry, 800 regular cavalry, and an uncertain number of spear-armed tribesmen. British intelligence reported, however, that the riflemen, the essential core of the army, were 'very badly trained and ill-equipped with ammunition'. This army was stationed at Al-Fasher, the capital of Darfur, and only when this was threatened by the advance of Kelly's column in mid-May was a decisive battle triggered. At 5.30 a.m. on 22 May, near the village of Beringia, about 12 miles from Al-Fasher, the Darfur Field Force advanced in square formation towards a line of enemy entrenchments. The country was covered in small sand hills which limited visibility to a few hundred yards. Fur horsemen and camelry were hovering. The enemy were shelled out of a forward position around 10.30, and the advance resumed. Kelly, aware that the main defences lay on the far side of the village, planned to pin the enemy with fire to the front while manoeuvring to flank them on their right. What made him uneasy were enemy cavalry and some detached units of enemy infantry on his own flanks. A moment of uncertainty and tension: the nerve-wracking climax of the two-month war.

Kelly recalled: 'the situation developed like a flash. Out came the whole of the enemy from all sides, and I saw a continuous line of men advancing to the double.' One camel company was exceptionally exposed: 'Personally, I never thought I should see many of them again alive.' But in fact, despite the fanatic bravery of the Fur, they were now exposed in the open to the lethal fire of mountain guns, Maxims, and magazine-rifles handled by trained modern troops. For 40 minutes, a torrent of Anglo-Egyptian fire tore through the attackers' ranks, driving them to seek shelter in such dead ground as they could find. Some got to within 10 yards of the square, but none closer. When they appeared to waver, Kelly ordered a counter-attack, and the army of Darfur disintegrated into rout, leaving 300 dead and seriously wounded in the 500 yards around the square. Kelly's column had suffered only 26 casualties. 'I had but little to do with the direction of the fight,' the commander later explained, 'which was brought on prematurely. The result was a most happy one, and what more can one want?'

Kelly entered Al-Fasher the day after the battle. The hunt for the fugitive Sultan continued for a further six months. He was finally run to ground by a flying column of 150 men under Major Huddleston. A dawn attack on the Fur camp on 6 November scattered the Sultan's followers in all directions. A mile or so further on, the pursuers came upon his body. The last Sultan of Darfur had been shot through the head.[29]

The British Empire contained the threat of anti-colonial *jihad* between 1914 and 1918 and emerged triumphant from the First World War. At Versailles and other post-war peace conferences, it hoovered up the colonies of its defeated enemies and swelled to its greatest extent. It had now developed more effective forms of counter-insurgency warfare based on light columns, motor cars, and airpower. These it now deployed in consolidating control over its enlarged empire. This was demonstrated immediately after the First World War on the North-West Frontier and in Somaliland.

King Habibullah of Afghanistan had been rewarded for his efforts in keeping his country out of the First World War with an assassin's bullet. His successor, King Amanullah, was more sympathetic to jihadist sentiment inside the Afghan armed forces and in May 1919 he ordered an invasion of British India. Though the Afghan regular army was formidable enough – 70,000 men organised in 78 battalions of infantry and 21 regiments of cavalry – the real danger was an uprising of Pathan hill-tribesmen on the frontier, and the possibility that this would trigger additional uprisings in the Indus Valley, where the struggle for independence had already drawn huge numbers of people into action. What increased British anxieties further was that the garrison was below strength because of the war, and many of the soldiers – wartime conscripts – were mutinous. Some Australian units had to be shipped home, and concessions had to be made to the British units – such as two weeks' pay in advance – before they would move out. Still, the Anglo-Indian counter-attack, backed by aerial bombing, quickly defeated both the Afghan forces and the tribal irregulars.[30] The war was over inside a month. Whatever else might happen to the Raj, it was not going to be overwhelmed by a tide of *jihad* flooding down the Khyber Pass.

The balance had shifted decisively against the Mullah of Somaliland as well. When a mass of 2,000 Dervishes attacked the coastal settlement of Las Khorai in May 1916, the British deployed HMS *Northbrook* to recover the town. As the Dervishes attempted to retreat, they were caught and massacred by naval gunfire, becoming a near stationary target as they crowded in their attempt to escape through a narrow pass. A second sharp defeat was suffered in October 1917, at the hands of the Camel Corps, when the Dervishes were cut down by machine-gun fire at Endow Pass, their traditional mobility lost as they attempted to escape with a large herd of stock. The Battle of the OK Pass in March 1919 was even more costly: the Dervishes fled precipitously, abandoning stock, rifles, and ammunition, leaving 200 dead on the field, in a fight that cost the British only 3 casualties.[31]

The Mullah's prestige was falling. His tribal allies were defecting. Imperial troops were available in abundance. The technology was appropriate and the doctrine was clear. The time seemed to have come to deliver the *coup de grâce*.

The newly formed Royal Air Force was playing a growing role in colonial repression. A flight of 12 aircraft, with 6 spare machines, commanded by Group-Captain Gordon, was attached to the Somaliland forces. The planes were De Havilland 9s, two-seater bombers able to remain in the air for four and a half hours and carrying two Lewis machine guns and a 460lb bomb-load. Back-up was provided by 21 motor vehicles, 30 medical personnel, and 160 ground crew. In the final campaign – a '21-day campaign' destined to end a 21-year war – Gordon's airmen were in action again and again. Early on the morning of 21 January 1920, they opened the campaign with an attack on Jidali and Medishe. This was war as the Mullah had never experienced it. He was almost killed by aerial bombs at Medishe – the only survivor, in fact, of a group that included his sister, his uncle, and ten riflemen – and he fled from the scene with a small group of followers. The bombing of the two Dervish camps continued for three days. Then Gordon switched tactics from aerial bombing to air support for the ground operations now under way. A succession of camps and forts were stormed in combined-arms operations. Typically, aerial bombing and strafing was used to traumatise defenders, while Stokes mortars and Lewis light machine guns on the ground gave covering fire to assault units. The Mullah, harried from place to place, fled further inland. By early February, British forces were closing in on Taleh, the Mullah's main stronghold. But the old jihadist retained his life-long instinct for survival. Driving back a covering force of 200 Tribal Levy, he and 80 mounted followers burst out of the north gate and disappeared into the bush before the British could catch them. The fort itself – some 90 Dervishes had been left to guard it – was taken within an hour; but the supreme prize still eluded the British.

Low-intensity operations continued against fugitive bands of Dervishes for several months. British Somaliland itself was soon cleared of rebels, though the Mullah and several hundred followers had retreated into Abyssinian territory. But his camp at Imi was hit by smallpox, influenza, and famine, and the last organised body of Dervishes slowly dissolved. The Mullah himself succumbed on 23 November 1920, following six days of illness, and his turbulent spirit was finally laid to rest in a small domed tomb. Nature had accomplished what the British, in 21 years of counter-insurgency warfare, had never quite managed: the death of the last of the great leaders of the First Modern *Jihad*.[32]

# CONCLUSION

Islam is neither reactionary nor progressive: social context is decisive. Colonel Arabi was, by all accounts, a devout Muslim. He was also a liberal nationalist who wanted to modernise and reform his country. His contemporary, Muhammad Ahmad, was also a devout Muslim. But he was a religious mystic and a supporter of slavery and *shariya* who wanted to return his country to an imagined medieval past. The Islamic faith was, and is, a framework for thinking about the world, for orienting oneself within it, for distinguishing right and wrong; the decisions Muslims make, in different places, at different times, is an open historical question, not one determined by their religion.

Islam, in this regard, is like other great religions. Christianity, for example, was represented in the 1960s by Martin Luther King and the Southern Christian Leadership Conference on the one hand, and by the Dutch Reformed Church on the other. The former spearheaded the civil rights struggle against racial oppression in the southern states of America. The latter was one of the main props of the Apartheid system in South Africa – dubbed 'the Much Deformed Church' by Christian anti-racists at the time. Religious form does not determine political content. God does not decide. We do.

Nor is the historical record of Islam any worse (or better) than that of any other great religion. It gave sanction to patriarchy, the slave trade, and wars of genocide and ethnic cleansing in East Africa over many centuries. Likewise, the Catholic Church gave sanction to patriarchy, the slave trade, and wars of genocide and ethnic cleansing in the Spain of the Inquisition and the Conquistadors. In either case, the victims – all sorts and conditions of women, dispossessed and enslaved indigenous people, the poor and powerless at the bottom of the heap, the many who formed 'the wretched of the earth' – they suffered.

What unfolded in North-East Africa in the half century or so between 1870 and 1920 was not a collision between progress and reaction, between civilisation and barbarism, but one between two systems of domination and oppression, one that was new – the coolie capitalism of European empires – and one that was old – the slave system of Middle Eastern potentates. But these were not the only alternatives. In the womb of an increasingly globalised market economy, the ideals of liberalism, nationalism, and even socialism were gaining traction. Some men and women aspired to remake their own countries in the image of the European powers that otherwise threatened them. Should they not industrialise, modernise, enact reforms, create the basis for national independence and prosperity, they asked, just as Britain and France had done? Should not Egypt draw upon its rich agricultural resources and the industriousness of its people to build its own future – not languish in debt-peonage to foreign bankers? But this, of course, was a threat to the whole expanding coolie-capitalist order, to the bondholders of London and Paris, to the mill-owners flooding the world with 'Manchester goods', to the diamond and gold magnates, to the railway and steamship capitalists, to the hustlers and chancers hanging out in every colonial outpost. So it was not to be: this alternative was smashed in short order by Admiral Seymour's ironclads and General Wolseley's cannon in 1882.

This created an opportunity for the otherwise marginal mystics of a fundamentalist Islam to make a turn to mass politics and become the leaders of militant movements of resistance to European imperialism. But, alas, movements devoid of any vision of a better world; movements, indeed, that merely sought return to traditional forms of oppression.

What really brought the First Modern *Jihad* to an end was not the success of the British Empire in containing it so much as the emergence of a far more compelling alternative. The Russian Revolution of 1917 detonated a global wave of mass revolutionary struggle – workers' struggles in the heart of Europe, and independence struggles among colonial people in the European empires – which lasted at least until 1923, and in some places, like China, for longer. That wave of revolt shook the world capitalist order to its foundations; never since has it come so close to collapse at the hands of its victims. And if the socialist revolutionaries eventually went down to defeat everywhere – which they did, even in Russia, where Stalinist counter-revolution had completed its work by the winter of 1927/28 – the upsurge left behind a powerful legacy of mass struggle and created a compelling model of state-directed modernisation and reform. That is why, for example, in the 1950s and 1960s, Third World leaders like Egypt's Gamal Abdul Nasser spoke of 'Arab socialism' or Ghana's Kwame Nkrumah of 'African socialism'; they meant that their countries should achieve full independence by pursuing a programme of national economic development comparable with that of Russia in the 1930s.

Few people in this period saw religion as anything other than a private matter. Few believed it might provide a suitable framework for political action. The fact that this has changed since the 1970s we can attribute to the success of Western imperialism in breaking the back of Third World 'socialism', toppling nationalist regimes, and opening economies to the ravages of neoliberal capitalism. This work of demolishing national development plans and programmes of social reform in what we now call 'the Global South' has been the work of 'structural adjustment programmes' imposed by the International Monetary Fund, the World Bank, and other international debt collectors. This is the new imperialism of the 'Washington Consensus'. But as before, in the period 1870–1920, economic coercion has been augmented by military force. The attack on Iraq led by US President George Bush and UK Prime Minister Tony Blair in 2003 can be considered a linear descendant of Gladstone's attack on Egypt in 1882 – similar in inspiration, similar in its self-delusion, similar in its dire consequences for the people of the Middle East and the world. And Bush and Blair, like Gladstone, have unleashed the genie of *jihad*.

This is how Pakistani scholar Aijaz Ahmad explains the eruption of irrational jihadist violence across the world since 9/11:

> The 'terrorism' that haunts the United States is that which comes about when the communist left and anti-colonial nationalism have both been defeated while the issue of imperialism remains unresolved and more important than ever. Hatred takes the place of revolutionary ideology. Privatised and vengeful violence takes the place of revolutionary warfare and national liberation struggles. Millenarian freelance seekers of religious martyrdom replaced disciplined revolutionaries. Un-Reason arises when Reason is appropriated by imperialism and is eliminated in its revolutionary form.[1]

It is worth reminding ourselves of what has transpired in the Middle East over the last two decades. When the two Western warlords launched their 'crusade' (as one of them called it) in March 2003, they claimed it was a 'humanitarian' mission. Blair, the more sanctimonious and self-deluding of the two, put it this way:

> We take our freedom for granted. But imagine not to be able to speak or discuss or debate or even question the society you live in. To see friends and family taken away and never daring to complain. To suffer the humility of failing courage in face of pitiless terror. That is how the Iraqi people live. Leave Saddam in place and that is how they will continue to live . . . the darkness will close back over them again . . .[2]

Blair may have believed his own propaganda. It hardly matters. In the affairs of the world, it is outcomes that matter, not spin.

The regime targeted by Bush and Blair was a nasty dictatorship with the full apparatus of repression – censorship, informers, secret police, praetorian guard, torture chambers, mass graves. But that is not why it was attacked. Lots of equally nasty regimes were left alone – including some that harboured jihadist terrorists, which Iraq did not. The problem was that Iraq had become too powerful and assertive in an oil-rich region vital to Western interests. Bush and Blair's war was an imperialist war.

In the almost two decades since, the outcomes are clear. Half a million people have been killed in the self-proclaimed 'War on Terror'.[3] More than 8 million people have lost their homes in Afghanistan and Iraq.[4] Millions of others have been plunged into unemployment and poverty as their societies are torn apart by sectarian conflict, political corruption, and rampant corporate looting. The shock waves of the War on Terror have spread far beyond the original targets, creating a swathe of geopolitical mayhem that stretches from Central Asia to West Africa; it is this region that today contains the great majority of the estimated 70 million people worldwide displaced by war.[5]

This is the legacy of Bush and Blair. And there is something else: from an almost forgotten past, they awakened the spectre of Islamic *jihad*.

When societies are torn apart by war and poverty, when people's lives become intolerable, the centre-ground, the status quo, cannot hold. Deep problems demand radical solutions.

In the 1950s and 1960s, most people in the Middle East looked to secular Arab nationalism, which carried a message of independence, modernisation, development, social betterment. Some, a radical minority, went further and worked for a socialist revolution of workers, peasants, and the poor. Very few thought the answers to modern problems were to be found in a medieval religious text. One prayed at the mosque, for sure, but one did not elect imams to run the country, and one certainly did not murder one's neighbours because they worshipped at a different mosque, or even a church. In fact, under the nationalist regimes, the grip of religion on daily life weakened. Young women, for example, got equal rights under the law, went out to work to earn a living, and stopped wearing the veil.

But Arab nationalism in its various forms, and more radical socialist groups on the far left, some of them waging guerrilla wars against Western-backed dictators, were a threat to the imperial order in a region which holds 70 per cent of the world's known oil supplies. So consistent Western policy has been to intervene in the region to knock back radical forces, strike down 'rogue states', build up client regimes, and keep the Middle East, as far as possible, internally divided. The methods have included direct military intervention (Suez), support for local proxies (the State of Israel), and economic aid for pro-Western states (Saudi Arabia). Western political inter-ference, Western-inspired 'structural adjustment', and the serial failure of the secular Arab nationalist tradition have combined to create fertile soil for religious fundamentalism. In societies eviscerated by war and neoliberalism, by mass displacement, unemployment, and poverty, a dystopian confronta-tion between Western imperialism and Islamic jihadism has played out.

If this book has any message for our troubled age, it may be this. It is not that we are incapable of learning from history. The film of the 1880s may have found its sequel in today's 'War on Terror', but the outcome of Bush and Blair's war was widely predicted, which is one reason that millions of people took to the streets in protest in 2003. But politicians who represent a system based on predatory corporate power cannot afford to learn the lessons of history. They must conform to the logic of global capital accumulation. They must deploy military power in defence of profit. They must visit mayhem upon the many in the interests of the few.

The lesson of history may be that the rulers of the world will continue to 'create a wilderness and call it peace' as long as we allow them to. The lesson may be that the people of the world need to act collectively to overturn the Lords of Capital and restore the Rule of Reason to human affairs.

# TIMELINE

| Date | Britain and the World | Africa and the Near East |
|---|---|---|
| c.570–632 | | Life of Prophet Muhammad |
| c.1740 | | Wahhabist movement founded in Central Arabia |
| 1789–1848 | 'Age of revolution' | |
| 1798 | | Napoleon's Egyptian expedition |
| 1804–8 | | Fulani *jihad* creates Sultanate of Sokoto |
| 1805–48 | | Reign of Muhammad Ali in Egypt |
| 1806–56 | | Reign of Sultan Seyyid Said of Muscat, Oman, and Zanzibar |
| 1807 | Abolition of slave trade in British Empire | |
| 1813 | Birth of Livingstone in Glasgow | |
| 1820–3 | | Turco-Egyptian conquest of Sudan |
| 1830–65 | Ascendancy of Palmerston | |
| 1833 | Abolition of slavery in British Empire | |
| c.1835 | | Senussi movement founded in Mecca |
| 1837–1901 | Reign of Queen Victoria | |
| 1838–48 | Chartist movement | |

| | | |
|---|---|---|
| 1839 | | British seizure of Aden |
| 1844 | | Birth of Muhammad Ahmad (later the Mahdi) in Dongola |
| 1845 | Publication of Engels' *Condition of the Working Class in England* | Sultan of Zanzibar outlaws overseas slave trade |
| 1848 | Year of revolutions Publication of *Manifesto of the Communist Party* | |
| 1848–75 | 'Age of capital' | |
| 1849–51 | | Livingstone's travels in Southern Africa |
| 1850–64 | Taiping Rebellion in China | |
| c.1850–90 | | Slave lord Tippu Tip active in Central Africa |
| 1851 | | |
| May–Oct. | Great Exhibition in London | |
| Aug. | | Livingstone reaches Zambesi |
| 1853–6 | Crimean War | Livingstone's travels along the Zambesi |
| 1854–5 | | Burton and Speke's Somaliland expedition |
| 1856 | | Al-Zubeir Rahma Mansour Pasha begins career as slave trader Birth of Muhammad Abdullah Hassan (the Mullah of Somaliland) |
| 1856–9 | | Burton and Speke's Great Lakes expedition |
| 1856–84 | | Reign of Mutesa of Buganda |
| 1857 | Publication of Livingstone's *Missionary Travels and Researches in South Africa* | |
| 1858–64 | | Livingstone's disastrous Zambesi expedition |

| | | |
|---|---|---|
| 1860–3 | | Grant and Speke's Great Lakes expedition |
| 1861–5 | American Civil War | Baker's first Sudan expedition |
| 1863–79 | | Reign of Khedive Ismail in Egypt |
| 1865 | Publication of Livingstone's *Narrative of an Expedition to the Zambesi and its Tributaries* | |
| 1866–71 | | Livingstone's Great Lakes expedition |
| 1866–87 | | Kirk serves as British vice consul/consul on Zanzibar |
| 1868–71 | | Schweinfurth's travels in Central Africa |
| 1868–73 | | Royal Navy East Africa Squadron anti-slavery campaign |
| 1868–74 | First Gladstone government Cardwell reforms of British Army | |
| 1869 | | Opening of Suez Canal |
| 1869–73 | | Baker serves as Governor General of Equatoria |
| 1870–1 | Franco-Prussian War | |
| 1870–99 | | Reign of Kabba Rega of Bunyoro |
| 1871 | | |
| 15 July | | Nyangwe massacre |
| 10 Nov. | | Meeting of Livingstone and Stanley at Ujiji |
| 1872 | Publication of Stanley's *How I Found Livingstone* | |
| 8 June | | Battle of Masindi (Equatoria) |
| 2 Aug. | | Battle of Fatiko (Equatoria) |

| | | |
|---|---|---|
| 1872–3 | | Livingstone's final journey |
| 1873 | | |
| 1 May | | Death of Livingstone |
| 9 May | Vienna stock market crash | |
| 6 June | | Sultan of Zanzibar outlaws slavery |
| Dec. | | Al-Zubeir Rahma Mansour Pasha appointed Governor of Shakka and Bahr al-Ghazal |
| 1873–6 | | Gordon serves as Governor General of Equatoria |
| 1873–96 | The Long Depression | |
| 1874 | | |
| 25 Oct. | | Battle of Manawashi (Darfur) Destruction of Sultanate of Darfur by Zubeir |
| 1874–6 | | Egyptian-Abyssinian War |
| 1875 | | |
| Dec. | | Zubeir enters Egyptian captivity |
| 1875–1914 | 'Age of empire' | |
| 1876–82 | | Egyptian financial crisis |
| 1876–1909 | | Reign of Ottoman Sultan Abdul Hamid II |
| 1876–1912 | | 'Scramble for Africa' |
| 1877 | | Anglo-Egyptian Slave Trade Convention |
| 1877–8 | Russo-Turkish War | |
| 1877–80 | | Gordon serves as Governor General of Sudan |
| 1878–9 | | |
| 28 Dec.–16 Mar. | | Battle of Deim Idris (Bahr al-Ghazal) |
| 1878–80 | Second Anglo-Afghan War | |
| 1879 | | Anglo-Zulu War |
| June | | Anglo-French coup in Egypt |

|          |                      | Replacement of Ismail with Tewfik |
|----------|----------------------|-----------------------------------|
|          |                      | Imposition of 'Dual Control'      |
| 14 July  |                      | Execution of Suleiman Zubeir Pasha |
| 1880–1   |                      | First Anglo-Boer War              |
| 1880–5   | Second Gladstone government |                             |
| 1881     |                      |                                   |
| 1 Feb.   |                      | Kasr el-Nil barracks armed nationalist demonstration in Cairo |
| 30 Apr.  |                      | Death of Romolo Gessi             |
| June     |                      | Mahdi (Muhammad Ahmad) declares his mission |
| 12 Aug.  |                      | Battle of Aba (Jazira)            |
| 9 Sept.  |                      | Abdin Palace nationalist revolution in Cairo |
| 8 Dec.   |                      | Battle of Jebel Gadir (Kordofan)  |
| 1882     |                      |                                   |
| 6 Jan.   |                      | Anglo-French 'Joint Note' published |
| 11 June  |                      | Riots in Alexandria               |
| 11 July  |                      | Bombardment of Alexandria         |
| 20 July  | Gladstone authorises invasion of Egypt |                 |
| 5 Aug.   |                      | Battle of Mehalla Junction (Egypt) |
| 28 Aug.  |                      | Battle of Kassassin (Egypt)       |
| 8 Sept.  |                      | Mahdist frontal assault on El-Obeid (Kordofan) |
| 13 Sept. |                      | Battle of Tel el-Kebir (Egypt)    |
| 25 Sept. |                      | Restoration of Khedive            |
| 1883     |                      |                                   |
| 19 Jan.  |                      | Fall of El-Obeid (Kordofan)       |
| Oct.     |                      | Battle of Om Waragat (Darfur)     |

**1884**

| | | |
|---|---|---|
| 5 Jan. | | Fall of Al-Fasher (Darfur) |
| 4 Feb. | | First Battle of El-Teb (Red Sea) |
| 18 Feb. | | Gordon returns to Khartoum |
| 29 Feb. | | Second Battle of El-Teb (Red Sea) |
| 12 Mar. | | Siege of Khartoum begins |
| 13 Mar. | | Battle of Tamai (Red Sea) |
| 28 Apr. | | Fall of Deim Suleiman (Bahr al-Ghazal) |
| 5 Aug. | Gladstone government authorises Gordon Relief Expedition | |
| 8 Aug. | | Mahdist army begins advance on Khartoum |
| 5 Sept. | | Battle of Umm Dibban (Jazira) |
| 26 Sept. | | Death of Colonel John Stewart |
| 23 Oct. | | Mahdist army arrives at Khartoum |
| 30 Dec. | | Desert Column sets out from Korti |

**1885**

| | | |
|---|---|---|
| 15 Jan. | | Fall of Omdurman to the Mahdi |
| 17 Jan. | | Battle of Abu Klea (Bayuda Desert) |
| 19 Jan. | | Battle of Abu Kru (Bayuda Desert) |
| 23 Jan. | | 'River dash' for Khartoum sets off |
| 26 Jan. | | Fall of Khartoum |
| 10 Feb. | | Battle of Kirbekan (Nile) |
| 22 Mar. | | Battle of Tofrek or McNeill's *zariba* (Red Sea) |

| | | |
|---|---|---|
| 13 Apr. | | Sudan campaign terminated |
| 22 June | | Death of Mahdi; succession of Khalifa |
| 30 Dec. | | Battle of Ginnis (Nile) |
| 1885–6 | First Salisbury government | |
| 1885–9 | | Sudanese-Abyssinian War |
| 1886 | Third Gladstone government | |
| 1886–92 | Second Salisbury government | |
| 1887 | | |
| 13 Nov. | Riot in central London | |
| 1888–91 | | Crisis of Mahdist regime |
| 1889 | | |
| 12 Mar. | | Battle of Gallabat |
| 2 July | | Battle of Argin (Nile) |
| Aug.–Sept. | London dock strike. Birth of 'New Unionism' | |
| 2 Aug. | | Battle of Toski (Nile) |
| 1891 | | |
| 19 Feb. | | Battle of Tokar (Red Sea) |
| 23 Nov. | | Abortive uprising of *Ashraf* at Omdurman |
| | | Supremacy of *Mulazimiya* and Baggara established |
| 1892–4 | Fourth Gladstone government | |
| 1895–1902 | Third Salisbury government | |
| 1896 | | |
| 1 Mar. | | Battle of Adowa (Abyssinia) |
| 7 June | | Battle of Firket (Nile) |
| 1896–1914 | *La Belle Époque/* Progressive Era | |
| 1897 | Diamond Jubilee of Queen Victoria | |
| 7 Aug. | | Battle of Abu Hamed (Nile) |

| 1898 | | |
|---|---|---|
| 8 Apr. | | Battle of Atbara (Nile) |
| 2 Sept. | | Battle of Omdurman |
| 25 Nov. | | Battle of Umm Diwaykarat (Kordofan) |
| 1899 | | |
| Aug. | | Mullah declares his mission |
| 1901 | | First Somaliland Expedition |
| 2 June | | Battle of Samala (Somaliland) |
| 1902 | | Second Somaliland Expedition |
| 3 Oct. | | Battle of Erigo (Somaliland) |
| 1903 | | Third Somaliland Expedition |
| 17 Apr. | | Battle of Gumburu (Somaliland) |
| 22 Apr. | | Battle of Daratoleh (Somaliland) |
| 1904 | | Fourth Somaliland Expedition |
| 10 Jan. | | Battle of Jidbali (Somaliland) |
| 1905 | | |
| 5 Mar. | | Italians and Mullah sign Illig Agreement |
| 1908 | | Young Turk Revolution |
| 1911–12 | | Italo-Turkish War |
| 1912–13 | Balkan Wars | |
| 1913 | | |
| 9 Aug. | | Battle of Dul Madoba (Somaliland) |
| 1914 | | |
| 28 July | Outbreak of First World War | |
| 31 Oct. | | Ottoman declaration of war |
| 14 Nov. | | Ottoman declaration of *jihad* |

| 19 Nov. | First attack on Shimber Berris forts (Somaliland) |
| 23 Nov. | Second attack on Shimber Berris forts (Somaliland) |
| 18 Dec. | British coup in Egypt |

**1915**

| 15–17 Jan. | Battle of Sarikamish (Caucasus) |
| 3–4 Feb. | Ottoman attack on Suez Canal |
| 4 Feb. | Third attack on Shimber Berris forts (Somaliland) |
| 25 Apr. | Gallipoli landings |

**1916**

| 26 Feb. | Battle of Agagiya (Western Desert) |
| 29 Apr. | British capitulation at Kut (Mesopotamia) |
| 22 May | Battle of Beringia (Darfur) |
| June | Arab Revolt begins |

**1917**

| late Jan./ early Feb. | Recapture of Siwah oasis (Western Desert) |
| 11 Mar. | Fall of Baghdad |
| 26 Mar. | First Battle of Gaza |
| 17–19 Apr. | Second Battle of Gaza |
| 1–7 Nov. | Third Battle of Gaza |

**1918**

| 19–25 Sept. | Battle of Megiddo |

**1919**

| May–Aug. | Third Afghan War |

**1920**

| late Jan./ early Feb. | '21-day campaign' in Somaliland |
| 23 Nov. | Death of Mullah of Somaliland |

# NOTES

## 1 HEART OF DARKNESS

1. Livingstone 1857/undated, 42; Seaver 1957, 116, 140–1.
2. Seaver 1957, 116, 140.
3. Ibid., 140; Jeal 1973/1985, *passim*.
4. Hobsbawm 1975/1985, 311–13; Milbrandt 2014, 21; Hutchinson 1874, 20–3.
5. Livingstone 1857/undated, 44.
6. Ibid., 44.
7. Livingstone and Livingstone 1865/2005, 385, 413, 440, 465.
8. Ibid., 439.
9. Gordon 1987/1992, 187–8, 147–9, 158–61, 172–8.
10. Loosemore 2014; Best 1971/1979, *passim*; Hutchinson 1874, 5, 20.
11. Brontë 1907; Harrison 1971/1979, 142–3; Dugan 2003/2005, 151–2; Victoria and Albert Museum 2018; Dickens 1851; Eric Hobsbawm defined the period 1789–1848 as 'the Age of Revolution', that of 1848–75 as 'the Age of Capital'; Churchill 1958, 57–8.
12. Frank 1978, 215; Best 1971/1979, 21, 25, 92, 103, 110, 255; Charles Dickens' *Christmas Carol* character Bob Cratchit earned 15 shillings a week, 1843/1971, 93.
13. See, for example, the collections at the Victoria and Albert Museum and the Geffrye Museum of the Home.
14. Wheen 1999, 109–13, 149, 166; Hunt 2009, 98–109; Faulkner 2013, 133–5; Nicolaievsky and Maenchen-Helfen 1936, 122–37; Marx 1848/1973, *passim*; Marx 1867/1976, 926.
15. Brontë 1847/2006, 108–9.
16. Scott 2012; Heaton 2017.
17. Joyce 2014; *National Geographic* undated; Burton 1872, vol. II, 413.
18. Burton 1872, vol. I, 273, 355–65, vol. II, 408–9, 413; Gordon 1987/1992, 187–8.
19. Schweinfurth 1874, 46–7.
20. Seaver 1957, 291; Livingstone et al. 1858, 1–24 *passim*; Milbrandt 2014, 5–6, 12, 25.
21. Jeal 1973/1985, 7–15.
22. Ibid., 34–85 *passim*.
23. Ibid., 58–61, 75, 106–12.
24. Ibid., 22–3.
25. Seaver 1957, 187–267 *passim*; Jeal 1973/1985, 106–55 *passim*.
26. Milbrandt 2014, 17–37 *passim*; Jeal 1973/1985, 197–9.
27. Milbrandt 2014, 17–105 *passim*; Jeal 1973/1985, 185–273 *passim*.
28. Jeal 1973/1985, 269–70.
29. Livingstone and Livingstone 1865/2005, 284–9, 430, 463–7, and *passim*.
30. Nicolaievsky and Maenchen-Helfen 1936, 261–4; Milbrandt 2014, 109–21 *passim*; Livingstone and Livingstone 1865/2005, 466.

## 2 THE MOUNTAINS OF THE MOON

1. Speke 1864/1967, 124–5; Maitland 1971, 34; Jeal 1973/1985, 146.
2. Speke 1864/1967, 126–42; Jeal 2011, 50–4.
3. Moorehead 1960, 1–5; Jeal 2011, 1–2.
4. Moorehead 1962/1963, 15–43 *passim*; Jeal 2011, 2.
5. Jeal 2011, 3–6; Conrad 1902/1973, 10, 111, and *passim*; 'the Age of Empire' was the third of the three main periods into which Eric Hobsbawm divided his 'long nineteenth century'.
6. Jeal 2011, 4–5; Hazell 2011/2012, 29–71, esp. 62.
7. Jeal 2011, 36–8, 42–3; Moorehead 1960, 19–21.
8. Jeal 2011, 54, 56–7.
9. Burton 1872a, 72–3, 84–94, 255–8.
10. Daggett 2016; Broich 2017, 69–70.
11. Burton 1972, vol. I, 312–13, 327–32, 353–65, 378–9, 462–6, 476–7; Hazell 2011/2012, 6–8, 15–17; Broich 2017, 131–2. Contemporary estimates of the population of Zanzibar varied wildly between 60,000 and a million. Burton's estimate of 300,000 (312n) appears to have been a stab in the dark. I have gone with Hazell's (and Moorehead's) 100,000.
12. Smee 1872, 495–6; Burton 1872, vol. I, 351–2, 453–4, 476–7; Hazell 2011/2012, 18–20.
13. Burton 1872, vol. I, 407–53 *passim*.
14. Burton 1872, vol. I, 259–60, 307, 352–3, 476–7; Hazell 2011/2012, 136; several portraits depict nineteenth-century Zanzibari sultans.
15. Burton 1872, vol. I, 462–5.
16. Lewis 1990/1992, 3–7; Broich 2017, v.
17. Gordon 1987/1992, 14–22; Lewis 1990/1992, 19–21.
18. It is necessary to stress this against some commentators who refer to the 'Muslim' slave-trade and imply that Islam is more sympathetic to slavery than Judaism or Christianity. This is a false perspective that smacks of orientalism and Islamophobia.
19. Lewis 1990/1992, 13–15.
20. Ibid., 11–12.
21. Ibid., *passim*.
22. Speke 1864/1967, 298, 305; Maitland 1971, 68–83; Jeal 2011, 84–92, 268.
23. Maitland 1971, 8–10, 13–18; Speke 1864/1967, 1–2; Jeal 2011, 45–7.
24. Jeal 2011, 67–8, 75–6, 81–2; Speke 1864/1967, 190.
25. Speke 1864/1967, 307; Jeal 2011, 92–100.
26. Maitland 1971, 86–111 *passim*; Jeal 2011, 101–28 *passim*.
27. Maitland 1971, 105, 111, 116, 121–2, 141; Jeal 2011, 131–2.
28. Speke 1863/1906, 72–3.
29. Ibid., 79, 87–8.
30. Ibid., 90–1.
31. *Hongo* is a Swahili word meaning 'tribute', 'toll', 'bribe', or 'gift'; the anthropological complexities make simple translation difficult.
32. Moorehead 1960, 50; Maitland 1971, 125–33 *passim*.
33. Speke 1863/1906, *passim*; Moorehead 1960, 43–4; Jeal 2011, 133–41 *passim*.
34. Maitland 1971, 140–2; Jeal 2011, 141–4.
35. Speke 1863/1906, 200, 231–8; Stanley 1878/1899, vol. I, plate facing 308; Jeal 2011, 166–7.
36. Jeal 2011, 144; Speke 1863/1906, 323–4, 331, 333–4, 338–9.
37. Speke 1863/1906, 241–2, 289, 301, 367; Maitland 1971, 161.
38. Jeal 2011, 165–9.
39. Ibid., 169–74.
40. Speke 1863/1906, 453–69.

### 3  A RUCKLE OF BONES

1. Jeal 2011, 212–13; Maitland 1971, 178–202 *passim*.
2. Jeal 1973/1985, 283–8.
3. Ibid., 296–7, 307–8, 315–16.
4. Ibid., 316–17.
5. Ibid., 283–8.
6. Livingstone 1874/2007, 123.
7. Ibid., 119–20.
8. Ibid., 121–5.
9. Ibid., 126–7.
10. Ibid., 143–4; Jeal 1973/1985, 334–5; Stanley 1872, 405–11.
11. Jeal 2007, 17–72 *passim*, 65–6, 84–5.
12. Ibid., 3–4, 53, 57–61, 75–8, 85–7; Harrison 1990, 166.
13. Best 1971/1979, 247–9.
14. Jeal 2007, 75–87, 90, 99; Foskett 1964, 138–9; Jeal 1973/1985, 337–40.
15. Jeal 2007, 99, 106–11; Stanley 1872, 308–9.
16. Stanley 1872, 405–11; Jeal 1973/1985, 311, 326–7.
17. Livingstone 1874/2007, 144–5.
18. Jeal 2007, 120–4.
19. Ibid., 126–9; Livingstone 1874/2007, 156–7.
20. Jeal 2007, 129–30.
21. Jeal 1973/1985, 357–66.
22. *New York Herald*, 2 July 1872.
23. Jeal 1973/1985, 355; Milbrandt 2014, 207.
24. Jeal 2007, 142–3; Stanley 1872, 627–8.
25. Milbrandt 2014, 208.
26. Milbrandt 2014, 208–9, 213–14.
27. Broich 2017, 1–3, 39, 55–9, 130–2.
28. Ibid., 7–9, 145–6, 195, 238.
29. Ibid., 151–2, 186–8, 203, 217–21, 226–7.
30. Broich 2017, 217, 221, 244.
31. Ibid., 230–6.
32. Ibid., 236–51 *passim*; Hazell 2011/2012, 239–43.
33. Hazell 2011/2012, 247–9.
34. Ibid., 249–55; Morris 1965/1972, 245–7.
35. Hazell 2011/2012, 164–5, 167, 169–74, 278, 283–5.
36. Hazell 2011/2012, 266–86; Broich 2017, 252; *Birmingham Daily Post*, 3 June 1873; *The Guardian*, 11 July 1873.

### 4  BAKER PASHA

1. Hutchinson 1874, 57–62.
2. Lewis 1990/1992, 163–6; Gordon 1987/1992, 158–61; Wright 1992, 181–2.
3. Hazell 2011/2012, 187–90; Stanley 1878/1899, vol. II, 74–6, 97, 99–101; Pakenham 1991/1992, 29–30; 318.
4. Hazell 2011/2012, 49–50, 136, 291; Hutchinson 1874, 26–30, 32; Gordon 1987/1992, 56–8, 79–104, 173; Mack 1992, 96–9, 100–1.
5. Baker 1879, 3–15.
6. Middleton 1949, 21–69 *passim*; Brander 1982, 11–46 *passim*.
7. Middleton 1949, 69–79 *passim*; Brander 1982, 48–64 *passim*.
8. Middleton 1949, 77–9.
9. Ibid., 80–146 *passim*; Brander 1982, 64–104 *passim*; Baker 1866/1962, 404.
10. Baker 1866/1962, 359–60.

11. Brander 1982, 52; Middleton 1949, 9, 65–6, 111; Baker 1866/1962, xli–xlii, 325.
12. Moorhead 1962/1963, 47–131 *passim*.
13. Ibid., 133–8.
14. Ibid., 170–84 *passim*; Prunier 1992, 129–30.
15. *Bastinado*, a widespread form of corporal punishment or torture, especially in the Middle East, involves beating the soles of the feet with a cane or whip.
16. Udal 2005, 14–31 *passim*, 43–6, 57; Prunier 1992.
17. Baker 1879, 5; Udal 2005, 85–117 *passim*.
18. Baker 1879, 120–1.
19. Baker 1866/1962, 68–9.
20. Ibid., 69–71.
21. Quoted in Middleton 1949, 210.
22. Baker 1879, 328–9.
23. Ibid., 348–9.
24. Ibid., 355–6.
25. A 'blue light' was an archaic form of pyrotechnic signal. Baker had a supply of these and deployed them as an improvised incendiary device.
26. Baker 1879, 362–5.
27. Ibid., 383; Allen 1931, 77.
28. Baker 1879, 388.
29. Ibid., 397–408.
30. Ibid., 412–14.
31. Ibid., 465–6.
32. Ibid., 472.

## 5 GORDON PASHA

1. Elton 1954, 94–6, 133–48 *passim*; Allen 1931, 1–2.
2. Allen 1931, 9; Gordon 1888, 90–1.
3. Allen 1931, 2–8; Elton 1954, 26–34 *passim*, 38–9.
4. Allen 1931, 3–5; Elton 1954, 43–88 *passim*.
5. Faulkner 2018, 242–5; Elton 1954, 73–82.
6. Elton 1954, 82–3.
7. Ibid., 97–136 *passim*, 284, 321; Allen 1931, 72.
8. Gordon 1888, 91; Allen 1931, 13, 18, 29, 45, 62; Hill 1885/1969, 79.
9. Allen 1931, 17, 27–8, 43–4, 47–8, map facing p. 45, map facing p. 74.
10. Hill 1885/1969, 131–2.
11. Allen 1931, 59–60; Watson 1929.
12. Allen 1931, 64–79 *passim*.
13. Elton 1954, 143–4, 146–7, 229.
14. Allen 1931, 23–6; Elton 1954, 88, 156–60, 182–6.
15. Elton 1954, 164, 216.
16. O'Fahey 2008, 261–74, esp. 274.
17. Hill 1885/1969, 20–4, 203; Allen 1931, 105–11; Elton 1954, 233–7.
18. Steevens 1900, 324–5.
19. Ibid., 325.
20. Allen 1931, 110; Udal 2005, 312.
21. Allen 1931, 110; Udal 2005, 312.
22. Gessi 1892/1968, 189–213 *passim*.
23. Allen 1931, 109–10.
24. Udal 2005, 328–32.
25. Allen 1931, 112, 154.
26. Ibid., 118.
27. Ibid., 103, 116–17, 139–41.

28. Hill 1959, 120–1; Udal 2005, 313–17.
29. Allen 1931, 138–9.
30. Ibid., 128–35.
31. Ibid., 144; Gessi 1892/1968, 182.
32. Gessi 1892/1968, 221.
33. Schweinfurth 1874, 411–27 *passim*; Gessi 1892/1968, 386–7.
34. O'Fahey 2008, 239–59 *passim*.
35. Ibid., 262–3.
36. Schweinfurth 1874, 361–2.
37. Hill 1959, 135; Udal 2005, 163–70; O'Fahey 2008, 263–7.
38. O'Fahey 2008, 267–75.
39. Udal 2005, 226–30.
40. Allen 1931, 117–23.
41. Ibid., 123.
42. Gessi 1892/1968, 307.
43. Ibid., v–viii.
44. Ibid., 200–6.
45. Ibid., 185–6, 232, 237, 240.
46. *Illustrated London News*, 23 Aug. 1879.
47. Gessi 1892/1968, 255; Griffith 1986, 38–9; Whitehouse 1987, 32–5.
48. Gessi 1892/1968, 209, 234–5, 239–40.
49. Ibid., 242–6.
50. Ibid., 247–54.
51. Ibid., 253–63.
52. Ibid., 263–4.
53. Ibid., 264–72.
54. Ibid., 270–1.
55. Allen 1931, 149–50.
56. Gessi 1892/1968, 322–4, 329; Allen 1931, 151–2.
57. Gessi 1892/1968, 332, 339, 359–64, 366–8.
58. Ibid., 386–8, 409, 418–19; Allen 1931, 153–63.
59. Gessi 1892/1968, 332–6.

## 6 EGYPT FOR THE EGYPTIANS

1. Royle 1899/2013, 19–20.
2. Blunt 1907, 12–18.
3. Newsinger 2006, 85–6.
4. Royle 1899/2013, 13; Newsinger 2006, 86–7; Toussaint 2016.
5. Grant 1886, vol. I, 22–3; Royle 1899/2013, 18; Blunt 1907, 13.
6. Blunt 1907, 94–8.
7. Ibid., 222–4, 263–4, 267.
8. Michael Barthorp, for example, in his 1984/2002 book *Blood-red Desert Sand*, entitled the relevant section 'The Cleansing of Egypt'. He concluded the section as follows: 'The best that could be done, indeed what a Liberal government should do, was to restore Egypt to stability, solvency, and security under the Khedive and his own ministers by a complete overhaul of all Egyptian institutions, guided and assisted by British advisors inspired by British standards of justice and humanity.' His Orientalist assumptions – that the Egyptians were incapable of governing themselves and that British imperialism was a benevolent force – are, of course, of nineteenth-century vintage. They are sustainable only on the basis of grotesque distortion of the truth about the events of 1881–2; specifically, denial that a liberal-nationalist revolution committed to social reform and enjoying mass popular support was smashed by British military aggression.

9. Blunt 1907, 75–80. See De Bellaigue 2017 on 'the Islamic Enlightenment' in general, a welcome corrective to the Islamophobic narratives that have predominated in the context of the 'War on Terror'.
10. Newsinger 2006, 85.
11. Barthorp 1984/2002, 24; Newsinger 2006, 88–9.
12. Blunt 1907, 99–107 *passim*.
13. Ibid., 101–7.
14. Ibid., 111–16.
15. Ibid., 116–17.
16. Ibid., 159–60.
17. Newsinger 2006, 84.
18. Churchill 1958, 242–3.
19. Newsinger 2006, 85; Blunt 1907, 180–1.
20. Hobsbawm 1968/1969, *passim*; Faulkner 2018, 264.
21. Churchill 1958, 244–9.
22. Faulkner 2018, 264–6.
23. Ibid., 266–8; Rosmer and Nagdy 2019. The figures quoted for rising British arms expenditure exclude the sharp spikes due to the Crimean and Boer Wars.
24. Blunt 1907, 138–49.
25. Royle 1899/2013, 46, 70–7, 120–1; Blunt 1907, 217, 247–50, 277.
26. Grant 1886, vol. I, 28–33.
27. Royle 1899/2013, 55–64; Blunt 1907, 236–8; Newsinger 2006, 91–2.
28. Newsinger 2006, 92.
29. Archer 1886, vol. I, 270–3; Royle 1899/2013, 77–80.
30. Archer 1886, vol. I, 274–6; Newsinger 2006, 92–3.
31. Barthorp 1984/2002, 35–7.
32. Grant 1886, vol. I, 19; Royle 1899/2013, 120–2, 136.
33. Quoted at www.historyandpolicy.org/opinion-articles/articles/dr-liam-fox-more-palmerston-than-blair (accessed 9 Jan. 2021).
34. Archer 1886, vol. II, 19–20; Royle 1899/2013, 122; Barthorp 1984/2002, 36–7.
35. Symons 1965, 9.

## 7 ALL SIR GARNET

1. Kochanski 1999, 4, 97; Brazier 2012, 36–8.
2. Kochanski 1999, 3–15.
3. Russell 1966/2008, 67.
4. Barnett 1970, 286.
5. De Watteville 1954, 137–63 *passim*; Barnett 1970, 272–91 *passim*.
6. Churchill 1958, 246.
7. Kochanski 1999, 15–131 *passim*; Brazier 2012, 36–8.
8. Wolseley 1869/1871, 1.
9. Wolseley 1869/1871, 240–3, 250–1; Stanage 2002.
10. De Watteville 1954, 163–9 *passim*; Barnett 1970, 299–310.
11. Wilkinson-Latham 1976, 6.
12. Barnett 1970, 343–4.
13. Williams 1967, 247–50.
14. Ibid., 256–7.
15. Ibid., 251–2; Barthorp 1984/2002, 47–8.
16. Williams 1967, 259–60.
17. Ibid., 251–2, 268.
18. Barthorp 1984/2002, 48.
19. Royle 1899/2013, 126–8.
20. Grant 1886, vol. I, 71.

21. Ibid., vol. I, 67.
22. Royle 1899/2013, 129–32.
23. Barthorp 1984/2002 48.
24. Whitehouse 1987, 34–5.
25. See Kiernan 1982 for the argument developed at length that it was the bourgeois social order, rather than industrial technology, that was decisive in the building of European empires.
26. Archer 1886, vol. II, 25–7; Grant, vol. I, 79–80.
27. Grant 1886, vol. I, 81–2.
28. Williams 1967, 263; Barthorp 1984/2002, 52–3.
29. Archer 1886, vol. II, 29–30; Williams 1967, 260–4; Barthorp 1984/2002, 51–2.
30. Williams 1967, 264–6.
31. Barthorp 1984/2002, 55–6; Featherstone 1978, 111, 116–22; Tylden 1969.
32. Williams 1967, 266–7.
33. Ibid., 267–8.
34. Wolseley 1869/1871, 245; Grant 1886, vol. I, 114–19.
35. Grant 1886, vol. I, 139–45.
36. Williams 1967, 270–1; Barthorp 1984/2002, 63; Grant 1886, vol. I, 159–60.
37. Grant 1886, vol. I, 155–6.
38. Williams 1967, 273; Grant 1886, vol. I, 81.
39. Grant 1886, vol. I, 159–60.
40. Ibid., 157, 162; Barthorp 1984/2002, 64–5.
41. Wolseley 1869/1871, 249; Emery 1986, 122–5.
42. Archer 1886, vol. I, 82–3; Barthorp 1984/2002, 68; Emery 1986, 123–4.
43. Grant 1886, vol. I, 174; Barthorp 1984/2002, 68; Emery 1986, 127–8.
44. Emery 1986, 129–30.
45. Ibid., 128–9.
46. Grant 1886, vol. I, 171; Emery 1986, 125–6.
47. Grant 1886, vol. I, 167–8, 170.
48. Blunt 1907, 281.
49. Grant 1886, vol. I, 57, 79.
50. Royle 1899/2013, 226, 234.

## 8  A MUSLIM PROPHET

1. Guillaume 1954/1990, 111–27.
2. Rogerson 2006, 349–52; Guillaume 1954/1990, 120–1.
3. Cohn 1957/1970, *passim*.
4. De Bellaigue 2017, *passim*, esp. xiii–xxxviii.
5. Ibid., 19–25.
6. Nicoll 2004/2005, 69–70.
7. Guillaume 1954/1990, 120–1; Nicoll 2004/2005, 70–1; Rogerson 2006, 350–2.
8. Nicoll 2004/2005, 50–2.
9. Lacey 1981/1982, 55–63; Howarth 1964, 13–23.
10. Faulkner 2016, 98–9.
11. Barraclough 1978/1986, 238–41; Nicoll 2004/2005, 72.
12. Nicoll 2004/2005, 89.
13. Ibid., 41–5.
14. Ibid., 34–5, 57–9.
15. Ibid., 13–43 *passim*.
16. Ibid., 73–6, 77–8.
17. Ibid., 83–8.
18. Allen 1931, 173–4; Nicoll 2004/2005, 90–3.
19. Nicoll 2004/2005, 97–8, 105.

20. Ibid., 106–14.
21. Wingate 1891/1968, map facing p. 32; Allen 1931, 170–1; Nicoll 2004/2005, 115–20.
22. Ohrwalder and Wingate 1893, 40–2; Nicoll 2004/2005, 125; plan of El-Obeid by C. Perron, 1885, accessed online.
23. Wingate 1891/1968, 22; Ohrwalder and Wingate 1893, 41; Nicoll 2004/2005, 125–6; plan of El-Obeid by C. Perron, 1885, accessed online.
24. Nicoll 2004/2005, 127–8.
25. Ibid., 128–9.
26. Ohrwalder and Wingate 1893, 59–61.
27. Wingate 1891/1968, 55 and *passim*; Nicoll 2004/2005, 128, 130.
28. Nicoll 2004/2005, 102–3.
29. Johnson 2007/2015, 16–17; Slatin and Wingate 1895/1930, 127–8.
30. Nicoll 2004/2005, 155–6.
31. Ohrwalder and Wingate 1893, 72; Wingate 1891/1968, 57–8; Nicoll 2004/2005, 101, 154–5, 157–8.
32. Ohrwalder and Wingate 1893, 10; Wingate 1891/1968, 11–12; Slatin and Wingate 1895/1930, 56–7.
33. Royle 1899/2013, 251; Nicoll 2004/2005, 161–3.
34. Nicoll 2004/2005, 160–8 *passim*.
35. Royle 1899/2013, 252–5; Nicoll 2004/2005, 168–70.
36. Wingate 1891/1968, 77; Bullock 2007/2015, 42.
37. Nicoll 2004/2005, 174, 176.
38. Wingate 1891/1968, 80–2; Ohrwalder and Wingate 1893, 87–9; Slatin and Wingate 1895/1930, 128–30.
39. Wingate 1891/1968, 80–2.
40. Nicoll 2004/2005, 184.
41. Ohrwalder and Wingate 1893, 89.
42. Ibid., 85–7, 98–9.
43. Wingate 1891/1968, 87–8; Callwell 1896/1906, 256–76 *passim*; Slatin and Wingate 1895/1930, 128–30; Nicoll 2004/2005, 184–5.
44. Wingate 1891/1968, 88.
45. Ohrwalder and Wingate 1893, 99–100.
46. Wingate 1891/1968, 88–9; Ohrwalder and Wingate 1893, 100.
47. Nicoll 2004/2005, 186.
48. Wingate 1891/1968, 89–90; Nicoll 2004/2005, 186–7.
49. Ohrwalder and Wingate 1893, 105–7.

## 9 A CHRISTIAN MYSTIC

1. Elton 1954, 324–5.
2. Allen 1931, 187–90.
3. Elton 1954, 325–7.
4. Hobsbawm 1987/1994, 53, 237–8.
5. Elton 1954, 329–36.
6. Allen 1931, 130–5, 162–3.
7. Ibid., 194–5, 205, 224–5.
8. Ibid., 227–32.
9. Allen 1931, 227–62 *passim*. The misunderstandings and recriminations around Gordon's final mission have been the subject of much learned (and not-so-learned) debate. I have chosen to follow Allen, whose scholarship appears to have been meticulous, and who formed the judgement that, much comment to the contrary notwithstanding, Gordon's actions were essentially rational and consistent within the framework of the instructions he believed he had received from the Liberal government in London and the British administration in Cairo.
10. Allen 1931, 214–15.

11. Royle 1899/2013, 286–7; Allen 1931, 205, 223–4.
12. Symons 1965, 35–7, 44–8; Nicoll 2004/2005, 219.
13. Gordon 1885, 309; Ohrwalder and Wingate 1893, 137–9; Allen 1931, 261, 267–8; Elton 1954, 377; Symons 1965, 37–8.
14. Allen 1931, 274–5; Symons 1965, 39–40; Nicoll 2004/2005, 226–7.
15. Ohrwalder and Wingate 1893, 136–7.
16. Allen 1931, 279–304 *passim*.
17. Nicoll 2004/2005, 188–93; Slatin and Wingate 1895/1930, 85–91.
18. Nicoll 2004/2005, 199–204.
19. Grant 1886, vol. II, 94–7; Royle 1899/2013, 270–1.
20. Archer 1886, vol. II, 217–19; Royle 1899/2013, 271–2.
21. Archer 1886, vol. II, 250–64 *passim*; Royle 1899/2013, 275–81 *passim*.
22. Archer 1886, vol. II, 268–70, 281; Royle 1899/2013, 281–2.
23. Royle 1899/2013, 267–8; Nicoll 2004/2005, 193–8 *passim*.
24. Nicoll 2004/2005, 247.
25. Royle 1899/2013, 292; Whitehouse 1987, 7.
26. Archer 1886, vol. II, 272–80 *passim*; Royle 1899/2013, 294–306 *passim*; Emery 1986, 133–6.
27. Royle 1899/2013, 307–21 *passim*; Whitehouse 1987, 24–5.
28. I am aware that this statement is controversial, but I am convinced of its truth, based on my knowledge of Gordon's behaviour, his more intimate letters, and the private comments of some who knew him. I do not subscribe to the widespread popular prejudice – not least among academics – against psychoanalytical insight. I certainly have no time for hagiographies informed by homophobic prejudice.
29. It was the title of a poem by Rudyard Kipling in 1899.
30. Allen 1931, 253.
31. Ibid., 309–15.
32. *Illustrated London News*, 13 Dec. 1984.
33. Allen 1931, 324–8.
34. Ibid., 331–2; Symons 1965, 59–60.
35. Allen 1931, 337–40.
36. Ibid., 347–9.
37. Bedri 1969, 1–21 *passim*.
38. A seminal study of men in battle is Marshall 1947/2000.
39. Bedri 1969, 24; Nicoll 2004/2005, 233.
40. Nicoll 2004/2005, 206.
41. Ibid., 205–6.
42. Ibid., 207–9.
43. Symons 1965, 40–2.
44. Allen 1931, 356–7; Symons 1965, 49–50, 74–5; Nicoll 2005/2005, 227–8.
45. Colvile 1889, vol. II, 33–4; Konstam 2016, *passim*.
46. Beresford 1914, 284–5.
47. Allen 1931, 361.
48. Colville 1889, vol. I, 7–13.
49. Wingate 1891/1968, 116.
50. Symons 1965, 76.
51. Allen 1931, 361–4.
52. Ibid., 364.
53. Ibid., 365.

### 10  A MODERN CRUSADER

1. Symons 1965, 67, 109.
2. Colvile 1889, vol. I, 25n, 29; Symons 1965, 65–6; Whitehouse 1987, 14.
3. Colvile 1889, vol. I, 59–61; Symons 1965, 139; Whitehouse 1987, 7.

4. Colvile 1889, vol. I, 61.

5. Ibid., 67–9, 200; Symons 1965, 112, 128–9, 241–2.

6. Colvile 1889, vol. I, 74–6; Symons 1965, 121–2.

7. Colvile 1889, vol. I, 43, 67, 71–2, 173–5; Symons 1965, 101–2.

8. Colvile 1889, vol. I, 71–4; Symons 1965, 139–44.

9. Colvile 1889, vol. I, 195–207 passim, vol. II, 1.

10. Beresford 1914, 251.

11. Archer 1886, vol. III, 261–4, 268; Colvile 1889, vol. II, 3.

12. Ohrwalder and Wingate 1893, 143–7; Allen 1931, 366–9; Nicoll 2004/2005, 239–41, 243–5.

13. Symons 1965, 80–1.

14. Gordon 1885, 69–71.

15. Ohrwalder and Wingate 1893, 142–3; Nicoll 2004/2005, 225–6, 241–3.

16. Wingate 1891/1968, facing 197; Slatin and Wingate 1895/1930, 198; Allen 1931, 405, 437; Nicoll 2004/2005, 244–5.

17. Nicoll 2004/2005, 237–9.

18. Allen 1931, 421–3; Symons 1965, 229–30.

19. Kochanski 1999, 159–60.

20. Colvile 1889, vol. I, 109; Symons 1965, 131–2; Wilkinson-Latham 1976, plate C, 38.

21. Symons 1965, 133.

22. Ibid., 133–4.

23. Ibid., 167–9, 184–5.

24. Wilson 1885, 9–11.

25. Colvile 1889, vol. II, 13–14.

26. Symons 1965, 203; Nicoll 2004/2005, 252.

27. Wilson 1885, 21–3.

28. Ibid., 23–5; Colvile 1889, vol. II, 16.

29. Colvile 1889, vol. II, 16–17; Symons 1965, 194–6.

30. Wilson 1885, 26–8; Colvile 1889, vol. II, 17–19.

31. Kochanski 1999, 270.

32. Symons 1965, 197.

33. Beresford 1914, 263.

34. Featherstone 1978, 63–5.

35. Beresford 1914, 263–4; Symons 1965, 199, 201.

36. Wilson 1885, 28–9; Beresford 1914, 264.

37. Colvile 1889, vol. II, 19.

38. Symons 1965, 199–200; Beresford 1914, 265–6.

39. Beresford 1914, 269–70; Symons 1965, 201–2.

40. Wilson 1885, 48; Beresford 1914, 271; Symons 1965, 203–5.

41. Wilson 1885, 47–56; Colvile 1889, vol. II, 22–4.

42. Colvile 1889, vol. II, 23–5; Symons 1965, 207.

43. Symons 1965, 207–11.

44. Beresford 1914, 276.

45. Wilson 1885, 76–8; Colvile 1889, vol. II, 26–7.

46. Wilson 1885, 92–8; Callwell 1899/1906, passim.

47. Colvile 1889, vol. II, 28–9; Beresford 1914, 281; Symons 1965, 212–14.

48. Colvile 1889, vol. II, 29–33; Symons 1965, 222.

49. Wilson 1885, 110–262 passim.

50. Ohrwalder and Wingate 1893, 152–3; Bedri 1969, 28–9; Nicoll 2004/2005, 255–7.

51. Nicoll 2004/2005, 257–8.

52. Bedri 1969, 29–31; Nicoll 2004/2005, 257–8.

53. Slatin and Wingate 1895/1930, 212; Nicoll 2004/2005, 258–9.

54. Ohrwalder and Wingate 1893, 154–7; Slatin and Wingate 1895/1930, 206; Elton 1954, 422; Nicoll 2004/2005, 259–61.

55. Symons 1965, 243–5; Kochanski 1999, 165–8.

56. Wolseley 1967, 136.
57. Ibid., 164–5.
58. Kochanski 1999, 177–8.
59. Symons 1965, 245–7; Kochanski 1999, 168.
60. Symons 1965, 247–9; Kochanski 1999, 169.
61. Colvile 1889, vol. II, 83–101 *passim*.
62. Ibid., 62–3, 96–7, 99–100.
63. Ibid., 101–9 *passim*; Symons 1965, 256.
64. Royle 1899/2013, 430–8 *passim*.
65. Ibid., 439–48.
66. Ibid., 453–7.
67. Colvile 1889, vol. II, 67–80 *passim*; Symons 1965, 260–6 *passim*.
68. Symons 1965, 266–8.

## 11 AN ISLAMIC CALIPHATE

1. Ohrwalder and Wingate 1893, 330–7; Slatin and Wingate 1895/1930, 266–8.
2. Nicoll 2004/2005, 268, 270–1.
3. Ibid., 271–4.
4. Ohrwalder and Wingate 1893, 316–20 *passim*; Slatin and Wingate 1895/1930, 308–21 *passim*; Zulfo 1980, 22–7.
5. Nicoll 2004/2005, 277; Zulfo 1980, 39–41; Slatin and Wingate 1895/1930, 347–53.
6. Zulfo 1980, ix.
7. Needless to say, the figures varied greatly over time; these are the estimates of Rudolf Slatin in 1895. Note that by this time the Red Banner had been dissolved, its leaders purged, its men absorbed into other units. Slatin and Wingate 1895/1930, 330; Zulfo 1980, 32–8.
8. Bedri 1969, 41–54, 143–9 *passim*.
9. Ohrwalder and Wingate 1893, 186, 393–8; Slatin and Wingate 1895/1930, 270–2; Bedri 1969, 69, 146.
10. Slatin and Wingate 1895/1930, 276–7, 301, 352–7; Ohrwalder and Wingate 1893, 337–43; Udal 2005, 496.
11. Udal 2005, 498–501; Nicoll 2004/2005, 275–6.
12. Ohrwalder and Wingate 1893, 249–56; Udal 2005, 478–81.
13. Ohrwalder and Wingate 1893, 209–19, 292–5, 383–7; Slatin and Wingate 1895/1930, 241–2, 304–6; Udal 2005, 494–5.
14. Udal 2005, 476; Royle 1899/2013, 471–6.
15. Udal 2005, 477–8.
16. Ohrwalder and Wingate 1893, 234–72 *passim*; Udal 2005, 481–4; Vaughn 2007; Herbert 2007.
17. Udal 2005, 485–6; Royle 1899/2013, 499–503; Bedri 1969, 63.
18. Udal 2005, 486; Bedri 1969, 62–74 *passim*.
19. Bedri 1969, 74–5.
20. Ibid., 77–8.
21. Royle 1899/2013, 504–10.
22. Udal 2005, 487–91; Royle 1899/2013, 513–14.
23. Ohrwalder and Wingate 1893, 306–15.
24. Nicoll 2004/2005, 279.

## 12 OMDURMAN

1. Churchill 1958, 302–3, 312.
2. Ibid., 284–300 *passim*; Faulkner 2018, 266.

3. Morton and Tate 1956, 174–6, 189–97.
4. Hobsbawm 1987/1994, 70; Pauwels 2016, 79–81.
5. Springhall 1971/3 *passim*; Morris 1971/3 *passim*.
6. Churchill 1958, 258; Morris 1971/3, 208.
7. Faulkner 2018, 264–8, 271–4.
8. Ibid., 268–71.
9. Churchill 1958, 303–4; Zulfo 1980, 48–50.
10. Zulfo 1980, 48–9; Magnus 1958/1968, 96–7, 115–16.
11. Magnus 1958/1968, 106; Zulfo 1980, 50.
12. Milner 1893/1894, vi–vii, 245–7.
13. Steevens 1900, 11–17; Wilkinson-Latham 1976, Plate D, 38–9; Simner 2017, 73–6.
14. Magnus 1958/1968, 41, 90, 116, 118–19, and 15–119 *passim*.
15. Ibid., 86, and 29–104 *passim*.
16. Steevens 1900, 7–8, 24–5; Magnus 1958/1968, 121, 143.
17. Magnus 1958/1968, 122; Simner 2017, 99–102.
18. Magnus 1958/1968, 123–9; Simner 2017, 102–8; Welsby 2011, 11–15.
19. Magnus 1958/1968, 128–30.
20. Steevens 1900, 22–3; Magnus 1958/1968, 132.
21. Magnus 1958/1968, 133–4.
22. Ibid., 131–3; Wolmar 2010, 97–9; Simner 2017, 80.
23. Magnus 1958/1968, 135–44.
24. Ibid., 145–6; Royle 1899/2013, 560; Featherstone 1978, 30–1.
25. Magnus 1958/1968, 147–50.
26. Steevens 1900, 140–51.
27. Magnus 1958/1968, 150–2.
28. Neillands 1996, 201; Bedri 1969, 222–9 *passim*.
29. Royle 1899/2013, 583–4.
30. Much of this account of Omdurman first appeared as an article in *Military History Monthly* in October 2012. It is based on Churchill 1899/1960; Royle 1899/2013; Steevens 1900; Falls 1967; Warner 1973/2000; Zulfo 1980.
31. Steevens 1900, 256–7.
32. Ibid., 263.
33. Churchill 1899/1960, 263.
34. Steevens 1900, 264.
35. Ibid., 265–6.
36. Quoted in Warner 1973/2000, 11–12.
37. Steevens 1900, 276.
38. Falls 1967, 297–8.
39. Steevens 1900, 282.
40. Churchill 1899/1960, 275–8.
41. Bedri 1969, 235–8.
42. Bennett 1899, 183–4; Newsinger 2006, 98–9.
43. Bedri 1969, 241.
44. Wingate 1955, 126; Nicoll 2004/2005, 280–2.

## 13 A 'MAD MULLAH'

1. Beachey 1990, 1–18 *passim*.
2. Ibid., 22–9 *passim*.
3. Ibid., 32–8 *passim*.
4. Jardine 1923, 39–47 *passim*. The British dubbed Muhammad Adbullah Hassan 'the Mad Mullah'. He was of course no 'madder' than, say, Livingstone or Gordon. It seems reasonable for history to remember him as 'the Mullah of Somaliland'. The term 'Dervish' was also a British coining, used to describe both Sudanese and Somali jihadists in this period.

I have used the term 'Mahdists' or 'Ansar' for the Sudanese jihadists, but, in the absence of a convenient alternative, have used 'Dervish' for the followers of the Mullah of Somaliland.

5. Beachey 1990, 48.
6. Jardine 1923, 61–75 *passim*.
7. Ibid., 75–7.
8. General Staff 1907, 104–8.
9. Jardine 1923, 85–6.
10. Ibid., 87–98 *passim*.
11. Ibid., 98.
12. Ibid., 92, 101–5; Beachey 1990, 51–2.
13. Jardine 1923, 106–15.
14. Ibid., 116–18, 120, 122–3.
15. Ibid., 124–5.
16. Beachey 1990, 55–7.
17. General Staff 1907, 250
18. Beachey 1990, 60.
19. Jardine 1923, 152.
20. Beachey 1990, 61–4.
21. Ibid., 70–4, 79–84.
22. Jardine 1923, 197–200.
23. Beachey 1990, 89–93.
24. Jardine 1923, 212–13.
25. Beachey 1990, 96.
26. Jardine 1923, 221–8.
27. Beachey 1990, 100–5.
28. Jardine 1923, 238–40; Beachey 1990, 106.
29. Jardine 1923, 240–3.

## 14 THE KAISER'S WAR

1. Buchan 1916/1999, 11–12.
2. Strachan 2001, 695–6.
3. Faulkner 2016, 64–5.
4. Ibid., 20.
5. Ibid., 57.
6. Strachan 2001, 696.
7. Faulkner 2016, 57–8.
8. Strachan 2003, 97.
9. *The Times*, vol. III, 284.
10. Ibid., 304–10.
11. Ibid., 316–17.
12. Nicolle 1989, 36–8; Rutledge 2014, 35.
13. Rutledge 2014, 29.
14. I have drawn mainly on my own *Lawrence of Arabia's War* (2016) in writing this section.
15. Faulkner 2016, 5–6.
16. Strachan 2001, 770–91 *passim*; Stewart 2012.
17. I have based this account of the Senussi war on *The Times*, vol. IX, 281–318 *passim*; MacMunn and Falls' *Official History* (1928), 101–45; Wavell 1928/1936, 35–8; and my own *Lawrence of Arabia's War* (2016).
18. MacMunn and Falls 1928, 113–14; Nicolle 1989, 6–7.
19. *The Times*, vol. IX, 297; MacMunn and Falls 1928, 107; Jafar 2003, 65, 69.
20. MacMunn and Falls 1928, 114–18; Jafar 2003, 80–3.
21. MacMunn and Falls 1928, 120–3; Jafar 2003, 85–6.

22. MacMunn and Falls 1928, 123–4.
23. Ibid., 126–8; Jafar 2003, 88–92.
24. MacMunn and Falls 1928, 128, 132.
25. Ibid., 135–45 *passim*.
26. Theobald 1965, 168.
27. O'Fahey 2008, 285–90 *passim*.
28. Theobald 1965, 163–4, 170.
29. MacMunn and Falls 1928, 145–53 *passim*; Theobald 1965, 176–207 *passim*.
30. Stewart 2011.
31. Beachey 1990, 119–20, 121–2, 127–8.
32. Beachey 1990, 130–40 *passim*, 153.

## CONCLUSION

1. Quoted in Bensaïd 2013/2015, 149.
2. *Hansard* House of Commons Debates, 18 March 2003.
3. *Al-Jazeera* 2018, 'US "war on terror" has killed over half a million people: study', 9 Nov., www.aljazeera.com/news/2018/11/wars-terror-killed-million-people-study-181109080 620011.html (accessed 18 Jan. 2021).
4. Crawford 2018.
5. Newey 2019.

# BIBLIOGRAPHY

Where two dates are given, they indicate date of first publication and date of the edition used.

Allen, B.M., 1931, *Gordon and the Sudan*, London, Macmillan & Co.

Archer, T., 1886, *The War in Egypt and the Soudan: An Episode in the History of the British Empire; a Descriptive Account of the Scenes and Events of that Great Drama, and Sketches of the Principal Actors in it*, vols I–IV, London, Blackie & Son.

Asher, M., 2005/2006, *Khartoum: The Ultimate Imperial Adventure*, London, Penguin.

Baker, S.B., 1866/1962, *The Albert N'yanza: Great Basin of the Nile and Explorations of the Nile Sources*, London, Sidgwick & Jackson.

Baker, S.B., 1879, *Ismailia: A Narrative of the Expedition to Central Africa for the Suppression of the Slave Trade Organised by Ismail, Khedive of Egypt*, London, Macmillan.

Barnett, C., 1970, *Britain and Her Army*, London, Allen Lane/Penguin.

Barraclough, G., 1984/1987, *The Times Atlas of World History*, London, Book Club Associates.

Barthorp, M., 1984/2002, *Blood-red Desert Sand: The British Invasions of Egypt and the Sudan, 1882–1898*, London, Cassell.

Beachey, R., 1990, *The Warrior Mullah: The Horn of Africa Aflame, 1892–1920*, London, Bellew Publishing.

Bedri, B., 1969, *The Memoirs of Babikr Bedri*, trans. Yousef Bedri and George Scott, London, Oxford University Press.

Bennett, E.N., 1899, *The Downfall of the Dervishes: Being a Sketch of the Final Sudan Campaign of 1898*, London, Methuen.

Bensaïd, D., 2013/2015, *An Impatient Life: A Memoir*, London, Verso.

Beresford, C., 1914, *The Memoirs of Admiral Lord Charles Beresford*, London, Methuen & Co.

Best, G., 1971/1979, *Mid-Victorian Britain, 1851–75*, London, Fontana.

Blunt, W.S., 1907, *Secret History of the English Occupation of Egypt*, London, Martin Secker.

Brander, M., 1982, *The Perfect Victorian Hero: The Life and Times of Sir Samuel White Baker*, Edinburgh, Mainstream Publishing.

Brazier, J., 2012, 'All Sir Garnet!', *Military History Monthly*, vol. 20, 36–42.

Broich, J., 2017, *Squadron: Ending the African Slave Trade*, New York, Overlook Duckworth.

Brontë, C., 1847/2006, *Jane Eyre*, London, Penguin.

Brontë, C., 1907, 'Visit to the Crystal Palace, 1851', in Clement Shorter, *The Brontes' Life and Letters*, at www.mytimemachine.co.uk (accessed 5 Jan. 2018).

Buchan, J., 1916/1999, *Greenmantle*, Oxford, Oxford University Press.

Bullock, D., 2007/2015, 'Weep for Hicks', in P.R. Wilson (ed.), *The Mahdist Wars Sourcebook*, vol. I, *1883–1885*, Oklahoma City, The (Virtual) Armchair General, 35–55.

Burton, R.F., 1872, *Zanzibar: City, Island, and Coast*, vols I and II, London, Tinsley Brothers.

Callwell, C.E., 1896/1906, *Small Wars: Their Principles and Practice*, London, HMSO.

Churchill, W.S., 1899/1960, *The River War*, London, Four Square Books.

Churchill, W.S., 1958, *A History of the English-Speaking Peoples*, vol. IV, *The Great Democracies*, London, Educational Book Company.

Cohn, N., 1957/1970, *The Pursuit of the Millennium: Revolutionary Millenarians and Mystical Anarchists of the Middle Ages*, London, Paladin.

Colvile, H.E., 1889, *Official History of the Sudan Campaign*, vols I and II, London, HMSO.

Conrad, J., 1902/1973, *Heart of Darkness*, Harmondsworth, Penguin.

Crawford, N.C., 2018, 'Human cost of the post-9/11 wars: lethality and the need for transparency', Cost of War, Watson Institute, Brown University, https://watson.brown.edu/costsofwar/files/cow/imce/papers/2018/Human%20Costs%2C%20Nov%208%202018%20CoW.pdf (accessed 18 Jan. 2021).

Daggett, A., 2016, 'The Indian Ocean: a maritime trade network history nearly forgot', at www.discovermagazine.com (accessed 1 Feb. 2018).

De Bellaigue, C., 2017, *The Islamic Enlightenment: The Modern Struggle between Faith and Reason*, London, Vintage.

De Watteville, H., 1954, *The British Soldier: His Daily Life from Tudor to Modern Times*, London, J.M. Dent.

Dickens, C., 1843/1971, *A Christmas Carol*, in *The Christmas Books*, vol. I, Harmondsworth, Penguin.

Dickens, C. (with Horne, R.), 1851, 'The Great Exhibition and the little one', in *Household Words*, 5 July 1851, at www.napoleon.org (accessed 5 Jan. 2018).

Dugan, S., 2003/2005, *Men of Iron: Brunel, Stephenson, and the Inventions that Shaped the Modern World*, London, Pan Books.

Elton, G., 1954, *General Gordon*, London, Collins.

Emery, F., 1986, *Marching Over Africa*, London, Hodder & Stoughton.

Falls, C., 1967, 'The reconquest of the Sudan, 1896–9', in B. Bond (ed.), *Victorian Military Campaigns*, London, Hutchinson.

Faulkner, N., 2012, 'Omdurman, 2 September 1898', *Military History Monthly*, vol. 25, 40–8.

Faulkner, N., 2013, *A Marxist History of the World: From Neanderthals to Neoliberals*, London, Pluto Press.

Faulkner, N., 2016, *Lawrence of Arabia's War: The Arabs, the British and the Remaking of the Middle East in WWI*, New Haven, CT and London, Yale University Press.

Faulkner, N., 2018, *A Radical History of the World*, London, Pluto Press.

Featherstone, D., 1978, *Weapons and Equipment of the Victorian Soldier*, Poole, Blandford Press.

Foskett, R. (ed.), 1964, *The Zambesi Doctors: David Livingstone's Letters to John Kirk*, Edinburgh, Edinburgh University Press.

Frank, A.G., 1978, *World Accumulation, 1492–1789*, London, Macmillan.

General Staff, 1907, *Official History of the Operations in Somaliland, 1901–04*, Uckfield, Naval & Military Press/Imperial War Museum.

Gessi, R., 1892/1968, *Seven Years in the Sudan: Being a Record of Explorations, Adventures, and Campaigns against Arab Slave Hunters*, London, Sampson Low, Marston, & Co.

Gordon, C.G., 1885, *The Journals of Major-General C.G. Gordon at Kartoum*, London, Kegan Paul, Trench & Co.

Gordon, M.A., 1888, *Letters of General C.G. Gordon to His Sister*, London, Macmillan & Co.

Gordon, M., 1987/1992, *Slavery in the Arab World*, unprovenanced, New Amsterdam Books.

Grant, J., 1886, *Cassell's History of the War in the Soudan*, vols I–VI, London, Cassell.

Griffith, P., 1986, *Battle in the Civil War: Generalship and Tactics in America, 1861–65*, Camberley, Fieldbooks.

Guillaume, A., 1954/1990, *Islam*, London, Penguin.

Harrison, J.F.C., 1971/1979, *Early Victorian Britain, 1832–51*, London, Fontana.

Harrison, J.F.C., 1990, *Late Victorian Britain, 1875–1901*, London, Fontana.

Hazell, A., 2011/2012, *The Last Slave Market*, London, Constable.

Heaton, B., 2017 (last updated), 'A history of the piano, 1157–2015', at www.piano-tuners.org (accessed at 13 Jan. 2018).

Herbert, E.J., 2007, 'The Abyssinian Army in 1886', in *The Mahdist Wars Source Book*, vol. II, *1886–1899*, Oklahoma City, The Virtual Armchair General, 30–2.

Hill, G.B., 1885/1969, *Colonel Gordon in Central Africa, 1874–1879*, London, Thomas de la Rue & Co.

Hill, R., 1959, *Egypt in the Sudan, 1820–1881*, London, Oxford University Press.

Hobsbawm, E., 1968/1969, *Industry and Empire*, Harmondsworth, Penguin.

Hobsbawm, E., 1975/1985, *The Age of Capital, 1848–1875*, London, Abacus.

Hobsbawm, E., 1987/1994, *The Age of Empire, 1875–1914*, London, Abacus.

Howarth, D., 1964, *The Desert King: A Life of Ibn Saud*, London, Collins.

Hunt, T., 2009, *The Frock-coated Communist: The Revolutionary Life of Friedrich Engels*, London, Allen Lane.

Hutchinson, E.M., 1874, *The Slave Trade of East Africa*, London, Sampson Low, Marston, Low, and Searle.

Jafar al-Askari, 2003, *A Soldier's Story: From Ottoman Rule to Independent Iraq: The Memoirs of Jafar Pasha al-Askari*, trans. Mustafa Tariq al-Askari, London, Arabian Publishing.

Jardine, D., 1923, *The Mad Mullah of Somaliland*, Uckfield, Naval & Military Press.

Jeal, T., 1973/1985, *Livingstone*, Harmondsworth, Penguin Books.

Jeal, T., 2007, *Stanley: The Impossible Life of Africa's Greatest Explorer*, London, Faber & Faber.

Jeal, T., 2011, *Explorers of the Nile: The Triumph and Tragedy of a Great Victorian Adventure*, New Haven, CT and London, Yale University Press.

Johnson, D., 2007/2015, 'The Jihadiyya: the Mahdi's marksmen', in P.R. Wilson (ed.), *The Mahdist Wars Sourcebook*, vol. II, *1886–1899*, Oklahoma City, The (Virtual) Armchair General, 16–18.

Joyce, C., 2014, 'Elephant slaughter, African slavery, and American pianos', at www.npr.org (accessed 13 Jan. 2018).

Kiernan, V.G., 1982, *European Empires from Conquest to Collapse, 1815–1960*, London, Fontana.

Kochanski, H., 1999, *Sir Garnett Wolseley*, London, Hambledon Press.

Konstam, A., 2016, *Nile River Gunboats, 1882–1918*, Oxford, Osprey.

Lacey, R., 1981/1982, *The Kingdom*, London, Fontana.

Lewis, B., 1990/1992, *Race and Slavery in the Middle East*, New York, Oxford University Press.

Livingstone, D., 1857/undated, *Missionary Travels and Researches in South Africa*, Memphis, TN, General Books.

Livingstone, D., 1874/2007, *The Last Journals of David Livingstone in Central Africa, from 1865 to His Death*, vol. II, *1869–1873*, Charleston, NC, BiblioBazaar.

Livingstone, D. and Livingstone, C., 1865/2005, *Narrative of an Expedition to the Zambesi and its Tributaries*, Stroud, Nonsuch Publishing.

Livingstone, D., Sedgwick, A., and Monk, W., 1858, *Dr Livingstone's Cambridge Lectures*, Cambridge, Deighton, Bell, & Co.

Loosemore, J., 2014, 'Sailing against slavery', at BBC Local, Devon, Abolition, 24 Sept. 2014, at     http://www.bbc.co.uk/devon/content/articles/2007/03/20/abolition_navy_feature. shtml (accessed 4 Jan. 2018).

Mack, B.M., 1992, 'Women and slavery in 19th-century Hausaland', in E. Savage (ed.), *Slavery and Abolition*, vol. XIII, no. 1, 89–110.

MacMunn, G. and Falls, C., 1928, *The Official History of the Great War: Military Operations, Egypt and Palestine, from the Outbreak of War with Germany to June 1917*, London, HMSO.

Magnus, P., 1958/1968, *Kitchener: Portrait of an Imperialist*, Harmondsworth, Penguin.

Maitland, A., 1971, *Speke*, London, Constable.

Marshall, S.L.A., 1947/2000, *Men against Fire: The Problem of Battle Command*, Oklahoma, University of Oklahoma.

Marx, K., 1848/1973, 'Manifesto of the Communist Party', in D. Fernbach (ed.), *The Revolutions of 1848*, Harmondsworth/London, Penguin Books/New Left Review.

Marx, K., 1867/1976, *Capital*, vol. I, Harmondsworth/London, Penguin Books/New Left Review.

Middleton, D., 1949, *Baker of the Nile*, London, Falcon Press.

Milbrandt, J., 2014, *The Darling Heart of David Livingstone: Exile, African Slavery, and the Publicity Stunt that Saved Millions*, Nashville, TN, Nelson Books.

Milner, A., 1893/1894, *England in Egypt*, London, Edward Arnold.

Moorehead, A., 1960, *The White Nile*, London, Hamish Hamilton.

Moorehead, A., 1962/1963, *The Blue Nile*, London, Reprint Society.

Morris, D.R., 1965/1972, *The Washing of the Spears: A History of the Rise of the Zulu Nation under Shaka and Its Fall in the Zulu War of 1879*, London, Book Club Associates.

Morris, J., 1971/3, 'Victoria's reign: the high noon of empire', *The British Empire*, vol. 5, no. 56, BBC/Time Life.

Morton A.L. and Tate, G., 1956, *The British Labour Movement, 1770–1920*, London, Lawrence & Wishart.

*National Geographic*, undated, 'The history of the ivory trade', at https://www.nationalgeographic.org/media/history-ivory-trade/ (accessed 13 Jan. 2018).

Neillands, R., 1996, *The Dervish Wars: Gordon and Kitchener in the Sudan, 1880–1898*, London, John Murray.

Newey, S., 2019, 'More than 70 million people forced to flee their homes because of war and persecution', *Telegraph*, 19 June, www.telegraph.co.uk/global-health/climate-and-people/70-million-people-forced-flee-homes-war-persecution/ (accessed 18. Jan. 2021).

Newsinger, J., 2006, *The Blood Never Dried: A People's History of the British Empire*, London, Bookmarks.

Nicolaievsky, B. and Maenchen-Helfen, O., 1936, *Karl Marx: Man and Fighter*, London, Methuen & Co.

Nicoll, F, 2004/2005, *The Mahdi of Sudan and the Death of General Gordon*, Stroud, Sutton.

Nicolle, D, 1989, *Lawrence and the Arab Revolts*, London, Osprey.

O'Fahey, R.S., 2008, *The Darfur Sultanate: A History*, London, Hurst & Co.

Ohrwalder, J. and Wingate, F.R., 1893, *Ten Years' Captivity in the Mahdi's Camp, 1882–1892*, London, Sampson Low, Marston, & Co.

Pakenham, T., 1991/1992, *The Scramble for Africa, 1876–1912*, London, Abacus.

Pauwels, J.R., 2016, *The Great Class War, 1914–1918*, Toronto, James Lorimer & Co.

Prunier, G., 1992, 'Military slavery in the Sudan during the Turkiyya, 1820–1885', *Slavery and Abolition*, vol. XIII, no. 1, 129–39.

Rogerson, B., 2006, *The Heirs of the Prophet Muhammad and the Roots of the Sunni–Shia Schism*, London, Abacus.

Roser, M. and Nagdy, M., 2019, 'Military spending', in *Our World in Data*, at www.ourworldindata.org/military-spending (accessed 11 Jan. 2021).

Royle, C., 1899/2013, *The Egyptian Campaign, 1882, and the Mahdist Campaigns, Sudan, 1884–98: The British Army at War in North Africa in the 19th Century*, no place of publication, Leonaur.

Russell, W.H., 1966/2008, *Dispatches from the Crimea*, Barnsley, Frontline Books.

Rutledge, I., 2014, *Enemy on the Euphrates: The British Occupation of Iraq and the Great Arab Revolt, 1914–1921*, London, Saqi Books.

Schweinfurth, G., 1874, *The Heart of Africa: Three Years' Travels and Adventures in the Unexplored Regions of Central Africa from 1868 to 1871*, vol. I, New York, Harper & Brothers.

Scott, D., 2012, 'The growth of the market for domestic music', at http://www.victorianweb.org/mt/dbscott/2.html (accessed 18 Jan. 2021).

Seaver, G., 1957, *David Livingstone: His Life and Letters*, London, Lutterworth Press.

Simner, M., 2017, *The Sirdar and Khalifa: Kitchener's Reconquest of the Sudan, 1896–98*, London, Fonthill.

Slatin, R. and Wingate, F.R., 1895/1930, *Fire and Sword in the Sudan: A Personal Narrative of Fighting and Serving the Dervishes, 1879–1895*, London, Edward Arnold.

Smee, T., 1872, 'Observations during a voyage of research on the East Coast of Africa', in R. Burton, *Zanzibar: City, Island, and Coast*, vol. II, London, Tinsley Brothers, 458–513.

Speke, J.H., 1863/1906, *Journal of the Discovery of the Source of the Nile*, London, J.M. Dent.

Speke, J.H., 1864/1967, *What Led to the Discovery of the Source of the Nile*, London, Frank Cass.

Springhall, J.O., 1971/1973, 'Rule Britannia! Hope and glory for armchair imperialists', *The British Empire*, vol. V, no. 55.

Stanage, J., 2002, 'The rifle-musket vs the smoothbore musket: a comparison of the effectiveness of the two types of weapons primarily at short ranges', https://scholarworks.iu.edu/journals/index.php/iusburj/article/view/19841/25918 (accessed 18 Jan. 2021).

Stanley, H.M., 1872, *How I Found Livingstone: Travels, Adventures, and Discoveries in Central Africa; Including Four Months' Residence with Dr Livingstone*, London, Sampson Low, Marston, Low, and Searle.

Stanley, H.M., 1878/1899, *Through the Dark Continent*, vols I and II, London, George Newnes.

Steevens, G.W., 1900, *With Kitchener to Khartum*, London, William Blackwood & Sons.

Stewart, J., 2011, 'Imperial pomp and Afghan nationalism: the third Anglo-Afghan War, 1919', *Military History Monthly*, vol. 4, 50–5.

Stewart, J., 2012, 'Mission to Kabul', *Military History Monthly*, vol. 26, 32–7.

Strachan, H., 2001, *The First World War*, vol. II, *To Arms*, Oxford, Oxford University Press.

Strachan, H., 2003, *The First World War: A New Illustrated History*, London, Simon & Schuster.

Symons, J., 1965, *England's Pride: The Story of the Gordon Relief Expedition*, London, Hamish Hamilton.

*The Times History of the War*, vols I–XX, London, *The Times*.

Theobald, A.B., 1965, *Ali Dinar: Last Sultan of Darfur, 1898–1916*, London, Longmans.

Toussaint, E., 2016, 'Debt as an instrument of the colonial conquest of Egypt', at https://www.cadtm.org/Debt-as-an-instrument-of-the (accessed 8 Jan. 2021).

Tylden, G., 1969, 'The accoutrements of the British infantryman, 1640 to 1940', *Journal of the Society for Army Historical Research*, vol. 47, no. 189.

Udal, J.O., 2005, *The Nile in Darkness: A Flawed Unity, 1863–1899*, Norwich, Michael Russell.

Vaughn, R., 2007, 'The Abyssinian Army', in *The Mahdist Wars Source Book*, vol. II, *1886–1899*, Oklahoma City, The Virtual Armchair General, 27–9.

Victoria and Albert Museum, 2018, 'The Great Exhibition', at www.vam.ac.uk (accessed 5 Jan. 2018).

Warner, P., 1973/2000, *Dervish*, Ware, Wordsworth Editions.

Watson, C.M., 1929, 'The campaign of Gordon's steamers', *Sudan Notes and Records*, vol. 12, no. 2, 119–41.

Wavell, A.P., 1926/1936, *The Palestine Campaigns*, London, Constable.

Welsby, D.A., 2011, *Sudan's First Railway: The Gordon Relief Expedition and the Dongola Campaign*, London, Sudan Archaeological Research Society.

Wheen, F., 1999, *Karl Marx*, London, Fourth Estate.

Whitehouse, H., 1987, *Battle in Africa, 1879–1914*, Camberley, Fieldbooks.

Wilkinson-Latham, R., 1976, *The Sudan Campaigns, 1881–1898*, London, Osprey.

Williams, M.J., 1967, 'The Egyptian campaign of 1882', in B. Bond (ed.), *Victorian Military Campaigns*, London, Hutchinson, 243–78.

Wingate, F.R., 1891/1968, *Mahdiism and the Egyptian Sudan: Being an Account of the Rise and Progress of Mahdiism, and of the Subsequent Events in the Sudan to the Present Time*, London, Frank Cass.

Wingate, R., 1955, *Wingate of the Sudan*, London, John Murray.

Wolmar, C., 2010, *Engines of War: How Wars Were Won and Lost on the Railways*, London, Atlantic Books.

Wolseley, G.J., 1869/1871, *The Soldier's Pocket-Book for Field Service*, London, Macmillan.

Wolseley, G.J., 1967, *In Relief of Gordon: Lord Wolseley's Campaign Journal of the Khartoum Relief Expedition, 1884–1885*, ed. Adrian Preston, London, Hutchinson.

Wright, J., 1992, 'The Wadai–Benghazi slave route', *Slavery and Abolition*, vol. XIII, no. 1, 174–82.

Zulfo, I.H., 1980, *Karari: The Sudanese Account of the Battle of Omdurman*, trans. P. Clark, London, Frederick Warne.

# INDEX

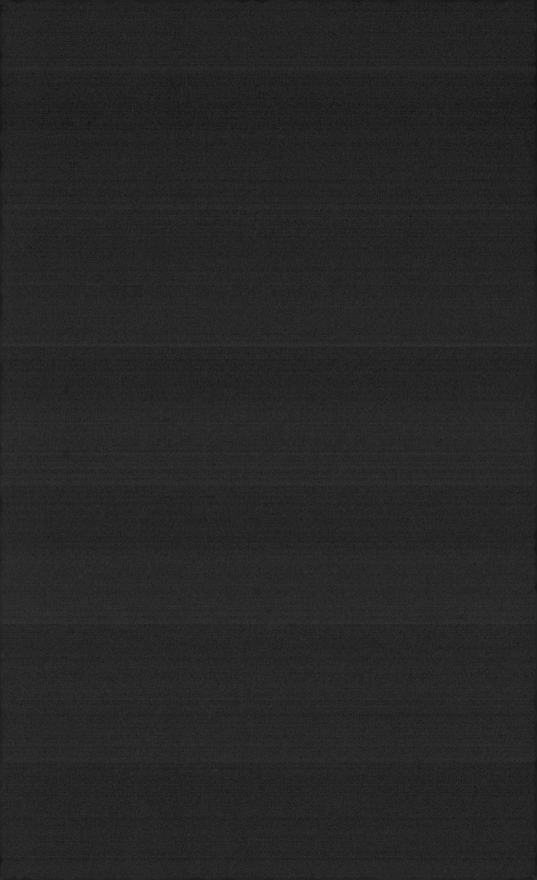